Bergson, Politics, and Religion

BERGSON, POLITICS, AND RELIGION

ALEXANDRE LEFEBVRE AND
MELANIE WHITE, EDITORS

DUKE UNIVERSITY PRESS
Durham & London 2012

Library of Congress Cataloging-in-Publication Data
appear on the last printed page of this book.

Frédéric Worms, "Le clos et l'ouvert dans *Les deux sources
de la morale et de la religion*" from *Bergson et la religion*.
© PUF, 2008.

Philippe Soulez, "Bergson philosophe de la guerre et
théoricien du politique" from *Bergson politique*.
© PUF, 1989.

"Anarchy and Analogy: The Violence of Language in
Bergson and Sorel" by Hisashi Fujita originally appeared
in *Etudes de langue et littérature françaises* 94 (2009).
© SJLLF.

An earlier version of "Asceticism and Sexuality:
'Cheating Nature' in Bergson's *Two Sources of Morality
and Religion*" by Leonard Lawlor was previously
published in *Philosophy Today* 46 (2002): 92–101.
© DePaul University.

Vladimir Jankélévitch, "Bergson et le judaïsme," from
Henri Bergson. © PUF, 2008.

Frédéric Keck, "Assurance et confiance dans Les deux
sources de la morale et de la religion" from *Bergson et la
religion*. © PUF, 2008.

G. William Barnard, "Tuning into Other Worlds: Henri
Bergson and the Radio Reception Theory of Consciousness," is reprinted by permission from *Living Consciousness: The Metaphysical Vision of Henri Bergson* by G.
William Barnard, the State University of New York Press.
© 2011, State University of New York. All rights reserved.

Paola Marrati, "James, Bergson et un univers en
devenir," from *Bergson et James, cent ans après*, ed.
Stéphane Madelrieux. © PUF, 2011.

CONTENTS

ACKNOWLEDGMENTS

We are grateful for the funding provided by the Social Sciences Research Council of Canada, the Faculty of Arts and Social Sciences at Carleton University, the School of Social Sciences at the University of New South Wales, and the School of Philosophical and Historical Inquiry and the School of Social and Political Sciences at the University of Sydney. We would like to thank the anonymous reviewers of the manuscript, in addition to our editor, Courtney Berger, whose support for this project was invaluable. We give warm thanks to Melissa McMahon who cheerfully responded to all manner of translation questions that went well beyond the call of duty. Joanne Lefebvre assisted throughout the preparation of the manuscript. This volume is dedicated to our daughter, Beatrice, who is continually opening and closing.

ABBREVIATIONS

The following abbreviations have been used throughout.
Page references are made first to the English translation,
followed by the corresponding reference to Henri Bergson,
Œuvres, ed. André Robinet, with an introduction by Henri
Gouhier (Paris: PUF, 1959).

   C *Correspondances*. Paris: PUF, 2002.
  CE *Creative Evolution*. Trans. Arthur Mitchell. New
      York: Dover, 1998 [1907].
  CM *The Creative Mind*. Trans. Mabelle M. Andison. New
      York: Citadel Press, 2002 [1934]; translation of *La
      pensée de le mouvant*.
   L *Laughter: An Essay on the Meaning of the Comic*.
      Trans. Cloudesely Brereton and Fred Rothwell.
      Rockville, MD: Arc Manor, 2008 [1900].
   M *Mélanges*. Paris: PUF, 1972.
  ME *Mind-Energy: Lectures and Essays*. Trans. H. Wildon
      Carr. Santa Barbara: Greenwood Press, 1975 [1919];
      translation of *L'énergie spirituelle*.
  MM *Matter and Memory*. Trans. Nancy Margaret Paul
      and W. Scott Palmer. New York: Zone Books, 1991
      [1896].
 TFW *Time and Free Will: An Essay on the Immediate Data
      of Consciousness*. Trans. F. L. Pogson. New York:
      Dover, 2001 [1889]; translation of *Essai sur les don-
      nées immédiates de la conscience*.
  TS *The Two Sources of Morality and Religion*. Trans. R.
      Ashley Audra and Cloudesely Brereton. Notre
      Dame: University of Notre Dame Press, 1977 [1932].

Bergson, Politics, and Religion

Alexandre Lefebvre and Melanie White

Henri Bergson is an extraordinary political philosopher. By this we mean two things: on the one hand, he is a philosopher who has had an extraordinary impact *on* the political, and, on the other hand, he is an extraordinary philosopher *of* the political. Now we are aware that this claim may seem doubtful to an English-speaking audience for whom Bergson's political thought is relatively unknown. Indeed, *Bergson, Politics, and Religion* is the first volume in English dedicated to the political and religious aspects of his thought. In order to introduce Bergson, let us turn to the historical record and begin with his influence on the politics of his time.

IMPACT ON THE POLITICAL

The first phase of Bergson's career is not especially "political," however one wishes to take the term. His early books, which established his reputation as the preeminent philosopher of France, do not expressly address political (or religious) themes: *Time and Free Will* (1889) develops a notion of time ("duration") from lived experience and extends it to mathematics; *Matter and Memory* (1896) addresses the age-old problem of the relationship between consciousness and matter through a new concept of memory; and *Cre-*

ative Evolution (1907) elaborates the idea of duration into a theory of evolution (the "*élan vital*"). In 1896 he was appointed to the Collège de France, where his public lectures enjoyed tremendous success. Packed with students and cultivated society, Bergson's lectures treated ideas already presented in the books that had made him famous (e.g., a course on memory in 1903, and another on freedom in 1904). In short, Bergson enjoyed the life of an extremely successful academic whose research and teaching concentrated on problems of philosophy and science.[1]

But in 1916 his life took an unexpected twist: the French government entrusted him with a series of diplomatic missions, first to Spain, and then again decisively, to the United States in 1917.[2] The purpose of this second assignment was to strike up a personal relationship with Woodrow Wilson in order to persuade the United States to enter the First World War. Here it is interesting to ask why France would entrust such a momentous task to a philosopher. Philippe Soulez and Frédéric Worms, Bergson's biographers, offer a startling answer to this question: Bergson was chosen precisely because he was a philosopher; because he could, in a sense, stand above the political fray and reflect back to Wilson his own (i.e., Wilson's) idealized vision of the end of war and the founding of an international community: "In essence, Bergson says to Wilson: 'you are philosopher, prophet, and king. For the first time in human history these three figures are one.' And if Bergson is persuasive, it is because he believes what he says. In this sense, Bergson is truly 'witness to the truth': he presents Wilson the very image he would like to have of himself. He is witness to Wilson's desire; or in other words, he guarantees Wilson's ideal self. *Only a philosopher can provide this guarantee.*"[3]

Thus it is perhaps misleading to divide Bergson's career into two distinct phases: first philosopher and then political figure, as if the latter was simply a different hat. Rather, if we follow Soulez and Worms, Bergson is an effective political actor—one who initiated, it is no exaggeration to say, a world historic event inasmuch as the United States' entry into the First World War was the decisive factor in ending the war—foremost because he is a philosopher, because he incarnates an ideal. This volume will explore the nature of this ideal in detail, but for now we wish only to signal this actualization of philosophy within politics.

Bergson's political career did not end with the First World War. During the drafting of the Treaty of Versailles, he continued to serve as a key intermediary between the French and American governments. But his

main postwar political contribution was his work with the Wilson administration to establish the League of Nations. In 1922 he was appointed
president of the League's International Commission for Intellectual Cooperation, which was precursor to UNESCO. The primary purpose of this
institution was to promote international collaboration between scholars
—such as the famous exchange between Freud and Einstein, "Why War?"
in 1932—in the hope that the spirit of internationalism would kindle in
the nations themselves. To this end, Bergson worked tirelessly to ensure
that the commission was not merely an abstract ideal and dedicated himself to practical down-to-earth tasks such as coordinating the international exchange of publications, bibliographies, and scientific results, as
well as ensuring financial support for the commission.[4] But driving these
practical activities we can see a principle dedicated to the prevention of
war through enhanced understanding, one that Bergson would later on
make explicit: "Anyone who is thoroughly familiar with the language and
literature of a people cannot be wholly its enemy. This should be borne in
mind when we ask education to pave the way for international understanding" (TS 286/1218). Thus, in these two positions—as emissary to the
United States and as president of the International Commission for Intellectual Cooperation—we can see the multifaceted nature of Bergson's
political accomplishment: a philosopher who affected the highest levels
of policy and an administrator who labored for a philosophical ideal.

PHILOSOPHER OF THE POLITICAL

Our claim that Bergson is an extraordinary political philosopher may
seem strange in light of the fact that he did not write a book of political
philosophy. Where his early work addresses the nature of time, memory,
and evolution, his last book—*The Two Sources of Morality and Religion*
(1932)—frames a series of political problems in terms of a treatise on
morality and religion. What, then, is the basis for our claim?

Here, two great readers of Bergson are especially helpful, both to assist
in understanding the nature of Bergson's political thought and, perhaps
more importantly, to know what to do with it today.

In a chapter translated for this volume, Philippe Soulez argues that it is
no coincidence that Bergson did not write a traditional book of political
philosophy. As he puts it, "it is doubtful in fact that Bergson was ever
tempted to write a book of 'political philosophy,' in the sense of a specific

philosophical *discipline*. What interests him are *problems* rather than a subject matter or discipline." Certainly this observation is borne out by Bergson's previous books. *Creative Evolution*, for example, engages the biological sciences according to its governing problematic of how to conceive of evolution as open-ended creative duration. Likewise *Two Sources* has its own organizing problem: to what extent can the drive to war be turned aside? *Two Sources*, then, can be considered a work of political philosophy because it treats political themes through the horizon of this problem. A goal of this introduction is to sketch Bergson's original formulation of the problem of war and observe how it transforms or even dissolves received political and religious problems.

Thus, on the one hand, while Soulez describes Bergson's own method of working through problems, Gilles Deleuze states that Bergson's contemporary relevance depends on renewing him along new lines of inquiry: "A 'return to Bergson' does not only mean a renewed admiration for a great philosopher but a renewal or an extension of his project today, in relation to the transformations of life and society, in parallel with the transformations of science. Bergson himself considered that he had made metaphysics a rigorous discipline, one capable of being continued along new paths which constantly appear in the world."[5] Deleuze gives us a directive of what it means to be Bergsonian: to extend, and indeed transform, Bergson's thought by cultivating new problems that respond to the challenges of today. In this sense, faithfulness is re-creation.

To carry on with Bergson, and to honor his way of doing philosophy, it is necessary to actualize his work through the invention of novel problems.[6] This is why a Bergsonian school of thought—whether in philosophy, psychology, or politics—is nonexistent and perhaps unthinkable. Take the case of Georges Sorel. *Reflections on Violence* (1908) is certainly the most famous text of political philosophy directly inspired by Bergson, and yet, for all that, Bergson (glowingly) denies, in a letter to Gilbert Maire in 1912, that Sorel was ever a disciple: "[He] is, it seems to me, too original and too independent an individual [*esprit*] to join this or that camp; he is not a disciple. But he accepts some of my views and, when he cites me, he does so as a man who has read me attentively and who has understood me perfectly" (M 971). In fact all of Bergson's great political readers—such as Charles Péguy, Karl Popper, John Humphrey, Gilles Deleuze and Félix Guattari, and William Connolly—could be similarly categorized: they are Bergsonians in the spirit of extending Bergson to new problems, rather than adhering to the letter of his text.

Soulez and Deleuze offer two perspectives that ground this collection's reassessment of Bergson's political and religious thought. On the one hand, the volume is exegetical. It identifies, clarifies, and develops the problems that occupy Bergson in *Two Sources*. Such work is timely as many of Bergson's core concerns are at the forefront of contemporary scholarship, such as the significance of emotion in moral judgment, the relationship between biology and society, and the entanglement of politics and religion. A key ambition of this book, therefore, is to foster Bergson's entry into these debates and demonstrate the importance of his contribution. On the other hand, this volume extends Bergson's thought in new directions. One benefit, of course, is to disseminate a Bergsonian perspective on problems hitherto unconsidered by him, but another, equally important benefit is to show that Bergson does not just offer a new solution to already established problems but, in keeping with the methodological privilege he gives to them, he dissolves or reconfigures the formulation of the problem itself. In short, the aims of this volume are to clarify central problems of Bergson's political and religious thought and connect them to current debates and to present Bergsonian scholarship that reconfigures problems in topics as diverse as human rights, Judaism, environmental ethics, sovereignty, and aesthetics.

THE PROBLEM OF WAR

We proceed in the next two sections to outline Bergson's formulation of the problem of war in *Two Sources*. Our aim is to make explicit a key point of reference that many of the chapters in this collection presuppose: the relationship Bergson establishes between biology or life on the one hand and politics and religion on the other.

We claim that war is the coordinating problem of *Two Sources*. Now, on a first reading of this text, it is not altogether obvious that Bergson is principally interested in *this* problem. The first three chapters are philosophical in tone and treat the topics of moral obligation, static religion, and dynamic religion respectively. Only in the final chapter, dedicated to a practical discussion of contemporary political issues, is the problem of war presented urgently in and of itself. But with it Bergson snaps the book into focus: "The object of the present work was to investigate the origins of morality and religion. We have been led to certain conclusions. We might leave it at that. But since at the basis of our conclusions was a radical distinction between the closed and the open society, since the tendencies of the closed society have, in our opinion, persisted, ineradicable, in the society opening itself up, and since all these instincts of discipline originally converged toward the war-instinct, *we are bound to ask to what extent the primitive instinct can be repressed or turned aside*" (TS 288/1220; emphasis added and translation modified).

Here Bergson makes it apparent that the search for the origins of morality and religion is in service of an immediate goal: to thwart the natural tendency to war. But why, might we ask, does Bergson find it necessary to bring such a formidable theoretical apparatus to the task? Because, he would say, we have an imprecise, all-too-comforting impression that war is irregular and unnatural: "Oh, I know what society says. . . . It says that the [moral] duties it defines are indeed, in principle, duties towards humanity, but that under exceptional circumstances, regrettably unavoidable, they are for the time being inapplicable [*suspendu*]" (TS 31/1000–1001). This view, common to liberalism at the turn of the century as well as today, is governed by two assumptions: first, that peace is normal and war exceptional; and second, that moral obligation extends to *all* human beings. Bergson's objection is that this view is at once imprecise and hypocritical. It is imprecise because it does not offer a satisfactory explanation for the outbreak of war. If we recognize basic moral duties to all, how could war so much as start? It is hypocritical because the cosmopolitan ideal that we claim to cherish is cast aside the moment it is most desperately needed. What Bergson has exposed is a false problem and its consequence: if we see moral obligation as universal but only suspended in times of war, then the origins of war are inexplicable, and our strategies to deter it are misguided.

War, therefore, exposes a dangerous confusion in our everyday idea of morality: on the one hand, moral duties are ostensibly universal, but, on the other hand, these same duties—as the fact of war brutally reveals—apply strictly to a specific group. In Bergson's terms our everyday idea of morality is composite: it misleadingly groups together tendencies that differ in kind (here, moral universalism and particularism). There is, in other words, a distinct moral tendency to preserve and protect the group exclusively and another distinct moral tendency to love, respect, and care for all human beings as such. Bergson calls the first tendency "closed" and the second tendency "open." The aim of *Two Sources*, then, is to achieve a clear and distinct view of each tendency, to warn against collapsing them, and, with these two tendencies in sight, to provide an appropriate solution—not in order to avert war as such, for as Bergson acknowledges this natural tendency is ineradicable, but to mitigate its effects and frequency by placing the two tendencies in opposition to one another.

BIOLOGICAL ORIGINS OF MORALITY AND RELIGION

If war is the practical problem that unites the myriad themes of *Two Sources*, the question of the origins of morality and religion is the philosophical problem that underlies them. As the very title *Two Sources* announces, morality and religion are not self-grounding. At the heart of the book is Bergson's claim that *the origin of morality and religion is life* (TS 101/1061). As we will see, it is in its connection to life that the problem of war receives its definitive formulation.

Life, for Bergson, is not a single source. Once again his title is instructive. It proclaims that there are *two* sources of morality and religion. He names these sources the "closed" and the "open" tendencies of life. These two tendencies are the origin of morality and religion.

Let us ask, as plainly as possible, why life has two tendencies. What does it mean to say that one tendency is "closed" and the other "open"? In using these terms, Bergson draws on two meanings of their ordinary usage. On the one hand, we say something is closed when it is bounded and exclusive. On the other hand, we say something is open when it is indeterminate ("open-ended") and inclusive. For Bergson, life exhibits both of these tendencies in both of their senses. In *Creative Evolution* he emphasizes the first sense of each tendency: boundedness and indeterminacy. Life tends toward self-preservation, reproduction and stability, *and* toward continuous and unpredictable change. In this way Bergson captures both the bounded stability and open-ended dynamism of evolution. In *Two Sources* Bergson picks up the second sense of each tendency: exclusion and inclusion. Human societies tend toward exclusion, group solidarity and war, *and* toward love and care that reaches beyond the limited bounds of the social group.

Let us pause and consider the relationship Bergson establishes in *Two Sources* between morality, religion, and war in the closed and open tendencies of life. The cornerstone of his reflections is that human beings are *living beings*. This means, first and foremost, that the defining aspects of human life—whether sociability, morality, religion, or reason—are products of evolution; they are evolutionary responses to vital needs. Consider morality and religion. The evolutionary function of morality, based on Bergson's account, is social cohesion: obligation creates the solidarity and discipline of the group. Because its purpose is to ensure the cohesion of a particular society, morality is always an in-group phenomenon.[7] Near the end of the book, Bergson gives a stark overview: "The closed society is that whose members hold together, caring nothing for the rest of humanity, on the alert for attack or defense, bound, in fact, to a perpetual readiness for battle" (TS 266/1201). The evolutionary function of religion intensifies that of morality but in a different register: it overcomes egoism and attaches the individual more firmly to the group, and through rites, ceremonies, and myths, it distinguishes the group from others (TS 206/1151). Given these functions of morality and religion, the nature of the war instinct comes to light. Bergson's originality, of course, does not lie in the claim that war is natural or that human beings have a natural propensity for it. Rather, his insight is that the evolutionary function of morality and religion inevitably leads us to war. Or, put in a different way, by virtue of their evolutionary origin, the love and affection characteristic of closed morality and religion is fully compatible with hatred: "*Homo homini deus* and *Homo homini lupus*, are easily reconcilable. When we formulate the first, we are thinking of some fellow-countryman. The other applies to foreigners" (TS 286/1219).

But this is not the whole story. It is a fact, one that Bergson never tires of recording, that throughout history individuals have existed who are able to love without partiality and exclusion. The significance of individuals such as Socrates, Jesus Christ, and Joan of Arc is that they exemplify, and also alert us to, a capacity that lies in each of us: to love beyond the narrow bounds prescribed by evolution.[8] Bergson calls these individuals "mystics." The closed tendency of life cannot account for them. But then what does?

Recall Bergson's evolutionary perspectivism: closed morality preserves the group by checking egoism and defending against enemies. What biological need, then, does love without preference—that is, "mysticism"— fulfill? Although Bergson does not explicitly make this point, the whole of *Two Sources* tends toward it: mysticism is life's solution to the problem of war. Love breaks us out of the rut of war.[9] Consider a loveless world, one without the means to transcend closure: "at once individual and social, the soul here moves round in a circle. It is closed" (*TS* 38/1006). Time and again in *Two Sources* Bergson favors the image of love as breaking us out of a cycle of hostility to which closed morality condemns us: "all aimed at opening what was closed; and the group, which after the last opening had closed [*repliait*] on itself, was brought back every time to humanity" (*TS* 267/1203); "there will be the hope that the circle may be broken in the end" (*TS* 53/1019); "you had a circle from which there would have been no escape, if one or several privileged beings . . . had not broken the circle and drawn the society after them" (*TS* 74/1038); "individual and society thus condition each other, circlewise. The circle, intended by nature, was broken by man the day he became able to get back into the creative impetus and impel human nature forward instead of letting it revolve on one spot" (*TS* 199/1144). Circle and cycle are always coordinated: society and individual form a tight-knit *circle*, which leads to a never-ending *cycle* of war. The paradox of closed morality is that it exists in order to preserve the species, and it also introduces a desperate need to transcend it. And, as Bergson makes clear, with the advance of deadly new technologies— indeed, he anticipates the atomic bomb (*TS* 312/1241)—this need has become imperative. Hence the urgency of the problem of war and the need to address it from the proper theoretical perspective: we must confront the fact that our natural morality has put us at a dire crossroads, and we must realize the source from which it can be effectively countered.

Now there are two key consequences to draw from love being an evolutionary response to the problem of war. On the one hand, Bergson's appeal to love is not abstract or sentimental. From his point of view, the root of major contemporary political institutions, such as human rights and democracy, is open morality or love. His point is that such institutions would be unimaginable (in terms of genesis) and incomprehensible (in terms of everyday practice) were we not able to see at their core a nonpreferential love irreducible to closed morality. In Bergson's treatment, therefore, love is a concrete and practical political force. Or, to put it another way, mysticism is not only present in politics but is also the foundation of the institutions that can divert war.

On the other hand, Bergson broadens the fact of open morality into a radical biological and theological argument. His claim is nothing less than that love transfigures, or indeed transcends, the human species: "Let a mystic genius but come forward, he will draw after him a humanity already vastly grown in body, and whose soul he has transfigured. He will yearn to make of it a new species, *or rather deliver it from the necessity of being a species*; for every species means a collective halt and complete existence is mobility in individuality" (TS 311/1240; emphasis added and translation modified). All species, for Bergson, are caught in a cycle of uncreative repetition: once created, they are fated to turn around and around on the same spot. But, as the means and ferocity of warfare demonstrate, the natural morality and religion of human beings traps us in a particularly destructive cycle. Love is a momentous fact for Bergson because it interrupts the logic of preservation, hostility, and closure. Hence his quite astonishing claim that the mystic—or rather, the mysticism dormant in each of us—has the potential to deliver us from the fate of specieshood as such. Or, positively put, love enables human beings to participate in the essence of life itself: creation, unpredictability, newness.

Bergson's originality is to devise an argument whereby human beings transcend the species without departing from animality or biology. The transfiguration of humanity is entirely immanent to life's powers, a fact reflected in the human species becoming creator. In sum, we are simultaneously animal and creator, a point captured in the remarkable closing lines of *Two Sources*: "Mankind lies groaning, half crushed beneath the weight of its own progress. Men do not sufficiently realize that their future is in their own hands. Theirs is the task of determining first of all whether they want to go on living or not. Theirs the responsibility, then, for deciding if they want merely to live, or intend to make just the extra effort required for fulfilling, even on their refractory planet, the essential function of the universe, which is a machine for the making of gods" (TS 317/1245). This incarnation of the theological in the political, and their essential entanglement, is a theme taken up repeatedly by the contributors to the volume. It is also a central reason why Bergson has been resisted by the mainstream tradition in Anglo-American political philosophy, to which we now turn.

BERGSON, POLITICS, AND RELIGION

If we are correct that Bergson is an extraordinary political philosopher, then it is indeed extraordinary that he has been ignored by an English-speaking audience. Our aim in this final section is to account for this neglect and, more importantly, to explain how each chapter in this collection renews the vitality of his political and religious thought.

This is the first volume in English dedicated to politics and religion in Bergson. We can think of at least three reasons why his work has been underappreciated. First, he does not treat standard themes of political theory head on. *Two Sources*, for example, rarely addresses subjects such as the justification and limits of power, or the principles of a just society, and even less so through the standard traditions in political philosophy. Second, *Two Sources* has had a difficult reception within continental philosophy. Its publication was initially met with mixed reviews and bewilderment for its reliance on mysticism;[10] Bergson's immediate successors such as Maurice Merleau-Ponty, Jean-Paul Sartre, and Georges Canguilhem were indebted primarily to his early works;[11] and in the contemporary revival of Bergson, due in large part to Deleuze, *Two Sources* is underplayed almost to the point of exclusion.[12] Third, while Bergson has never found much of a home within analytical philosophy, the argument of *Two Sources* intensifies the points of resistance. Bertrand Russell's attack on Bergson as an irrationalist seemed all the more warranted with the publication of *Two Sources*, in which love and creative emotion are given priority in morality and politics.[13]

Since this volume is intended for an English-speaking audience, it behooves us to explain why Bergson was initially resisted, and eventually forgotten, in the Anglo-American tradition. We focus on an exemplary piece of criticism that follows in Russell's footsteps: Judith Shklar's "Bergson and the Politics of Intuition" (1958). Our interest in this essay—a minor piece by a major liberal theorist and already more than fifty years old—is heuristic. We do not wish to criticize or refute it as such. Shklar's argument, in sum, is that Bergson is impertinent and dangerous for political theory. He is impertinent because he fails to engage with recognized and meaningful political categories, and he is dangerous because he imports "aesthetic" concepts—such as creativity, emotion, and mysticism— into the political realm.[14] For Shklar, Bergson is a dead end for the traditional problems that have defined politics.

The virtue of Shklar's essay for readers of Bergson today is that she has a keen sense of his originality. Time and again she zeros in on themes that make Bergson timely for contemporary thinking about politics and religion: the necessity of pluralism and creativity for political life, the centrality of affect for individual and group action, and the entanglement of politics and religion. And yet her assessment of Bergson is disappointing because it remains caught in problems and oppositions he had intended to upset. To bring out this impression, let us see how Shklar frames Bergson as destructive of political thought and life. She raises three distinct objections, which are coordinated by a single concern that Bergson transforms politics into a space of irrationality.

1 *Creativity eliminates political judgment.* As Shklar states: "Creativity is too indefinite a notion to be a standard of judgment in ethics. In political matters, it is, if anything, an even more meaningless term. In neither case, moreover, can creativity as such acquire concrete expression in some definable form of behavior. Ultimately any sort of exhibitionism can parade around as creative morality" (BPI 333).

2 *Emotion eliminates rational deliberation.* As with Russell, Shklar characterizes Bergson as a philosopher of "moods" rather than ideas (BPI 319): "Free actions . . . are not only personal, they are distinctly nonrational. They occur on those rare occasions when we act in defiance of reason and calculation to follow some inner urge of our hidden self. Above all, [for Bergson] freedom can only be felt, not discussed. . . . Certainly a form of freedom that defies discussion is not in the realm of social activity. In everyday life freedom depends on the number of genuine alternatives of action open to the individual, not on the possibility of creating a new, future self out of nothing, nor on the occasional moment of self-expression" (BPI 325).

3 *Mysticism eliminates the political.* On Shklar's account, mysticism, which she characterizes as prediscursive intuition, undermines philosophy and politics: "An inner apprehension of truth that is ineffable, unobstructed by the bonds of logic or communal expression can hardly be called philosophy. . . . [A mystic] could not be an actor on any political stage, which must necessarily be confining. He was, rather, the man who wants to end all politics, to dissolve the 'closed society,' and to create that 'open society' which embraces all mankind" (BPI 320, 333).

If Shklar is correct in her reading of Bergson, then no wonder she rejects him. But so too would Bergson! One way to put this is that they are both afraid of the same things: creativity, emotion, and mysticism as Shklar takes them to be. If creativity is seen as voluntarism, if emotion is seen to negate reason, and if mysticism is seen as the private and privileged access to truth, then Bergson would be the first to deny their place in political and religious life.

The heuristic value of Shklar's essay is that it shows that Bergson cannot be appreciated from the perspective of already given problems. If political philosophy, for example, has traditionally opposed emotion to reason and religion to politics, then Bergson's contribution is surely not to insist on the priority of emotion or religion within the terms of that opposition.[15] Our point is that to read Bergson effectively, perhaps nowhere more so than in politics and religion, his orientation to problems must be appreciated. His aim is to convert rather than intervene, to remake rather than accept.

The contributors to this volume exemplify this approach. The book is divided into three parts: "Closed and Open," "Politics," and "Religion and Mysticism." To introduce each part, we show how Bergson recasts the problems identified by Shklar and thereby clears the terrain for the collection's contributors.

Let us begin with the problem of creativity. In Shklar's reading of Bergson, creativity is a normative standard of political judgment: institutions are good to the extent that they foster creativity. Shklar places Bergson within a tradition of political philosophy—one that he inherits from Marx and another that he initiates with Sorel—that *recommends* change. The trouble with this interpretation, however, is that for Bergson creativity is an ontological rather than a normative category. In fact he anticipates such a misreading in *Creative Mind*: "Because I called attention to the mobility at the base of things . . . it has been said that my doctrine was a justification of instability. One might just as well imagine that the bacteriologist recommends microbic diseases to us when he shows us microbes everywhere. . . . A principle of explanation is one thing, a maxim of conduct is another" (SM 88/1328). Bergson thus shifts the place of creativity in politics and religion. He is not a voluntarist that urges change to a particular end; nor is he an advocate for change as such. His point is, rather, that the substrate of politics and religion *is* mobility, and successful institutions must acknowledge and work within that reality. As Bergson says, "One could almost say that the philosopher who finds mobility everywhere is the only one who cannot recommend it, since he sees it as inevitable, since he discovers it in what people have agreed to call immobility" (CM 88/1328). Bergson's genius, we might say, is at once to assert the reality of change and to exhort prudence in dealing with it.

The chapters in part I, "Closed and Open," begin from the necessity and reality of creativity. Frédéric Worms surveys the whole of *Two Sources* from the perspective of the distinction it introduces between closed and open. His claim is nothing less than that this distinction changes everything—not merely in the book but in our lives! He means this in two interrelated senses. On the one hand, *Two Sources* shows how this distinction has been effective throughout the history of morality, religion, and politics. Its purpose is to make this distinction explicit, to set out its criteria, and to demonstrate its force. And on the other hand, the goal of *Two Sources* is to show the immediate, practical, and everyday application of this distinction, such that ordinary people, then and now, can respond to the immediate challenges of mechanization and war. Suzanne Guerlac also insists on the urgency of the distinction between closed and open. This distinction allows Guerlac to affirm Bergson as "nonmodern," that is, as a thinker who refuses the classical antitheses of modern social and political thought, first and foremost among these, the distinction between nature and culture. Bergson offers, then, a nonmodern perspective on quintessentially modern problems. Guerlac's chapter first considers the problem of human rights through Bergson's critique of the French sociologist Emile Durkheim and proceeds to examine the problem of "the void," that is, the imbalance of a body empowered by modern technology and a soul as yet unequipped to guide it.

John Mullarkey's chapter uses the distinction between closed and open to present a concept of equality and democracy that affirms their essential openness and indeterminacy. Democracy, in this account, is productively "vague" in that it is the central political institution that provides latitude for the moral creativity and inventiveness that liberty and equality require. Bergson's contribution, says Mullarkey, is to provide a notion of equality that avoids the circularity at the heart of the concept: rather than equality "equaling" anything in particular, it ultimately remains open and receptive to the vagueness of politics. Claire Colebrook addresses the distinction between closed and open within aesthetics. She considers whether modernist art can create a sensibility able to release the human intellect from its self-serving, self-enclosed nature. In answering "yes," Colebrook uses Bergson to see in modernism the potential—always uncertain and liable to fail—to make contact with the open tendency of life, that is, with life irreducible to its already actualized forms, to yield an aesthetic sense that interrupts habitual rhythms of the intellect.

To introduce part II, let us consider the longstanding accusation that Bergson is an irrationalist, one that Shklar voices in a political register. Her criticism is that emotion kills rational deliberation in two ways. First, it makes dialogue pointless because it defies the reason and calculation upon which deliberation is built. Second, it makes dialogue impossible because it is prediscursive, private, and fractures the shared space of deliberation. On the basis of this strong opposition, emotion simply shoulders out reason, and politics is transformed into a space of irrationality. But this mistakes the nature of Bergson's problem, as Paola Marrati points out: "Bergson is not calling for a morality and a politics of irrational emotions or sublime sensibility. His claim is rather that no morality and no politics—be it Open or Closed—can ever take place within the limits of reason alone."[16] It is perhaps helpful to see the role of emotion in *Two Sources* as akin to what Montesquieu calls a "principle" in *Spirit of the Laws*: a set of affects that puts politics and religion in motion.[17] For example, at the root of human rights, democracy, and institutions under the sway of the open tendency more generally, love inspires action and universal fraternity (TS 234/1173–74). Closed morality and religion, for their part, are structured by fear, a fear of others, egoism, death, and uncertainty (TS 122/1078, 131/1086). The implications of Bergson's reconfiguration of the problem of emotion can be stated in different ways. In seeing the affective core of moral action, Bergson fills the motivational deficit that haunts practical philosophy. In so doing, he anticipates findings in neuroscience that people only reach decisions if they have an emotional attachment to the options before them.[18] Bergson also furnishes a distinctly post-Cartesian conception of the subject, in that emotion is no longer seen as a derivative modality of an essentially rational subject.[19] Indeed, for Bergson, human beings are sui generis not because of reason, language, or society but because of love: we are the animal that loves. Last, though we are defined by love, Bergson makes the devastating point that it is a fragile achievement, one that must be nursed. He thus transforms a natural and ineradicable tendency into an urgent project: it is altogether possible that human beings can lose, perhaps indefinitely, their love not only *of* the world (i.e., their attachment to life) but love *in* the world (i.e., those institutions that actualize it).[20]

The chapters in part II contend with the affective constitution of politics. Philippe Soulez's chapter is an impressive survey of Bergson's political thought. On the one hand, it distinguishes and interweaves

Bergson's remarks on the political (*le politique*—which are drawn primarily from the first three chapters of *Two Sources*) and politics (*la politique*—which are drawn primarily from the concluding chapter of *Two Sources*). And, on the other hand, it repeatedly situates Bergson within established traditions of political philosophy (Aristotle, Hobbes, Spinoza, and Rousseau), all the while demonstrating his originality. The major substantive preoccupation of the chapter is war, and it is in this context that the priority of emotion reveals itself. For in framing the problem of war in terms of countervailing affective "forces" or "energetics," Soulez shows that for Bergson it is only by highlighting the affective dimension of politics that we can confront the real and terrifying threat of extermination. Leonard Lawlor's contribution also concentrates on the problem of war in *Two Sources*, but he approaches it from the perspective of two distinct ways that human beings have "cheated" or exceeded nature: sexuality and love. Bergson's claim is that because modern sexual practice has separated pleasure from procreation, sexuality has become an end in itself such that our entire civilization has become "aphrodisiacal" (TS 302/1232; translation modified). For Bergson, this prepares the conditions of war because it yields a culture obsessed with luxury and the sterile repetition of pleasure. But following Bergson, Lawlor adds that this is not the only time that we have tricked nature. Love, that is, the unique human ability to love beyond the group, also cheats nature by escaping the original closure of morality and religion. War, then, is framed by the disequilibriums we have created, such that human beings are now enfolded by these two primary passions.

Hisashi Fujita directly confronts the political legacy for which Bergson has most often been termed an irrationalist: his influence on Georges Sorel. Fujita starts by questioning an opposition that interpreters from Schmitt to Shklar say marks Bergson as a "misologist": either rational discussion (i.e., parliamentarianism and deliberation) *or* immediate action (i.e., violence). But rather than accept this opposition between violence and language, Fujita argues that the true question for Bergson is the violence *of* language. This means two things: language is violent because it cuts up the world according to our needs, and any attempt to think with duration, that is, with "precision" and "clarity" in Bergson's sense, must do violence to language. It is here that Fujita establishes the link to Sorel. In *Reflections on Violence*, Sorel distinguishes the language of force from the language of violence. The first serves to maintain established powers, whereas the second, which includes myths and images that create bonds of sympathy between people, breaks through these powers to form a new social organization. The purpose of the chapter, therefore, is to observe that Sorel's Bergsonism consists in the idea that a new political articulation of the real confronts the language of force with the language of violence. Paulina Ochoa Espejo's chapter is a powerful example of how Bergson can be used to dissolve false problems. Here, Ochoa Espejo addresses a central paradox of contemporary democratic theory: the problem of the people. In a nutshell the paradox is that the demos appears to be both cause and consequence of the democratic people. On the one hand, democratic institutions must be created by the governed through their consent, but, on the other hand, for individuals to express their consent, democratic institutions must already exist. Ochoa Espejo escapes from this impasse by turning to Bergson to develop a concept of the people held together by habits and rules, but whose self-creative drive derived from the lived experience of time and nature enables them to evolve. It is this drive, called "creative freedom," that Ochoa Espejo argues is the suprarational, indeterminate foundation for democratic legitimacy and justification.

Carl Power's and Alexandre Lefebvre's contributions turn to the affective core of practical reason and human rights. Power's chapter carefully reconstructs Bergson's extraordinarily condensed criticism of the major schools of modern practical philosophy: Kantian deontology, empiricism, and rational intuitionism. Contrary to these rationalist positions, Bergson regards morality as lived before it is explicitly thought, as embodied in collective habits and emotions, and as immediately constituted by extrarational forces. Power concludes by comparing Bergson's views on human rights (and ethical universalism more generally) with those of Alain Badiou. Lefebvre's chapter argues that, despite the small number of pages Bergson dedicates to human rights, they are the culmination of his political philosophy and the institution that most purely embodies the open tendency. In practice, however, human rights are a composite phenomenon that actualizes both the closed and open tendencies of life. Because of this composite nature, Lefebvre argues that human rights have two essential and distinct functions: to *protect* human beings from our natural tendency toward closure, hatred, and war and to *initiate* human beings into open, universal love. Lefebvre defines human rights as the institution that protects us from hate and converts us to love.

To introduce part III, "Religion and Mysticism," let us attend to

Shklar's criticism that Bergson's concept of mysticism is designed to end politics. Mysticism, in her view, is essentially escapist. Concerned as it is with "an inner apprehension of truth that is ineffable," mysticism holds itself above, and is thus irrelevant to, the concrete cares and concerns of political life (BPI 320). Worse, because Shklar empties mysticism of any attachment to political reality, the call to realize the open society can only be a mysterious leap into an abstract "post-political" state. But we must remember that Bergson's starting position is not to oppose mysticism to politics but rather to insist on the mystical source of existing institutions. Consider how Soulez and Worms give voice to Bergson's interest in the League of Nations: "While we do not know *a priori* how far the League of Nations will go, we do nevertheless know where the idea comes from, and, in *Two Sources*, Bergson will trace it all the way up to a mystical and religious origin, higher than any political project."[21] Bergson thus remakes the problem. Politics and religion are neither opposed to one another as they are, say, in liberal political thought, nor are the concepts of modern politics secularized theological concepts. Instead, certain political institutions (such as human rights) are, in a sense, religious; they are the actualization, hence the bearer, of an irreducible mystical intuition.

Part III opens with a translation of a wonderful piece by one of Bergson's foremost interpreters: Vladimir Jankélévitch's "Bergson and Judaism," originally written in 1956. This chapter is concerned less with Bergson's specific observations on Judaism (say in TS 76–77/1039–40) and more with identifying the key points of contact between Bergsonism and Judaism. The chapter assesses the compatibility of Bergson's conception of time and that found in Jewish theology. Jankélévitch finds that while duration is at odds with biblical time, with its emphasis on absolute beginning and prophecy, it is in the notion of the "plenitude of becoming" (rather than the "plenitude of being" we find in Platonism and Christianity) that we recognize a deep connection between Bergson and Judaism. As Jankélévitch puts it, the plenitude of becoming, affirmed by both Bergson and Judaism, roots us in a condition of transience and immanence. Keith Ansell-Pearson and Jim Urpeth bring Bergson into dialogue with Nietzsche on the grounds that they are the two major thinkers to undertake a naturalistic account of religion that does not fall prey to a reductive sociobiology. The chapter begins with a comprehensive overview of Bergson's conception of static and dynamic religion and proceeds to treat key points of Nietzsche's evaluation of religion that both comple-

ment and challenge Bergson's analysis. Ansell-Pearson and Urpeth conclude with a discussion of the shared attempt by Bergson and Nietzsche
to fuse a theory of religion together with a theory of life.

Frédéric Keck and G. William Barnard both turn to the psychological
and spiritual dimensions of religion in Bergson. Keck's chapter analyzes
notions of assurance and confidence in *Two Sources* by situating them
within a genealogy of the French debate on responsibility that was fundamental to the French school of sociology. Keck argues that static religion
and dynamic religion sustain two different conceptions of assurance.
Static religion provides human beings with a sense of assurance necessary
to act in a world where outcomes are always uncertain. Dynamic religion,
on the other hand, transfigures assurance into confidence by making
perceptible the totality of the intellectual structures engaged in political
action. Barnard turns to the spiritualist dimensions of Bergson's thought,
and takes two lines of inquiry. First, Barnard carefully reconstructs the
spiritualist currents in Bergson's writings which, though central and vital
to his thought, are underrepresented in scholarship today. Second, Barnard proposes a bold rereading of *Matter and Memory* toward a tentative
explanation of extraordinary religious phenomena. In particular he uses
Bergson's "filter" theory of perception, along with what he calls the "radio
reception theory of consciousness," to envisage the etiology of a wide
range of non-ordinary experiences such as telepathy, clairvoyance, mediumship, possession states, mystical states, and so on.

The volume concludes with a chapter by Paola Marrati on time and
openness in Bergson and William James. Her contribution directly challenges a picture of time deeply embedded within theology. Whether
called teleology, finalism, or eschatology, Marrati criticizes that family of
concepts that takes the future to be guided by a divine plan. Contrary to
this picture, Marrati argues that James and Bergson's affirmation of the
openness of time undercuts not only the foundation of finalism but with
it any psychological correlate of optimism or pessimism for the future.
Marrati is especially concerned with countering the impression of James
and Bergson as ontological optimists. There is, in their philosophy, nothing to sustain a belief in the necessity of progress (nor, of course, a belief
in the necessity of regress). A genuine philosophy of time cannot sustain
a political or theological temperament of "optimism" or "pessimism." It
leaves us only with an affirmation of openness and a place for responsibility and hope.

NOTES

1 See Lawlor and Moulard, "Henri Bergson."
2 On Bergson's political missions to Spain and the United States, see Soulez, *Bergson politique*.
3 Soulez and Worms, *Bergson*, 160.
4 See ibid., 186.
5 Deleuze, *Bergsonism*, 115. See also Deleuze and Guattari, *What Is Philosophy?*, 28. For a similar statement by Jankélévitch, see *Premières et dernières pages*, "Bergson did not want us to do again *what* he did, but to do it *as* he did" (92).
6 See Lefebvre, *The Image of Law*, 51–52. For a reading of Deleuze that applies this principle, see Patton, *Deleuzian Concepts*, 10–11.
7 Contemporary debates in biology reflect this line of argument. See in particular Frans de Waal's claim that "morality likely evolved as a within-group phenomenon in conjunction with other typical within-group capacities, such as conflict resolution, cooperation, and sharing. . . . The profound irony is that our noblest achievement—morality—has evolutionary ties to our basest behavior—warfare" ("Morally Evolved," 53, 55). See also his *The Age of Empathy*.
8 These are Bergson's examples but other figures come to mind, real and imaginary: Prince Myshkin, Nelson Mandela, the speaker in Walter de la Mare's poem "The Titmouse," who sees a titmouse as company, Donkey from *Shrek*, and many more. Indeed, it is an open question as to whether the open tendency is confined exclusively to human beings. For Bergson, we take it that the answer is yes: human beings alone have the capacity to love beyond preference. But if we turn to contemporary primatology, it is perhaps not so clear-cut. What should we make of a case such as Kuni, a bonobo at Twycross Zoo in England? "One day Kuni captured a starling. Out of fear that she might molest the stunned bird, which appeared undamaged, the keeper urged the ape to let it go. Kuni picked up the starling with one hand and climbed to the highest point of the highest tree where she wrapped her legs around the trunk so that she had both hands free to hold the bird. She then carefully unfolded its wings and spread them wide open, one wing in each hand, before throwing the bird as hard as she could towards the barrier of the enclosure. Unfortunately, it fell short and landed onto the bank of the moat where Kuni guarded it for a long time against a curious juvenile" (de Waal and Lanting, *Bonobo*, 156).
9 See John Rawls's insightful reading of the essential boredom and repetition of war for Thucydides (*The Law of Peoples*, 28n27).
10 Waterlot, "Penser avec et dans le prolongement des *Deux sources de la morale et de la religion*," 4–5.
11 We note here the important exception of Emmanuel Levinas who repeatedly states his debt to *Two Sources*. See Levinas, *Entre Nous*, 223–24; and de Warren, "Miracles of Creation." For the relation between Bergson and phenomenology in general, see Kelly, *Bergson and Phenomenology*.
12 Deleuze's *Bergsonism*, for example, dedicates only a few concluding paragraphs to *Two Sources* (110–12). To date, the growing and excellent English scholarship on

Bergson has by and large not treated *Two Sources*. Although Mullarkey's *Bergson and Philosophy* and Lawlor's *The Challenge of Bergsonism* each devote a chapter to it, Ansell-Pearson's *Philosophy and the Adventure of the Virtual*, Guerlac's *Thinking in Time*, Mullarkey's edited volume *The New Bergson*, and Grosz's *In the Nick of Time* seldom make reference to it. In France this situation is changing with a rush of recent publications on *Two Sources*. See, for example, Worms's *Bergson ou les deux sens de la vie*, his edited volume *Annales bergsoniennes I*, Waterlot's edited volume *Bergson et la religion*, and the new critical edition of *Deux Sources de la morale et de la religion* (2008), edited by Waterlot and Keck.

13 Russell, "The Philosophy of Bergson."

14 Shklar, "Bergson and the Politics of Intuition," 320 (hereafter cited in text as BPI).

15 See Lefebvre and White, "Religion within the Bounds of Mere Emotion."

16 Paola Marrati, "Mysticism and the Foundations of the Open Society," 600.

17 Montesquieu, *The Spirit of the Laws*, 3.1.

18 See Damasio, *Descartes' Error*.

19 See Marion, *The Erotic Phenomenon*, 7.

20 See Pippen, *The Persistence of Subjectivity*, 149.

21 Soulez and Worms, *Bergson*, 187.

PART I

Closed and Open

ONE

The Closed and the Open in
The Two Sources of Morality and Religion

A DISTINCTION THAT CHANGES EVERYTHING

Frédéric Worms
Translated by Alexandre Lefebvre and Perri Ravon

It may appear presumptuous to maintain, as I will do here, that a distinction—especially one set out in a philosophy book—could change everything, that is, even change everything in our lives. I must therefore immediately make clear that it is not the book itself that changes everything; Bergson, in publishing *The Two Sources of Morality and Religion* in 1932, would certainly not have made such a claim!

If there is something that changes everything, as Bergson does in fact claim and as I also believe is the case, it is not his book of philosophy, nor even a distinction inside that book, even one between the "closed" and the "open," if by that one means that the book creates the distinction out of thin air. If something changes everything, it is the distinction between open and closed moralities, religions, and societies inasmuch as this distinction *effectively exists*: one effectively appears, observable and active. If something changes everything, it is the difference between the closed and the open, not as it appears in a book but first of all *in life and in human history*, to the point of becoming, perhaps today more than ever, its primary and ultimate source of *orientation*.

But this does not mean that a book of philosophy, or philosophy itself, is good for nothing and changes nothing—

quite the contrary! For if the distinction appears in history, and even if as soon as it appears we immediately sense its full significance, this does not mean that we find it explicitly set out there alongside its criteria, that it is demonstrably established as primary, and that it does not also run into concurrent forces that cloud its effect. The role of philosophy and the philosopher may well be secondary compared to those who bring this distinction to life in history, but it is no less an essential one: in setting out and establishing this distinction in its specificity and scope, it also contributes to its practical effect. This is, without a doubt, Bergson's goal in *The Two Sources of Morality and Religion*, right down to its title. The book will change something, while establishing that a distinction changes everything.

This certainly explains, in any case, why the distinction between the "closed" and the "open" by itself commands the *whole* of Bergson's *Two Sources*.

Once again, perhaps more than ever, a fundamental "intuition" is expressed through a distinction that in turn governs a whole field of experience, according to Bergson; an intuition to be grasped both at the most intimate level *and* in the widest variety of its effects and consequences. Such was the case (in his earlier works) with duration and space, with memory and perception, and with life and matter. The distinction between the closed and the open will also express an intuition and a simple act that goes even beyond philosophy this time, and, through philosophy, it will resonate throughout the field of morality, religion, and society.

But if this is the task of philosophy and of writing *Two Sources*, it is also the task of understanding or reading it. This is therefore my goal here: to grasp the meaning or structure of the whole book based on the distinction—it being understood that the one expresses the other.

In order to do this, I will begin from the end of the work. Indeed, it is at the end of the book, more specifically at the beginning of its fourth and last chapter, just when he draws out the consequences of the theory of morality and religion he has just presented, that Bergson brings it back, *explicitly* and *in its entirety*, to the difference between the "closed" and the "open."

Taking this indication as my guide, we will proceed in *four stages*:

- We will start from the beginning of the fourth chapter, in order to understand how Bergson subsumes the *whole book* under this difference.
- We will then return to morality and to religion, respectively, which were presented in the three previous chapters; that is, I will return to

the *moral criterion* of the difference between the closed and the open
and then to the *religious expansion or deepening* of this difference.

- ← We will then be able to go back to the fourth chapter in order to
understand what this distinction changes in practice, *in our lives and
history*, both in 1932 for Bergson and also for us today.

THE CLOSED AND THE OPEN:
THE CONCLUSION AND OPENING OF *TWO SOURCES*

It is only at the beginning of the fourth and last chapter of *Two Sources*,
titled "Final Remarks: Mechanics and Mysticism," that one fully grasps
the scope of the difference between the closed and the open that has been
established in the three previous chapters.

More specifically, here Bergson explicitly entrusts it with a double role.
It must first sum up everything that came before. As the first sentence of
chapter 4 states: "One of the results of our analysis has been to draw a
sharp distinction, in the sphere of society, between the closed and the
open" (TS 266/1201). It is therefore both morality *and* religion that are
taken up anew here. Thus, with respect to closure: "This religion, which
we called static, and this obligation, which is tantamount to a pressure,
are the very substance of closed society" (TS 266–67/1202). But this is
not enough.

This distinction must also open up new perspectives that form the
true object of Bergson's last chapter, which is thus not only conclusive, or
rather not only "final" (to take up the first part of its title), but also itself
remains open. That is why what are here described as final are just
"remarks," an unusual term for Bergson: it is an invitation to go further.
Or more precisely still, here is what the new problem is from the perspective of this fundamental difference: "Now, is the distinction between the
closed and the open, which is necessary to resolve or remove theoretical
problems, able to help us practically" (TS 271/1206)?

It is of course important to underline the urgency of this "now," which
is not simply a logical step to one consequence among others. What must
"now" be faced are the practical problems of the present moment, in 1932
as the "us" also emphasizes. But this may seem surprising all the same.
While it is true, with regard to morality and then religion, that Bergson
has been addressing theoretical problems—the *criterion* of morality, the
principle of religion—we were hardly removed from practical concerns.

On the contrary, Bergson had dismissively criticized all theoretical morality; he even defined "complete mysticism" as the transition from contemplation (or ecstasy) to action. How then do we make sense of the fact that this practical dimension remains in a sense wholly untouched, at least for "us," on the threshold of these "Final Remarks"? How do we make sense of the fact that, of everything that came before, all that apparently remains is the distinction between "the closed and the open" as twin guiding threads, conclusive from a theoretical perspective but still "prospective" from a practical one? This is the double question that ought to be answered.

To do this I will first have to reconstruct Bergson's trajectory, in other words, retrace the steps that lead to this conclusion, before trying to understand what it also opens up for our action.

Before proceeding we shall make one last preliminary remark in order to avoid a serious misinterpretation regarding Bergson's fourth chapter itself. It concerns its title, the first part of which I have already discussed but whose second part must also be analyzed in order to rule out a potential misunderstanding and, more importantly, to elicit a new positive guideline for our inquiry. What, in effect, after the indication of "Final Remarks," does the phrase "Mechanics and Mysticism" mean? Let me immediately stress, before demonstrating it later on, that *the distinction between mechanics and mysticism in no way overlaps the distinction between the closed and the open*! It is not the case, in other words, that mechanics would be "closed" and mysticism "open." On the contrary, the entire goal of Bergson's chapter is to show how "mechanics" or technology "calls on" a form of mysticism *and* how mysticism "demands" a form of mechanics. They can, indeed must, proceed in the same direction, even if there is risk or danger that precisely consists in the possibility of them being separated! Everything that is at stake in this chapter lies within this. Mechanics and machines are described there as the stage reached by a humanity that has always, for Bergson, been defined by technical ability and intelligence—*homo faber*—but that "now" finds itself, more than ever, torn *between* the closed and the open! This then is the significance of the practical utility for "us," "now." The closed and the open can and must assist the direction we give to this modern, super-powerful technology, which can either lead to unheard of destruction on the side of closure or turn more strongly than ever toward openness.

Bergson therefore in no way condemns us to a terrible choice between a purely warlike "mechanization" and an ecstatic "mysticism" without any technical support! We can leave that to others. The freedom of humanity, "now," requires this new alliance between mechanics and mysticism, one beyond the dark, doubly closed one made by war, where technological power serves not mysticism but myth, mythology, ideology, and "fabulation." To get there, however, the distinction between the closed and the open first has to, as we shall see, run through the morality and religion of Bergson's previous chapters. To these, therefore, we must return.

A MORAL CRITERION

It is once again with a consummate writerly art and sense of "the composition of a book" that Bergson introduces the distinction between the closed and the open in the first chapter of *Two Sources*: it is a genuine *coup de théâtre*, or burst of thunder, heralded moreover by the witches of *Macbeth*!

Everything had effectively moved at the speed of light up to that point. Without any preamble, Bergson had moved from the fact of "obligation" to the immediate location of its double social principle, indeed vital principle, in a "virtual instinct" required by life to counterbalance the disorder introduced by human freedom. "Morality" seemed thereby to be given a foundation: a biological foundation, to be sure, but nevertheless one that is universal, omnipresent, and in any case in every society. Bergson even insists on this point: "What is natural is in great measure overlaid by what is acquired; but it endures, almost unchangeable, throughout the centuries. . . . To it we must revert . . . to explain what we have called obligation as a whole. Our civilized communities, however different they may be from the society to which we were primarily destined by nature, exhibit indeed, with respect to that society, a fundamental resemblance" (*TS* 29–30/999–1000). The logical conclusion then is that the principle of obligation does not change with history; it is the same everywhere. Its necessity and universality are thus confirmed; there is no distinction to be drawn between "primitive" and "civilized"; on the essential point, they are alike, equivalent. Yes, but the "resemblance" the paragraph concludes with is not the one you would expect. The "whole" of obligation is transformed with extreme abruptness into a wholly different thing in the next sentence!

Here is the resemblance between these "natural" human societies, whatever their place in history: "For they too are closed societies" (TS 30/1000).

Why does the "whole" of obligation turn into closure, totality into limitation? Why is this fact fundamental, so fundamental that it actually calls for a whole other morality, one that is not only universal this time in virtue of its (vital) foundation but also in virtue of its object, in virtue of those for whom it is valid or to whom it speaks. What is it that immediately proves this difference?

What immediately proves it to us, according to Bergson, is a simple fact that turns everything on its head, the reversal of values precisely heralded by the witches of *Macbeth*: *"Fair is foul, and foul is fair."* This fact is war: "we need only think what happens in time of war." And what effectively happens during a war? This: "Murder and pillage and perfidy, cheating and lying become not only lawful, they are actually praiseworthy" (TS 31/1000). If such a reversal of values is possible, it nonetheless has a simple explanation according to Bergson, summed up in the term "closure."

Certainly morality has not lost its validity; it simply reveals that it was only valid for the members of a given society to the exclusion of others: it reveals their limits or closure through its own. Such is the very simple and literal definition of closed societies: "They may be very vast ... [but] their essential characteristic is none the less to include at any moment a certain number of individuals, and exclude others" (TS 31/1000; translation modified).

What could be simpler? A closed society is one that does not include *everyone*, that marks a spatial limit, a frontier, an exclusion. But this spatial closure is immediately moral. Where the society stops so too does its morality. This closure, therefore, is not just a simple fact but also a serious problem. It is not simply a case of Pascalian relativism: "Truth this side of the Pyrenees, lies on the other"; it is even more serious: "Thou shalt not kill on this side of the Pyrenees, thou shalt kill on the other side." The boundary does not represent a relative difference but an absolute change: not truth here and lies there, but a prohibition here and an obligation there not only to lie but also to steal and kill. These are not two relative truths, but two absolute imperatives that contradict each other. And the boundary can fall within the same territory as soon as it isolates groups and identities. In short this fact revealed by another fact—the closure revealed by war—is not just one aspect among others of societies that hitherto considered themselves "moral," or of the "whole" of obligation that seemed so self-assured: it radically upsets them. Everything is thus clear-cut.

But we need to go a step further. It is obvious that this closure is not directly conscious of itself or at least not conscious of itself as "immoral." On the contrary, there is a sense in which we can only perceive, articulate, and, in any case, *denounce* this closure from another point of view, one that defines or rather calls for *another* morality! It is only from the perspective of this other morality, whose object is what Bergson calls here straightaway "man as man," or "the whole of humanity," that closure can be taken as a limit—not only a factual and spatial one but moral and absolute (TS 87/1048). Thus, it is not only closure that is revealed but also, by the same stroke or with the same indignation, the openness that is radically opposed to it.

We mustn't believe, however, as Bergson immediately stresses, that the difference between the two is not absolute. If the closed only appears as closed from the point of view of the open, it doesn't mean there is not what Bergson calls here a "difference of kind and not simply degree" between them (TS 32/1002)! Quite on the contrary: in the very feeling revealed to us by the fact of war, or our indignation before it, an absolute leap is revealed. And immediately the move from a closed society to an open society, from a limited society to a limitless society, cannot appear as a simple expansion, because it would then have to include that extreme, and also immediate, figure of closure: the enemy. The fact of war alone already prohibits us from conceiving the passage from closed to open as a simple expansion.

But Bergson has to insist on this point, and us with him: "Between the society in which we live and humanity in general there is, we repeat, the same contrast as between the closed and the open; the difference between the two objects is one of kind and not simply one of degree" (TS 32/1002).

Even the *image* of closed and open, with their suggestive spatial force, leaves no room for doubt: it is all or nothing. We can invoke another figure here who, like Pascal, hovers behind the scenes throughout this admirable book. It is the same here as in Rousseau's *Discourse on the Origin of the Inequality of Men*, where he imagines "the first man who, having enclosed a piece of land," invented property. With a single enclosure, all is closed. For Bergson too, this is how history can radically shift. The same principle is at play here, but it also runs in the opposite direction. For Rousseau, we move from a hypothetically open origin (the so-called state of nature) to an enclosure that inaugurates history. For Bergson, we move from a factually *closed* origin to an openness that demands effort and action but that similarly represents the real start of history or, in other words, the only thing that is truly new under the sun.

A genuine, crucial problem is thus raised: how do we attain open morality? While its criterion is given in a single stroke, it is also so demanding that we must surely postpone its possibility or its reality and achievement. But perhaps we should say the opposite. For Bergson it is precisely *because* this morality has already been realized and made possible that today we have a sense of it, and this is the reason why war or hate, even if we can't always avoid them, *at least make us indignant*! But, in this paragraph where everything is transformed and decided, he is more or less satisfied to raise the problem and to abstractly indicate two possible solutions: "Whether we speak the language of religion or the language of philosophy, whether it be a question of love or respect, a different morality, another kind of obligation supervenes, above and beyond the social pressure. So far we have only dealt with the latter. The time has come to pass to the other" (TS 33/1002).

There are two possibilities, therefore, for the universal: reason or love, philosophy or religion. But there are also two mistakes to avoid:

- First of all, even if Bergson comes down in favor of religion and love, it will certainly not be by way of relegating reason and philosophy to the side of closure! From Socrates to Kant, via Spinoza, the various moral philosophies are already on the side of the open, even if, according to Bergson, they lack its most active principle. But they already, and decisively, break ranks with the war instinct.
- But in addition, Bergson does not philosophically "deduce" or construct religion or even open morality. These exist as a matter of fact; the philosopher cannot invent them. This is what the rest of the first chapter demonstrates in its discussion of the "great moral figures" (TS 68/1032). Without them, the philosopher would not conceive of the criterion of the closed and open any more than we would be scandalized even by war.

It is nevertheless true, having stressed these two points, that from this point on there is something like a call to the problem of religion. To this we therefore must turn.

A RELIGIOUS DEEPENING

The transition from "morality" to "religion" is not, in *Two Sources*, the transition from a fact to its "foundation," but rather it is a transition *from one problem to another*: one that may be deeper but is still analogous and turns on the same principle and the same distinction implied by this principle. It is by going back over the same grooves that the distinction between the open and the closed takes on even greater scope, and, just as the moral criterion is amplified by religious experience, so this experience in turn continues to draw on the moral criterion, which will retain a *definitive*—in all senses of the word—character throughout the entire book.

What then is this new problem? Why have the stakes involved—not only in openness but also in closure, as is too often forgotten—increased here (an immediate sign being the division, this time across two chapters, between "static" and "dynamic" religion, respectively)? A brief attempt to answer these questions is required here.

The problem that religion responds to is in effect analogous to the one to which morality, for its part, offers a response. As indeed the whole start of the second chapter of *Two Sources* shows, human "intelligence" introduces not one but a *double* imbalance into life. It not only introduces freedom, to which "obligation" already represented some kind of response. It also introduces risk, doubt, a whole series of representations that threatens to distance humans, alone among all the species, from what Bergson no longer calls—as in his other books—"attention," but rather "attachment to life." Humans are the only beings—or only animals, if you prefer—who can entertain doubts about life. Hence the most general function of religion, which Bergson sets out in two stages:

- "*Looked at from this first point of view, religion is then a defensive reaction of nature against the dissolvent power of intelligence*" (TS 122/1078).
- "*Looked at from this second standpoint, religion is a defensive reaction of nature against the representation, by intelligence, of the inevitability of death*" (TS 131/1086).

As we know, Bergson will distinguish *two ways of responding to this double problem*: "static" and "dynamic" religion, respectively. The first will consist in countering representation with representation drawn from within thought itself, drawn even from human intelligence: namely the fictions and myths resulting from the "fabulation function." These fill the role of reassuring us and renewing our attachment to life, but they don't take us outside the sphere of human nature, of the species—even if there is an appearance of historical progress in the myths of the Greek pantheon, for instance, we remain in the realm of fable, which every child rediscovers and reinvents without knowing it. Dynamic religion, however, proceeds in an altogether different manner. It does not compensate the representations of intelligence with representations from the imagination; it goes beyond them by way of contact with the very source of life. This contact can be contemplative and simply free us from our doubts; it can be active and make us go beyond the very limits of human action. But in every case of what Bergson calls "mysticism," dynamic religion provides us not only with security but serenity, not only fiction but experience, not only a fable but a genuine narrative.

But what is too often forgotten, and what I want to stress here in a few words, is the way that the very distinction between static and dynamic in religion—and perhaps within each religion—is actually a revival and intensification of the distinction first established in morality between the closed and the open.

Here again, Bergson's writing style is striking. It is at the start of the third chapter, at the moment we get to "dynamic" religion, that once again all the results of the previous chapter are brutally put into perspective and turned on their head by the eruption, once again, of war: "The contrast [between the two religions] is striking in many cases, as for instance when nations at war declare that they have God on their side, the deity in question thus becoming the national god of paganism, whereas the God they imagine they are evoking is a God common to all mankind, the mere vision of Whom, could all men but attain it, would mean the immediate abolition of war" (*TS* 215/1157–58).

Thus, what must be stressed is that static religion not only fulfils its own function in a "static" way but also completes "closed" morality by further reinforcing the pressure that unites a group both within itself and against its enemies: "What binds together the members of a given society is tradition, the need and the determination to defend the group against other groups and to set it above everything. To preserve, to tighten this bond is incontestably the aim of the religion we have found to be natural. ... The fact that religion, such as it issued from the hands of nature, has simultaneously fulfilled ... the two functions, moral and national, appears to us unquestionable" (TS 206/1151).[1] What we need to take into account here is that it is not just a case of one fact that ties in with another; it is a *force* that joins up with another, magnifying what becomes an ever more formidable obstacle. It is truly myth that welds the community together. Bergson speaks of fabulation, which may have drawn wry smiles. What of it? But this is serious business. What is constantly highlighted throughout the chapter is the "ideo-motor" force of these imaginary representations, which compensate on a practical level for a practical defect of our intelligence. Fabulation has, and is, a power. It was this that was already cause for amazement on the impressive first page of the second chapter: "Religion has been known to enjoin immorality, to prescribe crime" (TS 102/1061).

Not only does the same amazement return but so too does the same criterion, this time redoubled. Of course, it may be argued that Bergson also suggests that the open has by the same token gained in strength and intensity. And as a matter of fact this will indeed be the case with mysticism. But before we even reach that point, it is important to stress the exceptional character of mysticism, even if it finds a place, or awakens an echo, in us all. In reality, what Bergson calls "natural" religion here doesn't disappear anymore than the "morality" of the same name, even if it encounters its radically opposed other. It will continue to offer resistance. Who can gainsay Bergson on this point?

But what is more often forgotten, and more seriously still, is that the very criterion of mysticism is to be sought, in the first instance, within the openness that would thus be opposed, more than ever, to closure! We rightly seek to characterize the metaphysical implications of mysticism. We wonder about the distinction Bergson makes between mystics. And yet if there is one criterion of mysticism that ensures that not just anyone can call him- or herself a mystic, that ensures there can be no mistake about the matter, it is surely the distinction between the closed and the open. Of course, it is possible to say that open morality is only fully open if it draws its strength from its contact with the principle of life, which only the mystic accomplishes. But conversely, this contact, especially for the complete mystic, expresses itself first and foremost in the aspiration to open morality. Thus, according to Bergson, the peak of mysticism is attained in Christianity. Nothing is more laconic than the nevertheless central declaration—the cutting edge of the whole book—in the third chapter: "Let us merely say that, if the great mystics are indeed such as we have described them, they are the imitators, and original but incomplete continuators, of what the Christ of the Gospels was completely" (TS 240/1179).

In the first chapter on morality, Bergson had stated in advance what he meant by this: "The morality of the Gospels is essentially that of the open soul" (TS 59/1024). He added: "Such is the inner meaning of the antitheses that occur one after the other in the Sermon on the Mount: 'You have heard it that it was said . . . I say unto you . . . ' On the one hand the closed, on the other the open" (TS 59/1025). The same is true of the other mysticisms. I have elsewhere shown that each mysticism seeks, however incompletely, to deliver humanity from one of its limits and essential sufferings (_souffrances vitals_): metaphysical problems, life sufferings, and moral injustice are thus in a sense the angle of attack for the Greek, Oriental, and Jewish mystics.[2] But all this had already been announced in the first chapter of the book through the lens of the closed and the open. Attention is thus usually riveted on a single page in the third chapter where Bergson, having spoken about Christianity, speaks about Israel's prophets. But how can we forget what he had already said in this regard in the first chapter: "Let us recall the tone and accents of the Prophets of Israel. It is their voice we hear when a great injustice has been done and condoned. From the depths of the centuries they raise their protest" (TS 76/1039). It is almost as if we were—and in our opinion we are—hearing Charles Péguy talking about Bernard Lazare during the Dreyfus affair.

It is therefore indeed the opposition between the closed and the open that governs Bergson's theory, both of religion as well as morality. Yet far from this opposition finding only a foundation in mysticism, it also finds a further difficulty: for while there have been mystics (without whom access to the distinction itself would have been impossible), once again they are both definitive and exceptional, unimpeachable and met with resistance. The greater the effort, the greater its reach, the more it reveals the force of the obstacle, which ceaselessly returns. This is also why it should no longer come as a surprise, at this stage of our journey, that the book does not end with its third chapter! Certainly, in principle, everything has been said; we can even say that the absolute has made its entrance into history or has opened up what finally, in the evolution of life, becomes history. In fact, however, everything remains to be done. We have at our disposal not only the words, example, and action of the mystic but also a distinction, along with its philosophical force, to confront problems that can no longer wait.

THE CLOSED AND THE OPEN: PRACTICAL PERSPECTIVES

Here we are then, back to our starting point, on which I will present three brief series of perspectives, by way of conclusion, in order to understand the practical implications of the distinction between the closed and the open, not only in the last chapter of *Two Sources* but beyond.

Everything effectively takes place as though the fourth chapter of the book was caught in a sort of in-between state, an in-between that is explicit and claimed as such, as well as being caught up in an extreme state of *urgency*. On the one hand, the distinction between the closed and the open changes everything; more specifically, open morality and religion institute a definitive break and novelty. On the other hand, however, it is precisely only the mystic or great moral figure who can practically implement the distinction in reality. So much so that in their absence—their exceptional and unpredictable absence—the distinction precisely falls back into a distinction that, while certainly not empty, while still real, risks being merely theoretical and ahead of its effects. The goal of the fourth chapter is thus, explicitly, to show that we cannot wait: in other words, that we can and even must immediately determine points of application that are accessible to ordinary people, insofar as they are themselves caught in the in-between that is opened up by the distinction: the in-between of intelligence, technology, and institutions. Furthermore, we must do so because these problems don't have to be invented. They are there: the war, its "reasons," its "means," and its dangers—on which we can thus act, in a sense, by default. We can't do everything; only mystical effort is capable of that. But we can't do nothing: the dangers have become extreme. We must therefore act: by diagnosing the problems (mechanization and war); by using the distinction to orient ourselves (the mechanical calls on the mystical and vice versa in the direction of openness, away from closure); by showing the fact of the oscillation between the two extreme poles in human history, an oscillation on which we can lean (dichotomy, double frenzy). In short, the whole fourth chapter invents a sort of politics of the in-between that is neither metaphysical nor without any metaphysical implications. In so doing, it takes a stance on problems that are both essential and urgent (the meaning of technology, the nature of democracy, contemporary war). This in-between, too often misunderstood, is far from being a weakness; it is instead a means of precision, strength, and a step forward.

But everything happens as though the reception of the book had to side one way or the other.

For example, there is the demand to immediately realize mysticism. But Bergson had seen the resistance of closure and the strength of the "mythical" as opposed to the "mystical." Far from what has too often been thought, it is because there are these two forces—infra-rational and warlike on one side, supra-rational and democratic on the other—that as long as the latter has not definitively defeated the former, with which it cannot be confused, we must rely on reason and intelligence! *Two Sources* is thus clearly a treatise of all three orders: the infra-rational, rational, and suprarational. How could anyone have thought that Bergson favored just any form of irrationality? He distinguishes two, more radically than ever! Hate and love. When he states in a now famous interview that "Hitler proved the truth of the two sources,"[3] that is indeed what he is talking about. Only Jesus, as always, and all the "heroes" of openness will answer him and win. But if their strength at a given moment is no longer enough, reason, although less powerful in itself, cannot but take up the baton, the weapons, and responsibility of history.

If pure mysticism is inaccessible, however, it would also be a mistake to give an entirely non-metaphysical significance to the distinction between the closed and the open, as did Karl Popper in *The Open Society and Its Enemies*, nevertheless one of its most profound adaptations.[4] For Popper, the distinction becomes that between totalitarianism and democracy, the latter defined first and foremost by the "openness" of speech, information, and verification and refutation based on the model of science. He thus explicitly makes use of Bergson's distinction, without its metaphysical foundation, in his own remarkably pertinent and powerful fashion.

But it is possible that today, without necessarily returning to Bergson's metaphysics and the in-between it outlines as a horizon for action, we may not be satisfied with a quasi-technical distinction that does not refer to a radical and ever-returning obstacle against which one must constantly struggle. This is at least the case in the three domains the book covers one by one. First, in the religious domain: more than ever, the distinction between the closed and the open seems to us to cut like a sword—not between religions but within each religion. It shows the extent to which religion is not necessarily what frees us from closure, from the conflict between identities, and from hatred, but what further strengthens these, while at the same time it is also, in virtue of the strength of an effort that exists in each one, what is opposed to all these things. It is thus both poison and antidote at the same time, not blended together but as two clearly opposed directions, Bergson being one of the few to have set up an opposition between them. This is also quite true of the political domain: democracy, as Bergson shows, is a direction more than an institution, an effort to be renewed rather than an established structure. Its imperfection and readiness to fall back into closure should lead us not to abandon it but to return to it!

But I will conclude with a moral observation. Namely that the experience of closure and openness takes place not only in the transition from the closed group to the whole of humanity but also in every relationship between men and at all levels, from the vital individual relationship to the global relation on the scale of the planet. In this sense this experience does not presuppose any transcendent metaphysics; it is rather the experience itself that gives a metaphysical significance—that is, an absolute polarity—to all immanent relationships. In this sense, finally, it certainly does not change "everything" in a single stroke, as if that were possible, as if "everything" were not a fiction. But it absolutely does change, everywhere, something—not only through the philosopher who states it but also through those who, without even having to state it, make it happen.

NOTES

1 Significantly, this section of the text is titled "The Function of Static Religion." [Translator's note: the English edition of TS omits the section headings.]

2 See my " 'Terrible réalité' ou 'faux problème'?," esp. 384.

3 See Chevalier, *Entretiens avec Bergson*, 215.

4 Popper, *The Open Society and Its Enemies*.

TWO

Bergson, the Void,
and the Politics of Life

Suzanne Guerlac

"Just when everyone has stopped believing in them," Nietzsche writes of truly great texts, "they begin to speak to us in a new voice."[1] But we have to listen carefully. *The Two Sources of Morality and Religion* (1932) can produce a distinct feeling of estrangement, even in admirers of Bergson's earlier works. Its argument is deeply embedded in the discourses and events of the interwar decades, an intellectual context that no longer seems to us quite modern. We imagine that the demands placed upon thought by the Holocaust—Adorno expressed them most poignantly—have rendered the intellectual concerns of the interwar years of the twentieth century negligible, that we have moved well beyond them.[2] But have we? Is it possible that Bergson's final work, through the very sense of estrangement it produces, might throw into relief the contours of the intellectual fabulations we have inherited from the second half of the twentieth century, ones that might no longer prove adequate, when examined closely, to the challenges of the twenty-first century? In what follows, I examine, and attempt to reinvigorate, Bergson's challenge to the modern intellectual framework.

THE MODERN AND THE BARELY MODERN

If *Two Source* strikes us as unmodern today it might be because Bergson takes Emile Durkheim—in many respects a quintessentially modern thinker—as his target here.[3] When he writes in *Two Sources* that moral philosophy is traditionally vague about the relation between duties toward one's fellow citizens and duties toward mankind he puts his finger on a particularly vulnerable moment in Durkheim's sociological analysis of ethics, the articulation of real structures of social affiliation with the ethical ideal of human rights for all humanity: "A moral philosophy that does not insist on this distinction," he adds, without referring to the sociologist by name, "cannot be true [*est à côté de la vérité*]" (TS 31/1000).[4] The problem is how to extend what Durkheim calls "attachment" to the political group of which one is a part to humanity generally or, in other words, how to reconcile nationalism with cosmopolitanism.[5]

In *Moral Education* Durkheim identifies three levels of group affiliation: the family, the fatherland or political group (*la patrie*), and humanity.[6] He states that the three groups "can be superimposed on one another without mutual exclusion" (ME 74). Each represents a different phase in human social and moral evolution, phases that "have mutually prepared one another" (ME 74). He goes so far as to declare that man "is not morally complete unless he undergoes this triple action" (ME 74). Having made this high-minded claim however, the sociologist is immediately forced to backtrack from it in order to remain consistent with the argument of his general theory. We are only moral beings to the extent that we are social beings, and for this to be the case, we must belong to a social group that actually exists. Mankind cannot be considered such a group, for it is merely an abstract term (ME 76). It is an ideal that the progress of civilization attempts to realize. Although civilization implies an eventual progressive expansion from family, to patrie, to humanity, the nation-state, Durkheim affirms, is "presently the highest organized human group that exists" (ME 76). Acknowledging the urgency of the debate between nationalism and cosmopolitanism, Durkheim takes the side of nationalism, arguing that "it seems to be impossible to subordinate and to sacrifice a group that exists, that is a living reality at the present time, to a group that does not yet exist, and which, very likely, will never be anything but an idea of reason [*un être de raison*]" (ME 76). Forced, for the sake of the coherence of his broader argument, to acknowledge the distinction between a real and an ideal human group, and to align himself with the former, he nevertheless tries to blunt the opposition between nationalism and cosmopolitanism. To resolve the antinomy between the two, he suggests, "the State need only give itself, as a principal objective ... the aim of realizing within itself [*dans son sein*] the general interests of humanity, that is, to ensure the reign [*faire régner*] of more justice [*plus de justice*], a higher morality" (*ME* 77). While Durkheim comes down on the side of nationalism (albeit with apparent reluctance), Bergson, as we shall see, will argue resoundingly in favor of cosmopolitanism—we might even say in favor of a certain cosmopolitics.

In a light version of the distinction Bergson will deepen and theorize as structurally fundamental to his argument in *Two Sources*, Durkheim delineates two different national characters, one egotistical, materialistic, and predatory, the other spiritual, generous, and inclined toward the ideal of humanity. An evolutionary progress leads from the former, which Durkheim paints as primitive, to the latter, which he identifies with civilized societies that take the ideal of humanity (and of human rights) as their guiding principle. He considers the generous, or spiritual, state character to be the highest form of collective association, one that becomes possible historically only among "states which have achieved the same degree of moral development" (*ME* 77). The more civilized a nation becomes, the more it tends toward the realization of the universal ideal of humanity. The modern state, Durkheim concludes, is "the highest approximation of this human society, presently not realized, and perhaps unrealizable, but which constitutes the ideal limit that we tend toward, indefinitely [*dont nous tendons à nous rapprocher indéfiniment*]" (*ME* 81). Thus a certain Kantian feature returns within Durkheim's analysis: an ideal of humanity that serves as a regulative idea in relation to a social teleology, one that overlaps with the European discourse of civilization that François Guizot synthesized in the 1830s.[7] The implication is clear: European nations (and they alone) are spiritual states on their way to realizing, to one degree or another, the ideal of humanity.

History would sorely disappoint Durkheim on this score within his lifetime: the First World War provided the definitive counterexample to his assumptions about the civilized societies of Europe. In an essay published just after the war, "L'Allemagne au-dessus de tout: La mentalité allemande et la guerre" (Germany above all: the German mentality and the war), Durkheim analyzed the collective personality of Germany as it revealed itself during the war, expressing astonishment that the Germans "were able to belie the principles of human civilization to his point."[8] Durkheim is dismayed to find barbarism lodged in the heart of Europe and at the cutting edge of modernity.[9] The German state, he concludes, and the "monstrous war machine that it launched on the world in an attempt to dominate it," is an aberration, a case of social pathology that he refers to as a "morbid hypertrophy of the will."[10] The analysis of the German exception, however, reveals a fundamental character of the state in general; it emphasizes the amorality of state sovereignty in time of war and simultaneously affirms the inevitability of war in a world of economic competition. Durkheim's conclusions are damning to the argument he had confidently proposed in his lectures on moral education before the war. He has come to recognize that the right to declare war is the special attribute of national sovereignty: "It is by this right that it distinguishes itself from all other human groups." "Without war," he now concludes, "the State is not conceivable."[11]

This statement might well have served as the point of departure for *Two Sources*. The First World War confirmed for Bergson that the evolutionary story of development from the primitive, or barbaric, to the modern—the story of civilization as a narrative of moral advancement— was but a fable. In *Two Sources* he builds his analysis of the closed society around the very features Durkheim analyzed in relation to the pathological case of Germany. Although he affirms a limited agreement with Durkheim's broader argument concerning moral obligation—"the moral domain begins where the social domain begins" Durkheim had affirmed (*ME* 60); "social necessity [*l'exigence sociale*] lies at the basis of moral obligation," Bergson writes in *Two Sources* (*TS* 30/1000)—Bergson restricts this conception of the social, and of moral obligation, to the framework of the closed society that divides "us" from "them" and renders war inevitable. To the (actual) closed society he then opposes a (virtual) open one, on the basis of which he will elaborate another foundation of ethics and another conception of the social.

Having essentially quarantined Durkheim's analysis of social obligation within the structure of the closed society, Bergson proceeds to deconstruct the ethical pretensions of the rational ethics associated with it. Although society may claim an obligation to humanity, Bergson argues, in times of war the notion of humanity vanishes into thin air and moral imperatives reverse themselves, much as Durkheim had demonstrated in his essay on Germany. When actions are directed against an enemy, Bergson writes, citing Shakespeare, "Fair is foul and foul is fair" (*TS* 31/1000). The ends justify the means; all that matters is the victory of us against them. "Between the nation, however great it might be, and humanity" Bergson concludes, "there exists the distance that separates the finite from the indefinite [*le fini de l'indéfini*], the closed from the open" (*TS* 32/1001).

Bergson is not just saying that we have a long way to go before achieving a peaceful world. He has already left this attitude behind, after his unsuccessful efforts in connection with the League of Nations and the International Commission for Intellectual Cooperation.[12] The key feature of Bergson's analysis, and the one that most radically challenges the Durkheimian (modern) position, is the assertion that the two kinds of society—the closed and the open—are different not simply in degree (i.e., in degree of inclusiveness, of civilized culture, or of approximation to the ethical ideal) but in kind. What this means is that there is no continuous passage from one to the other and hence no rational access to the latter. Through this formal distinction Bergson essentially shuts down the narrative of civilization. What is at stake in the difference between the closed or the open—or the nation and humanity—is a more or less perpetual threat of war and, as we shall see, the very possibility of a universal secular ethics. It is a mystification, Bergson holds, to construct an ethics (or a politics) based on the hope of a progressive realization of a rational ideal, since there is no rational way to get from the closed society to the open one. It is because his theory of the difference in kind between the closed and the open implies a rejection of both Kant and Durkheim that Bergson can strike us as barely modern.

If the closed society precludes a realization of the ideal of humanity, this realization is the very definition of the open society: "a society that would be humanity [*qui serait alors l'humanité*]" (*TS* 212/1155). The open society neutralizes the opposition between "us" and "them" not because it reaches beyond this distinction to all of humanity but because it reaches beyond humanity altogether to embrace all living beings. Whereas the closed society coincides with Durkheim's analysis of the social, the open society is "supra-social" (*TS* 66/1030). Instead of obligation, which Bergson and Durkheim agree is founded by the social, this supra-social obligation implies the supra-obligation associated with the "open soul" (*TS* 59/1024), whose emotion of love is characterized as a love of creation that ultimately coincides with the forces of life itself. This "supra-intellectual" (TS 84/1046) emotion enjoys ontological status.

In *Moral Education* Durkheim dismissed *"la charité"* as a moral force, claiming that it operates only on the level of the individual and that social ills can only be addressed collectively—"there is no true moral motivation a part from attachment to the group" (ME 82). On this basis, it has been easy to set up an opposition between the social thinker (Durkheim) and the individualist one (Bergson), the sociological thinker on the one hand and the psychological one on the other. But this would be to miss the point. For although Bergson attributes the force of charitable love to the individual he calls the mystic or the "privileged soul," this individual has a distinctly social function in *Two Sources* (TS 52/1000). He or she acts powerfully on others as a model of imitation that imposes itself with irresistible force.

In this deconstruction of the opposition between the individual and the social Bergson is playing Gabriel Tarde (1843–1904; briefly Bergson's colleague at the College de France) off against Durkheim. If we have heard relatively little about Tarde until quite recently, this is because Durkheim's stellar rise in the academy cast the thought of his senior colleague into the shadows.[13] In *The Laws of Imitation* (1890) Tarde defined society as "a collection of beings as they are in the process of imitating one another."[14] He held that "the social being [*l'être social*], as social, is essentially an imitator" (LI 54), affirming that "everything that is social . . . has imitation as its cause" (LI 12). In his opposition to Durkheim, then, Bergson does not pit an individualist, or psychological, perspective against a social one; he opposes one conception of the social (and of sociology) to another. Bergson plays Tarde off against Durkheim in his elaboration of the formal distinction between the open and the closed society and between static and dynamic religion. These structural oppositions take the place of the diachronic opposition between the primitive and the modern—the civilization story—at work in modern thinkers such as Durkheim, Lucien Lévy-Bruhl, and Marcel Mauss.

According to Tarde, repetition is a fundamental structure of being, an ontological structure. If repetition occurs in the social world as imitation, it also occurs in the material world as vibration and in the organic, or human, world as heredity (LI 12).[15] Repetition proceeds energetically from events of innovation that produce new models of imitation and open new series. On the social level, Tarde's analysis of imitation concerns forces of belief and desire that "have their source in the living world" (_LI_ 159) and penetrate energetically into the very fabric of being. Energy, Tarde affirms, "is always dual in its manifestations." A dualism between "the static and the dynamic . . . divides the whole universe in two" (_LI_ 159). A structural opposition for Tarde, the static and the dynamic return in _Two Sources_ to mark the qualitative difference associated with Bergson's formal opposition between the closed and the open: the closed society is static, the open dynamic. Bergson's open society will be associated with the imitative forces of dynamic religion (mysticism) as against the static religions of closed societies that depend upon a fabulatory function.

THE LIMITS OF REASON: THE LEAP

We owe to Bruno Latour the possibility of contesting a modern epistemology without having to adopt a postmodern perspective. In _The Politics of Nature_ (where he characterizes his own perspective as "nonmodern" or "unmodern")[16] he criticizes a conceptual framework he refers to as "modern" that depends on the oppositions between nature and culture on the one hand and the subject and the object on the other. Durkheim is one of the figures he names in conjunction with what he calls the "epistemology police" that defends this framework.[17] He attempts to displace this modern framework toward a new paradigm of political ecology.

When Bergson writes, "the social is, fundamentally, a function of the vital [_est au fond du vital_]" (_TS_ 119/1075) he performs the distinctly unmodern gesture of collapsing culture into nature by subjecting the notion of society to a biological interpretation. Sociability, he argues, is a natural tendency, one at work in communities of ants and bees as well as humans. This social instinct, which operates on behalf of the conservation of the species, "always implies [_vise toujours_] . . . a closed society" (_TS_ 32/1001). Nature, in other words, requires a closed society where moral obligation, a function of habit and adaptation, occurs through various pressures imposed by natural necessity in accordance with evolutionary forces and constraints. Bergson introduces this perspective in his first chapter of _Two Sources_ and returns to it in his discussion of war in the concluding chapter of his study: humans are designed for war, an inevitable consequence of the closed structure of human society, itself required by nature for purposes of survival.[18]

To this natural obligation Bergson heuristically proposes another, one that would require a detour around the pressures of nature. He suggests two possible trajectories: the "detour" of rational philosophy that proposes "universal acceptance of a law" (TS 34/1002) or "the leap" [bond] (TS 33/1002) of religion that implies "collective [commune] imitation of a model" (TS 34/1003). He proceeds to launch a major assault (in his gentle manner) on the first path, picking up the thread of the second in his third chapter.

Bergson's first line of attack against the theoretical foundation of ethics on the basis of the "universal acceptance of a law" (TS 34/1002) concerns the difference between theory and practice. Ideas in and of themselves have no power to affect the real world—"as if an idea could ever categorically demand its own realization!" (TS 96/1057) Bergson exclaims with uncharacteristic sarcasm. To become "effective" (agissante) (TS 78/1040) an idea must be able to take hold affectively, thereby creating a desire for its own realization.[19] Plato, he reminds us, had an idea of man that could have lead to a conception of humanity and been the basis for a philosophy of human rights (TS 77/1040). But his idea did not become fully elaborated in this way because ancient Greek philosophers were unwilling to challenge the institution of slavery. Political interests protected this institution and encouraged the notion that strangers to the elite community of the city, as well as slaves, were barbarians; as such they were excluded from the very concept of man. It took religion (Christianity), Bergson argues, "for the idea of universal fraternity . . . to become effective [agissante]" (TS 78/1040). Ideas alone are powerless against the political forces that oppose them. Rational ethics is ineffectual in the face of egoism and the political pressures of powerful interests. This is what is revealed in times of war when the principles of rational ethics—universality, for example—are overridden and the very notion of humanity disappears into thin air. It is ultimately impossible to sort out the limits between self-interest and the general interest, Bergson maintains, largely because intelligence itself is egotistical and self-interested. This was one of the lessons of Creative Evolution. Here Bergson makes it explicit that the intelligence of the philosopher will produce "an ethical morality where the interpenetration of personal interest and the general interest is demonstrable [démontrée]" (TS 93/1054), at least in retrospect.

Reason alone cannot determine ends. Those ostensibly invoked by a rational ethics are, for the most part, actually derived from existing practices. Bergson demystifies the notion that there might be pure moral ideas accessible to reason. "Obligation does not come down from above, as one might think," with maxims rationally deduced, "it rises up for below ... from the depths of the pressures [*pressions*] ... on which society rests" (TS 91/1048). The most important philosophical consequence of this argument is that there is no rational foundation for the notion that reason is universal. To believe that it is, and that this universality itself has a rational foundation, Bergson concludes, is an illusion—the "illusion common to all rational ethics [*morales théoriques*]" (TS 92/1053), including that of human rights—"in short, it cannot be a question of founding ethics on the cult of reason" (TS 89/1050).

Critics have emphasized the impact of the First World War—"whose horror," Bergson writes, "exceeded anything one believed possible (TS 285/1218)—on *Two Sources*. In a quite different context, Hannah Arendt reminds us that this war had a devastating effect on the authority of human rights discourse. In the wake of the First World War, she writes, there emerged minorities and stateless people (populations unprotected by any state authority to uphold claims to human rights) in such numbers that "the very phrase 'human rights' became for all concerned—victims, persecutors and onlookers alike—the evidence of hopeless idealism or of fumbling feeble-minded hypocrisy."[20] In the wake of the war, "peoples suddenly appeared whose elementary rights were as little safeguarded by the ordinary functioning of nation-states in the middle of Europe as they would have been in the heart of Africa."[21] The real shock, then, concerned the inability to protect human rights among peoples *within Europe*. The lack of protection for human rights in so-called backward cultures had been attributed to a cultural primitiveness (as Durkheim's analysis implied). In *The Origins of Totalitarianism* Arendt forcefully affirms that the notion of "some inborn human dignity," upon which the theory of human rights is usually founded in the Kantian tradition, is "possibly the most arrogant myth we have invented in our long history."[22] Arendt, then, like Bergson before her, calls into question a certain theoretical foundation of human rights, though not its practice.

More recently, Jacques Derrida has criticized the democratic ideal of fraternity associated with human rights discourse for its unwitting complicity with a politics of exclusion based on factors such as race, class, and gender. When he writes that it "privilege[s] ... the masculine authority of the brother ... genealogy, family, birth, autochthony, and the nation," and that it leads to war and genocide, he transposes the thrust of Bergson's analysis of the closed society into a new key.[23] Yet the difference between Bergson and Derrida's critiques of fraternity is revealing. Derrida's response to the closed structure of fraternity is to replace the figure of the brother with that of the friend, shifting from the rational framework of fraternity (as characterized by Arendt) to an affective register, just as Bergson does. But if Derrida needs to further nuance this figure by evoking the figure of the "true friend"—the friend loved after death, in mourning—this is because he focuses on the (intersubjective) object of love.[24] Given that, in Hegel, the intersubjective relation implies a structure of recognition that entails the violent reduction of the other to a subordinate version of the same, it becomes necessary for Derrida to safeguard the alterity of this object of love—this friend—by situating him or her within a horizon of absence and mourning. Bergson, on the other hand, is interested in the *action* of love, not its object. Indeed, the specific feature of mystical love in *Two Sources* is that it has no object; Bergson invokes "an active love [*agissant*] that would address . . . nothing" (*TS* 255/1192). The structure of the open requires this objectlessness and also affects the status of the subject. Bergson's musical metaphors for the emotion of love in the register of the open suggest that the love of all living creatures would occur on the level of a Tardean vibration, that is as a mode of attunement or a kind of transposing. Bergson dispenses with the subject-object relation altogether in his account of the ethics of the open. In *Two Sources* resistance to the closed and static structure occurs as a force of energy (love) that comes, as it were, from the outside—from being as time—and passes right through others (in the plural) on the way to touching all humans, animals, and plants, indeed all of nature—"charity would subsist in the one who possesses it even if there were no other living creature on earth" (*TS* 38/1007). With Bergson it becomes possible to think beyond fraternity in a mode that is not melancholic but rather involves an experience of joy—a "resonance of feeling" (*TS* 40/1008) that exceeds any dialectics of pleasure.

THE LIMITS OF THE LIVING: FROM EMANCIPATION
TO SUSTAINABILITY (AND BACK)

The nineteenth-century French feminist militant Flora Tristan invoked a right to life that had nothing to do with women's reproductive choices but rather concerned the right to work and so to sustain oneself by means of a living wage.[25] We might call it the right to go on living. Today, this right is at risk not only for economic reasons associated with the global economy but also because we now face threats to the conditions that sustain life on a planetary scale, threats that concern climate change, the water supply, and the disruption of ecosystems due to reduced biodiversity. These risks seem to defy political or legal solutions either because of their transnational character, because they evolve over exceptionally long time spans, or because they imply an interaction between global corporate "persons" that are not easily held responsible under the law. In other words, these contemporary challenges to the right to go on living escape the paradigm of emancipation. In the face of such threats we can no longer rely on categories that isolate human (or intersubjective) relations, upon which discourses of emancipation depend, from dynamics of ecological organization that go beyond those limits.

To translate Bergson's perspective into more contemporary terms, we could say that *Two Sources* argues that one cannot get to a discourse (or practice) of sustainability by simply extending the discourse of emancipation; nor can we realize emancipation on the scale of humanity without a practice of sustainability. This is just what it might mean for Bergson to be unmodern. In this respect Bruno Latour could be said to pick up where Bergson left off. Latour (whose *Politics of Nature*, he reveals, was in part prompted by the Kyoto talks) argues that the modern epistemological framework is outdated to the extent that it depends on the oppositions between subject and object on the one hand and between nature and culture on the other; neither one is appropriate to the world of information networks and crises of sustainability that is now ours. He proposes replacing the traditional position of the subject with the term "humans and nonhumans" and referring to the object (or fact of nature) as a "matter . . . of concern."[26] He challenges the ideological power of a monolithic science, deconsolidates its authority, and redistributes it through various social protocols (consultation, politics, ethics, etc.) that he models on the experimental practices of the sciences (in the plural) that he continues to prize.

From this perspective our reading of *Two Sources* has opened up; however, neither the shift from a knowledge to an information model, nor the displacement from the category of the human subject to that of "humans and nonhumans," necessarily alters the framework of what Bergson calls "intelligence" and critiques as intrinsically instrumental and egotistical. If we can thank Latour for the opportunity to approach Bergson as at once nonmodern and contemporary (that is, contemporary precisely in as much as he is nonmodern), reading Latour with Bergson in mind suggests that perhaps Latour's own fable of political ecology might not be unmodern enough.[27] We are struck by what Latour avoids in his attempt to leap out of the modern framework. He carves out a function for what he calls the "ethical worrier" in *The Politics of Nature* without stopping to wonder on what basis the worrier worries or about what. Nor does he concern himself with the activity, or point of view, of the economic knowledge workers, whose disciplinary territory (and political presuppositions) remains unexamined. What appears to be left out of Latour's somewhat bureaucratic account of cosmopolitics, or political ecology, are egotism and the institutional sedimentation of interests and powers, which, as we have seen, Bergson diagnoses so skillfully in his critique of the closed society. These appear to be the blind spot of Latour's vigorous intellectual challenge to the politics of modernism that—and here Latour and Bergson would appear to agree—reveal themselves to be entirely inadequate to the challenges of the present moment.

If Latour shies away from economic and political issues, Bergson addresses them head on in the conclusion of *Two Sources*. He emphasizes that colonial rivalry leads to war, with specific reference to Morocco, where conflict over energy resources was a prelude to the First World War. In other words he critiques colonialism from a perspective that remains pertinent in a postcolonial context, one that concerns the pillaging of nations in a competition for the energy resources required by a global economy that, according to his analysis, produces comfort and profit for the few instead of addressing the basic needs of all. He emphasizes the extent to which economic interests manipulate desires and needs, creating artificial needs and profiting from the satisfaction of them. Critics have characterized this as an ascetic ideal, a term that, by association with a religious conception of the mystical, marginalizes an analysis that presents a prescient critique of subsequent developments in global capitalism. Bergson does not object to technology but to the ends it serves in the context of (closed) industrial societies. His analysis acknowledges the domination of capitalism (as it functions in relation to the structure of the closed society) as the horizon of threats to living beings.[28] To this extent, far from being marginal—merely proposing an "ascetic ideal"—his analysis of the impact of technology in the contemporary social and economic framework can be read as a step toward the recognition of capitalism as "the only totalitarianism that has succeeded."[29]

THE VOID

In the bleak months leading up to the outbreak of the Second World War, Bergson analyses the problem this way:

> But machines that run on oil, coal, or white coal and that convert potential energies accumulated over millions of years into movement, have endowed our organism with an extension so vast and a power so formidable, so disproportional to its dimension and its force, that surely nothing like this was foreseen in the structural plan of our species: here was a unique stroke of luck, the greatest material success of man on the planet. A spiritual impulse had perhaps been transmitted at first: the extension occurred automatically, facilitated by a chance blow of the pickaxe which struck a miraculous treasure underground. Now in this inordinately swollen body, the soul remains what it was, too small now to fill it, too weak to guide it. Whence the void between the two [*entre lui et elle*]. Whence the formidable [*redoubtables*] social, political, and international problems that are but so many definitions of this void, and which provoke so many muddled and ineffectual efforts to fill it [*le combler*]: we must make new reserves of potential energy, moral energy this time.[30] (TS 309–10/1238–39)

Bergson continues, saying that "now in this inordinately swollen body, the soul remains what it was, too small now to fill it, too weak to guide it" (TS 309–10/1239). This image, which appears dense, even a bit overwrought in the passage cited above, has haunted Bergson, in one form or another, since the First World War. He has produced numerous versions of it, all of which inform this passage. In speeches intended to stir up patriotic feeling in his countrymen and to energize them for the war effort, Bergson figured German military force as a mechanical body and French patriotic sentiment in terms of a vital or moral energy. In a second iteration (still in the war context) the figure for France became a "moral energy . . . that continually reconstitutes its instrumentality [*instrument organisé*] as the soul reconstitutes its body." Bergson, who has been soliciting American intervention in the First World War in support of France, invites the soul (France) to strengthen its body in order to triumph over the soulless, material force of the enemy. Here we have a confrontation between two bodies, one mechanical and non-regenerating and the other a material force invigorated by a vital moral energy. A third iteration emerges after the First World War. One body, the body of mankind, becomes a figure for the origin of war itself, which, Bergson wrote, is caused by a disproportion between the body of mankind, "inordinately [*démesurément*] extended by technology [*la technique*]," and the human soul, "which has not undergone the same growth [*croissance*]." In a penultimate version of the figure (before *Two Sources*) Bergson asks whether "the soul [would] have the force to master this monstrous body?"[31] Here the body becomes the monstrous term, the implication being that if humanity cannot reign in its powers of destruction it will be destroyed by them.

"On the level of the statement 'there is information,'" Peter Sloterdijk has argued that "the old image of technology as heteronomy and the enslavement of matter and persons loses its plausibility."[32] Up to this point we might say that Bergson has been reworking this kind of metaphysical opposition, one central to his image for the comic in his *Laughter* as "mechanism superposed upon life" (L 28/405). He has slid, perhaps, toward black humor. But a shift occurs in the elaboration of the image in *Two Sources* where the relation between the mechanical and the living is no longer a laughing matter. A puzzling new element appears: a void. An emptiness has opened up between the monstrously swollen, over-empowered, artificial body and the soul that, in comparison, now appears shrunken.

The organism as a whole now appears monstrous to the extent that it includes a void within itself. What is more, this void is paradoxical. It is empty and, at the same time, overfull: an excess of formidable social and political challenges are not only lodged within it but "amount to so many definitions of this void" (TS 310/1239). The void is defined by what fills it, both the myriad social and political problems associated with it and the "muddled [*désordonnés*] and ineffectual efforts" (*TS* 310/1239) made to resolve them. Bergson's conclusion follows from this image of overfull emptiness: "we must create [*il faudrait faire*] new reserves of potential energy, this time moral" (*TS* 310/1239).

This last version of the monstrous body image does not appear to conform to what Sloterdijk called the "old image of technology as heteronomy and the enslavement of matter."[33] For there appear to be three terms at play here, not two. The monstrously distended mechanical body is disproportionate not only with respect to the soul but also to the organic body, for it presents a vast "extension and a power . . . disproportionate to its [i.e., the organism's] dimension and force" (*TS* 309/1239). The allusion to the organism's dimension and force implies an organic body. The passage proposes that the monstrously overextended body is not merely a mechanical extension—or prosthesis—of the organic one but rather a second, artificial body, separated from the first by a void, one that depends upon energy resources that stand in for the animating principle of the soul.

The image has shifted to become an economic figure that carries philosophical force. It now tells us that industrial production on a grand scale requires a consumption of time: it is a question of the conversion into movement of "potential energies accumulated over millions of years" (*TS* 309/1239). Bergson has characterized life as time passing through matter. Coal and oil and white coal, which animate the artificial industrial body and massively extend its reach in the passage cited, are figures for life in just this sense. These potential energy resources imply time held materially in the past and then consumed to give to our "organism . . . the greatest material success of man on the planet" (*TS* 309/1239). The void that lodges at the heart of Bergson's image is created by consuming reserves of time as energy, time accumulated (and reserved) in matter over a very long duration. This void strikes a chord with us today. "Everything that earlier was merely 'given' becomes 'explicit," Bruno Latour writes, "air, water, land, all of those were present before in the background: now they are explicitated because we slowly come to realize that they might disappear—and we with them."[34] Today, as we dig deeper and deeper in the sea for oil, even beyond the capacity of our instrumental knowledge to address the unintended consequences of this deep reach, and as the planet becomes increasingly emptied of its reserves, Bergson's premonitory figure becomes ever more haunting.

Bergson's image proposes the emergence of the technological body from the organic one as a kind of mutation, one that occurred as a "unique chance"—"surely nothing like this had been foreseen in the structural plan of our species [*il n'en avait rien été prévu dans le plan de structure de notre espèce*]" (TS 309/1239). At this point we recognize that the entire thrust of *Two Sources* concerns precisely the possibility of a parallel mutation, one that would enable the human species to accede to an ethical and political realization of the notion of humanity—and to leap from the closed to the open. "Life might have stopped there," Bergson writes, "and done nothing more than constitute closed societies" (TS 95/1055). What proves that it hasn't done so is the appearance within history of the mystic individual who exists, Bergson writes, in "contact with the very principle of nature, which amounts to [*se traduit par*] a whole other attachment to life" (TS 214/1157). The privileged soul enjoys an "overflow of vitality [that] flows from a source that is the source of life itself [*coule d'une source qui est celle même de la vie*]" (TS 232/1172). The appearance of this figure within history—its empirical reality—is compared to the "creation of a new species" (TS 95/1056). With the appearance of these privileged souls, evolution in a sense reboots itself and becomes capable of creating new life energy and new forms of social life. They anticipate an evolutionary direction, "a result that could not have been obtained all at once for the whole of humanity" and that is enabled through this "overflow [*débordement*] of vitality" (TS 95–96/1056). Just as physical energy reserves lie buried in the earth for millions of years, the mystic lodges memories of the possibility of opening in a collective (or historical) memory. If, as we have seen, the artificial, or technological, body is produced through a consumption of time, Bergson's solution to the monstrous imbalance of the hybrid he has figured is to replenish the void with a kind of time energy, a reserve of virtual energy to be stored up for a future time. La charité would be the moral equivalent of the energy resources consumed to activate the technological body. But instead of being stored up in the past like an oil deposit, this force emerges from the future and is therefore unlimited. It is an unlimited force of love, a love of life that comes from life and from the opening of time. It is a question of a direct infusion of duration into the hybrid of the organic and the artificial, an infusion of pure time, free of matter, which *Two Sources* thematizes as love—la charité—and figures by the vibrations of music: "When music cries, it is all of humanity and all of nature that cries with it" (TS 40/1008).[35]

A few questions remain. Where is Bergson with respect to the difference between the closed and the open at the conclusion of *Two Sources*? When he writes, "it would be necessary to create new reserves of potential energy, this time moral" (TS 310/1239), does his voice convey the pressure of a necessity (as in the closed structure) or is it an *appel*—an appeal or inspiration (as in the open one)? The need for moral energy appears to have become a natural necessity, in a strange intertwining of the closed and the open. Is this a call to support the leap from the closed to the open? Or does the grotesque image of the monstrous hybrid convey a bloating of the closed society, an extension of its reach on a planetary scale, such that the closed no longer finds the enemy outside itself but within, an example of what Derrida would call autoimmunity?[36] Has the closed society become its own enemy?

"Humanity suffers [*L'humanité gémit*]," Bergson concludes, "half crushed under the weight of the progress it has made. It does not fully realize [*ne sait pas assez*] that its future depends on it . . . that it is up to it to determine [*voir*; could also be translated as "see"] first of all if it wants to continue to live" (TS 317/1245). Humanity appears here no longer as a virtual term, an ethical or political one, but as a kind of empirical totalization of all humans, closed together within one planet. Is it a question of an expansion of the closed to the planetary scale? Or are we to read this as an appeal to that other meaning of "humanity"—that of the open society that would be a society of humanity. We have come up against the logic of a "we" that we don't quite know how to think about in Bergson's terms. The "we" of the closed society has become its own worst enemy, unlikely to be capable of any choice or vision. Is it then a question of the glimmer of a we—humanity—that Bergson's *Two Sources* has brought into the open through the figure of the mystic: a notion of "we" in the very broadest sense, which is to say "we the living" or, quite simply, "life"? We reach a point here of a strange encounter between the structure of the closed and the reach of the open, between politics, in other words, and life. Does a leap to the open become an option only when the closed society has reached a condition of autoimmunity on a grand scale, such that the imperative—or the call—of humanity has also become the imperative—or is it the call?—of sustainability: the imperative of life itself?

Bergson claims that "we must make [*il faudrait faire*] new reserves of potential energy, this time moral" (TS 310/1239). What the figure of the hybrid calls upon us to do is to replace time (the time consumed in the depletion of material energy reserves) with love, the life energy of the privileged soul that lodges in collective memory. To replace time with love: this is precisely what Bergson could be said to do in *Two Sources*. This is the move he makes that veers off slightly from, or exceeds, the path of *Creative Evolution* (TS 256/1193). This is what he calls the probable or speculative hypothesis of *Two Sources*. Since *Time and Free Will*, for Bergson, time has been a form of energy.[37] Time was the ontological term in *Creative Evolution*, which has been read as an exteriorization of the inner experience of duration elaborated in *Time and Free Will*.[38] Here love, as a kind of dynamic double love in open circulation, both internal and external, becomes the energy of the *élan vital* as the vital energy of being and becoming. This is the step Bergson evokes as a hypothesis, distinct from the philosophy of his previous works. But it is a hypothesis based on the empirical fact of the presence of mystic individuals in history, which Bergson now considers as having experimentally confirmed the thrust of his philosophy.

I plead guilty to having pushed my reading of Bergson to elicit a maximum of critical force. I have engaged with *Two Sources* to test the limits, or reveal the contours, of various contemporary ways of being nonmodern. A number of questions remain. What is the precise relation between the terms "nature" and "life" in *Two Sources*? How do the two sources, the closed and the open, articulate with each other and with the concept of life?[39] Finally, we might ask, given Bergson's early diagnosis of the limits of the modern (and, as I have implied, even of the challenges of the posthuman), does the difference in kind between the closed and the open remain pertinent?

Some critics now place "information" as a third term between matter and spirit, but in a context that continues to implicitly privilege a framework of cognition or knowledge. Bergson's position presents an illuminating contrast. He seems to propose "emotion" as a third term in relation to the metaphysical opposition between matter and intelligence. Just as the displacement from mind to memory was not a simple gesture and ended up deconstructing the opposition between mind and matter in *Matter and Memory*, so the displacement of intelligence to emotion (an intensification, it seems, of the displacement from intelligence to intuition that was his signal gesture from *Time and Free Will* on) displaces, and in a sense undoes, the opposition between matter and mind. Bergson's appeal to the flow of the emotional energy of la charité, which he identifies here with the élan vital itself, reveals the extent to which the notion of information, for the most part, leads back to a quite metaphysical privilege of intelligence (whether natural or artificial) and to logics or discourses of reason. Network theorists have recently discovered Gabriel Tarde, whose later work, which examines statistical analyses, particularly inspires them.[40] Given Tarde's contribution to Bergson's theory of the open, we might wonder what would happen if network theorists turned their attention to Tarde's early work, which emphasized desires and interests and met up with the thought of psychologists such as Emile Myers?[41] What would happen, in other words, if instead of "inter-intelligently condensed networks" we considered a hybrid that included "inter-affectively condensed networks" with an emphasis on the energies of la charité? At the very least Bergson invites us to entertain such thoughts and to consider why it is so difficult for us to seriously explore them. This is perhaps where the distinction between the closed and the open might remain not only valid but also urgent. In comparison with Bergson some of our cutting-edge nonmodern thinkers appear, perhaps, not quite unmodern enough.

NOTES

1 Cited in Ansell-Pearson, "The Transfiguration of Existence and Sovereign Life," 141.

2 See Rabinow and Rose, "Biopower Today," 200.

3 See Keck, "Bergson et l'anthropologie," 195; and Lefebvre and White, "Bergson on Durkheim."

4 I have frequently modified and retranslated the passages cited from the English editions of Bergson's works.

5 In *Moral Education*, Durkheim writes that "attachment to the group" is one's "obligation par excellence [*le devoir par excellence*]" (110).

6 Durkheim, *Moral Education*, 73–74 (hereafter cited in text as ME; I have frequently modified and retranslated the passages cited).

7 Guizot, *Histoire de la civilisation en Europe*.

8 Durkheim, "L'Allemagne au-dessus de tout," 4.

9 The pathology of the German case, in other words, amounted to a dangerous regression toward the primitive within the precinct of preeminently civilized nations. Bergson rejects the notion of cultural evolution from "primitive" to "modern" society. In *Two Sources* he presents an extensive critique of Lévy-Bruhl's notion of a primitive mentality. See Sitbon-Peillon, "Bergson et le primitif," 175.

10 Durkheim, "L'Allemagne au-dessus de tout," 44.

11 Ibid., 11.

12 See Soulez, *Bergson politique*, 290–91.

13 See Latour, *Reassembling the Social*, 14–15.

14 Tarde, *Les lois de l'imitation,* 73 (hereafter cited in the text as *LI*; all translations are mine).

15 Tarde could be said to go further than Bergson in the direction of what Latour calls political ecology to the extent that he goes beyond any distinction between the living and the inanimate (a distinction that always remains pertinent to Bergson).

16 Latour, *The Politics of Nature,* 191.

17 Ibid., 15.

18 On this point he agrees with Kant who writes in *Perpetual Peace,* "the natural state is one of war."

19 If religion trumps reason it is not because of its message but because of its medium, which, being affective, touches our will and is therefore more pragmatic. Bergson was very much aware of the dangers of false or counterfeit mysticism to exacerbate nationalistic feeling.

20 Arendt, *The Origins of Totalitarianism,* 168.

21 Ibid., 288.

22 Ibid., 435.

23 Derrida, *Rogues,* 58.

24 Derrida, *The Politics of Friendship,* 12.

25 Tristan, *The Workers' Union.*

26 Latour, *The Politics of Nature,* 22–24, 72–76.

27 Ibid., 1–8, 20–22.

28 "It is irrefutable," writes Soulez, "there is a critique of economic liberalism in *Two Sources.* Bergson critiques the primacy of the market" (*Bergson politique,* 299).

29 Surya, *De l'argent,* 94, 110. Capitalism implies total domination in today's world to the extent that "no one opposes it anymore" (89).

30 The original French reads as follows: "Mais des machines qui marchent au pétrole, au charbon, à la "houille blanche," et qui convertissent en mouvement des énergies potentielles accumulées pendant des millions d'années, sont venues donner à notre organisme une extension si vaste et une puissance si formidable, si disproportion-née à sa dimension et à sa force, que sûrement il n'en avait rien été prévu dans le plan de structure de notre espèce: ce fut une chance unique, la plus grande réussite matérielle de l'homme sur la planète. Une impulsion spirituelle avait peut-être été imprimée au début: l'extension s'était faite automatiquement, servie par le coup de pioche accidentel qui heurta sous terre un trésor miraculeux. Or, dans ce corps démesurément grossi, l'âme reste ce qu'elle était, trop petite maintenant pour le remplir, trop faible pour le diriger. D'où le vide entre lui et elle. D'où les redoutables problèmes sociaux, politiques, internationaux, qui sont autant de définitions de ce vide et qui, pour le combler, provoquent aujourd'hui tant d'efforts désordonnés et inefficaces: il yfaudrait faire de nouvelles réserves d'énergie potentielle, cette fois morale" (*TS* 1238–39).

31 Mossé-Bastine, *Bergson, éducateur,* 103, 104, 105, 106.

32 Cited in Ansell-Pearson, "The Transfiguration of Existence and Sovereign Life," 150.

33 Ibid.

34 Latour, "A Plea for the Earthly Sciences," 74. He explains the notion of "explicitation" this way: "History was never about 'modernization' or about 'revolution,' but was rather about another phenomenon . . . 'explicitation.' As we moved on, through our technologies . . . through the extension of our global empires, we rendered more and more explicit the fragility of the life support systems that make our 'spheres of existence' possible. Everything that earlier was merely 'given' becomes 'explicit.'"

35 Bergson consistently characterizes emotion in terms of the vibrations of music and dance. See TS 40/1008–9, which picks up the theme of the dancer in the opening pages of the *Essai sur les données immédiates de la conscience*.

36 For the notion of autoimmunity, see Derrida, "Faith and Knowledge."

37 See Guerlac, *Thinking in Time*, 77.

38 See Deleuze, *Bergsonism*.

39 Worms addresses these questions in *Bergson ou les deux sens de la vie*.

40 Latour, *Reassembling the Social*, 15.

41 William James was an admirer of Emile Myer's psychology of the subliminal self. Myers, who associated with Mesmer and Charcot, studied hypnosis or "somnambulisme." "Social man," Tarde writes, "is a veritable sleepwalker [*somnambule*]" (LI 83). See Blackman, "Reinventing Psychological Matters."

THREE

Equally Circular

BERGSON AND THE VAGUE
INVENTIONS OF POLITICS

John Mullarkey

PHILOSOPHICAL CIRCLES

"Equality," comes from *aequlis*, from *aequus*, meaning "even," "level," or "equal." Etymologically driven arguments can only go so far before becoming lexically circular (referring us back to the start) or vaguely ostensive. With an abstraction like equality, moreover, the inadequacies of the more seemingly exact, lexical strategy, are nonetheless informative. To say that equality means x, y, or z necessitates a willful blindness toward one dimension of this semantic equivalence—equality *equals x, y*, or *z*. This chapter follows a number of ideas from Henri Bergson concerning the circularity of all *philosophical* equivalences and focuses in particular on what Bergson calls intellectual analysis. It looks specifically on the circularity found in a number of theories of equality that Bergson would dub "intellectualist," as well as the means by which one might break out of this recursiveness. To come to the point directly, Bergson's response to this challenge is to state that an escape can only be achieved through an inventive thought (creative emotion or metaphysical intuition). The solution to the impasse of circularity (the impassible) is *movement*, a performative practice or inventive thought that breaks the circle of analysis, that invents a new meaning or thought of equality simply by *implementing* it. Yet, for Bergson specifically, this means that the general, political meaning of democracy must indeed become vague or indefinite, only with vagueness now understood positively as an unforeseeable democracy now existing in the future anterior of what *will have been*.

Bergson's duality of metaphysical intuition and philosophical analysis is found in his "An Introduction to Metaphysics" of 1903 and *Creative Evolution* of 1907. In the case of intuition, concepts emerge *from* the object rather than being applied *to* it (as analysis does), according to the earlier text, while in 1907 Bergson makes clear his view that "every other method of philosophy," apart from metaphysical intuition, involves a "vicious circle" (CE 193/659). "Pure intellectualism" can never extend philosophy into "something different," into something that is not already given, as "it is of the essence of reasoning to shut us up in the circle of the given" (CE 192/658): "In using the intellect to transcend the intellect, we find ourselves turning in a real circle, that which consists in laboriously rediscovering by metaphysics a unity that we began by positing a priori, a unity that we admitted blindly and unconsciously by the very act of abandoning the whole of experience to science and the whole of reality to the pure understanding" (CE 197/663). In contrast to this, by expanding the findings of a narrow, analytic science (or a philosophy reduced to such a naturalistic science), metaphysical intuition belongs to the *Absolute*, a Real in which "we live and move and have our being" (CE 199/664).

The intuitive method Bergson uses to describe the Real may appear vague to some, yet it is, he says, the only precise manner in which we can understand the Real (CM 42–43/1285–86). Intuition is precise in virtue of the fact that it *instantiates* the Real rather than represents it. If the intellectual concept is a fixed picture *of* reality, then Bergson wants no part of it. The inflexibility of the ready-made concept carries within it a "practical question" that forces reality to answer with only a yes or no (CM 189/1420). All that can follow is a never-ending dialectic and the various oppositions of traditional philosophy: phenomenon and noumenon, substance and accident, being and appearance (CM 176–77/1409–10). But the bivalency of the answer is merely the necessary response to the narrowness of the question: what is missed entirely between the two is the polyvalency of a vital Real that does not allow for such rigid antitheses. The static representational concept requires a separation between knower and known. But intuitive knowledge, Bergson argues, can "coincide with the generative action of reality" (M 773). But "coincide"

here does not mean "correspond": the relationship is mereological, belonging to the same process reality, not one of representation between
rigid concept and fixed referent.

So, given our aim of extrapolating the concept of equality in light of
these views, we will want to see how the Bergsonian method avoids the
circularities of traditional philosophical analysis. To do that, we must
sketch three examples of such circularity in operation. Certainly, the
question of equality—its nature, origins, and current impediments—is a
pressing one among those forms of philosophy increasingly focused on
politics: Does it exist in some kind of sovereign property or power, a
possession (Peter Singer), or in the lack of any such power (John Llewellyn)? Or is it based on a mathematical quantity opposed to any particular
quality (Alain Badiou)? We choose these three even though they may not
be numbered among political theorists as strict egalitarians on a par with,
say, G. A. Cohen or Amartya Sen. Rather, it is because their respective
attempts to give a philosophical (or even ontological) grounding to egali-
tarian thought are among the most intellectually rigorous.

For Bergson it will actually be the *kind* of thinking of equality that is
most important to resolving this set of questions, for we can only understand equality through a performative thought, a movement or vital action rather than an intellectualist representation of it. From the perspective of traditional philosophy, this movement is vague and unhelpful,
while for Bergson such an indefinite understanding of equality—and its
concomitant notion of democracy—is the only precise means of understanding it (see CM 42–43/1285–86). It is precisely this kind of movement
that Bergson offers us in response to the problems of equality in his *The
Two Sources of Morality and Religion* through a new *vitalist* model of thinking—creative emotion.[1] Positing any *defined and definite* (intellectualist)
essence to equality—in mathematics (Badiou), sentience (Singer), or
vulnerability (Llewellyn)—is too preemptive. Equality, to be noncircular,
must be invented (or thought) anew and immanently within each and
every situation. Moreover, what emerges of equal significance when applying Bergson's vitalist critique of intellectualism within the *political*
situation is that such abstract models fix their notions of equality and
democracy at a level of life (most often *human* life) that misses what is
living about life: it is not that life is human (and abstract, sentient, vulnerable) but that it is creative and that makes it democratic. In a remarkable

economy of thought, what is vital *in* life is that it is creative and unforesee-able; but that is also what makes democratic equality truly itself—that it is creative and unforeseeable too.

In the following sections, I sketch three examples of circularity from prominent and rigorous theories of equality.

ALAIN BADIOU: EQUALITY AS MATHEMATICAL QUANTITY

At the heart of Badiou's philosophy—and of his political philosophy—is an intellectualist axiom of equality. It posits a model of mathematics (set theory) and mathematical ability as the key to equality. Badiou is at-tracted to set theory because it is a pure and empty formalism and involves no particular qualities. His formalism allows no particular thing to be privileged, and correspondingly, every particular thing is affirmed *equally and universally*. The politics of set theory (against privilege, for universality) is as important as its mathematical abstractness, but, per-versely, what allows it to work is a quality, an *ability*: the spark of infinite rationality that (at least in principle) makes mathematicians of us all (all humans, that is). In short it is axiomatic for Badiou that all humanity— "generic humanity," as it were—is mathematically gifted.[2]

But immediately this poses a problem: in actuality mathematical power comes in degrees across a range of species. *Meno*'s slave and I can both do some math, but there will be as many differences of *degree* be-tween us, as between both of us (his is a younger brain) and a mathemat-ics genius like Henri Poincaré, and between all of us and a chimpanzee, a rat, or a dog. Pointing to the apparent *empirical* fact that Poincaré, the boy, and I are all *defined* as human only begs the question—for Badiou, it is our universal mathematical abilities that make us exceptional.

Through Badiou's presumption that all—and only—human beings are equally gifted, he shuts down the political process of transformation (the event) at an arbitrary stage: *human* equality; this despite his notion of the universal *should be* unqualified by virtue of being grounded in *pure* quan-tity or Number. In short Badiou's theory is marked by an unnecessarily anthropocentric dogmatism, one that also makes a highly dubious induc-tion, to wit, that animals cannot think mathematically. By virtue of Badiou's formula—being equals ontology or ontology equals mathematics—non-human animals are discounted from being equals because they cannot count (even though all the evidence points in the opposite direction).[3] The circularity of his thought—defining equality through a predefined ability in mathematics—guarantees an anthropocentric outlook. It is also symptomatic of the intellectualist approach that Bergson wishes to sidestep.

PETER SINGER: EQUALITY OF INTEREST

In contrast with this most abstract conception of equality, the egalitarianism found in Peter Singer's conception of the political is much more socially embedded, and yet it is no less intellectually rigorous. Singer's proposal is that there is no need to establish the principle of equality on the basis of either an *empirical* equality (everyone having the same abilities, or color, or gender, etc.) or an a priori equality (being a member of a certain species, nation, or other classification): all that is required to ground a genuine ethic is the notion of *equality of interest*. The chief prerequisite for any ethical behavior for Singer is that we treat all sectional interests on a par with our own, no matter whose interests they are: "ethics requires us to go beyond 'I' and 'you' to the universal law, the universalizable judgement, the standpoint of the impartial spectator or ideal observer."[4] No empirical fact or a priori principle (such as the "sanctity of human life") can be used to exclude any interest: only those or that without interests at all can justly be excluded.

Giving equal consideration to every interest, however, need not always lead to equal treatment: where there are significantly different interests at hand, commensurably different treatments ought to follow. As Singer writes in his essay, "All Animals Are Equal": "since a man cannot have an abortion, it is meaningless to talk of his right to have one. Since a pig cannot vote, it is meaningless to talk of its right to vote."[5] To allow the alternative, whereby only certain interests abide within a theory of equality, is simply inconsistent. Its most radical inconsistency indicates "a prejudice or attitude of bias in favor of the interests of members of one's own species and against those of members of other species." This is what Singer famously labels "speciesism."[6] Yet this begs the question of how "we" learn of these interests. According to Singer, if members of a species can indicate a preference for the avoidance of suffering or continued existence, then the onus is on us to respect that preference. *But how do we recognize this "indication"?* Can such a recognition of interest itself be disinterested, impartial, or equal? Is it not already anthropocentric (and so speciesist) to ground a value on how things appear to *us* (which simultaneously leaves open the matter of who constitutes this "us")? There must be, again, a circular presupposition of human interest *as* disinterested (objective) in order to construct a system of ethics that is deemed, by fiat, impartial and thereby ethical.

<h2>JOHN LLEWELYN: EQUALITY IN VULNERABILITY</h2>

It is just such a critique of misplaced objectivism that John Llewelyn overtly embraces in his theory of equality. Part of Llewelyn's rejection of an ethics such as Singer's is its reliance on objective powers enjoyed by a sovereign subject: consciousness, sentience, memory, expectation, and so on. In order to avoid the pseudo-objectivism of such a stance, Llewelyn adopts a position close to that of Emmanuel Levinas. Indeed, following Levinas, Llewelyn seeks a *passive* principle of one's *infinite* responsibility toward the other in his or her *vulnerability*.

Llewelyn goes beyond Levinas's humanism of the other: for Llewelyn, ethics cannot value the human, or any other entity, as something of greater *comparative* worth (than an ape, for example), for that is to measure an infinite value as though it were a commodity—to objectivize it and thereby transform ethics into economics. There should be no comparative evaluation of the other: in saying—as both Levinas and Llewelyn do—that the other counts "more" than myself, one should not understand that "more" comparatively but as a structural claim about ethics itself.[7] The condition of possibility of any genuine ethics is that the moral realm is *unconditional*, that it is not reducible to ontology or epistemology. Ethics *must be* first philosophy, if it is not to be reducible to or supervene on either epistemological or ontological categories ("do I know you?," "who are you?," "what are you?," etc.).

Yet Llewelyn reads this theory of incommensurable alterity as a requirement to view animals, plants, and even the inanimate as others too. Each and every being has a claim on me on account of its own "that it is" rather than "what it is." There need be no qualitative similarity (having consciousness, sentience) between us for there to be an ethical responsibility between us. Moreover, there is no need for sympathy for this other to maintain my ethical obligation. All the same, Llewelyn does not extend political rights to animals or stones (correctly or incorrectly) but simply shows where the primordial basis of any ethical notion of right, obligation, or justice lies.[8]

So where does this proto-ethical responsibility leave us: do we have the same moral obligations toward the human fetus, as well as its mother, toward the cancer virus, or even the gas chamber? They are all beings after all. Llewellyn's answer is yes. There was never a guarantee that theorizing equality would be easy or simple. Indeed, equality, like liberty, is difficult, and Llewelyn has simply revealed to us how difficult ethics really is through this hyperbolic egalitarianism.[9]

Yet it is still arguable that Llewellyn's charity to *all* leads to such an aporia, an impasse for *any* ethical action, that, as with Zeno's excessive focus on the conceptual minutiae of walking, all movement is rendered impossible. Unless, of course, the very possibility of such an egalitarianism, irrespective of its latent difficulties, is still regarded as *theoretically* possible. Even in this most (morally) realist of philosophies, it is, again, an *intellectual* possibility—that of the condition of possibility of any ethics— that Llewelyn prioritizes over the actual movement required by an ethics of equality. It is Llewellyn's logical deduction (following Levinas) that ethics *must be* first philosophy (if it is not to be reducible to epistemology or ontology) despite the intractability of practicing such a position (and all it implies) in actuality. It is the intellectualism of Llewellyn that demands that, if ethics as first philosophy is possible, it is also *necessarily* real. Yet this shift from the possible to the real begs the question as to why a deductive movement should translate into a real one (at least from the perspective of a nonintellectualist stance such as Bergson's).

In Bergson's notion of "open morality," however, we will see a model of ethical equality that is able to keep all that might be interested in sight while still being able to move about in actual reality (rather than only in intellectual possibility), because any conceptual aporias, its own impossibilities, are dissolved (sidestepped) by creative moral action.

FROM THE CLOSED TO THE OPEN

"In order to speak of 'all citizens' it is necessary that somebody not be a citizen of said polity," writes Etienne Balibar when formulating his own rigorous concept of equality:

> Equality in fact cannot be limited. Once some Xs ("men") are not equal, the predicate of equality can no longer be applied to anyone, for all those to whom it is supposed to be applicable are in fact "superior," "dominant,"

"privileged," etc. Enjoyment of the equality of rights cannot spread step by step, beginning with two individuals and gradually extending to all: it must immediately concern the *universality* of individuals. . . . This explains . . . the antinomy of equality and society for, even when it is not defined in "cultural," "national," or "historical" terms, a *society* is necessarily *a* society, defined by some particularity, by some exclusion, if only by a *name*.[10]

With this attempt to counter any "limited equality," Balibar also rediscovers Bergson's concept of the "closed society" from *Two Sources*. According to Bergson's text, every form of group identity implies "a choice, therefore an exclusion." The most salient trait of social obligation is that it immediately installs a "closed society, however large" (TS 32/1001).

It is in the nature of the closed to form social groupings like the family, the class, the nation, the race, and so on, each of which acts as an intermediary reinforcement of persisting social mores. Within each grouping, all are regarded in a comparatively equal light and all are allowed similar rights and freedoms. What is essential about such bounded domains, however, is that they are more or less closed to some kind of outside. A social formation may be very broad and even grow broader by incorporating previously ostracized minority groups; all the same, such formations remain closed in the type of movement they instantiate: "their essential characteristic is nonetheless to include at any moment a certain number of individuals, and exclude others" (TS 30/1000).

And here's the rub: even the idea of a "humanity in general" only occupies the broadest and most abstract of these concentric circles surrounding the self.[11] For it too is constituted through exclusion: be it the nonpolitical animal or the nonreciprocating animal, something must be excluded.

The closed society (and its internal, closed morality) consists of a fixed set of rules and balances, pressures and obligations, that bear down on the individual (TS 39/1008, 205/1150, 207/1151). Everything is organized, balanced, neutralized, and static. Given this rigidity, Bergson asks how such a closed society might transform itself into an open one (rather than simply enlarge itself at the expense of some new outside). It cannot, according to Bergson; or at least it cannot do so *intellectually*: it is impossible for abstractions such as "universal love," for example, to change a movement of closure into one of openness. Universal love cannot transform any social egoism into a genuine altruism, for the two are as incommensurable as the steps of Achilles are with those of the tortoise in Zeno's paradox (TS 36/1005).

Behind the command to "love all" lies something else, Bergson claims: the desire for openness, specifically the desire *to be open toward openness*. He talks of the "extreme limit" of this desire as follows:

> The other attitude is that of the open soul. What, in that case, is allowed in? Suppose we say that it embraces all humanity: we should not be going too far, we should hardly be going far enough, *since its love may extend to animals, to plants, to all nature.* And yet no one of these things which would thus fill it would suffice to define the attitude taken by the soul, for it could, strictly speaking, do without all of them. Its form is not dependent on its content. We have just filled it; we could as easily empty it again. "Charity" would persist in him who possesses "charity," though there be no other living creature on earth. (TS 38/1006–7, emphasis added)

Even the inclusion of "all humanity" is not enough. Pure openness sympathises "with the whole of nature," but it is also a contact with a *principle of nature* that expresses itself in a quite different attachment or sympathy than that found in closed morality (and hence, it is not a simple extension of the latter). It is described as an *objectless* emotion that loves who or what it does only "by passing through" them rather than aiming for them (TS 52/1019, 39/1007, 254–55/1191–92). An ethic of distributive justice, by contrast, is only a matter of reciprocity and equivalence—a mathematical balancing act of quantity with quantity, quality with quality. Such a relative justice creates a form of equality that remains set against the outsider (TS 69–79/1033–42). An absolute justice, on the other hand, has another source altogether: it refuses to let even one individual suffer for the good of *any* group. The welfare of "all humanity" would not be enough.

As a consequence of Bergson's stance in *Two Sources*, it is not by a process of "intellectualist" gradual extension that we pass from the closed to the open. An "open morality" is not about recalculating a (more equal) distribution of justice: it is a "disposition of the soul"—an affective change that breaks the circles (both logical in methodology and thematic in content) of intellectualist theories of equality (TS 32/1001, 38/1007, 59/1024). Naturally, little of this will lie well with those discourses that do place an emphasis on political emancipation through intellectual reformation. All the same, Bergson has no confidence in the value of increasing the bound-aries of enfranchisement through winning larger and larger associations through logic (consistency, rationality); instead, an action is required to dissolve our *spatialized* discourse of "boundaries" entirely. What is needed is another *kind* of discourse altogether, a metaphysical thinking that en-acts or performs this new politics of equality. And it is this that intuition captures, be it as a thought that comes from the real object (in the lan-guage of "An Introduction to Metaphysics"), that exists *in* the Absolute (in the language of *Creative Evolution*), or that is a creative emotion partially coinciding with Life itself (in the language of *Two Sources*). Throughout, however, it is a thought that will be as intellectually vague as it is actually real.

THE OPEN AND THE VAGUE

It is usually said that Bergson offers a religious formula—"dynamic reli-gion"—to explain radical transformations of society, that is, the shift from closed to open. Yet Bergson's religious formula is used only as one place-holder for a much broader, indefinite movement in his thought. Open-ness is a necessarily vague formulation that requires continual creativity to fill out its content in any one situation; one should see it as a moving position with no essence. The basis of equality in the concept of Number (Badiou), sentience (Singer), or vulnerability (Llewellyn) remains too presumptive and abstract for Bergson. Despite their apparently "univer-sal" nature, their content also remains all too substantive in contrast with Bergson's necessarily indefinite expression. The form open morality takes "is not dependent on its content." Its "aim" is only to pass through its object. In other words, the evolution *to* openness is not teleological (strictly speaking) but, in a self-referential manner, an evolution that places itself at issue, that performs itself.

In political terms democracy is the name given to this vague evolution. The idea of democracy, for Bergson, rests in the attempt to reconcile liberty and equality. But this can only be achieved through what *Two Sources* also calls "fraternity" or love rather than through reason. The vagueness of the democratic formula provides latitude for the moral creativity and inventiveness that will work empirically to reconcile con-cepts of freedom and equality that are presently unforeseeable, and per-haps even inconceivable too. After all, any new actual liberty for one individual or group (emerging, say, on the back of a new technology or social attitude) will almost inevitably encroach on the liberty of *some* other or others. But *how* the two conflict cannot be predetermined a priori, for those others may adapt their behavior in recognition of this new liberty, that is, through a reflexive feedback mechanism that subverts any possible algorithm for political change (TS 79–80/1041–42). The contemporary idea of a democracy "to come," therefore, reinvents Bergson's idea of a vague democracy perfectly. As Simon Critchley puts it: "Democracy is an indeterminate political form founded on the contradictions of individual freedom versus . . . [among other things] complete uniformity. . . . *Democracy does not exist*; that is to say, starting from today, and every day, there is a responsibility to invent democracy, to extend the democratic franchise to all areas of public and private life."[12]

Democracy is an ongoing invention that cannot be predicted (even through a notion of "extension," as Critchley imports). Now read Bergson: "Objections occasioned by the vagueness of the democratic formula arise from the fact that the original religious character has been misunderstood. How is it possible to ask for a precise definition of liberty and of equality when the future must lie open to all sorts of progress, and especially to the creation of new conditions under which it will be possible to have forms of liberty and equality which are impossible of realization, perhaps even conception, today" (TS 282/1215).

This notion of the vague should not be seen as only a side issue in Bergson's social philosophy. The vague, or indefinite, is a technical idea at work throughout his writings. Contra the terms of the current dispute between philosophers of finitude and philosophers of the infinite, Bergson forwards the idea of the indefinite as an ongoing, creative process (upon which both the finite and the infinite are merely two static perspectives). Indefinites (or "dynamic definitions") are found throughout his work—in intuition, duration, virtual memory, the *élan*, and his own preference for metaphorical language to express all these ideas. Reality as a whole, he says, is neither finite nor infinite but "indefinite" (see CE 84–85/567; CM 211/1442; TS 296/1227). The infinite, by contrast, would be the substantialization of the indefinite. The indefinite captures best the processual moment at issue. Whereas to say that x is infinite is to *decide* its being, to say that it is indefinite is to *leave it open*, to let it be beyond the finite or infinite as states or things.

THE AFFECTIVE CREATION OF POLITICS

So, while it is true that liberty and equality are always in tension for Bergson, how they are reconciled each time cannot be anticipated. These reconciliations can only be invented by what Bergson names "moral creators" (TS 80/1042). He also calls these creators "mystics," though the notion of an ascetic contemplative is far from what he has in mind. These mystics are social inventors and interventionists, transgressing the boundaries of life, mind, and society through their very real and active political advocacies. What is termed "complete mysticism" is wholly for the other, an advocacy of the other, rather than self-absorbed: "true, complete, active mysticism aspires to radiate, by virtue of the charity which is its essence" (TS 309/1238). How it radiates is through the contagious properties of a "creative emotion," that "infectious like all emotions . . . [is] akin to the creative act" (TS 53/1019). The etymology of emotion should be taken into account here: again, Bergson is not describing the private ecstasy of a contemplative but a type of "movement" rich in activity, a movement of openness (TS 61–62/1026–27).

Let me explain further. When Bergson looks at the non-philosophical origin of ethics in *Two Sources*, he finds that: "Alongside of the emotion which is a result of the representation and which is added to it, there is the emotion which precedes the image, which virtually contains it, and is to a certain extent its cause . . . an emotion capable of crystallizing into representations and even into an ethical doctrine" (TS 47/1015). Out of such affectivity come new (intellectual) doctrines within ethics and politics. The affectivity in question is not any supposedly dumb feeling but precisely the affective, performative thinking *in* time that precedes its spatialization into doctrine (with an inside and an outside, insiders and outsiders): "Antecedent to the new morality, and also the new metaphysics, there is the emotion . . . neither has its metaphysics enforced moral practice, nor the moral practice induced a disposition to its metaphysics. Metaphysics and morality express here the self-same thing" (TS 49/1016).

It is this creative emotion that generates a new kind of thinking with itself: an advocacy for *all, equally*, in its actual performance rather than its intellectual content—a type of thought and action in one, which *invents* the equalities that it thinks (and so escapes any vicious circularity).

CONCLUSION: THE FUTURE ANTERIOR OF EQUALITIES

We can relate this seemingly vague equality to what Bergson writes of the future anterior of art in his essay "The Possible and the Real." When asked for his view of what "the great dramatic work of the future" will be, his reply was that "the work of which you speak is not yet possible." Rather, "it *will have been possible*" in the future anterior: "That one can put the possible there [in the past], or rather that the possible may put itself there at any moment, is not to be doubted. As reality is created as something unforeseeable and new, its image is reflected behind it into the indefinite past" (CM 101/1340). This idea, recently reinvented by Slavoj Žižek and Badiou, not only underpins the novelty of creation in Bergsonism but also explains the origins of the intellectualist temptation to reduce that novelty to a conceptual premise.[13] The movement toward equality is always reinventing itself and is as such vague or indefinite (undefined), creating a democracy that is always "to come," with new equalities in the future anterior—of what *will have been* equal. More than this, however, this indefinite movement (action-emotion) *makes* both its future and *its own possibility*: it is this retrograde movement of possibility that legitimizes the intellectualist strategy of forwarding an unchanging principle, premise, and logic *through which* all future equality must be negotiated.

Yet we have seen how the intellectualist thought of equality can undo itself in myriad different versions, from Badiou through Singer to Llewellyn. We can axiomatize one kind of equality as an intellectual principle (of mathematics, of sentience, of vulnerability), but then the thought of equality becomes circular (as intellectualism always does for Bergson). However, the best way to prove the reality of movement is simply to walk away, as Bergson recommended to Zeno. Hence, an action can "break the circle" of Parmenidean and sufficient reason (Bergson prefiguring Laruelle here) when we enact a new kind of thought. The solution to any impasse is *movement*: for the matter in question, it is the performative practice or inventive thought that breaks the circle of analysis simply by inventing a *new* meaning of equality, by implementing a new thought of equality. With that, then, there might come different "logics" of equality altogether, ones that some would find it hard to call a logic or even a "thought" at all, looking more like actions as they do. Yet it is these actions (involving creative emotions) that perform an openness and equality in the only noncircular manner possible according to Bergson: by invention.

NOTES

1 Of course, *Two Sources* is an exercise in sociobiology as well, but it grounds both ethics and religion in the inventiveness of life, a conception of life that is necessarily incomplete and indefinite. There is no reduction of the *socius* to a determining *bios*, but quite the opposite: the indetermination of all social forms are on account of their immanence within a creative life. As we will see, there is a "radical democracy" inherent within Bergson's metaphysics of life, but it is one that is grounded in a simultaneously moral and metaphysical intuition.

2 See Badiou, *Being and Event*, 353.

3 See Dehaene, *The Number Sense*. Of course, there are differences: even the famous case of Sheba, which resolutely shows that a chimpanzee can manipulate *abstract* number—it is not a case of conditioning—is still behind the mathematical abilities of a human child. But it is not an *absolute* difference: mathematics is not unique to the human, and humans do not all have the same *actual* mathematical prowess. Indeed, even rats can represent number "as an abstract parameter that is not tied to a specific sensory modality, be it auditory or visual" (24).

4 Singer, *Practical Ethics*, 12. That ethics must be universalizable gives us good reason, Singer believes, for favoring a broadly utilitarian position. Singer's reasoning is that, in conflict situations, impartiality demands that one *weigh up* the opposing *interests* and "adopt the course of action most likely to maximise the interests of those affected" (13).

5 Singer, "All Animals Are Equal," 2.

6 Singer, *Animal Liberation*, 6. The term was coined by Richard Ryder. The principle of equality leads to some startling implications, and Singer is never fearful of pursuing these ideas to their logical conclusion. Significantly, the most important interests possessed by individuals are independent of the categories "human" and "nonhuman": pain, for example, is suffered and avoided by all regardless of color, gender, or species. If we are ever forced to favor one individual's interests when they are in conflict with those of another, it can only be on the basis of those respective properties that *affect the interests either might have*.

7 Llewelyn, *The Middle Voice of Ecological Conscience*, 260, 249–50.

8 For Llewelyn, the idea of exclusive human rights, in fact, is a restriction of the term "right" in general. See *The Middle Voice of Ecological Conscience*, 254–55, 257, 261.

9 Llewelyn, *The Middle Voice of Ecological Conscience*, 263.

10 Balibar, "Citizen Subject," 50.

11 Here Bergson is unique, for political theory, from Aristotle to Rawls, maintains an anthropocentric system of justice based on an opposition toward the inhuman.

12 Critchley, *The Ethics of Deconstruction*, 209, 240.

13 "If—accidentally—an event takes place, it creates the preceding chain which makes it appear inevitable" (Žižek, *First as Tragedy, Then as Farce*, 151). See *Creative Evolution* for how "action breaks" the "circle of the given" (202–3/658).

FOUR

The Art of the Future

Claire Colebrook

> When music weeps, all humanity, all nature, weeps with
> it. In point of fact it does not introduce these feelings
> into us; it introduces us into them, as passers-by are
> forced into a street dance.
>
> HENRI BERGSON,
> *The Two Sources of Morality and Religion*

In some respects Bergson could be *the* philosopher of a posthuman future. He does, after all,
locate the human intellect within a broader trajectory of life
and creative energy. And the intellect, far from being the
reason and telos of life, is a stultifying pause in an otherwise
greater and greater expansion of complexity. There is, set
alongside this opening out to inhuman life, Bergson's curious privileging of spirit, as though only humanity's proper
potential could overcome the very inertia the intellect imposed upon life. Yet even here one might say that *spirit* is
that point at which humanity overcomes all those aspects of
its being that had seemingly defined its essence: calculative
reason, mastery of nature, distance from animality, generalizing concepts, the formalization of time and space, located point of view, personality, and moral communities
that extend self-interest by way of altruism.

Bergson was not the first thinker to suggest that humanity, by its very nature, harbored the potential to diminish or
corrupt the power it possessed to transcend material life.
Since Kant argued in his *Critique of Pure Reason* that the
very categories that enable reason lead to internal illusions,
there have been more strident post-romantic attacks on the
intellect as a deadening and calculative power that precludes the expansion of life beyond the limited subject of

instrumental reason. These include a wealth of literary critiques of *life*, such as P. B. Shelley's "Triumph of Life," in which something like a natural course of organic and efficient existence (along with the power and self-serving interest it brings in tow) would be set against an always fragile capacity for thinking beyond actuality and the given. It is possible to locate Bergson in a context of modernity and modernism in which the intensity of life (not reducible to any bounded organism, mind, or completed form) would have been defeated by the living, the egoistic strivings of organisms that could do nothing other than represent the world according to their own limiting and limited ends.[1]

Bergson was not the only thinker to consider self-annihilation, or the destruction of the bounded, autonomous and self-constituting being as imperative if something like life were to be released to achieve something —anything—beyond already actualized measures. Not surprisingly, then, a certain modernist motif of art—where art is an antibourgeois attack on the enjoyment of consumption—could not only be found within Bergson's own writing but would also seem to characterize the milieu within which he was writing. Art and Man would be bound together in an impossible, always mutually defeating cycle of creation and destruction.[2] Man, as a living being spurred on by creative energy, would produce greater and more complex forms in order to escape the rigidities of animal life, and yet it would be precisely the sophistication of those created techniques that would also render life so utterly efficient that its forward creative movement would be halted. What could awaken the human intellect from its self-serving, self-enclosed myopia in which its only perception of the outer world is reduced to its own interests in externality? The modernist artwork would, according to its own self-reflective theorization, react against bourgeois enjoyment and consumption. It would not further the living but would somehow make contact with Life, outside its already actualized forms. This raises (at least) three questions.

1 Is Bergson simply *of his time*, part of an early twentieth-century sense of civilization's arrival at a point of self-paralyzing inertia, whereby all the perceptual technologies that had furthered life (language, images, social forms, familial desires, artistic genres, and conventions) now tie life to a present of ever sameness? And if this were so, how would we begin to think about an epoch that begins to perceive the limits and limiting nature of the very humanity within which it is located and upon which it seeks to wage war?

2 How would this epoch communicate with the singularity of the twenty-first century? If Darwinian evolution was tied to a moment in which humanity was first perceived to have a beginning within life, an equally counter-narcissistic blow has occurred in the last decade or so. Humanity now has a perceived end: in addition to talk of the "anthropocene era," there are also numerous calculations and imaginations of the incalculable yet certain extinction point of humanity.[3]

3 If it is humanity's extension via techne that has led to the domination of life evolving into the annihilation of life, is the technical revolution of the *art object* a way out of the instrumentality of reason, and how would one judge the mode of this aesthetic renovation?

Even though Bergson's philosophy may appear to be expressed in some of high modernism's most canonical works, there is nevertheless a distinction to be drawn between the way that Bergsonism influenced or mobilized aesthetic production and the function the image of the work of art serves within Bergson's own philosophy. For what Bergson allows us to do is revisit modernist aesthetics, intuit another potentiality of modernism, and then read that tendency in contemporary aesthetic production that is both chronologically and art-historically postmodern.

THE EPOCH OF BERGSON

How is it possible for a thinker to undertake a critical attitude toward thinking and thinking's constitutive temporality? For Bergson, as for Husserl, thinking *is time*.[4] This postulate of a temporality that has no outside, that cannot be located *within* living nature, can take two forms. For phenomenology, temporality is the condition for something like the living. But temporality is transcendental, not natural, and is subjective—even if the subject is impersonal and opposed to any concrete psychophysical individual. Phenomenology shares with Bergsonism its criticism of the rigid image of the intellect as mind *within* life. Phenomenology, like Bergsonism, will tellingly appeal to the example of music or melody to disclose living time's proper nature. Husserl argues that when one listens to a melody one must focus both on the unfolding of elements through time and the retention of the past into the future; we become aware of the synthesis of time.[5] Despite this example of music, and an eventual criticism of logic as a rigid rather than dynamic system, phenomenology remains wedded to mind *as reason* discovering its destiny in the universal truth of the world.[6] Phenomenology is critical of the intellect or mind as some substance within the world, but rather than refer to some broader life of which the mind would be an expression, Husserlian phenomenology presents the transcendental subject as the ultimate ground of synthesis or "origin for all being."[7]

By contrast Bergson's project of freeing the intellect from its seduction by naturalism (the illusion that mind is simply a part of the world alongside material objects) requires a release of thought from its intellectual trajectory and a transition from humanity toward some spiritual tendency of which humanity is capable. Even if Bergson will seek time in its pure state, liberated from the needs of the organism, this will nevertheless—*as endurance*—be a time of rhythms: there is no time in general, nor is time some abstract whole within which speeds and movements would be located relatively; time is composed of distinct living durations. A living potentiality unfolds in relation to other potentialities, becoming in its own manner, according to the potentialities it encounters, and the whole is just this highly complex, highly differentiated, constantly altering, constantly creative, openness.

On the one hand, then, this would align the Bergsonian criticism of mechanical chronological time (a time of units) with a history of organicism: for there is no such thing as a distinct part, sufficient and complete unto itself. Organicism has *always*—going back to mythic and theological distinctions between good and evil—privileged a life of fluid and dynamic interrelatedness with a disconnected, mechanical, and merely quantitative world of atomism.[8] Everything that is exists in relation; relations are dynamic and have no ground or systemic imperative outside the ongoing creativity of living and individuating action. On the other hand, it is precisely the organism—the bounded living being that seeks to maintain and preserve itself by perceiving the world only according to its own reifying systems—that has led to the enclosure of life within the generalizing intellect.

Today, in critical theory, identity politics, and philosophy, there has been an alarming retreat to the normativity of the organism: there is now an emphasis on the bounded living body as the foundation of all sense and relations. Often, phenomenology and Bergson are enlisted to insist that life and being are always already embodied and meaningful. Phenomenology is now naturalized and aligned with the origins of meaning emerging from the living body.[9] There can be an orthogonal or converg-

ing relation between the moralism of the organism and organicist aesthetics. Bergson and phenomenology were both critical of conflating life
with the organism, insisting on a process of synthesis that not only exceeded the living body but also organic life in general: Husserl oriented
mind and subjectivity to universal truths of reason not reducible to nature, while Bergson's near-mystical affirmation of religion was not only
impersonal but directed toward an open whole beyond naturalism.

Criticisms of the self-enclosed natural organism might be furthered by
an organicist aesthetics: the natural living body would overcome its physical limits by intuiting the universe as an interconnected whole. Today's
emphasis on the earth as one sympathetic living system is a mode of organicist aesthetics that aims to supplant the myopia of the organism.
Organicist aesthetics—whereby one perceives the rhythms other than oneself in terms of a dynamism, creativity, and relatedness that is not one of
the mapping and representing mind—is the only way that life might overcome the limits of the organism. Organicist aesthetics sublates the lures of
the organism. It is the tendency of the organism to reduce the world (and
its image of itself) to so many actual things, locating all other potentialities within its own enclosed timeline. There is, however, a counter-
organicist aesthetic that is more critically aware of the narcissistic projections of the human organism: the capacity for the human animal to view
the earth as one great living body.

Such a counterargument can be discerned in what Bergson refers to as
the "aesthetic sense." It is not surprising that he often has recourse, like
Husserl, to the listening required by musical apprehension; the units are
not *partes extra partes* but unfold according to a duration that is neither
imposed by the auditor, nor mappable by clock time, for it is the *melody
itself that bears its own tempo and unfolding in which time is necessary, and
not simply the time taken for information to appear*: "That an effort of this
kind is not impossible, is proved by the existence in man of an aesthetic
faculty along with normal perception.... In default of knowledge properly
so called, reserved to pure intelligence, intuition may enable us to grasp
what it is that intelligence fails to give us, and indicate the means of
supplementing it" (CE 176–77/645). Bergson seeks *another* temporality
for thought, he does not merely regard thought as temporality tout court
but as one specific mode of temporality: one in which time is distinguished according to different speeds and economies. And it is precisely
here that one might tie Bergson's thought to the future in a manner that

would *not* be the same for a series of other antibourgeois, anti-instrumental, antinaturalizing thinkers.

To look further into where this might go aesthetically we might say that there is not an object or subject who acts but action as such, incapable of being stabilized into any entity. There is no distinction between dancer and dance or, as in organicist aesthetics in its most radical mode, there is not a creative artisan who then expends energy on some external object. Rather, there "is" performing creativity as such, without distinction between subject and object. And this is, indeed, both how modernism often imagined artwork and artist *and* how Bergson imagines art from within his own philosophy: one does not perceive an isolated object but perceives (or senses) the *becoming* in dynamic relations of an ongoing creative process, without distinction between selfsame subject and altering states or action:

> The aesthetic feelings offer us a still more striking example of this progressive stepping in of new elements, which can be detected in the fundamental emotion and which seem to increase its magnitude, although in reality they do nothing more than alter its nature. Let us consider the simplest of them, the feeling of grace. At first it is only a perception of a certain ease, a certain facility in the outward movements. And as those movements are easy which prepare the way for others, we are led to find a superior ease in the movements which can be foreseen, in the present attitudes in which future attitudes are pointed out and, as it were, prefigured. . . . Thus the perception of ease in motion passes over into the pleasure of mastering the flow of time and of holding the future in the present. A third element comes in when the graceful movements submit to a rhythm and are accompanied by music. For the rhythm and measure, by allowing us to foresee to a still greater extent the movements of the dancer, make us believe that we now control them. . . . Thus a kind of physical sympathy enters into the feeling of grace. . . . It is this mobile sympathy, always ready to offer itself, which is just the essence of higher grace. Thus the increasing intensities of aesthetic feeling are here resolved into as many different feelings, each one of which, already heralded by its predecessor, becomes perceptible in it and then completely eclipses it. . . . we might ask ourselves whether nature is beautiful otherwise than through meeting by chance certain processes of our art, and whether, in a certain sense, art is not prior to nature. (TFW 11–14/11–13)

Bergson's speculatively postulated beginning of life, before the genesis of human intellect and mind, offers a way of thinking about life that intimates not only a future without humans but also a future of different economic velocities. If art may be prior to nature this is not because intellect or mind constitutes objectivity but because mind and matter unfold from something like potentiality or creativity as such, before any mode of life—organic or otherwise.

Consider, here, Bergson's distinction among plants, animals, and the intellect: this describes not a difference in degrees of sophistication but a different relation between stored energy, expenditure, and anticipation. Such distinctions of kind can only be thought if we imagine Bergson's opening postulate in *Creative Evolution*: in the beginning is energy as such, explosive in its creativity and not yet halted or mired in any stability or identity. The plant, then, would be a storing of energy, allowing us to think a difference between an influx of power (sunlight, water, soil nutrients) and the pool of energy that remains in itself, without outflow. The animal, thought of in terms of instinct, expends energy for the sake of retrieving a greater gain, exerting its own metabolism for the sake of living on with a range of further movement and exertion that goes beyond mere static survival. The animal's relation to other rhythms is thus one of delay, having to indulge in minimal calculation and strategy to move one way rather than another, to seek one prey or object rather than another, and to use one means rather than another. Instinct does not leave the animal stable in itself but gives direction or movement that will then shore up the organism's being. The intellect achieves a different relation between speed, expenditure, survival, and strategy. It is through technical extension (or procedures that take the body's expenditure beyond an immediately perceived range and calculation) that an entirely different economy is opened.

"Humanity" occurs as an extension of the intellect rather than spirit. In humanism others are imagined, in a manner of generalization, as alter egos. Humanism's *extension* of sympathy—whereby others are similar versions of myself—enables general laws of humanity that ultimately enhance bodily survival (either the body of the individual or the population of man). The thought of the world as generalizable matter, of other persons as quite like myself, of an ongoing identity whose maintenance I am prepared to work upon: this is what constitutes humanity as an *intellectual* system or machine. It not only has its concomitant speed and technology of clock time (where the "now" of the present can be imagined as analogous to the "now" of the past); it also has its accompanying technology of art. Great art appears in a series of master works—classical, romantic, and modern—each with their own way of imagining one common humanity. What is occluded is an intensive art history, in which each creation would alter the whole. One would have a different Milton after each new poem, each new film, and each new apocalyptic miniseries. Every painting would rewrite the history of painting; every word would alter the canon of literature. Whereas an extensive art history of humanism occurs by way of consumption, assembling a corpus of great works for edifying pleasure, an intensive art history creates new perceptions drawing spectators into a rhythm beyond the time of living bodies.

Art (of humanity) may be considered via an economy of enjoyment: an expenditure that exceeds merely material survival but nevertheless gives man a sense of himself, tying him to a world that he can imagine as his own. Despite Kant's distinction between sensual enjoyment and a properly reflective judgment of taste, one would have to include Kantian aesthetics in the modes of art consumption that Bergson's work would seek to surpass. For Kant, even if the artwork is not pathologically enjoyable and cannot be reduced to highly particular and bodily pleasures, art nevertheless yields a *feeling* of harmony: it is because the intuited content is not yet conceptualized but *feels* as though it is destined for conceptual formation that we are given a sense of the harmonious relation between the world as it is and the world as it is for us. It is because we do not simply perceive the world through concepts but are affected by our own potentiality for conceptualization that art is not *mere* enjoyment. It is both an indication of our synthesizing powers and a prelude to our properly moral self-legislation, freed from all particularity. For Bergson, another direction is indicated whereby we might find a way beyond perceiving the world according to our own rhythm. Art may shore up our intellectual economy, strengthen the ways in which we have mapped the world according to our own interests, and may also be highly moral—allowing us to imagine a world of others as similar to ourselves and therefore worthy of our care. Like other human social practices, art would extend the energy we expend beyond considerations of simply organic survival (beyond animality), and it would do so by way of speed and delay. We would not consume immediately and directly but would allow for the production of technologies (language, art, symbols, moral figures) that would ultimately create community survival. But this would not yet allow for something like spirit and genuine duration, for we would still be tied to the preservation of an actual humanity—man as we imagine him to be, with art and morality allowing us to sympathize with others as being somewhat akin to the image we have of ourselves.

Bergson may, then, suggest some way of thinking beyond the problem that dominates the present: how does humanity, witnessing its own end, save itself? If Darwinian evolution gave form to the sense that humanity had a beginning in time, recent events in various disciplines (from climate change studies and archaeology to cosmology and future studies) are forming a sense of humanity's end in time. How might we be interested in this end? At present, the problem takes the form of humanity striving to achieve the survival or extension of its current and already actualized form: we must use fewer resources or develop more efficient technologies in order to eke out the spending of energy we have now for a longer period. And if art served any purpose here it would be to extend the range of our survival-serving sympathy, allowing us to feel more for nature or ecology.

We might, though, begin to see this problem of human survival as a false problem, and a false problem to do with the very tendency that Bergson identified in the intellect: the tendency to fix the world according to stable images and to manage the mind itself as one more object within the world. The very intellectual power that allowed for a speed and economy outside of instinct and vicious survival also encloses humanity within itself. We can see the brain as an organ with certain functions (language, representation, imagination, morality) and make this the basis for human sciences and then use these sciences to manage our future. We might be able to manage ourselves better and thereby extend our survival; we might develop an ecological or global awareness, become less consumerist or more "mindful."

There have been forms of literary study or supposed literary criticism that pursue just this postulate: that art is an *extension* of survival mechanisms. Joseph Carroll and Brian Boyd, whose work we will consider in more detail below, have each argued for forms of literary Darwinism. Against what they see to be the constructivism or arbitrariness of theory, they want to ground the creation of artworks in the survival mechanisms of organisms. Such a postulate is worthwhile as long as one remains with an extensive theory of time and life and ignores the possibility of what Bergson refers to as differences in kind. A quantity can be increased—one can become more and more intelligent—but a threshold might occur where increasing intellectual activity might tend toward a difference in kind. What if the technologies of art—drawing and writing in order to formalize and manage the world—developed according to their own trajectories, independent of the organism, to create new rhythms, durations, and multiplicities irreducible to organic life? This would be a different mode of Darwinism, where evolution would not be for the sake of bodies and identities but for traits and divergent lines of synthesis.

Bergson's "creative" evolution is destructive of the creativity of humankind and instead places creativity in processes of proliferation outside already formed bodies. Art, intuited from such a point of view, would yield an "aesthetic sense": not the creation of a common humanity in which I feel the world *as if* it accorded with my own human rhythm but an annihilation of my sensory-motor rhythm, an annihilation of personality, and a feeling of duration beyond that of the self. This aesthetic sense as described by Bergson bears two salient features. First, it is a strict form of antihumanism, but an antihumanism that has always accompanied humanism. That is, it is the very essence of the human animal to be other than its animality or to have no essence—insofar as it is human—other than its existence. So, even if the intellect that distinguishes humanity from animality takes the form of rendering the world determinable, calculable, and manipulable in a reified image humanity has of itself, this very stultifying power *also* has the potential to release its own creativity and produce rhythms that are not reducible to sensory-motor efficiency. Second, Bergson's antihumanist ethics and aesthetics both accords with and overturns Kantian aesthetics. Like Kant, Bergson's proper humanity is not that of man as an object within the world who can be known and theorized: the properly human is antihuman, not a thing within time and space but a power that can be felt only after its mapping of the world as spatiotemporal (feeling itself as other than spatiotemporal). Like Kant, there is a distinction between the ethical and spiritual and the aesthetic; but this distinction is also an intimate connection. The aesthetic sense can either lead us to believe that there is a single human order to the world and that morality is nothing more than living according to some natural harmony, or it can release humanity from the natural attitude, allowing a *feeling* of the distinction between the rhythms of perception and the rhythms of the world itself. That is, if one can feel oneself feeling, then one begins to approach a sense of oneself as being affected, as being distinct from and yet related to a world that is *not oneself*.

The Kantian approach to aesthetics would appear, then, to lead ultimately to modernism: the body that simply perceives and acts as an organism in the world can be reduced through processes of mechanization and generalization, but it can also—through art—become aware once again of its power as originally creative and synthetic. Tear ordinary language and perception apart, destroy the already synthesized and allow subjectivity to emerge, *not* as a distinct thing but as a potentiality to create distinction. Any implied author or voice would not be a stable substance so much as a retreating and impersonal effect that would be posited after the event. From the fragments of an artwork one would deduce a synthesizing power that must have once been present but that itself cannot be presented. Modernism will present both a fragmented, mechanized, and dispersed reality *and* imply an artist "above and beyond" fragments.[10] "Humanity" in its actual mode would be so much mechanized waste; yet something like a humanizing potentiality might be discerned only after fragmentation has done its work and demanded a revitalization or activation of a subjective power. A humanity beyond humans, or a synthesizing power beyond synthesis, would be intimated by a fragmentation that does not appear as the fragmentation *of* some lost or prior wholeness.

For all its similar emphases on the overcoming of everyday functionality and instrumental reasoning, Bergson's mode of distinguishing the aesthetic sense takes a different route, leading to a different way of thinking about modernist aesthetics. To be more accurate: aesthetic sense destroys functional, generalizing, and *human* distinctions—those that have served the intellect and its extension of the organism—in order to allow something like *distinction itself* to emerge. Art would tend toward impersonality, but not so that one might achieve a subject so free and creative as to be above and beyond all work. Rather than emphasize fragmentation that would allow for the subjective synthesizing power to be regenerated after a century or more of industrialism and the mechanization of the sensory motor apparatus, Bergson places the aesthetic sense close to an overcoming of active synthesis. The mind does not feel its *own* power, nor even its own harmonization with a world with which it happily accords. It is in the merger of self-annihilation and perceptual intuition that another (radically futural) rhythm might emerge. This is not man re-finding himself but a destruction of actual humanity for the sake of a virtuality that is distinct from any already possible power.

This would be a radically destructive and explosive aesthetic. If "life" begins—as Bergson speculates—with a power of explosive difference in which there is no opposition between the differentiating, destructive, and pulverizing power and some matter or stability that is the object of this propulsive force, then this pure power would be regained at a higher level in the aesthetic. There would be no distinction between creative power and object created, just creative rhythm itself, not grounded in the stabilizing point of view of subject or observer.

THE EPOCH OF EXTINCTION

Why should this problem of proper names, of aesthetics, and of modernist aesthetics concern us *now*, when so much more is at stake? Consider the two problems posed by the traditions of Kantian and Bergsonian aesthetics both of which are embedded in a modernist tradition that inflects theory and criticism today. For Kant, art may indeed be explained and experienced *pathologically* as the way in which it affects the bodily organism, causing it pleasure or pain. But there is another way of thinking about the aesthetic. Kant, after all, was the master thinker of the shifted problem, whereby we transpose the terms of the question to a different register (and here Bergson was similarly critical of the ways in which badly posed problems led to frozen intellectual battles). Rather than look at the bodily pleasure or function of art in terms of the organism, how might we consider art from the point of view of the art object: *not* in terms of the ways in which it affects and serves my organic being, but art as a conduit to a world given in intuition—independent of the concepts we use to organize thought? Reflective judgment occurs *not* when we feel the pleasures of our organism and its furtherance, such as the pleasures of bodily consumption, but when we feel the intuited world as not already conceptualized *for us*, and yet as though it possessed a harmony conducive to conceptualization in general. This Kantian theory of reflective judgment has implications for science, art, and morality. We proceed scientifically as if the world's order would be in accord with our ongoing research and inquiry. We accept that we cannot know the world as it is in itself, but we proceed *as if* its being were indeed aligned with the way in which it is received by us. This allows for *theoretical* knowledge: an awareness of the distance between our concepts and the world in itself, with the acknowledgment that this conceptualized world (known only as given) is the only world we have. There could be no better or more accurate knowledge outside concepts, for knowledge (as experienced and experienceable) is essentially conceptual.

Aesthetic experience, by contrast, is not conceptual; it is proto-conceptual. It is the presentation of intuitions that demand, but do not yet receive, a generalized conceptual mode and therefore indicate conceptuality as a power. We act ethically *as if* we could imagine ourselves as *subjects*, regardless of any received intuition or inclination: the aesthetic would be a prelude to ethics precisely in an opening of a gap between subject and object. Can we think of ourselves *as if* we were not beings within some affecting, conceptualized, knowable, manipulable, and historical world? How would one act if one were nothing more than the power to decide as such? In terms of modernist aesthetics, as already suggested, the idea of thinking of art as destructive of enjoyment and pathological pleasure and as somehow activating a critical power capable of thinking not of man, not as an animal within the world, but of a worldless humanity was opened up. How would we act if not tied to community, habit, sympathy, tradition, context, and concept?

Bergson's destructive aesthetic does not annihilate man as organism in favor of a decisive subject and does not regard the aesthetic sense as liberating perception from actual concepts in order to disclose a conceptualizing or legislating power. His aesthetic is proto-ethical in its destructiveness of organic pleasure, but rather than yielding a transcendental subject of decision it intimates a radically inhuman thought of difference in itself dislocated from any location, *as if we could become one with what we perceived, not in terms of our own organic rhythms but in line with the beat or pulse of life outside any general harmony.*

Thus Kant and Bergson sought to shift the problem and relation between aesthetics and morality and did so by waging a war on the morality of the organism. This may, of course, have been for theological reasons and sentiments: could we think of life as pure action not determined by any form other than that of its own creative flowing forth? But there was also a destructive motif within both their notions of the aesthetic sense that is worthy of consideration as we witness the edge of the anthropocene era. Man, as organism, has a tendency to be a pleasure machine with a thermodynamic economy: expend a bit of effort here to receive a reward there. The problem with such an economy is the paucity of its way of posing problems, all of which become a question of more and less. Eat a little less, live a little longer. Work a little harder to receive a little more. Feel a little bit more sympathy for nature and animals (make them a little more human) and have a better (more sustainable) world. This thermodynamic bubble of our survival economy is hurtling us toward an extinction that we cannot think because our imagination is only one of degrees (living longer, sustaining, adapting, mitigating, becoming more viable, surviving, and trading). How would we act, think, or feel if we abandoned the idea of humanity as it actually is in favor of what Bergson indicated through spirit and the aesthetic sense? The virtual would be tied crucially to the aesthetic sense insofar as *feeling* would take us away from the body and its interested point of view toward the rhythms and timelines of the universe without us.[11]

We can begin to conclude by noting that Kant and Bergson provide different ways of thinking an aesthetic annihilation of the human organism: for Kant the body is vanquished by a virtual intimation of humanity as it *would be if it could imagine itself as an end with nothing other than its own will and decision in view*. It is not as though feelings yield a proper humanity; it is in thinking about humanity, as disembodied or nonpathological, that I can then feel respect for this virtual self I might become. For Bergson the body becomes affected in a way that takes it beyond the concepts it has of itself to a universe without man, even if that universe in its purest perception may only emerge from a humanity capable of annihilating itself virtually. Both Kantianism and Bergsonism are attacks upon a humanity of the organism: Kantianism yields a higher organicism, or sense of life and community beyond the individual body, whereas Bergsonism aims to think the explosiveness of life beyond system and harmony, beyond any organicism.

Despite the crucial role that *counter-organicism* and human annihilation possess for both these thinkers, the opposite path—a reactive organism of the organism—has been the one that is increasingly followed and often in the name of Bergson and Kant. Modernism always had two sides: an antibourgeois disgust for a humanity intent on destroying enjoyment and "man" and a redemptive valorization of *the* aesthetic that would revive subjective potentiality by retrieving perceptual activity. It is the latter, redemptive, crypto-theological path that has become increasingly dominant, often through craven or retreating readings of Kant and Bergson. Kant has, after all, become the source of a liberal theory of ethics and politics in which morality is grounded on normativity and personality, on the integrity of remaining true to who I am.[12] Kant and Bergson could, and should, provide opportunities for contemplating the capacity for thinking through an aesthetic (or nonconceptual) experience of humanity's limit and end, its virtual nonexistence, that would enable it to imagine life beyond its own organic frontiers. Instead, in the mode of a reaction formation, the very concepts created by Kant and Bergson have a re-humanizing, reorganizing, neo-organicist tendency.

In addition to a widespread and increasingly vehement insistence on the embodied mind, the extended mind, the global brain,[13] and a series of other motifs that project the human image of the bounded organism onto life as a whole, there have been even more reactive and putatively "evolutionist" attempts to tie the aesthetic sense to the human organism. That is, not only is the world now seen as one vast interconnected organism (as a macro-human, or worse, as a goddess Gaia figure), literary events are seen as extensions of the sensory-motor apparatus' striving for self-maintenance. Either the world is one vast body, or human bodies are seen as the foundation from which techne extends. (What is not considered is what Bergson referred to as creative evolution or the tendency for lines of difference to break free from their organic origin.)

Brian Boyd, for example, has tied literary production to storytelling, and this in turn to adaptation (and therefore an extension of organic survival tendencies). For Boyd there is no difference in kind between body-serving cognition and aesthetic perception and production. Boyd's work is typical of a current tendency to see all art as a cognitive "treadmill": we have perceptual and cognitive powers that help us to map the world and that become elaborated and extended in art. What Bergson referred to as the "aesthetic sense" or the capacity to intuit rhythms other than those of one's organic being is reduced by many "literary" evolutionists to a richer form of cognitive processing: "One sign of a cognitive adaptation is that limited perceptual input yields rich conceptual output: the mind automatically processes information in elaborate ways. In fiction we repeatedly make inferences that far outstrip evidence."[14] This may indeed be true; we may, indeed, tend to create and reduce art in ways that serve our own projections rather than the world as it is (or might be). But it is for just that reason that a tradition of modernism emerged: to destroy easy cognitive processing, to annihilate the storytelling power, to reverse the relation between perceptual input and conceptual output, to jam that efficiency machine.

To take another example, Joseph Carroll appeals to "literary Darwinism" to turn the humanities back to scientific grounding and to locate information and literary objects in the historicism of the human mind.[15] In doing so, these trends of literary Darwinism avoid the thrust of the counter-organic creativity that Bergson drew from Darwinian evolution. Carroll argues that poststructuralism is a form of "wishful thinking" that cannot face up to the realities of biology, nature, and power, and he appeals to literary Darwinism—grounding literary study in what we know of the evolving human organism—as a wake-up call:

> Transformation involves renovation from the ground up, eliminating the endemic confusion of "pluralism" and carrying through on the implications of a Darwinian vision. It is not the case that there is nothing outside the text. It is not even the case that there is nothing outside of life. Before life evolved, there was a physical universe in which it could evolve. It is the case, though, that there is nothing in life outside of evolution. That means both less and more than it might seem to mean. It does not mean that the forms of literary development—genres and traditions—exactly parallel the macrostructures of evolutionary development. It does not mean that all human experience is driven in a simple and direct way by the biblical injunction to go forth and multiply. It does not mean that all literary characters exemplify average or species-typical forms of behavior. It certainly does not mean that all authors, even ancient, medieval, Renaissance, and neoclassical authors, are crypto-Darwinists. What it does mean is that all humans past and present have evolved under the massively constraining force of adaptation by means of natural selection.[16]

Such an appeal to natural selection, and the natural selection of humans, precludes what Bergson referred to as creative evolution, or what Darwin referred to as sexual selection: traits develop, connect, proliferate, and become detached from their organic genesis.[17] Aesthetic production may have one side turned toward organic survival, but it also has an explosive element that takes the organism into other rhythms. By turning production back to natural selection, literary Darwinists cannot consider lines of difference beyond organic survival or the maintenance of fit types. They diminish the aesthetic radicalism of the epoch of extinction.

If Darwinism dealt a blow to human narcissism by locating a human emergence within time, Bergson's epoch (and beyond) has increasingly intimated an end to human existence within time. This ranges (at least) from the modernist intimation of a world and time after humanity (Conrad's atavism, Woolf's moment outside human organicism, Eliot's pure time, Lawrence's Dionysian antihumanism) to the current postmodern thought of a world of perceptions outside the human visual apparatus. For Carroll, by contrast, the challenge of the present is one of turning back to the extension of the mind and the human organism: "Authors are people talking to people about people. Most stories are about people seeking resources and reproductive success—fortune and love. But they are also about people seeking to perceive meaning in or impose meaning on the events of their own lives and the lives of every person they know."[18] (One wonders whether Carroll stopped reading literature after Jane Austen.)

The recent "turn to affect," far from opening out from the organism to perceptions and relations that are not centered in a single conceptualizing body, has become a way of returning life and thought to the emotive body, to feeling, to individuals and identities. The "affective turn" is proclaimed to be a correction of an overly linguistic literary theory or idealism; affects are the expression of embodied individuals. For Bergson, by contrast, affect needed to be distinguished from the emotions of the sensory-motor apparatus: on the one hand there is affect—or a certain force of relations—and then there is the domesticating and registering of that affect in emotions and actions. Bergson therefore distinguishes between nature's affects and those of art; the former are ways in which our nervous system can adapt to its world, and the affects of art take on a life of their own, drawing us into other rhythms. As Bergson remarks:

> If musical sounds affect us more powerfully than the sounds of nature, the reason is that nature confines itself to *expressing* feelings, whereas music *suggests* them to us. Whence indeed comes the charm of poetry? The poet is he with whom feelings develop into images, and the images themselves into words which translate them while obeying the laws of rhythm. In seeing these images pass before our eyes we in our turn experience the feeling which was, so to speak, their emotional equivalent: but we should never realize these images so strongly without the regular movements of the rhythm by which our soul is lulled into self-forgetfulness, and, as in a dream, thinks and sees with the poet. (*TFW* 15/14)

We need to see Bergson's epoch of modernist aesthetics as having *one* side turned back to a theological spiritualism, in which art would somehow allow for an image of pure, flowing, self-furthering life, liberated from any fixed form and yet fully distinct and self-individuating, and *another* Bergson who opened the problem of a life that was radically explosive and destructive of closed forms *without* any end in view.

The *aesthetic* would not be a sensation or feeling enabling attunement but a force or power not yet oriented to any relation. Deleuze, for one, saw the liberation of affect from the systematizing sensory-motor apparatus as both a way of liberating images and perceptions from the moralizing figure of the human animal and as an intimation of a life freed not only from organicism but also from spiritualism and higher organizing syntheses.[19] One might lament that Deleuze, like Kant and Bergson, has seemed to license a new literalism and organicism, and yet if one takes up what Deleuze referred to as "Bergsonism," the challenge of intuiting the distinct and individuating tendencies that common sense conflates into generalizing figures, we would need to distinguish the explosive tendency that Bergson located in something like life itself from the organizing and binding tendencies that led Bergson to posit a finalizing spirit grounded in a self-surpassing humanity—a humanity that would find itself properly through "the aesthetic," through feeling itself feeling life as such.

THE EXTINCTION OF ART

These concerns can now take us beyond Bergson and Bergsonism to a present that seems to bear all the features of a world in which a "vulgar" modernist aesthetic has won the day. Rather than a generalized world of passive and uniform consumption in which individuals move, think, and are manipulated as machines, and rather than a *simple* biopolitics in which humans are regarded as nothing more than genetic material to be maintained and managed, what appears to be valued above all else is the living act of pure becoming, freed from any external or transcendent domination. In popular culture there is a widespread celebration of active and self-aware consumerism, with individuals now able to use new technologies to orient consumption to their own rhythms and able to enter the domain of production themselves (via YouTube, social media, and other interactive modes). In contemporary political debate there is a retreat from the older models of identity politics (identifying "as a . . ." in favor of a performativity in which the self is nothing other than its de-stabilizing and disturbing action, never a subject subtending or preceding action).[20] In theory—ranging from Hardt and Negri's celebration of "homo homo humanity squared,"[21] to Agamben who wishes to "return thought to its practical calling,"[22] and a celebration that we have over-come the linguistic paradigm—all this can be read as a reaction forma-tion. Precisely at the time when humanity is accelerating the intellectual trajectory that has enclosed it within its own organic interests, it becomes unable to read indications of another life and another time. Current evolutionary affirmations of *art* as the object that discloses the organism's capacity to extend itself and live its own world *as its own* domesticate the technicity or creativity of evolution in a highly psychotic manner. In the face of increasing evidence of evolution's tendency to develop beyond organic survival there are ever more shrill assertions of the organism's tight bond with the self-furthering life of art objects.

You would not have to look very far to see that by any definition of art there has been a counter-human or superhuman trajectory of creation that does *anything but* further the life of the intellectual or efficient organ-ism. One would not have to go as far as looking at Don DeLillo's *Point Omega*, which theorizes—within narrative and the genre of the novel—the human eye's captivation by screens, images, unfolding sequences of cinema, and installation art. Delillo's novella opens with a character view-ing an art installation (often playing to an empty room) that plays a radically slowed-down sequence of Hitchcock's *Psycho* (a film that has already placed the eye and brain's mesmerized paralysis by the screen within its own frame): "The original movie has been slowed to a running time of twenty-four hours. What he was watching seemed pure film, pure time. How long would he have to stand here, how many weeks or months, before the film's time scheme absorbed his own, or had this already begun to happen?"[23] Art is no longer *for* the organism or the eye but plays in its own time, indicating the capacity for image synthesis beyond any per-ceiver.[24] Art, *at least since modernism*, has turned back upon the supposed sufficiency of images and framed and thematized the ways in which the human brain's own technical objects also bear a suicidal or brain-paralyzing tendency. Jane Austen's *Northanger Abbey*, after all, parodied the capacity for an over-consumption of gothic novels to diminish critical judgment. But these critical and self-reflexive aspects of aesthetic culture in which art attacks its own narrative and pacifying lures are accompanied by a widespread cultural anxiety witnessing the brain's (and organism's) self-destructive trajectory. The capacity for digital, gaming, and Internet culture to destroy the brain's life and development have been widely noted,[25] but this occurs alongside an equally redemptive and enthusiastic embrace for nonnarrative and cerebrally mesmerizing modes of cultural consumption. Precisely at the moment at which the human animal becomes aware of its self-accelerating end, it manufactures and embraces (in equal measure) a widespread denial of its self-enclosure (including the denial of climate change and the return to various modes of communitarian humanism) and a fascinated anticipatory witnessing of its own brain death (including disaster epics and postapocalyptic narratives of life after humans). In short, art, intellect, brain, and futurity are what Bernard Stiegler refers to as pharmacological: they are at one and the same time potentials for productive complexity *and* the means by which life short-circuits and encloses itself in its own death. Bergson's appeal to the aesthetic sense is, for our time, a philosophy of the future that is beyond good and evil. If there is a future then it cannot be *for us*: it cannot ground itself upon man as some good life-furthering form. Rather, it would need to consider—at one and the same time—the organism and intellect as self-enclosing forms of suicide by myopia *and* as self-destructive futurity by creation.

NOTES

1 See Antliff, *Bergson.*

2 I refer here to "man" rather than "humanity" precisely because the concept is sexually differentiated; there has never been a "humanity" that is not sexed and is not defined through all the predicates of masculinity.

3 These range from ecological claims that the tipping point of destruction has already passed (see Lovelock, *The Vanishing Face of Gaia*; and Greer, *The Ecotechnic Future*) to imaginative projections and thought experiments of a world after humans (see Weisman, *The World Without Us*).

4 See Husserl, *The Phenomenology of Internal Time-Consciousness.*

5 Carr, *Interpreting Husserl*, 38.

6 Bergson also uses examples of watching dance or listening to music, but he focuses less on the subject's synthesis or activity and more on music or dance's capacity to draw the spectator or listener into *another* duration (TWF 44/32; see Barden, "Method in Philosophy," 34).

7 Fink, *Sixth Cartesian Meditation*, 4.

8 Ricoeur, *The Symbolism of Evil.*

9 See Hansen, "Becoming as Creative Involution?"

10 See Ellmann, *The Poetics of Impersonality*.

11 One could contrast this possibility, opened by Bergson, with the correction of "Descartes' error" as posed by Antonio Damasio. For Damasio, and some Deleuzians who follow him, the correct direction for thought (and, for some, *political* thought) is the relocation of point of view, mind, and thinking in the feeling *body*. See Damasio, *The Feeling of What Happens*; and Connolly, *Neuropolitics*.

12 See Korsgaard, *The Sources of Normativity*; and O'Neill, *Acting on Principle*.

13 See Varela, Thompson, and Rosch, *The Embodied Mind*; Menary, *The Extended Mind*; and Bloom, *The Global Brain*.

14 Boyd, *On the Origin of Stories*, 189.

15 Carroll, "Three Scenarios of Literary Darwinism," 58.

16 Ibid., 61–62.

17 See Grosz, *The Nick of Time*.

18 Carroll, "Human Nature and Literary Meaning," 90.

19 See Deleuze, *Cinema 2*.

20 See Butler, *Gender Trouble*.

21 Hardt and Negri, *Empire*, 204.

22 Agamben, *Homo Sacer*, 4.

23 DeLillo, *Point Omega*, 6.

24 See Cohen, *Hitchcock's Cryptonymies*.

25 See Carr, *The Shallows*; and Greenfield, *I.D.*

PART II

Politics

FIVE

Bergson as Philosopher of War
and Theorist of the Political

Philippe Soulez
Translated by Melissa McMahon

We have already shown that Bergson maintained close relations with the leading politicians of his time and was engaged in a specific kind of political activity at a particularly crucial moment in world history.[1] We have shown how he conceived those contacts and this activity. But is Bergson by that token a theorist *of the political*? One can very well be an "intellectual," intervening in the affairs of the city, even be an advisor to the Prince, without for all that developing a properly political *philosophy*. This discrepancy may even partly explain Bergson's unease in relation to himself as *Homo loquax*. Is he expressing his philosophy, in particular his political philosophy during this period? The answer to this question is not simple. Bergson's discourses on war share enough similarities with his previous philosophy for us to recognize "Bergson" in them. But the partisan nature of the arguments, the sign of a "polemical" and political *activism*, shows that Bergson does not reflect on *the political* [*le* politique] per se during the war.[2] In fact, after *Two Sources* his political thought will continue to operate on two distinct planes. In this work Bergson distances himself from the wartime polemics (TS 285–86/1218) and places the phenomenon of war at the very center of his analysis. Subsequently, and more especially in 1939, Bergson will continue to intervene in the political arena. He will even republish one of his discourses on war.[3] Bergson has not therefore renounced any of his previous positions. The two planes are not however entirely unconnected. We can show how the main themes of the discourses on war are both reprised and criticized in *Two Sources*. Bergson, a philosopher *in* times of war, thereby becomes a philosopher *of* war. From being the intellectual he was, Bergson becomes a theorist of the political.[4] We should note that by the same token, he tries, as a philosopher, to overcome his own duality.

The first objection we should address could be expressed as follows: how can a book devoted to "morality and religion" be a political treatise? It is not difficult to answer this objection, although it has had its historical impact. The work *The Two Sources of Morality and Religion* is not a book about morality and religion but a book about the *sources* of morality and religion, precisely insofar as there are *two* of them. It is from the analysis of the sources that the reflection on the political emerges. The first pages of *Two Sources* should already have put the reader on alert. The question of prohibition being posed in the first few lines of the text, Bergson's train of thought continues with a reflection on *order*, on the social order insofar as it is distinct from the natural order while also resembling it. With this remark Bergson revives the diagnosis of the discrepancy between being and appearing that was Rousseau's point of departure in the *First Discourse* in the area of moral and political philosophy:

> And yet everything conspires to make us believe that this regularity is comparable to that of nature. I do not allude merely to the unanimity of mankind in praising certain acts and blaming others. I mean that, even in those cases where moral precepts implied in judgments of values are not observed, *we contrive that they should appear so*. Just as we do not notice disease when walking along the street, so we do not gauge the degree of possible immorality behind the exterior which humanity presents to the world. It would take a good deal of time to become a misanthrope if we confined ourselves to the observation of others. It is when we detect our own weaknesses that we come to pity or despise mankind. The human nature from which we then turn away is the human nature we have discovered in the depths of our own being. The evil is so well screened, the secret so universally kept, that in this case each individual is the *dupe*

of all: however severely we may profess to judge other men, at bottom we think them better than ourselves. On this happy illusion much of our social life is grounded. (TS 11–12/983; emphasis added)

The paragraphs that follow are devoted to the analysis of obligation. Faithful to its etymology, Bergson presents obligation as a "bond between men" (TS 15/986) that binds us to them because it binds us in the first place to ourselves. Bergson's thesis is that there is only a social bond because society has a "hold" within each of us (TS 15/987). If obligation binds us to other men, does it bind us to *all* men? "To find an answer," says Bergson, "we need only consider what happens in time of war" (TS 31/1000; translation modified). This methodology shouldn't surprise us. The Bergsonian problem of morality, as a problem concerning its "sources," is a problem concerning *energetics*. Bergson asks himself *what force* makes men act morally. He analyzes obligation as a fact of social and individual behavior. It is thus enough for him to "look at" (TS 31/1001) what naturally social individuals do to conclude that war is natural and normal. Bergson's reference to biology will help him moreover to counter the objection that argues from the rare or exceptional character of the war to decide its normality. Disease, too, is rare and exceptional; it is nevertheless just as "normal" as health. Even better, we can in fact define health as a constant effort "to prevent disease or avoid it" (TS 31/1001). Bergson thus performs a conceptual reversal in how we conceive the relationship between war and peace. It is peace that is the interruption of war and not vice versa. This conceptual reversal from a phenomenological point of view is also, within the ethical order, a reversal of day and night. "Fair is foul, and foul is fair," says Bergson in relation to war. He thus anticipates the analyses of Roger Caillois, Georges Bataille, or René Girard on war as a festival and an irruption of the sacred into the monotony of everyday life.

With war it is the notion of the enemy that appears at the center of the phenomenology of morality. Moral obligation aims to forge an attitude of discipline within us in the face of the enemy (TS 31/1001). Morality, *closed* morality to be precise, and politics are one. Bergson makes no secret of this and recalls the Latin adage, *salus populi* ("the health of the people") (TS 75/1039). We could for that matter add that closed morality, politics, and religion are one, since (closed) religion merely uses fabulation to compensate for what may be less than perfect about human justice in the eyes of the closed society itself (TS 13/985, 98/1058).

Bergson's methodology, both descriptive ("consider," "look at") and genealogical (going back to the source of the force), is an almost perfect application of the usual method, or "Bergsonism." Bergson is effectively required to start by criticizing the false synthesis that makes up ordinary morality (mixed morality and combined sources). This criticism of the synthesis is a critique of "comprehension": on the pretext that humanity quantitatively "comprehends" a greater number of individuals than the city, which itself comprehends a larger number of individuals than the family, we believe that we can move by a process of expansion from the family to the city and from the latter to humanity (TS 32–33/1001–2). A serious mistake, says Bergson: only the first move is intended by nature. The fact of war shows that the second move is not intended by nature.

By criticizing "comprehension," Bergson criticizes the notion of "human society" (TS 30/1000) that was at the heart of the problem addressed by the discourses on war and peace (those given by Bergson just after the declaration of peace, reproduced in the *Œuvres* volume and elsewhere, as well as those given in the context of the International Committee on Intellectual Cooperation). There is no longer any teleology of the species for him that would drive humanity to unite. The balancing act between individuation and association (CE 259/715, TS 117/1074) can certainly continue to illuminate the circle of the individual and society (TS 15–19/985–90). It no longer suggests any promise of the unification of humanity.

Having criticized the false movement of "comprehension," Bergson rejects a vain attempt, in his view, to explain obligation (TS 22/991). Having accepted obligation as a fact, we might be tempted to provide a rational foundation for obligation *in reason itself*. But since chapter 4 of *Creative Evolution* Bergson can no longer reenlist the idea of reason on his side. On the contrary, he sees the idea of Reason, as well as the transcendental subject that supports it, as a substitute for God, a god brought down to more modest proportions (CE 356/796). Henceforth, Bergson recognizes only "intelligence." There is no doubt that this is a force (TS 92/1053), but it can't be a categorical one. There are thus three forces involved in the energetics of morality: pressure, aspiration, and intelligence. The force that is intelligence is intelligent enough, as it were, to see that it has an interest in submitting to obligations that in return give it rights over others, not to mention the fact that approval in the eyes of others forms part of self-interest (TS 93/1055).

But Bergson denies that utilitarianism, properly understood, leads intelligence as a force to sacrifice itself without any return. At the moment of the supreme sacrifice, this force could rebel and say that it doesn't understand its interest in this way. And who better than intelligence can judge how its interest is to be understood? When it comes to morality, intelligence will thus at best be a strategist but always in the final analysis self-centered. Thus if intelligence sacrifices itself, it is because it has felt the pressure or attraction of another force besides itself and has rationalized this pressure or attraction (or both), turning a blind eye to its origin.

Moving away from the plane of phenomenological and genealogical analysis, and abandoning the search for a foundation because such a search is illusory and unconscious of its own presuppositions (TS 89–90/1050–51), Bergson takes off in another direction to find what he thinks is the true explanation of obligation. From the very first pages of *Two Sources*, the organic metaphor made its appearance. Bergson very quickly poses the question of whether this metaphor is just a "comparison" or if it doesn't rather have an ontic foundation (TS 9/981). The philosopher of the *élan vital* is naturally inclined to be in favor of the second interpretation. We must in effect explain what is categorical about obligation. But *Creative Evolution* already stated very clearly that the order of intelligence was hypothetical in nature and that of instinct categorical (CE 149/621). All Bergson then has to do is transpose this observation to the problem of the social bond itself. Even though Bergson still uses the word "consider," it is clear that we are no longer in the descriptive-phenomenological realm, nor even the genealogical one, but in the realm of hermeneutics, since Bergson "interprets" an "intention of nature" (TS 116/1073; translation modified).

The biological interpretation provides the explanation we were looking for. In order to explain obligation we have to ask ourselves what human society *would have been* if human society had been purely instinctive instead of being intelligent (TS 28/996–97). Of course, human society is not instinctive in nature, but we can understand in this way that habit is to freedom what instinct is to animals. Each of our habits is contingent, but the need to contract them is not:

Let us consider two divergent lines of evolution with societies at the extremities of each. The type of society which will appear the more natural will obviously be the instinctive type; the link that unites the bees of a hive resembles far more the link that holds together the cells of an organism, coordinate and subordinate to each other. Let us suppose for an instant that nature has intended to produce at the extremity of the second line societies where a certain latitude was left to individual choice: she would have arranged that intelligence should achieve here results comparable, as regards their regularity, to those of instinct in the other; she would have recourse to habit. Each of these habits, which may be called "moral," would be incidental. But the aggregate of them, I mean the habit of contracting these habits, being at the very basis of societies and a necessary condition of their existence, would have a force comparable to that of instinct in respect of both intensity and regularity. This is exactly what we called the "totality of obligation." This, be it said, will apply only to primitive societies at the moment of emerging from the hands of nature. It will apply to primitive and to elementary societies. But however much human society may progress, grow complicated and spiritualized, the original design, expressing the purpose of nature, will remain. (TS 26–27/996–97)

The value of Bergson's explanation of obligation is tied to that of his "biological interpretation." The "comparison" that underlies the whole of chapter 1 of *Two Sources* has its limits. We can ask whether these limits are sufficiently marked. The conclusion of chapter 1 gives us pause for thought in this regard: "Everything is obscure if we confine ourselves to mere manifestations, whether they are all called indiscriminately social, or whether one examines, in social man, more particularly the feature of intelligence. All becomes clear, on the contrary, if we start by a quest beyond these manifestations for Life itself. Let us then give to the word biology the very comprehensive [*compréhensif*] meaning it should have, and will perhaps have one day, and let us say in conclusion that all morality, be it pressure or aspiration, is in essence biological" (TS 100– 101/1060–61; translation modified). Bergson commits a fault here, in terms of strict Bergsonian methodology: a philosopher has the right to play on the *plurality* of meanings of an ordinary language term, but he has no right to extend (expand) *the* meaning of that term,[5] especially if, as in the case of "biology," it is a technical term. He runs the risk, as we have seen, of turning it into a mere "conventional sign." The use of the term "comprehensive" in this context, given Bergson's criticism of "comprehension," does not bode very well. There is no doubt, for example, that the concept of "virtual instinct" is interesting. But we can't avoid noting that the reference to "biology"—a biology moreover brought down to the level of prejudices that are not necessarily "philosophical"—alienates Bergson from some of his most precious intuitions. To take just one example that relates directly to the political, is it adequate to conceive the "enemy" as simply a useless—or no longer useful—"troublemaker"? There is no doubt that politics [la politique]—which, let us remember, is the domain of the attachment to life for Bergson—is highly utilitarian, when it is not in fact a sordid affair, but the exclusion of the other precedes and subordinates the evaluation of "utility." This is precisely what Bergson's phenomenology of the political demonstrates. We could even say that Bergson overlooks what is suggested *in his own text*.[6] The massacre of the enemy takes place precisely so it can become the subject of a "story" and be "engraved" for posterity. The function of the "vision of horror" is not illuminated by zoology, because the cruelty of animals is very little beside that of man. Moreover Bergson is the first to criticize the idea that we fight to avoid "starvation." Anxiety about one's "standard of living" has no zoological equivalent in other species. It is the contemporary, industrial form of *amour-propre*, prestige and glory. Bergson suggests this, without realizing it perhaps, when he describes it as the thing without which "life would not be worthwhile" (TS 286/1218). It is not in the problem of need, defined biologically, that we will find the origin of animosity. At the very most we would find a justification there or, as Bergson says, a "rational motive" (TS 288/1220).

Whatever the status of this criticism and of the more or less legitimate expansion of the concept of biology, the biological interpretation allows Bergson to affirm that there is a human nature, since humans are a species or, more precisely, since they are *only* a species. The recourse to the élan vital allows us to imagine what the revival of the creative effort—of which the species represents an immobilization—might be. Some humans, mystics, are a species unto themselves—better, they are what exempt humans from being a *species* (TS 220–21/1162, 257/1194, 268/1203). *Two Sources* is thus a quite original work in the history of philosophy: a political work regarding the *natura naturata*, a work of mysticism regarding the *natura naturans* (TS 58/1024).

The notion of "mysticism" has given rise to a host of misunderstandings, despite Bergson's efforts to, in a way, "demystify" it. Shifting the problem of the origins of morality onto the field of education, Bergson makes a very interesting qualification: "Two ways lie open to the teacher. The one is that of training, in the highest meaning of the word; the other the mystic way, the term being taken here, on the contrary, in its most modest sense. By the first method is inculcated a morality made up of impersonal habits; by the second we obtain the imitation of a person, and even a spiritual union, a more or less complete identification" (*TS* 97/ 1057–58; translation modified). Mysticism in its most modest sense, Bergson's qualification here is very much analogous to the one he made for the term intuition: "there is nothing mysterious about this faculty" (*CM* 235/1431). In this sense all men have an experience of "mysticism." And Bergson has made it clear that the concepts of the "closed society" and the "open society" are the result of a passage "to the limit" (*TS* 84/1046).

Contrary to what a rather sectarian rationalism might believe, Bergson's description here is very close to the Freudian problematic of identification.[7] Regarding the point that more particularly concerns us here, we can see that the mystical, as it is conceived by Bergson, forms part of the problem of the "man of action" and creation. Like the artist, the mystic is a genius of creation. With his creation he creates the conditions for its reception (*TS* 75/1038).

The mystic thereby sets the moral *level* (*TS* 85/1047) of a society or, if you prefer, the acceptable degree of openness. Who is the mystic then from the point of view of the tradition of political philosophy? The question arises because by setting the moral level, the mystic exerts undeniable political influence. Is it the ruler? Nothing in Bergson's text allows this interpretation. The mystic is not the "leader." He very much resembles what Rousseau calls "the Lawgiver." The allusion to the "wise men of Greece" (*TS* 77/1040) confirms this interpretation. The comparison is all the more striking for the fact that Rousseau clearly considers Moses to be a "lawgiver." We thus see the problem of the "philosopher king" shift and move away from the domain of rhetoric to become even more clearly aligned with that of prophecy. This shift is very clearly observable in the very limited place henceforth reserved for Marcus Aurelius (*TS* 77/1040). Emperor *and* philosopher, he lacked the superhuman dimension that would have allowed him to transform the Roman Empire. The mystic is not however to be confused with the lawgiver, because in Christianity he is concerned with man. As Henri Gouhier has shown, Bergson has a perfect recollection of Rousseau's distinction between the religion of the citizen and the religion of man.[8] But he is less pessimistic than Rousseau concerning the contribution of the religion of humankind to that of the citizen, which is precisely what is indicated by the notion of "level."

The status of the "Final Remarks" in *Two Sources* has often been pondered.[9] Few commentators have really committed themselves to understanding this text. From our standpoint this is nevertheless quite understandable. Bergson moves from a reflection on the *political* [*le* politique] to "considerations," to use his own words, on *policy* [*la* politique]. We only have to pay close attention to the movement of the text to be persuaded of this. Bergson begins by "emphasizing" (*TS* 268/1203) the distinction between the closed society and the open society in order to stress the critique of intellectualism one last time, but for the first time he raises the question that will dominate the rest of the text: "Now, is the distinction between the closed and open, which is necessary to resolve or remove theoretical problems, able to help us practically" (*TS* 271/1206)? From being a theorist of the political, Bergson thus becomes, as a good "Bergsonian," a thinker of *particular* political problems. He intervenes in the political area on his *own initiative* as a philosopher, selecting the questions that strike him, *as a philosopher*, as the most important.

Let us dwell for a moment on this movement itself (from the political to politics). The philosophies that have attempted to affirm the existence of an invariant principle in the political domain, whatever their differences in terms of how this invariant is described, have had a common goal: to criticize those theories and political practices that, in setting themselves the task of creating an "other man," have aimed in fact at something other than a man, to use an expression of Julien Freund's. This is in our view the meaning of Bergson's critique of Kant in the "Final Remarks." Democracy is not the work of reason, because reason would never have discovered "human rights" if its own ideal were not in fact underpinned by a religious one, an evangelical disposition, namely a mystical disposition in Bergson's sense. But mysticism concerns the superhuman, not humans as a species. Bergson stresses the millenarian dimension of Kant's philosophy, which Kant himself recognized at least once.[10]

Going in the opposite direction, if we take up the interesting distinction between millenarianism and utopia,[11] Bergson's criticism of Kant is not unlike Aristotle's criticism of Plato's *Republic* in books I and II of the *Politics*. In Aristotle's view, Plato disregards certain constitutive givens of man, for example, the difference between the family and the city, and commits himself to a form of politics that is unsustainable and indeed unworkable. If Bergson made much use of the "Plato and Aristotle" pairing in the context of his critique of metaphysics, the same does not apply in the context of his reflections on society.[12] No doubt Bergson would make less of the city than Aristotle, a difference specific to man. For Bergson, man is a "political animal" in the first place because he is an animal.[13] But perhaps Aristotle himself did not make "the political" as specific to man as a whole philosophical tradition would have it. Whatever the case, it is quite deliberately that Bergson, at the beginning of chapter 2 of *Two Sources*, takes up the expression "political animal" for his own purposes *against Durkheim*. But it isn't only this phrase that Bergson takes up. He places the distinction between "living" and "living well" at the center of his analysis, and it is on this distinction that the *Two Sources* concludes (ᴛꜱ 317/1245). Bergson had made it his own since *Laughter*. With the notion of "good sense," Bergson returns to an Aristotelian set of problems around the notion of "prudence."[14] Generally speaking, the presence of Aristotle's text can be clearly felt in *Two Sources*.[15]

But Bergson would not be the author of *Two Sources* if he were content to simply discuss the "ineradicable" givens (ᴛꜱ 288/1220) of human nature. The description of the natura naturata is accompanied by a prospective analysis of what a return to the natura naturans in politics could be. Here we have, we believe, the key to the three-part plan, clearly visible in the text, of the "Final Remarks."

1   The first part (I) (ᴛꜱ 266–75/1201–9) strongly reaffirms the distinction between the closed society and the open society and insists on the need to "rediscover" the "schema" of human nature insofar as this nature is political. It ends on the question of the "practical conclusions" we are entitled to draw from the schema.

2   The second part (II) (ᴛꜱ 275–92/1209–23) develops the outline of the schema and applies it to the problems of our time (democracy, war, and international organizations). The general line of this second part is that the "expansion" (or "broadening") of societies, combined with the means provided by the growth of science and technology, makes them ungovernable and dangerous given the persistence of warring instincts.

3   The third section (III) (ᴛꜱ 292–317/1223–45), in a typically Berg-

sonian move, ponders the question of whether we might resolve with a return to "simplicity," to the creative source itself, what politics isn't able to contain in the infinitely scattered detail of its "regimentation." If mysticism implies mechanism, mechanism in turn calls for a return to the hot spring of the source.

The reader cannot fail to be struck by the fact that Bergson outlines an entirely classical "political philosophy" *in terms of the subject matter* it addresses.[16] Bergson begins by explaining the lack of true statesmen (II, § 1); then he asks: what are the dimensions of a society "as ordained by nature" (II, § 2); which political system complies with nature (II, § 3); what is a leader (II, § 4); what relationships hold between the rulers and the ruled (II, § 5); which political system is consistent with the ideal (II, § 6); why does war exist (II, § 7); what are the different forms of war (II, § 8); can international organizations put an end to war (II, § 9); what are the rational motives for war (II, § 9–10); and in which areas can international organizations intervene (II, § 11)?

When considered from this angle, the eleven paragraphs of the second part come across as a synopsis of a treatise on political philosophy that Bergson has not had the time to write. Some of Bergson's more private comments in fact point in this direction.[17] But it is doubtful in fact that Bergson was ever tempted to write a book of "political philosophy," in the sense of a specific philosophical *discipline*. What interests him are *problems*, rather than a subject matter or discipline. As interested as Bergson was in "psychology," he also never wrote a treatise on psychology, and even *Two Sources* should be considered more as a work that attempts to solve a set of problems confronting Bergson's philosophy than a moral treatise. Thus Bergson constantly *assumes* political philosophy as a known quantity.[18] It would be entirely possible to situate Bergson in relation to the tradition of political philosophy, and the way he reconciles Hobbes and Spinoza, *homo homini lupus* and *homo homini deus*, shows that such an undertaking would not encounter insurmountable obstacles. On one point in particular it is clear that Bergson takes a stand in favor of the theory of natural sociability over the theory of conventional sociability (as the outcome of a contract) (TS 105/1063).[19] Such an undertaking would only have one drawback: it would in fact go against the spirit of Bergsonism. It would sign up Bergson's political philosophy to the game that is played out between the different political philosophies. Bergson would then just become one more player.

But when Bergson concerns himself with a subject, this is not how he proceeds. We can't understand Bergson if we do not ask what new, unavoidable problem confronts him (см 67–68/1309). This problem is none other than that of extermination.[20]

The last paragraph of *Two Sources* is perfectly clear in this regard: "whether we go bail for small measures or great, a decision is imperative. Mankind lies groaning, half crushed beneath the weight of its own progress. Men do not sufficiently realize that their future is in their own hands. Theirs is the task of determining first of all whether they want to go on living or not. Theirs is the responsibility, then, for deciding if they want merely to live, or intend to make just the extra effort required for fulfilling, even on their refractory planet, the essential function of the universe, which is a machine for the making of gods" (тs 317/1245). The phrase "theirs to decide whether they want to live" has not been sufficiently commented on. Humanity could therefore not want to live or even *decide* not to live. Bergson is perhaps the first *major philosopher* to become aware of this new possibility already in 1932. He senses the coming of the atomic bomb.[21] Bergson was wrong, we think, to explain massacres by comparing the "ferocity" of humans with that of the bees. But in saying that massacre is a *ratio prima* and not *ultima*, he was right to show that the exclusion of the other, which characterizes the political per se, carries the seed of extermination, precisely when the other is seen as a different and of course inferior species or biological race. Racism is, in this sense, the commonest thing in the world (тs 71/1035, 279–80/1213). It is the flipside of the refusal to "know" the other (тs 77–78/1040, 285–86/1218), namely to acknowledge or "recognize" him. Naturalizing the difference (by biologizing it) opens the way to extermination. And science provides the means.

The *Two Sources* thus ends on a double alternative: die or live, merely live or live well. Bergson's philosophy of history thus becomes clearer. We have commented elsewhere that Bergson's discourses on war, specifically the one dated December 12, 1914 (*The meaning of the war*), envisaged the possibility of a "perverse" evolution of humanity.[22] This possibility is taken up again here in a radicalized form. The thermodynamics of death, "thanatocracy," has reached its limit point: the extinction of humanity itself and no longer just the enemy. The reassuring perspective that returned in *Mind-Energy* disappears once and for all. "Life" no longer drives societies via the clash of wills toward their integration in a finally reunified humanity. The break with Kantian teleology is absolute. Nature no longer knows, better than man, what man needs. War is no longer a ruse of reason. Bergson constantly insists on man's ability to outwit a nature that is "so simple-minded" (TS 56/1022), in particular on the energetic level, which is precisely the level the survival of humanity will be played out on (TS 310/1239).

Does this mean that all notions of progress have disappeared? Will Bergson conclude his interrogation of this notion, which dates back in his work to at least *Creative Evolution* (CE 272/725) and is recognized in an interview of February 1914, with a simple negation (M 1039)? Certainly not. We have to take into account here the intersection of two Bergsonian motifs: the analysis of the retrograde movement of truth and the distinction between the closed and the open—the first motif alone would make a *teleological* conception of progress very problematic. The mechanism of nature does not lead humanity unawares toward the fulfillment of the ideal. Progress can only be observed after the fact. The second motif certainly revives a progressive outlook but for the purposes of prophesy. The criticism of the Kantian Idea is not a criticism of the ideal. On the contrary, Bergson tends to interpret the Idea as a "translation" of the Ideal in the language of Reason (see TFW 232/151–52; TS 33/1002). Kantian philosophy is for Bergson a speculatively questionable translation of a mystical "emotion" that is perfectly legitimate. Far from philosophy being able to judge religion within the limits of reason alone, it is religious sentiment (qua mystical) that gives us the criterion that allows us to assess Kantian philosophy as a false "critique"—false as a critique but a true expression of the religious emotion on the ethical level. In other words, it is Judeo-Christianity that gave Kantianism the idea of the Idea!

Bergson can thus give a genealogical explanation of everything that touches on "human rights," not only as a regulative principle of the ideal but also as a political practice or, if you prefer, a form of "activism":

> Humanity had to wait till Christianity for the idea of universal brotherhood, with its implication of equality of rights and the sanctity of the person, to become operative. Some may say that it has been rather a slow process; indeed eighteen centuries elapsed before the rights of man were proclaimed by the Puritans of America, soon followed by the men of the French Revolution. It began, nevertheless, with the teachings of the Gospel, and was destined to go on indefinitely; it is one thing for an idea to be merely propounded by sages worthy of admiration, it is very different when the idea is broadcast to the ends of the earth in a message overflow-

ing of love, invoking love in return. Indeed there was no question here of clear-cut wisdom, reducible, from beginning to end, into maxims. There was rather a pointing of the way, a suggestion of the means; at most an indication of the goal, which would only be temporary, demanding a constant renewal of effort. Such effort was bound to be, in certain individuals at least, an effort of creation. The method consisted in supposing possible what is actually impossible in a given society, in imagining what would be its effect on the soul of society, and then inducing some psychic condition by propaganda and example: the effect, once obtained, would retrospectively complete its cause; new feelings, evanescent indeed, would call forth the new legislation seemingly indispensable to their appearance, and which would then serve to consolidate them. The modern idea of justice has progressed in this way by a series of individual creations which have succeeded through multifarious efforts animated by one and the same impulse.—Classical antiquity had known nothing of propaganda, its justice had the unruffled serenity of the gods upon Olympus. Spiritual expansion, missionary zeal, impetus, movement, all these are of Judaic-Christian origin. (TS 78–79/1041)

Bergson practically ignores the current sense of the term "ideology." This may have detracted quite a few contemporaries from reading his work. But when he refers to the mystical origin of the great principles, he criticizes them (in terms of the rational foundations that the Enlightenment philosophers believe they can assign them) and justifies them at the same time, insofar as they define the method by which progress becomes possible. The fact that ideologies can take over from historical religions does not in any way invalidate the distinction between the closed and the open. The dogmas and stories have just taken on a different aspect. We should add moreover that an ideology of universality always runs the risk of having as its enemy an ideology that understands universality a little differently![23]

Such a definition of the ideal and its method of realization allows us to understand what Bergson says about "democracy" and international organizations. By defining democracy as an "ideal, or rather a signpost indicating the way in which humanity should progress" (TS 282/1215), Bergson shows that it never properly applies to a particular regime, nor ultimately to the idea of "regime," insofar as this idea implies a determinate content and is thus opposed to the ideal that is by definition indeterminate. The democratic precepts are "convenient" for "overthrowing" a status quo; it is less easy, says Bergson, "to gather from them the positive indication of what is to be done" (TS 283/1216). The actual content of a "democratic" regime assumes the "transposition" of the grand principles in terms of the common interest, which always tends to "bend" toward private interests. Such remarks show that Bergson has a perfect understanding of the stock criticism applied to regimes that claim to be democratic: the demonstration that the grand (universal) principles simply conceal private interests. But this kind of criticism makes sense only if one has previously accepted the validity of the principles.

Bergson is thus careful not to confuse democracy and parliamentarism. He sees the role the grand principles play in this context as a constitutional reference. "Principles sit with the opposition" (TS 293/1224), which legitimizes the "negative" role of the opposition. Thanks to changes in ruling parties the principles themselves change in meaning, because the opposition has had time to change the content of its ideas while allowing the government to practice them. We are more in the realm of a constitutional ruse here than that of the ideal. And Bergson very lucidly sees parliamentarism as a clever way of managing "discontent" (TS 292/1224). In fact it is in relation to this aspect that he speaks about the State explicitly for the first time in the text. Parliamentarism compensates for the discontent that is "congenital" in modern societies (TS 275/1209), because they have grown beyond nature's intention and also because of the lack of great statesmen that results from this expansion.

"Expansion"—this is certainly the key concept of the "Final Remarks." Expansion denotes a quantitative process. It represents a limit case in Bergson's philosophy of the nontransition from quantity to quality. This should be kept in mind when we consider the philosophical status or otherwise of the "Final Remarks." The more you increase the size of a society quantitatively, Bergson essentially says, the more you complicate its government, but you do not thereby change the nature of the social bond.[24] There is a difference in kind between expansion and openness. No finite number can specifically characterize "openness." Were there only one mystic on earth, openness would nevertheless remain what it is in its essence (TS 38/1007).

We have referred to the ungovernable nature of civilized societies. What then of humanity considered as a global entity! The interest of Bergson's text lies in the fact that he examines two or three conceivable versions of the League of Nations. He first of all pays homage to Wilson and, if we look at the text "Mes Missions," to Wilson alone (M 1565).

Given what we have presented elsewhere on this subject,[25] we can say that Bergson continues his dialogue with Woodrow Wilson even beyond the latter's death. As in "Mes Missions," Bergson refuses to consider the League of Nations as a "chimera." On the contrary he applies to the League of Nations the same "political method" defined in chapter 1 of *Two Sources* that he applies to democracy: a method that, by anticipating the desired end result, is able to realize it at least partially. This is the meaning of the phrase: "Like all great optimists, they began by assuming as solved the problem to be solved" (TS 287/1219).

Bergson first examines the version of the League of Nations that could be called "diplomatico-judicial," the one that was closest to Wilson's plans. The League of Nations would be a sort of permanent diplomatic congress designed to serve as a court of justice, in that it would encourage participants to settle their differences through arbitration. But it would not only arbitrate. It would also have a permanent task force at its disposal, substantial enough to curb the behavior of recalcitrants who violated its rules. Bergson raises a technical objection to the task force: "even so the recalcitrant nation would still have over the League the advantage of the initial impetus; even so the unexpectedness of a scientific discovery would render increasingly unforeseeable the nature of the resistance the League of Nations would have to organize" (TS 287/1220). This is not the essential problem for Bergson, no more than the absence of means of constraint to oblige enemies to use the League of Nations as a common arbitrator. Two different peoples in dispute are not in an identical situation to that of two individuals in conflict. Society exerts pressure on individuals so that they accept a common judge. Nothing of the sort exists for two peoples. By definition, two peoples have no common judge. Extending Bergson's thought slightly, we could even add that it is precisely in order to avoid this pressure that peoples separate and refuse to be acquainted. In these circumstances, where is the common rule that would allow their dispute to be arbitrated? No difference in language, standard of living, geographical or historical difference, and so on automatically results in the exclusion of the other. It is rather in the light of this exclusion that the multiple concrete differences, sometimes very small, become insurmountable barriers. From that point we have a *differend*, in the sense that there is no shared idiom acceptable to both sides that would allow the injury that one side believes it has suffered to be translated into the language of the other. Translating, for our part, Bergson's thought into the philosophical "idiom" of Jean-François Lyotard, we could say that for Bergson between the individuals of the one society there is only "litigation," however serious this may be, and between peoples there are "differends," however minimal the stakes may appear in the eyes of a third party or of posterity. It is precisely this third-party perspective that is denied. If it were accepted, there would hypothetically be a shared idiom and social bond. Given this, almost anything can be the cause of a war—cloves, for example (TS 303/1234).

Thus we see Bergson, *qua philosopher*, formulate objections of principle to the Wilsonian version of the League of Nations. But he doesn't stop there and in fact proposes another version, that of economic cooperation and population control. Bergson's approach is quite understandable in terms of philosophical consistency: if we can't uproot the instinct, we can get around it by trying to control the "rational motives" the instinct attaches itself to. Bergson brings together two senses of the word "rationalization" in his text. We have to distinguish rationalization in the Freudian sense, namely the reasons man gives to himself and others to "justify" (TS 284/1217) what he does. These reasons are rarely the "real" ones. On this point Freud and Bergson are close. But there is also rationalization in the sense given to it by Max Weber. This second sense is not at all neglected by Bergson, whether or not he was familiar with Weber's thought —a question we won't attempt to settle here. Rationalization in this second sense means that the domain of prediction and consequently of calculation has to be applied to an increasing number of phenomena that regulate themselves "spontaneously" by a supposedly natural intention or an unplanned statistical effect and thus appear "natural." Bergson understands that the domain of planning will keep expanding in order to be applied, for example, to demography (TS 290/1222). The two senses of the term can be legitimately linked. If the "standard of living," for example, does not represent the "real" reason of war, this justification is nevertheless a constraining factor in the order of the arrangement of means and ends. The drama of humanity comes from the fact that technical rationality organizes its heavy investments around motives that are not the real reasons behind the desire,[26] and that also do not correspond to what an ethical consciousness would have determined as the priority (not to starve) for humanity considered as a whole (TS 305–6/1235).

Given this, technical rationality can very well be animated unawares by the war instinct and lead the whole of humanity to the final catastrophe.

While the "rational" will may manage to repress the instinct in its effects, the sensation of emptiness, a gap, can only continue to grow (see TS 309– 10/1209) as long as a new moral energy doesn't convert the instinct itself. Already considerable on the level of the civilized societies, the "discontent" that expresses this emptiness will assume global dimensions.[27]

This diagnosis seems singularly lucid and prophetic. The role of the League of Nations for Bergson can only be to increase the "regimentation" (TS 290/1222) of humanity, the inevitable complement to its "rationalization." Bergson clearly sees that in order to do this it is not necessary to abandon the principle of sovereignty. It is enough to bend it in "individual cases" (TS 290/1222). This is exactly what we see happen, less at the level of global organizations—although some of them *in their foundation* have considerable powers (WHO)—but rather at the level of certain regional or specialized organizations (EEC, OECD, OPEC, COMECON). Of course some states can exert that pressure to bend a little more than others, but the awareness of a greater level of interdependence now seems to be taken for granted. We find again here the debates that took place during the First World War. Everything happens as if against the American choice of 1919, Bergson recalls the suggestions of Albert Thomas, who demanded that the organizations created due to the demands of war be maintained. The Second World War would demonstrate the validity of this option. We can see here moreover the reappearance of the problem of "federal imperialism" that the Germans accused the Allies of during the First World War. "Effective" cooperative organizations are not global ones. Expansion is not opening.

But openness can contribute to the viability of expansion,[28] and Bergson, clairvoyantly, places international organizations on the side of the "small means" available to mankind in order to avoid self-destruction! There is a wide gap between Wilson's quasi-religious project and Bergson's analysis, but the question of how far one can go in rejecting international organizations is one to be addressed elsewhere.[29]

The pages Bergson devotes to the "twofold frenzy" will perhaps seem less convincing in terms of their prophetic value. In the absence of historical confirmation (but on the scale Bergson works on, isn't it too early to judge?) they implement Bergsonism's most basic schema, its very symptom, namely duality or splitting in two (*dédoublement*). We cannot therefore undervalue them, especially given the general approach we have taken to Bergson. Everything happens as if, faced with an ultimate impasse, Bergson tries one last time to deploy the most fundamental structure of his whole oeuvre and show it in its transparency—like an open book, so to speak. In this sense these pages are highly instructive from the more general point of view of the history of philosophy reflecting on its own methods. There is always a moment in an author's work when his schemas go astray (or seem to go astray). It is the moment when the explanatory power that represented the strength of these principles, in being applied to other fields, is both exhausted and revealed at the same time.[30] In Bergsonian terms it is the moment where "comprehension" trumps explanatory force. No philosophy can explain everything.

But perhaps the issue will become clearer if we allow ourselves to ask what *philosophical* problem Bergson is trying to solve. The reference to the élan vital allows Bergson to think the schema of human nature qua political animal. Bergson defines an invariant that is bound to the species. No doubt the human species—and this is part of the invariant—shows a far greater *variability* than other species. The question is whether the effects of this variability simply amount to pure variety or even a simple object of "curiosity" (TS 297/1228). If there is a concept of history or "story" in *Creative Evolution*,[31] and if this concept allows us to conceive the history of the creation of different species, Bergson has almost no resources for thinking the history of *one* species. He thus tries two schemas (in the Kantian sense) in succession. The first schema is that of the balancing act between individuation and association. Drawing the *philosophical* lessons of the war of 1914 and his presidency of the International Committee on Intellectual Cooperation, Bergson definitively abandons its application to human history in *Two Sources*. He then tries another schema even more internal to the problem posed by *Creative Evolution*. Because humanity is stuck in an impasse, a guiding principle needs to be found that would allow us to conceive, against a background of discontinuity, the continuous and historically identifiable sequence that gave birth to industrial society, but without thereby abandoning the idea of conserving what has been picked up along the way. Bergson first of all identifies a continuous process: the Renaissance, the Reformation, the eighteenth century.[32] Banalities? Perhaps, but for whom?

To grasp the interest of this framing perspective, which of course contains an element of retrospective illusion—Bergson has sufficiently explained himself on this point for it to be raised as an objection (TS 308/1238)—we have to leave the terrain of philosophy proper. First of all, Bergson chooses his side in terms of the internal ideology. Charles Maurras also assimilated the Reformation and the French Revolution, but in order to denounce them.[33] Bergson thus chooses the republican, modern, and secular side. But he also chooses sides on the international level. Ever since the French Revolution, there have been ideologues in Germany with a mission to set up an opposition between the Reformation and the French Revolution. The Bergsonian sequence is thus not accepted by everyone in Europe. Bergson knows very well that the "ideas of 1914" in Germany are deliberately and vehemently antirevolutionary.

The process analyzed by Bergson seems to lead to the impasse of industrial society. Must this impasse lead us to dream of an impossible return to origins? This is where the law of twofold frenzy, the heir to the law of dichotomy (CE 105–6/585) in *Creative Evolution*, will be useful for us. At the origin of the modern world there is a legitimate reaction against the frenzy of asceticism that characterizes the Middle Ages for Bergson (TS 298/1229). But since the essence of a tendency is to deviate in relation to its origin, it is less the deviation than the origin itself that needs to be considered. Since humanity (European and henceforth global) is at an impasse, why isn't there a reaction symmetrical to that of the Middle Ages? It is of course impossible to give a categorical answer to such a question, but given the "political method" of the ideal, the simple fact of hypothetically formulating the answer is a way of contributing to its practical realization. Reasoning in this way, Bergson has perhaps contributed more than is generally thought to the "philosophy of action" that he is accused of not providing in *Two Sources*. If we want to escape the fatalism to which many philosophers of history have indirectly contributed, the only credible prophecies are those whose pronouncements work toward their realization. The Bergsonian philosophy of history is one of these. It is perhaps at the point where it is closest to Hegelian philosophy, because the twofold frenzy is "dialectical" insofar as it comprises both negation and conservation (TS 297/1228), that their difference is seen most clearly. Bergson's philosophy of history is entirely oriented toward an interrogation of the future. The very idea of an "end of history" would be totally foreign to it.

At this point it is difficult for us to assess the hypothetical degree of the return to the "simple life" that Bergson proposes in conclusion of the *Two*

Sources. If our anxiety about our standard of living has not exactly diminished, our *way of life* has certainly become simpler, partly for technical reasons: the modern system of communications is hardly compatible with the ceremonial of civilities. The already detectable trend in the First World War to criticize the overly formal rituals of diplomacy has only intensified. But certainly the standout point of Bergson's analysis in relation to our own "current state of affairs" is how it clearly anticipates the critique of consumer society.

How do we classify Bergson "politically"? We don't want to evade this question at the end of a piece devoted to Bergson's "political theory." A political theory would be futile if it sidestepped the imperative to take a side. It is not easy to politically categorize a thinker endowed with an "international mind" like Bergson, precisely because in France taking political sides tends to ignore or pretend to ignore foreign policy. We have seen that this was on the contrary Bergson's specific arena of intervention. It was moreover in this arena that he crossed paths with some socialists. Will this priority given to foreign policy be interpreted as the sign of a "right-wing" thought? This would inevitably lead, in order to be consistent, to judging all parties in power as "right-wing"—it would cost them too dearly to disregard the international scene for too long. No ruling party escapes the need for conservation, be it of its own revolution. It would be more pertinent to ask whether, faced with a social or political crisis of great magnitude, Bergson would prefer disorder to injustice. In effect, nothing we have been able to glean from his correspondence leads us to believe that he ever preferred disorder to injustice. But for how long can you prefer, in practice and not just verbally and occasionally, disorder to injustice? Very quickly the need to reestablish an order ends up overriding all other considerations, including taking into account the abuse that is at the origin of the crisis. A political thought cannot wholly consist of "overthrowing."[34] At the same time, the denunciation of the motto of the closed society, the invocation of "Judeo-Christianity" in the political method of the ideal, doesn't allow us to consider Bergson as a "man of order" above all. His final political philosophy may have been more progressive than his life, and we can certainly see this in how *Two Sources* was received.

To analyze the reception of *Two Sources* would be a task deserving to be undertaken for its own sake. Its impact has been considerable in religious circles, more particularly Catholic ones. Much ink has been spilled over Bergson's "conversion." Nobody has ever asked whether it is not rather Bergson who contributed to the conversion of the Catholics themselves. From the nostalgia for the Ancien Régime to "Christian socialism" (which has also been the object of a certain amount of criticism) the political path of the Catholic Church in France in less than a century has been considerable. It is partly due to Bergson. We can't demonstrate this here in historical terms, but to give an indication we reproduce here a letter from a social worker whose name does not seem to have been remembered by history. This unpublished reading of the *Two Sources* strikes us as highly representative of the Christian progressivism that will grow through the Resistance and the Liberation.

> Regarding "mechanism and mysticism," you say that if "in the case of two contrary but complementary tendencies, we find one to have grown until it tries to monopolize all the room, the other will profit from this, provided it has been able to survive; its turn will come again, and it will then benefit by everything that has been done . . . against it." This passage makes me think of Russian communism. The great anguish for us Christians is that if Bolshevism becomes widespread, it would threaten to kill faith. Did not Christ not say: "When I return, will there still be faith on earth? . . ." And yet we feel in an obscure way that perhaps the new humanity cannot be born without passing through communism. Russia certainly seems to be moving towards the liberating mechanization you refer to and towards a return to the simple life. Will it go beyond its current stage to return to spirituality and God? This strikes me as the crucial problem of our time. I would appreciate hearing your thoughts on this subject.[35]

By affirming in *Two Sources* that the freely agreed surrender of a freedom is still a freedom, liable moreover once its effects are realized to give the impression of greater freedom (TS 79–80/1042, also 316–17/1245), Bergson gave ammunition to those religious believers who wanted to opt for "structural reforms" in economic terms. It is indisputable that *Two Sources* contains a critique of economic liberalism—Bergson criticizes the primacy of the market (see TS 306/1236). Objecting to the very expression "crisis of over-production" (TS 306/1235; translation modified) he calls for a central "organizing" intelligence. We no longer find any reference in the *Two Sources* to the "struggle for life" in society, an expression that appeared in *Laughter* (L 16/395). Bergson takes a clear stand against invoking "the force of circumstances" (TS 307/1237). Politically, Bergson's thought provides a rare example of a political thought that evolves toward "the Left" as it develops its position on certain points.

Nothing shows this evolution better than the issue of France's depopulation. Bergson, unlike his statements in his report to the *Foundation Carnot*, adopts a position in favor of state intervention and for a system of family allowances. It will be said that this is an ambiguous example, because it is not just for the sake of social justice that Bergson supports this idea, as the rest of the text makes clear, since he suggests a negative allowance system for countries with runaway population growth! But this is where on the other hand Bergson's thought could offer some criticism of the official lore of the Left. Does anyone believe that social measures are not also measures in support of national solidarity, which is to say, measures taken inside a closed society? By making no distinction, moreover, between collective property and private property (see TS 284/1217), Bergson shows indirectly that the collectivization of the means of production is not in itself a deterrent to war. The wars conducted before our eyes by states where collectivization is quite advanced provide empirical evidence of this. In more general terms what Bergsonian thought can contribute to a "left-wing" thought is that the stereotyped repetition of formulas and recipes is inadequate for pursuing the realization of an ideal whose content is in principle *indeterminate*.[36] It is consistent with the political method of the ideal to make revisions without thereby abandoning its achievement or weakening the will.

We have referred to the considerable influence of *Two Sources* on Christian believers. We would be limiting the philosophical scope of this work to only consider it from this perspective, as essentially a matter "between believers," as if indeed all men were not in a certain way "believers." Bergson wrote his text in such a way that it could also offer food for thought to those for whom God is not an "existent."[37] Whether we like it or not, the affirmation that God exists is posited in *Two Sources* as "probable" (TS 256/1193), not as necessary in any way. Given this, Bergson's phenomenology and genealogy of the political becomes all the more interesting. By placing politics between the human-all-too-inhuman of the political animal and the aspiration to the Other via an "other man," it shows the two dimensions that any effective politics must take account of, without forgetting the specific dangers that arise precisely from their uncontrolled interference in a revolution. For simplicity's sake we can call these two dimensions ferocity and enthusiasm.[38]

NOTES

1 See Soulez, *Bergson politique*.

2 [Translator's note: Soulez uses a distinction between *"le* politique" and *"la* politique" at several points. "Le politique" is the adjectival noun, "the political" is a concept; "la politique" is the noun "politics" (also "policy"), the actual and practical expressions of "the political."]

3 "La force qui s'use," first published in 1915 and reprinted in *Le Temps,* 8 January 1940. See M 1593.

4 The term "theorist of the political" is to be understood literally. It seems to us that Bergson identified *the political* as a specific and irreducible object, thus as an "essence." Since he describes and wants to explain this object, it is truly a genuine theory we are dealing with. But Bergson is not for all that a "political philosopher," if we take "political philosophy" to mean an area of specialization. We mention a little further on why Bergson could not become a "specialist" *in that particular sense.*

5 What applies to the concept does not apply to the ideal. We can see why Bergson wants to reduce the two terms to one. But if everything is "life" and consequently all science "biology," what difference is there to the metaphysics so radically criticized in *Creative Mind* (CM 55–56/1290–91)?

6 For more on this subject, see TS 279/1212, on murder as the *ratio prima* and not *ultima* of politics.

7 See Freud, *Moses and Monotheism,* and the question of "The Great Man" (chapter 3).

8 Gouhier, *Les méditations métaphysiques de Jean-Jacques Rousseau.*

9 See among others Jacques Maritain, *De Bergson à Saint Thomas,* 67.

10 "One sees that philosophy could also have its chiliasm" (Kant, "Idea for a Universal History with a Cosmopolitan Aim," 116).

11 Jean Servier, *Histoire de l'utopie.*

12 Chapter 1 of *Two Sources* contains very clear references to the *Republic,* which Bergson clearly places on the side of the closed society. Bergson first of all alludes to the myth of the three races (TS 71/1035), then the cycle of political regimes (TS 73–74/1037) in the long passage devoted to the analysis of the concept of "justice" (TS 69–81/1033–43). We may even wonder whether Bergson does not make the *Republic* the idealized prototype of the "closed society" itself. Is it not a perfect model of the order of fixity, hierarchy, and the rejection of the foreign, a model that would achieve the always-unsatisfied dream of closure? Closed religion moreover is presented from the beginning of the chapter as fulfilling a function similar to that of the "Platonic Ideas" (TS 13/985).

13 See in this regard the use of the expression "political animal" to introduce the analysis of the ferocity of the "leader."

14 Like *phronesis,* "good sense" is wisdom, but practical wisdom. It is "more than instinct, but less than science" (M 359). It is an "attitude" (M 360), which brings it even closer to the Aristotelian *exis.*

15 We could from this point of view compare TS 290/1222 ("Antique mythology realized this when it coupled the goddess of love with the god of war. Let Venus have her way, and she will bring you Mars") and Aristotle, 1269 *b* 27–30 ("It appears, indeed, that it is not without reason that the primitive mythology has matched Ares and Aphrodite, as military men turn out all strongly inclined to love, either with men or with women"). The beginning of the two passages in question is almost identical, but the reference to the Ares-Aphrodite couple is inflected differently by Bergson and Aristotle. Bergson places the stress on the problem of demography and the risk of overcrowding, Aristotle poses the question of power between men and women by drawing attention to the risk, less paradoxical than it seems, of gynocracy in warmongering societies. But if we pursue the reading of the passage from Aristotle, we see demography appear in turn, with the analysis of the depopulation of Sparta. Would Bergson have "classical mythology" say the opposite of what Aristotle made it say? Should we "in return" apply to France, a country named in Bergson's text, the Aristotelian analysis of the causes of depopulation (excessive valorization of military courage and the hoarding of wealth by a minority of owners [1271 *a*])? We have in any case here a fine example of "intertextuality."

16 Bergson doesn't miss the opportunity to make use of certain classical terms from the Greek tradition, excusing himself for applying them to a "barbarian" state (TS 277/1211; translation modified). He constantly opposes the classical concept of nature to the one he created in *Creative Evolution*. Hence the provocative use of the terms "natural" religion, "natural" society, "natural" regime, "natural" war, in a sense that is deliberately opposed to the Greek understanding as well as that of the Enlightenment. Living according to "nature" can only lead societies toward horror in Bergson's view.

17 See Chevalier, *Entretiens avec Bergson*, 155.

18 See TS 283/1216: "But it is not necessary to catalogue the objections raised against democracy nor indeed the replies to those objections." Similarly, in his text on French philosophy, Bergson writes, "everyone knows how in eighteenth-century France the general principles of political science were elaborated, and more particularly the ideas that would bring about a transformation of society" (M 1164).

19 Hence his return to Aristotle beyond Kant and Rousseau.

20 Needless to say that Bergson's thought, with everything that is published about "Auschwitz" and "Hiroshima" as symbols, proves to be singularly current.

21 "At the pace at which science is going, that day is not far off when one of the two adversaries, through some secret process which he was holding in reserve, will have the means of annihilating his opponent. The vanquished may vanish off the face of the earth" (TS 287). This passage can be usefully compared to that which Bergson speaks of "limitless powers" available to mankind, "when science is able to liberate the force that is enclosed, or rather condensed, in the smallest particle of ponderable matter" (TS 312/1241).

22 Soulez, *Bergson politique*, 140–41.

23 This is moreover a problem that Bergson grapples with in light of the ideology of the League of Nations.

24 He is less sensitive in this sense than Rousseau and Durkheim to the loosening of the social bond that they attribute to larger societies. Bergson insists instead on "intermediaries" that habit has "interpolated" between the individual and society (family, occupation), see *TS* 18/899–900. Bergson is aware of the destructive effects of solitude (*TS* 105/1064), but he doesn't have any premonition, it would seem, of the problem of the "lonely crowd" as an effect of industrial society.

25 Soulez, *Bergson politique*, part I, "Les missions du philosophe."

26 See Bergson's remarks about pleasure as "a means whereby we can snap our fingers at death" (*TS* 317/1245).

27 For Bergson, discontent is ultimately the *verbal* compensation for the frustration felt by instinct when external factors are sufficiently powerful to repress its *manifestations* (see *TS* 275/1235).

28 We note the subtle distinction between this "imitation" as applied to patriotism and the "counterfeit" (of "true mysticism") when applied to imperialism (*TS* 310–11/1239–40). If Bergson thus confirms his patriotism in *Two Sources*, he no less clearly distances himself from colonialism and all forms of imperialism (see in particular the statement: "A country considers itself incomplete if it has not good ports, colonies, etc." [*TS* 289/1221]). Bergson thereby distinguishes two kinds of mission, the legitimate mission of the mystic "instrument of God" and the illegitimate one that imperialist nations claim for themselves.

29 Soulez, *Bergson politique*, part I, chapter 4.

30 The law of twofold frenzy responds to an internal imperative of the structure of Bergson's thought, just like Nietzsche's eternal return. It is moreover also an ethical imperative: "Act in such a way that the machine contributes to the really important needs of man." Like the eternal return it is thought under the sign of *necessity* (*TS* 293–94/1225) *and* of indeterminacy (*TS* 299/1230).

31 See in this regard the definition of the concept of history in the letter to Harald Höffding dated 15 March 1915: "The essential argument that I oppose to mechanism in biology is that it does not explain how life unfolds a *story*, which is to say a succession where there is no repetition, where every moment is *unique* and carries within it the representation of the whole of the past" (*M* 1149).

32 We would be tempted to write Renaissance, Reformation, French Revolution, but Bergson did not write it like that and quite intentionally, because he distrusts the revolution as an instance of overthrowing the status quo, even as he praises it as a moment of proclamation of the great principles.

33 See Maurras, *De la politique naturelle au Nationalisme intégral*, especially 100–20.

34 Bergson sees very clearly that the idea of human rights is a thought of "overthrow" and by that token is not a *political* thought, which is to say, a thought whose purpose is to establish an order that is as stable as possible, without nevertheless being rigid (*TS* 283/1216).

35 Signed Marie Solomon, letter to Bergson, 2 May 1932.

36 Indeterminate in Bergson does not mean "vague." Indeterminacy pertains to the inadequacy of any content in relation to the ideal, "vagueness," the difficulty in

specifying (using symbols) the contours of a reality that is nevertheless determinate (mind for example, see CE 177/645, 268/722).

37 In an interesting passage, Bergson begins by noting that "the quality of love will depend on its essence and not upon its object": "Such a sublime music expresses love. And yet it is not love for any particular person. Another music would be another love" (TS 254–55/1192; translation modified). He thus sees the difficulty clearly. But when he adds that a love addressed to nobody would not be active or "at work," he doesn't resolve the issue. The fact that the mystic *believes* he is addressing someone does not *prove* that this addressee is an existent being. But this does not thereby mean that the mystic is "unbalanced." Let us say rather that the mystic resolves the questioning of the Other by telling himself that it is the Other who needs him: a very significant reversal that Bergson is right to point out.

38 In this sense Bergson's analysis of the analysis of the French Revolution as a concomitant experience of the sublime of the great principles and an awakening of ferocity is very convincing. It would be quite possible to do a Bergsonian analysis of terror. Terror occurs when a political elite tries to impose a degree of "openness" greater than a society can allow at a given point in its history. Such an analysis would encompass the very famous Hegelian analysis as an individual case. "Absolute freedom" is not the only thing that produces terror, but also any figure of the "new man," when a significant portion of *the masses* cannot follow. Given the "religious" dimension of the problem, the problem is definitely more in the masses than in the real or supposed "resistance" of the former propertied and/or ruling classes. See what Bergson says about the coincidence of violence and enthusiasm (in relation to feminism) in Bernstein, *With Master Minds*, 104.

SIX

Anarchy and Analogy

THE VIOLENCE OF LANGUAGE IN
BERGSON AND SOREL

Hisashi Fujita
Translated by Melissa McMahon

VIOLENCE AND LANGUAGE

The work of Henri Bergson represents a point of intersection for the quite agitated discussion in the first half of the twentieth century on the theme of "violence and language." The famous French literary critic Jean Paulhan, for example, labelled as "terrorists" the contemporary authors and critics who were wary of language as, in their opinion, inherently dangerous to thought—"the simplest definition one can give of the Terrorist is that he is a *misologist*"[1]—and mentioned Bergson as the person who gave philosophical expression to this terrorism. At a time when those interested in language were thereby led to the problem of violence, others discussing violence were led to the question of language. Drawing a contrast with the fact that the supporters of the parliamentary system under the Third Republic, mostly left wing, were very often Cartesian, François Azouvi writes: "Bergsonian France recruits its largest battalions from the nationalist and conservative right, ready opponents of the parliamentary system, sometimes even openly anti-Republican, but also—at least until 1914—from a left that is also anti-parliamentarian, a revolutionary or anarchist left."[2]

As it happens, almost the same observations were made in Germany by more or less contemporary political thinkers.[3] Let's examine here the sharpest of these, from Carl

Schmitt. Not only does he make the observation that Bergson influenced both the extreme Right and the far Left, he also highlights the fact that their shared interest in Bergson was an antiparliamentarism that refuses all rational discussion. In *The Crisis of Parliamentary Democracy* (1923), Schmitt devotes the whole of chapter 4 to analyzing the "irrationalist theories of the direct use of force (the theory of myth in Georges Sorel; the mythical image of the bourgeois; class struggle and national myths in Bolshevism and Fascism)." According to Schmitt, Bergson is an enemy of parliamentarism and a friend of the irrationalism that, starting with Sorel, calls for "the direct use of force" by refusing the discursive effort of forming a consensus:

> One cannot object to the fact that Sorel relies on Bergson. His antipolitical (i.e., anti-intellectual) theory is based on a philosophy of concrete life, and such a philosophy has, like Hegelianism, a variety of practical applications. In France Bergson's philosophy has served the interests of a return to conservative tradition and Catholicism and, at the same time, radical, atheistic anarchism. . . . One could say that philosophy has its own real life if it can bring into existence actual contradictions and organize battling opponents as living enemies. From this perspective it is remarkable that only the opponents of parliamentarism have drawn this vitality from Bergson's philosophy.[4]

This image of Bergson—that is, his "antipathy to *Homo loquax*" (CM 67/1325)—comes directly from the "misologist" image that haunts him throughout his philosophical career: "My initiation into the true philosophical method began the moment I threw overboard verbal solutions, having found in the inner life an important field of experiment" (CM 71/1329–30). Hence the alternative: rational discussion or immediate action, language or violence. A certain (distorted from our point of view) image of "the political Bergson" thus presupposes the (mis-)interpretation of Bergson's theory of language. From language to violence, from violence to language—either way, something crucial took place on this very subject, and precisely around Bergson, in the first half of the twentieth century. The present piece attempts to show how what is required and appropriate in order to disentangle this problem of violence and language is, on the one hand, economics (anarchy) rather than politics and, on the other hand, analogy as well as metaphor. Hence the title: anarchy and analogy.

First we will give a quick overview of Bergson's theory of language, in order to try to show that it does not in any way imply the false alternative between language and violence but rather his singular vision of the *violence of language* and of *trope* (metaphor and analogy), which brings us to the economic dimension. Once this is done, we propose, second, to re-examine the much-discussed Sorelian notion of "violence," which has too often been interpreted as a form of physical violence or direct action such as a "general strike," whereas for Sorel it concerns above all a *language of violence*, namely what he calls *myth*.[5] If the intellectual dialogue between Bergson and Sorel takes place around the issue of "violence and language," we go a step further by seeking out what makes it possible: the very foundation of Bergson's theory of language. Although this last stage can only be sketched out, we will at least try to stress the decisive importance of analogy not only in Bergson's theory of language but also for the whole system of his philosophy.

FROM LANGUAGE TO VIOLENCE: BERGSON'S TROPOLOGY

At first glance Bergson seems contradictory when he addresses the question of language. We know on the one hand his avowed hostility toward language: "In short, the word with well-defined outlines, the rough and ready word, which stores up the stable, common, and consequently impersonal element in the impressions of mankind, overwhelms [*écrase*] or at least covers over the delicate and fugitive impressions of our individual consciousness" (TFW 132/87). But on the other hand, Bergson is known for his elegant style and his sophisticated linguistic practice, making good use of metaphors, analogies, images, figures—in short, *tropes*. Let us briefly remind ourselves of a few examples. The image of *duration*: "If I want to mix a glass of sugar and water, I must, willy-nilly, wait until the sugar melts" (CE 9/502). The figure of the inverted cone as planes of consciousness and *memory* (MM 162/302). The metaphor for life and the *élan vital*: "All the living hold together, and all yield to the same tremendous push. The animal takes its stand on the plant, man bestrides animality, and the whole of humanity, in space and in time, is one immense army galloping beside and before and behind each of us in an overwhelming charge able to beat down every resistance and clear the most formidable obstacles, perhaps even death" (CE 271/724–75).

And finally, the analogy of *emotion* as life's force of attraction: "When music weeps, all humanity, all nature, weeps with it. In point of fact it does not introduce these feelings into us; it introduces us into them, as passers-by are forced into a street dance. Thus do pioneers in morality proceed" (TS 40/1008). How should we understand this apparent contradiction? Bergson himself was fully aware of these two sides of language that, even if they always appear inextricably connected, are able to be distinguished: "To maintain the struggle on equal terms, [the impressions of our individual consciousness] ought to express themselves in precise words; but these words, as soon as they were formed, would turn against the sensation which gave birth to them, and, invented to show that the sensation is unstable, they would impose on it their own stability" (TFW 132/87).

We are thus naturally led to the hypothesis that there are two violences of language in Bergson's philosophy. On the one hand, the violence criticized by Bergson is the *symbolic abstraction* that ordinary language operates on reality. We simply don't realize that the spatial understanding of the world through language is already a violence that cuts up reality arbitrarily with a view to the convenience of action. On the other hand, there is a violence that language undergoes, a violence that writers and thinkers practice on it in order to rediscover the reality that is thus distorted, a violence that takes the form of metaphors, analogies, images, figures, in short, a new style. This is what we call *metaphorical attraction*. Diverted in this way from ordinary usage, forced and inflected, language also serves the philosopher in order to suggest a more intense dimension of life, to broaden and deepen human life. Bergson speaks of a need to "shatter the framework of language" (TFW 134/89; translation modified), to "remold language and get the word to encompass a series of experiences instead of an arbitrary definition" (TS 263/1199; translation modified): "we have to violate words" (TS 254/1191; translation modified). What is important here is that when he analyzes phenomena related to language, Bergson often uses economic metaphors. With respect to *Creative Evolution*, for example, Sorel writes: "When Bergson wishes to clarify his thought, he often borrows from economists their considerations on convenience, economy of effort, and, of course, interest."[6] For our part, let's just cite one example. In a passage in *Two Sources*, where he is explaining the creative force of mystical love, Bergson compares two attitudes that the writer can take to writing. To clarify his point, he makes use of an economic analogy:

[Intellectual writing] will be but an increase of that year's income; social intelligence will continue to live on the same capital, the same stock. Now there is another method of composition, more ambitious, less certain, unable to say when it will succeed and even if it will succeed at all. . . . To obey it completely new words would have to be coined, new ideas would have to be created, but this would no longer be communicating something, it would not be writing. Yet the writer will attempt to realise the unrealisable. . . . He will be driven to strain words, to violate speech. . . . But if he does succeed, he will have enriched humanity with a thought that can take on a fresh aspect for each generation, with a capital yielding ever-renewed dividends, and not just with a sum down to be spent at once. (TS 253–54/1190–91, translation modified)

The intellectual and analytical writing that provides a *ready-made* language by combining existing words and concepts, namely the violence of what we earlier called "symbolic abstraction" is compared to the finite increase of the year's revenue, which draws on the same core capital and the same stock. On the other hand, there is another form of writing, an intuitive, synthetic, and creative writing that crafts *tailor-made* language with the violence of metaphorical attraction that is compared with the proliferating movement of capital. These are only metaphors of course, but the fact remains that when it comes to explaining linguistic phenomena, Bergson prefers metaphors of an economic kind much more than ones that have a political dimension.[7]

Sociopolitical thinkers, beginning with Carl Schmitt, are too inclined to editorialize Bergson, pushing him toward an alternative between "language or violence." The questions become: Was the extremist reading, Right and Left, that used Bergson to reject a form of parliamentarism based on rational discussion a complete misrepresentation? Or is it in fact true that Bergson's philosophy has a fascistic and/or anarchistic side? But doesn't such an alternative itself show the limits of the political point of view? And as such it does not manage, in our view, to grasp Bergson's theory of language, or even the real terms of the problem of "language and violence." Isn't the Bergsonian tropology, which represents the two violences of language as finite growth on revenue and infinite proliferation of capital, better understood from the economic point of view? Adopting this hypothesis, we will analyze Bergson's theory of language from the economic point of view.

On the sociopolitical aspect of Bergson, there have been just a few readings but serious ones.[8] As for the economic aspect, there are only two people to our knowledge who touch on it: Ernst Bloch and Georges Sorel. We'll just give a brief summary of the first briefly here and analyze the second in a little more detail in the next section.

In *The Heritage of Our Times* (1935), Bloch observes that Bergson, having reached the summit with *Creative Evolution*, takes a "surprising, unpredictable turn" in order to effectively show "something new" in his last book *Two Sources*. Bloch's observation, while not itself very original, nonetheless has the invaluable merit of containing an analysis of both of these two phases of Bergson's from an economic point of view. Parodying the famous metaphor according to which Bergson is trying to do philosophy in the haute couture style of the "made to measure," Bloch sees in the first Bergson an entrepreneurial spirit that relentlessly strives for progress and excellence through effort: "Only 'intuition' does justice to life with tailor-made suits (instead of with quantitative ready-made clothing); it strikes as *élan logique* the same zest of life outside in real terms. . . . *Elan vital* in Bergson himself [as opposed to Sorel and Gentile] is still that of a bourgeoisie . . . at this level [it] still has the entrepreneur in the fullest bloom of zest."[9]

The first Bergson, with his "élan vital of the bourgeoisie," thus incorporated the logic of capitalism. In contrast, the last Bergson, as represented in *Two Sources*, is described as "very Marxist" in its sympathies with the planned economy and thus the logic of anticapitalism: "Thus Bergson's philosophy has attained two faces; and the second one, even in 1932, does not extol any flight from technology of consciousness (as would surely have been expected of the great vitalist). . . . The creator of the philosophy of life is no stranger to the courage of the most advanced technology, indeed he aims, even if in mysterious terms, at an equally anti-individual and antinational—planned economy."[10] Bergson does in fact propose some sort of planned economy in chapter 4 of *Two Sources* (TS 306/1236). It is not a matter of whether Bloch's analysis of the "turning point" in Bergson is pertinent or not. The important thing for us here is that Bloch offers a coherent reading of Bergson's entire oeuvre from an economic point of view, and that we find elements in his philosophy that lead us to both the logic of capitalism and of anticapitalism. We will see with the example of Sorel that the Sorelian strike also contains these two logics, at first glance antagonistic.

FROM VIOLENCE TO LANGUAGE:
THE SORELIAN MYTHOLOGY

George Sorel, often considered as the "thinker of violence," is one of the most famous figures influenced by Bergson in the social, political, and economic domain. But on precisely what level do Sorel and Bergson meet? Is it that Sorel simply misread Bergson, or interpreted him in a violent way? Our hypothesis is that Sorel, impressed by his reading of *Creative Evolution* in 1907 and having published his masterpiece *Reflections on Violence* in 1908, had indeed understood Bergson in a certain way, namely on the level of "the violence of language," a level that concerns us here. Isn't it rather that the reader of Sorel as a thinker of physical violence has misread him? Here again, an unfortunate interpretation of language produces an unfortunate political theory. It is true that, in a series of reviews on *Creative Evolution*, Sorel declares, "We will now attempt to establish that Bergson's creative evolution simply imitates the history of human industry. . . . The true place for Bergson's philosophy is in social studies, especially those concerning the present day."[11] Moreover, Bergson himself seems aware of Sorel's singular interpretation.[12] But there are two points to clarify. The first is that Sorel's point of view is *economic*. Citing a passage from *Creative Evolution* ("a species which claims the entire earth for its domain is truly a dominating and consequently superior species" [CE 134/608]), and offering an interpretation that would wipe out virtually the whole volume ("what biology can only assume, economic history directly puts its finger on"), Sorel states, "here is a thesis that obviously originates in economics and whose full meaning is only found within economics." Thus, it is not surprising to see Sorel reading *Creative Evolution* in constant parallel with Marx's *Communist Manifesto* and *Capital*: "We could apply what Bergson says much better to capitalism than to man."[13]

The second point to emphasize is that Sorel's economic interpretation tends to stress the aspects involving technology and human intelligence: "Bergson bases his doctrine of intelligence on labor-related considerations, which cannot fail to strike those aware of the role Marx assigns to technology in history."[14] This view has as its flipside in the categorical rejection of the whole philosophy of evolution and biology in general: "In ending this study, I express my wish that Bergson would abandon the largely infertile applications of his philosophy to the natural sciences and instead apply it to the problems raised by the great social movements."[15] Bergson's error is, according to Sorel, not to have taken his theory of *homo faber* to "as significant consequences as we might have hoped, because he is obliged, by the very nature of his project, to apply it as much to animals as to man and therefore goes outside of economic history." The line separating Bergson and Sorel—connecting animal intelligence with that of man (or not) and thus merging (or not) the two kinds of knowledge, scientific and subjective—is precisely aligned with notions of "style," "analogy," "image," and, in the end, of "language." For Bergson, as Sorel construes him, scientific knowledge amounts to so much abstract "stylization."[16] For Sorel, the sin of evolutionist philosophies lies in "moving from analogies drawn from physics to explaining life wholly through physics."[17] This analogy creep (we would be tempted to say in French *mal d'analogie*) drags us into a labyrinth of images: "In reality, when we talk about the intelligence of animals, we always proceed by way of images, asking ourselves what we would have done in the same circumstances as them. We move from image to image, . . . we cannot observe this effort in any phenomenon."[18] To navigate this labyrinth, Ariadne's thread is nothing other than *language*: "I must try to show how language could have originally depended on work, because Bergson accords language a decisive importance in the development of intelligence."[19] Let us simply make two remarks here. First, Sorel takes up Bergson's theory of language[20] in order to develop it in his own direction. He gives special status to the verb: "[In relation to the rudimentary languages of primitive people, which often lack verbs] the addition of the verb was a great step forward, allowing different forms of labor to be more clearly distinguished; . . . the verb defines the activity of the worker. The verb is, in some ways, the psychological element of the sentence; . . . the verb was not intended to highlight man's will, but to *accentuate* the tool, to clarify the meaning of its operation."[21] Second, the mobility of linguistic signs—which will be at stake in our concluding section on analogy—is elucidated in Bergson using observations on children, whereas Sorel explains the same phenomenon in reference to technological or instrumental examples: the mobility of language comes from the fact that archaic craftsmen would use the same tool for several different jobs, that traders designated exotic tools based on analogies drawn from local usage, and so on. Hence, "technological considerations form the basis of all this figurative language."[22]

It is precisely in this context that we can refer to two letters from

Bergson to Sorel. The first is dated 25 April 1908. This long letter was a response from Bergson to the series of five articles by Sorel that were published in the journal *Le mouvement socialiste*. After noting "in particular the views you [Sorel] present on language in general, and especially on the verb," Bergson continues by taking up Sorel's interrogation of his discursive strategy: "You observe that I most often resort to images. But in what other way could I have expressed myself? Outside of the image, there is only the concept, which is to say a general heading under which we classify different objects. . . . If the concept, the intellectual instrument par excellence, is, like intelligence itself, a product of life's evolution, how can life's evolution enter into our concepts? . . . And this is precisely why it was impossible to proceed by subsuming under concepts, or reducing to concepts; I had to proceed by way of suggestion, and suggestion is only possible by way of images" (c 195). The second letter is dated 18 May 1908: "Thank you for thinking to send me your latest book [*Reflections on Violence*]; I had already read it in the form of the articles, but as soon as I have a little more free time, I shall reread it in this new form. Your conclusions on the subject of violence disturb me a little, I confess, but I am very much interested in the method that led you to them. And I was also very interested in your introduction, which I read right away, and which contains a number of suggestive positions. It gives the lie throughout to your protest at one point that you don't know how to write. Thank you for the kind allusions you make there to my classes and my work. Your obedient servant" (c 202). Bergson states unambiguously that his interest lies not in the conclusions regarding the general strike but in the process and methodology that led Sorel to these, and that his interest is also drawn to the paradoxical style Sorel shows in the preface, an elaborate style that denounces cleverness in writing. It is always on the level of methodology and language that Bergson sees the existence of the philosophical problem in Sorel.

Now that we have seen their relationship, it's time to tackle Sorel's central notion: "violence." As we know, Sorel distinguishes "force," which works to maintain established power, and "violence," which breaks through this established power in order to move toward a new form of social organization: "We should say, therefore, that the object of force is to impose a certain social order in which the minority governs, while violence tends to the destruction of that order."[23] This distinction between bourgeois force and proletarian violence makes possible another distinction, according to Sorel, between true socialism and the bourgeois tendency that lurks within socialism itself. What is noteworthy here is that this distinction corresponds for him to one between the political and the syndicalist (i.e., the antipolitical and economic): "The method which has served us to mark the difference that exists between bourgeois force and proletarian violence may also serve to solve many questions which arise in the course of research about the organization of the proletariat. In comparing attempts to organize the syndicalist strike with attempts to organize the political strike, we may often judge what is good and what is bad, i.e., what is specifically socialist and what has bourgeois tendencies" (RV 172). Note that the difference between false political socialism and true economic socialism is expressed directly in their different attitudes toward language. When he says that "against this noisy, garrulous, and lying socialism . . . stands revolutionary syndicalism, which endeavors, on the contrary, to leave nothing in a state of indecision," Sorel denounces the situation where political socialism, by rallying to the parliamentary system, delays in his view the revolutionary decision (RV 112). What type of violence is practiced by Sorelian socialism then? It is "the organization of the image" that Sorel calls "myth": "[The general strike is] the *myth* in which socialism is wholly comprised, i.e., a body of images capable of evoking instinctively all the sentiments. . . . The general strike groups them all in a coordinated picture and, by bringing them together, gives to each one of them its maximum intensity. . . . We thus obtain that intuition of socialism which language cannot give us with perfect clearness. . . . This is the global knowledge of Bergson's philosophy" (RV 118). At first glance Sorel seems to oppose images to language. At the very least his hostility toward language and discussion would seem beyond any doubt: "To estimate, then, the significance of the idea of the general strike, *all the methods of discussion* which are current among politicians, sociologists, or people with pretensions to practical science, must be abandoned" (RV 117; emphasis added). Nevertheless, the alternative here does not reside between language and images but between the intellectual and analytical language that forms the foundation of political *force* and the intuitive and imagery-laden language that forms economic *violence*. The proof: "A myth cannot be refuted since it is, at bottom, identical to the convictions of a group, being the expression of these convictions in the language of movement" (RV 29). Since we have seen the two violences of language in Bergson's philosophy earlier on, there is nothing surprising in seeing his name at the very heart of this Sorelian theory of language and violence:

> Ordinary language could not produce these results in any very certain manner; appeal must be made to collections of images which, *taken together and through intuition alone*, before any considered analyses are made, are capable of evoking the mass of sentiments. . . . This method has all the advantages that integral knowledge has over analysis, according to the doctrine of Bergson; and perhaps it might [not] be possible to cite many other examples which would demonstrate equally well the worth of the famous professor's doctrines. . . . I believe that it would be possible to develop still further the application of Bergson's ideas to the theory of the general strike. (RV 113; translation modified)[24]

We have thus seen that this Sorelian mythology of the general strike is in no way a form of propaganda for physical violence but rather a form of praise of images and metaphors (the "language of movement") as violence. What Sorel calls "violence" is not the political violence that pushes us wordlessly toward immediate action but a violence in the economy of language, a violence that prompts us to act. It is a "myth," namely, an "organization of images," a discursive strategy that works in a mysterious way on the emotions so that a bond of sympathy is easily established between people. If this is the case, this language-like operation of images is intimately and necessarily linked with the violence of metaphorical attraction. It is precisely in this sense that Sorel has inherited the "violence of language" from Bergson. In other words we would be almost tempted to say that what makes Sorel a thinker of violence is neither Proudhon, nor Marx, but Bergson.[25] Whatever the case, what is certain is that Bergson and Sorel share the same theoretical terrain of the "economy of language," and that the Sorelian strike, unlike other strikes shot through with the logic of anticapitalism, is also a radical form of the logic of capitalism that makes an entirely positive form of economic development possible. Let us cite as proof a passage from chapter 7, which is the conclusion of *Reflections on Violence*: "The preceding explanations have shown that the idea of the general strike, constantly rejuvenated by the sentiments provoked by proletarian violence, produces an entirely epic state of mind and, at the same time, bends all the energies of the mind towards the conditions that allow the realization of a freely functioning and prodigiously progressive workshop; we have thus recognized that there is a strong relationship between the sentiments aroused by the general strike and those which are necessary to bring about a continued progress in production" (RV 250). The amazingly progressive workplace where one works freely is a realization of the continual progress of production. In this sense the Sorelian conception of the strike goes toward the logic of capitalism at the same time as the logic of anticapitalism. The "ethics of the producers" (title of chapter 7) overcomes the opposition between socialism and capitalism.

We have thus seen that the most fruitful theoretical contribution that Sorel received from Bergson is his considerations on language. We have gone with Bergson from language to violence and returned with Sorel from violence to language. It remains for us to understand what makes the Bergsonian violence of language possible, which itself makes possible the Sorelian language of violence.

THE ORIGINAL ANALOGY

This amounts to examining the relationship between the two violences of language, between the utility of ordinary language and the heuristic effectiveness of metaphor. Elements of an answer are found, it seems to us, in chapter 2 of *Creative Evolution*, more specifically in the three paragraphs where Bergson characterizes human language in relation to intelligence, namely in its difference from the language of animals (CE 158–61/629–32). While animals, like humans, have a language whose function is to generalize, the signs that make up this language must nevertheless each remain invariably attached to a certain object or a certain operation. The signs of human language, for their part, while not able to be infinite in number, can be extended to an infinite number of things. Hence the crucial importance of what we could call the *original analogy* [*analogie originaire*]. To understand the Bergsonian economy of language, it would be essential to read these three paragraphs in great detail, but we shall be happy here just to indicate the direction of our reading. To start with, the first paragraph: "This tendency of the sign to transfer from one object to another is characteristic of human language. It is observable in the little child as soon as he begins to speak. Immediately and naturally he extends the meaning of the words he learns, availing himself of the most accidental connection or the most distant analogy to detach and transfer elsewhere the sign that had been associated in his hearing with a particular object. . . . What characterizes the signs of human language is not so much their generality as their mobility" (CE 158/629).

If normally we understand by analogy a relational connection or a structural similarity between several terms ($A{:}B = C{:}D$), here it is a question of a completely different kind of analogy, since it is an analogy that opens up the very horizon of human language through a process of radical displacement. It is analogy as modulation, which, through the addition a heterogeneous element, reveals a completely different face of the previously formed totality. It is analogy as metamorphosis, which brings disparate elements into an environment where they can exchange their determinations, in short where they can enter a pure becoming. If this original analogy is the key to clarifying, if not solving, the problem of the economy of language, that is, the relationship between the two violences of language, it is because it clearly shows the common and commonly creative root not only of imagery-laden language but also ordinary language. If the mobility of language liberates the faculty of reflection in relation to the human intelligence that initially appears rigid, so that intelligence can examine itself what it does, this analogy deserves to be qualified as "original" or even "creative." Let's move on here to the second paragraph: "An intelligence which reflects is one that originally had a surplus of energy to spend, over and above practically useful efforts. . . . Without language, intelligence would probably have remained riveted to the material objects which it was interested in considering. . . . Language has greatly contributed to its liberation. The word, made to pass from one thing to another, is, in fact, by nature transferable and free" (CE 159/629–30).

The language that has given intelligence the opportunity to break free of its own obsession with utility, prompts a certain logic of "surplus," not in the narrow sense of "surplus value" within political economy but as "surplus energy to expend" in the sense that Georges Bataille in *The Accursed Share* would ascribe to the "general economy" in contrast to the restricted economy. This surplus of intelligence and language could not in any way be regarded by any political point of view (above all not the Schmittian decisionism of "language or violence"), but by an economic point of view in the broad sense of the complex relationship between "language and violence." On the other hand, this mobility, by clearing pathways and leaving traces, can only determine the direction it may take with intelligence. This is how Bergson describes it: "Language itself, which has enabled it to extend its field of operations, is made to designate things, and nought but things: it is only because the word is mobile, because it flies from one thing to another, that the intellect was sure to take it, sooner or later, on the wing, while it was not settled on anything, and apply it to an object which is not a thing and which, concealed till then, awaited the coming of the word to pass from darkness to light. But the word, by covering up this object, again converts it into a thing" (CE 160/630–31).

The fact that language is not simply mobile is something that needs to be stressed, especially when there is a tendency to overestimate the effectiveness of metaphors and images. As soon as intelligence discovers a hitherto unheard of reality, language pins it down and reifies it. Symbolic abstraction is another name for this fixation and reification. Without fixation and reification, language would not be able to provide intelligence with a fulcrum to act on reality. It would thus have no utility or convenience. But more attention must be paid to the fact that it is mobility itself, analogy itself, that makes this fixation and reification possible. Let's reread the passage: "it is only because the word is mobile, because it flies from one thing to another, that the intellect was sure to take it, sooner or later, *on the wing*, while it was not settled on anything." It is in virtue of this dual nature that the original analogy can be a form of creative violence different from metaphorical attraction. If ordinary language is not something that Bergson can easily do away with, it is because its foundation lies in this double-sided mobility. This is why we definitely do not adopt the point of view that ordinary language is simply unproductive and conservative. In any case, what we have suggested, however schematically, with the conceptual couple of the "two violences of language," what we have called "symbolic abstraction" and "metaphorical attraction," namely the analogy that informs us of the generality of the relation and the metaphor that uses images to suggest the singularity of being, will help to renew the too often hasty image of Bergson's theory of language and its influence on social philosophers.

BY WAY OF CONCLUSION: THE PLACE OF
ANALOGY IN BERGSON'S PHILOSOPHY

Bergson had social and political influence over the extreme Right as well as the far Left. But this is not due to an alternative between "parliamentary discussion or immediate action," between "language or violence," in short because of a supposedly Bergsonian hostility toward language, but it is due to his singular vision of language, which allows us to ask the question: "what kind of violence of language?" He considers the problem from the economic point of view when he contrasts symbolic abstraction with metaphorical attraction, the finite increase on revenue with the infinite proliferation of capital. Accused of forcing his interpretation of Bergson and regarded as a thinker of violence, Sorel sees at the heart of the opposition between political force and the economic violence of the strike the opposition between an intellectual and analytical language and an intuitive language rich with images. Sorel's language of violence extends a Bergsonian idea: that a new (political) articulation of the real confronts the language of force with the language of violence. If Sorel's "language of violence" is at work within the dimension of economic anarchy that leads as much to the logic of anticapitalism as to the logic of capitalism, Bergson's "violence of language" derives from the original analogy that determines the complementary economy of language as mobility and fixity.

Before ending, let's go one step further by noting that Bergson expresses a wish to work this original analogy into the very methodology of his own philosophy. When he draws on analogy it is often to overcome the absolute distinction between inside and outside, between the fact of consciousness and the objective phenomenon. We won't get anywhere by demanding full, rigorous, and mathematical evidence in the domain of consciousness, says Bergson. To have certain knowledge that a being is conscious, we have to be able to coincide with it, to be it (otherwise, as for Descartes watching unseen the people crossing the street in Amsterdam, these people would be automatons). This is why Bergson urges us to "follow the thread of analogy" with him: "Between us there is an evident external resemblance; and from that external resemblance you conclude by analogy there is an internal likeness. Reasoning by analogy never gives more than a probability; yet there are numerous cases in which that probability is so high that it amounts to practical certainty. Let us then follow the thread of the analogy and inquire how far conscious-ness extends, and where it stops" (*ME* 7/819).

If Bergsonism is, as Deleuze says, a philosophy of probability, we would further say that it is a philosophy of the original analogy. Harald Höffding, a contemporary of Bergson's, wrote: "Mr Bergson's method is not solely intuitive; intuition is just the first step, analogy must take the next ones."[26] To develop this subject, to "follow the thread of analogy," we would have to analyze the materiality and incorporeality of language in Bergson, namely the relationship between meaning, image, and schema, between the "motor schema" and the "dynamic schema." But that's a story for another time.

NOTES

An early version of this text was presented in Japanese at the Société japonaise de langue et littérature françaises (SJLLF), May 25, 2008. A Japanese version appeared in the *Études de langue et littérature françaises*, no. 94 (March 2009): 119–31. I translated this essay from Japanese to French prior to its being translated into English.

1 Paulhan, *The Flowers of Tarbes*, 34.

2 Azouvi, *La Gloire de Bergson*, 17. Azouvi's schema couldn't be more clear-cut: "Berg-son's friends are not Descartes,' and vice versa. There is therefore no overlap be-tween Bergsonian France and Cartesian France; we could even say there are two Frances opposed to each other, two Frances that have neither the same political roots, nor the same intellectual aspirations, nor the same artistic references."

3 Apart from Schmitt and Bloch who we mention in the present piece, we can list a few German works that address this sociopolitical aspect of Bergson's philosophy: Mannheim, *Conservatism*; Horkheimer, "On Bergson's Metaphysics of Time"; and Arendt, *The Human Condition*.

4 Schmitt, *The Crisis of Parliamentary Democracy*, 109–10.

5 Whether or not Sorel was a fascist is one large question (which we will nevertheless leave to one side); whether or not Sorel owed anything to Bergson is another. The analysis of *Reflections on Violence* has already revealed the key elements; reading Sorel's long review of *Creative Evolution* will further strengthen our point of view. But let's make one thing clear: we are not saying that Sorel did not advocate violence in the physical sense; rather, our claim is that the most important thing Sorel received from Bergson concerns language and the image.

6 Published in *Le mouvement socialiste*, this series of reviews appeared in five succes-sive journal issues, 191 (15 October 1907: 257–82), 193 (15 December 1907: 478–94), 194 (15 January 1908: 34–52), 196 (15 March 1908: 184–94), and 197 (15 April 1908: 276–94).

7 See Goux, *Symbolic Economies*.

8 Besides Azouvi mentioned above, there are at least two other studies. The first is

Soulez's *Bergson politique*. Soulez calls the social thinkers who lay extensive claim to Bergson "ideological Bergsonisms," and he observes that they fall into the same contradiction: "They have made the notion of intuition into a faculty of a practical nature. Yet ... intuition is a faculty that is theoretical and even speculative in nature" (347). We agree with Soulez in saying that intuition is not simply "practical," but we would not agree with his claim that it is purely theoretical or speculative—for the simple reason that this characterization of intuition does not explain why such speculation could seduce the social thinkers obsessed by the practical question. We claim rather that the crucial distinction for Bergson is not between the theoretical and the practical but between the useful that regulates life (symbolic abstraction) and the effective that intensifies life (metaphorical attraction), and that while not directly practical, intuition is nevertheless effective. The second important study is Lafrance's *La philosophie sociale de Bergson*. This study, which carries the same title as an article published in 1948 by Georges Gurvitch in *Revue de métaphysique et de morale*, approaches the task literally. With the aim of "drawing out the fundamental elements of Bergson's social philosophy and situating them in relation to their contemporary intellectual climate" (7), Lafrance offers internal analyses of *Laughter* and *Two Sources*.

9 Bloch, *Heritage of Our Times*, 319–20.

10 Ibid., 321, 322.

11 *Le mouvement socialiste* 191 (October 15, 1907): 275.

12 On this matter, Jacques Chevalier, a disciple of Bergson's, made a note of his master's private remarks. On 5 January 1937: "I have seen Georges Sorel a few times, Bergson tells me. He's a curious man, this old engineer, whose thought had such an effect on Lenin and Mussolini. What he has tried to find in my work is the idea of a generative myth. But he had his own ideas in mind more than my own." On 3 January 1938: "In this regard, Bergson explained where Georges Sorel got the idea of the vital importance of *myth* from. 'The myth of the general strike, the myth of the proletariat revolution, etc., has become the driving force of Marxist socialism. Sorel said that he owed it to me. He was attending my class on Plotinus at the Collège de France at that time. In the course, I showed the primordial role myth plays in Plato's philosophy, and how Plato, having climbed, by way of the dialectic, from sensible things to Ideas, found himself obliged, when he wanted to move from Ideas to things, to appeal to myth. This idea made a great impression on Sorel, and it is from this, he tells me, that he drew his notion of myth as the driving force of humanity'" (Chevalier, *Entretiens avec Bergson*, 254, 265). Our analysis attempts to shed further light in this direction.

13 *Le mouvement socialiste* 191 (15 October 1907): 277.

14 *Le mouvement socialiste* 193 (15 December 1907): 478.

15 *Le mouvement socialiste* 197 (15 April 1908): 294.

16 "If social phenomena are able to be known scientifically, we must nevertheless note that this knowledge can take place only on the condition it is specially adapted to study them. We need to adopt special views on those aspects that lend themselves to regularity, and *stylize* those forms. . . . We can clearly see the appearance here of

the contempt that philosophers of freedom have for these stylized views, without which scientific knowledge is impossible" (*Le mouvement socialiste* 197 [15 April 1908]: 289, 291).

17 *Le mouvement socialiste* 197 (15 April 1908): 293.

18 *Le mouvement socialiste* 193 (15 December 1907): 480.

19 Ibid., 486.

20 "Whether the movement be qualitative or evolutionary or extensive, the mind manages to take stable views of the instability. And thence the mind derives, as we have just shown, three kinds of representations: (1) qualities, (2) forms or essences, (3) acts. To these three ways of seeing correspond three categories of words: *adjectives, substantives,* and verbs, which are the primordial elements of language" (CE 303/751).

21 *Le mouvement socialiste* 193 (15 December 1907): 487.

22 Ibid., 489.

23 Sorel, *Reflections on Violence,* 165–66 (hereafter cited in text as RV).

24 The qualifier "not" is inserted here in accordance with the original French text and the English translation of 1950.

25 The following quotation shall serve as the circumstantial evidence that Sorel was always sensitive to the question of language, and that Marx was not in the best position to create a concept of "myth" or "violence" either: "Marx had acquired in Germany a taste for very condensed formulas and these formulas were so admirably suited to the conditions in the midst of which he worked that he naturally made great use of them.... He was happy therefore to be able to find in German academic writing a habit of abstract language which allowed him to avoid all discussion of detail" (RV 130–31).

26 Höffding, *La philosophie de Bergson,* 137.

SEVEN

Asceticism and Sexuality

"CHEATING NATURE" IN BERGSON'S
THE TWO SOURCES OF MORALITY AND RELIGION

Leonard Lawlor

"Asceticism and Sexuality" is a strange, perhaps even jarring, title if you know anything about Bergson's works. Yet I think that Bergson's *The Two Sources of Morality and Religion*, published in 1932, his last and only work entirely devoted to ethics, revolves around this duality or this doubling: asceticism and sexuality.[1] Obviously, such a title makes us think not of Bergson but of Foucault, and indeed my reflections on *Two Sources* are partly inspired by Foucault. So, in the introduction to his second volume of *The History of Sexuality*, subtitled *The Use of Pleasure*, Foucault says, "It is philosophical discourse's right to explore what might be changed in its own thought through the practice [*l'exercise*] of a knowledge that is foreign to it. The 'essay' [in the sense of *une épreuve*, a test] . . . is the living body of philosophy, at least if we assume that philosophy is still what it was in times past, i.e., an *askesis*, an exercise of oneself in thought."[2] At a minimum, this comment means that Foucault is defining thought as a kind of exercise. But there is more. As the title to the series indicates, Foucault is implying that exercises concerning sensing—pleasure— generate thought, that is, these exercises in sense generate new forms of thought or new forms of subjectivities.[3] If Foucault is right that thought itself consists in a kind of asceticism of pleasure, then it seems necessary to investigate the discourses on asceticism. Like Foucault—and especially if our most general project consists in the renewal of thinking—we can ask: what kinds of practices are still available that can be used to generate new forms of thinking? Obviously, with Foucault in mind, one thinks of Nietzsche. But one can also go to a less well-known source and that is Bergson, as I said, his *The Two Sources of Morality and Religion*.

In the scholarship on Bergson much has been written on the well-known themes of *Two Sources*: the distinction between open morality and closed morality; the distinction between static religion and dynamic religion; dynamic religion being defined by mysticism; the "return to simplicity" of "Final Remarks."[4] Yet I am going to present a thesis that is not found in the scholarship, at least the scholarship with which I am acquainted.[5] Repeatedly, Bergson qualifies his investigation of the two sources of morality and religion with the word "today" (*TS* 286/1219, for example). Therefore, I am going to claim that *Two Sources* is a book about "today," about the then-contemporary political and moral problems. As I said, this book first appeared in 1932, and that means it appeared between the two world wars of the twentieth century. Thus what Bergson was concerned with, so to speak, "yesterday," is the problem of war. But war never seems to be a thing of the past; it is always, as we know all too painfully, a problem of *today*. For Bergson, war, that is, what he calls "essential war," is generated out of need, the most obvious of which is the need for food. The need for food increases with population, but this is true of all material needs. Thus for Bergson war is generated by overpopulation. But as we can see already, if war is ultimately caused by overpopulation, and if the contemporary problem with which *Two Sources* is concerned is war, then *Two Sources* really concerns *sexuality*. Asceticism, therefore, comes on the scene for Bergson as a kind of "counterweight" for what he calls the "aphrodisiacal" nature of our entire civilization.[6] As we are going to see, the aphrodisiacal nature of any culture does not consist in what we commonly call perverse sexual practices, but rather in a practice of repetition. But more importantly, as we shall also see, the very counterweight of asceticism also consists in the exact same repetition. This role of repetition means that the two sources of morality and religion, the two practices of asceticism and sexuality, are really one. As always with Bergson, the dualism is a monism and vice versa. So, what is at stake here is what we are going to call the "paradox of the double." In Bergson's own words what is at stake here is "cheating nature." In any case, if it is correct to say that *Two*

Sources concerns the relation of asceticism and sexuality, a relation that we can understand only on the basis of the paradox of the double, then we must identify clearly the problem with which the book is concerned. To identify this problem is the purpose of the present text. I have already mentioned that I think the problem is war. But to identify this problem is not as easy as one might think. Unlike his *Matter and Memory*, for which Bergson provided a preface fifteen years after its first publication in 1896, *Two Sources* possesses, unfortunately, no such guide. So, we shall begin our investigation with identifying the purpose of this long and rather unwieldy book. Then I am briefly going to turn to this "cheating nature."

THE PRACTICAL AND THEORETICAL OBJECTIVES
OF *TWO SOURCES*

In the "Final Remarks" of *Two Sources*, Bergson states explicitly that "the objective of the present work was to investigate the origins of morality and religion" (TS 288/1220). What is important here is that Bergson does not rest with the *theoretical* conclusions about these origins. He asks, "Can [the origins of morality and religion] help us *practically*?" (TS 271/1206; emphasis added). As is well known, Bergson was involved actively in world politics during and after World War I, with practical matters such as the formation of the League of Nations. And just as the League of Nations was intended to prevent war, here in *Two Sources*, Bergson's practical aid consists in showing how what he calls the "war-instinct . . . will be able to be repressed or turned aside" (TS 288/1220). Bergson's explanation of the war instinct depends on the idea of a "frenzy," a frenzy for luxury, in particular, which means that the frenzy is based on the artificial extension of the vital need for food (TS 298/1229). But for Bergson, the frenzy is double (TS 296/1227). And just as there is now—"today," he says—a frenzy for luxury, there was in the Middle Ages a frenzy for asceticism. According to Bergson, the double frenzy works like a "pendulum" (see TS 292/1123–24). The frenzy for luxury will eventually (but not necessarily) swing back toward asceticism. We are going to return to this double frenzy a little later. But what we should notice now is that Bergson describes the two positions of the pendulum as "frenzies." The word "frenzy"—Bergson uses the word "frénésie"—derives from the Greek "phrenesia," which means "inflammation of the brain," in a word, madness.

With this double frenzy in mind, we can now determine three interrelated theoretical objectives that Bergson is pursuing, each one corresponding to the three chapters in which *Two Sources* consists. In "Final Remarks" Bergson says that the frenzy of asceticism "evokes mysticism" (*TS* 308/1238). So, to understand the frenzy of asceticism, we must understand mysticism. And indeed, chapter 3, "Dynamic Religion," concerns precisely Bergson's definition of mysticism. But in order to define mysticism, Bergson must distinguish it from the normal view of it; normally what we see in mysticism is only "pathological [mental] states" (*TS* 245/1183); in other words, Bergson distinguishes what he is calling mysticism from mental illness, from unbalanced states, states of "disequilibrium" (*déséquilibrés*) (*TS* 245/1183).[7] The reason we associate mysticism with unbalanced states consists in the fact, which Bergson admits, that the mystical states are "abnormal" (*TS* 228/1169). The "morbid states" of "a lunatic" (*un fou*) resemble mystic raptures and ecstasies (*TS* 228–29/1169). Bergson distinguishes between mystic abnormality and morbid abnormality by trying to show that the great mystics themselves (such as Joan of Arc) do not define themselves by the mystical visions and emotional disturbances they undergo. The visions and emotion are only a "systematic rearrangement aiming at a superior equilibrium." Most importantly, this systematic equilibrium results in action. Action, for Bergson, defines mysticism. If we define mysticism as action, then we can distinguish the frenzy of mysticism from what Bergson calls "charlatanism" (*charlatanisme*) (*TS* 246/1184; see also *TS* 229/1169). The word "charlatanism" literally means to prattle, to engage in idle talk, and therefore not to act. Now this charlatanism brings us to Bergson's second theoretical objective in *Two Sources*. This theoretical objective is located in chapter 2, "Static Religion."

Bergson begins chapter 2 with an obvious fact. He says, "The spectacle of what religions were, and of what certain religions still are, is humiliating for human intelligence. What a tissue of error and absurdity!" (*TS* 102/1061; translation modified). What Bergson is calling here "static religion" refers not only to all the polytheisms such as the religion of ancient Greece, not only to all the forms of paganism, but also to all superstitions including the belief in evil spirits and magic. Here, for Bergson, in these nonmystical religions we really have madness. So, Bergson's second theoretical objective consists in showing why rational beings, "*Homo sapiens*," are the only beings who believe in "irrational things" (*des choses déraisonnables*) (*TS* 102/1062). He will explain these aberrant beliefs by means of the fact that human beings, unlike animals, possess intelligence. In other words, intelligent beings like human beings are the only creatures to believe in superstitions (*TS* 1067/109). For Bergson, intelligence consists in the ability to manufacture tools, but this ability to manufacture tools requires reflection (*TS* 210/1153). Reflection then produces two kinds of dangers (*TS* 210/1153–54). On the one hand, reflection gives humans a kind of "foresight" (*prévision*) that allows them to be aware of future dangers, in particular, death. The result of this vision of death is that humans become depressed; they then lose "confidence" (*TS* 130/1085) in their ability to act and finally detach themselves from life. Because of intelligence, beings like us become unbalanced. But we become unbalanced in a second way. So, on the other hand, reflection allows humans to reflect on themselves. And, according to Bergson, as soon as we begin to think of ourselves, we become egoistical. Nature, however, has generated humanity to live in societies and societal life demands disinterestedness. Thus in two ways things need to be set right again. To do this, according to Bergson, nature uses one of intelligence's functions, a specific form of the imagination, the "fabulation function" (*TS* 107–9/1066–67). The fabulation function invents images, "voluntary hallucinations" (*TS* 195/1141), out of the feeling that there exists an invisible but efficacious presence which has "its eyes always turned towards us" (*TS* 176/1124). Eventually, the images of this efficacious presence become individual gods. The gods, on the one hand, intervene in human affairs to ward off the future dangers that we cannot control. On the other hand, the gods intervene in human affairs in order to forbid egoism and thereby ensure social cohesion. The gods therefore restore the balance lost through intelligence.

Now Bergson thinks this restoration of balance occurs naturally and that there is no madness here. This is not where the madness is. The madness occurs when an individual is afraid or feels a need (*TS* 136/1090). For example, an enemy in a distant city threatens the individual or disease has destroyed his crops; the individual can neither reach the distant enemy in order to strike back nor obliterate the disease. Confidence is lost. Then the fabulation function takes over and starts to produce images of evil spirits to attack the enemy or to explain the ruined crops. We are now in the domain of magic.[8] These first images of evil spirits, according to Bergson, are extended in the direction of the magical "recipes" or "formulas" that are used to conjure the spirits up. Here we return to the idea of charlatanism. The magician is a charlatan, that is, he is not just an imposter but also someone who merely talks, who merely utters "incantations." The magician does not engage in scientific research to cure the disease; he does not go to the distant city and attack his enemy. In short, he does not act. But even this idle chatter is not quite madness, for Bergson. At first we had the images of the evil spirit; these images were extended in the direction of formulas. But then the images continue to extend themselves. As if under the influence of the magic incantation "like is equivalent to like" (see TS 169/1118), the first images attract more, similar ones. Eventually, for this individual, the entire world ends up being "peopled" with evil spirits. This unstoppable "proliferation" (TS 169/1118) of images is "monstrosity" (TS 1091/137); Bergson also calls it "decadence" (TS 140/1094).

On the basis of this consideration of the first two theoretical objectives, we can see already why Bergson called his book *Two Sources of Morality and Religion*. We have seen two sources or origins of religion. On the one hand, nature is the source of static religion. That is, the evolution of nature has produced intelligence, but intelligence unbalances the individual. This unbalance produces a natural need which in turn develops the fabulation function in order to restore the balance. On the other hand, a certain kind of psychological state, which is abnormal, is the source of dynamic religion; that is, a mystical rapture unbalances the normal balance of the individual resulting in a different kind of balance. Superior equilibrium results in action. Obviously since both sources—nature and mysticism—concern different kinds of balances and equilibriums, we are again speaking of the image of the pendulum. But just as obviously, if we think only of the title of this book, we can see that one of its theoretical objectives is to differentiate between these two sources. But why do they need to be differentiated? This question brings us to the third theoretical objective.

The third theoretical objective is located in the first chapter of *Two Sources*, "Moral Obligation." Unlike the titles to chapters 2 and 3—"Static Religion" and "Dynamic Religion"—which together indicate a difference, the title for chapter 1 indicates a unity, within which, nevertheless, Bergson is going to make a difference. This difference is that of closed morality and open morality. Closed morality is the morality of a group, the morality of the city, and here we should keep in mind the old walled cities of Europe. The closed morality aims only at self-preservation of the group and thus social cohesion. It consists in customs. Society therefore trains the individual in these customs to the point where the individual is habituated. The closed morality is entirely about habituation, even automatism. In contrast, the open morality is entirely about creation. For Bergson, the open morality refers to the great moral initiators, the mystics, and in particular, Jesus. Jesus gives us the image, according to Bergson, of an individual who loved all humanity, not just one's friends, not just the group. In fact, the openness of this love is such that it has no object and thus extends to infinity, to every single thing. Here we do not have customs but an example (the image of Jesus given in the Gospels) to follow or, more precisely, to which one aspires. Here, in the open morality, we do not have habits, but emotion and therefore for Bergson effort. As I said, the title of the first chapter, "Moral Obligation," implies a kind of unity. The two kinds of morality, the open and the closed, can come to be mixed together and therefore be indistinguishable.

But also, the title of the first chapter quickly makes one think of duty and thus of Kant's moral philosophy.[9] According to Bergson, Kant has made a "psychological error" that has, as Bergson puts it, "vitiated many theories of ethics" (TS 20/991). The psychological error is this: In any given society, there are many different, particular obligations. The individual in society may at some time desire to deviate from one particular obligation. When this illicit desire arises, there will be resistance from society but also from his habits (TS 21/992). If the individual resists this resistance, a psychological state of tension or contraction occurs. The individual, in other words, experiences "the rigidity" (la raideur) of the obligation. Now, according to Bergson, when philosophers such as Kant attribute a severe aspect to duty, they have "externalized" this experience of the inflexibility of the obligation. In fact, for Bergson, if we ignore the multiplicity of particular obligations in any given society, and if instead we look at what he calls "the whole of obligation" (TS 25/995), then we would see that obedience to obligation is almost natural. According to Bergson, obligations, that is, customs, arise because of the natural need an individual has for the stability that a society can give (TS 15/986–87). As a result of this natural need, society "inculcates" habits of obedience in the individual (TS 97/1057). And habituation means that obedience to the whole of obligation is, in fact, for the individual, effortless (TS 19/990).

The psychological error then consists in externalizing an exceptional experience—which Bergson calls "resistance to the resistance"—into a moral theory. Duty becomes severe and inflexible. But there is more to this error. Philosophers—and again Bergson has Kant in mind—"believe that they can resolve obligation into rational elements" (TS 22/992). In the experience of resistance to the resistance, the individual has an illicit desire. And, since the individual is intelligent, the individual will use intelligence, a "rational method," to act on itself. According to Bergson, what is happening here is that the rational method merely restores the force of the original tendency to obey the whole of obligation that society has inculcated into the individual. But as Bergson says, the tendency is one thing, and the rational method is another (TS 22/993). The success of the rational method, however, gives us the illusion that the force with which an individual obeys any particular obligation comes from reason, that is, it comes from the idea or representation, or better still, from the formula of the obligation.

But it is this rationalization of the force of closed morality into formulas that really leads to the need to differentiate between the closed and the open morality. The open morality, for Bergson, is identical with the dynamic religion, with mysticism. Here too we have a force. This second force is what Bergson calls "the impetus of love" (élan d'amour) (TS 96/1057). Here too we must speak of an experience, but one that is different from the experience of resistance to the resistance. When a mystic has the experience of the impetus of love, this mystic, according to Bergson, undergoes a specific emotion and specific images (TS 229/1170). Both the emotions and images can be, and indeed must be, explicated into actions and representations. But this process of explication can be extended. The representations that the mystic explicates can be further explicated into formulas, for example, the formula of each person being deserving of respect and dignity. These formulas, which are the expression of creation and love, are now able to be mixed with the formulas which aim solely to ensure the stability of any given society. Since we are now speaking only of formulas, this mixture of creation and cohesion is found on, as Bergson says, "the plane of intelligence"; the two forces now are mixed together, in other words, in reason. As before, where the rational method used in the experience of resistance to the resistance comes to explain the force of obedience, here in the mystical experience of the impetus of love, the formulas come to explain the force of creation. A reversal has taken place. The very forces, which Bergson says "are not strictly and exclusively moral" (TS 96/1056), that have generated the formulas are instead now being explained by the formulas. We can see the difficulty that rational moral theories encounter. How could "some representation of intelligence have the power to train the will"? How could "an idea demand categorically its own realization"? As Bergson says, when we "re-establish the duality [of forces], the difficulties vanish" (*TS* 96/1057).

All I have been trying to do so far is determine the objectives of Bergson's *Two Sources*. There are four objectives, each one corresponding to one of the book's four chapters: (1) We saw that Bergson has a practical objective, which consists in finding a method to repress the "war-instinct." Then there are three theoretical objectives: (2a) Corresponding to chapter 3, there is the theoretical objective of differentiating between two unbalanced psychological states, between mystical states and morbid states. The difference is that mystical states result in action, while the morbid ones do not. (2b) Corresponding to chapter 2, there is the theoretical objective of explaining why the only beings with intelligence believe in irrational things. It is intelligence itself that brings about this belief since intelligence unbalances the individual. (2c) Corresponding to chapter 1 there is the theoretical objective of righting the relation between intelligence or reason and the forces of morality. Again, as Bergson says, when we "re-establish the duality [of forces], the difficulties vanish" (*TS* 96/1057).

Now, immediately after this passage that I just quoted again, Bergson says, "Reinstate the original duality [of forces] and the difficulties vanish. And the duality itself will be absorbed into the unity, since 'social pressure' and the 'impetus of love' are but two complementary manifestations of life." For Bergson, there is a unity of life that always manifests itself in duality. Bergson at times calls this unity "*sens*" (see *TS* 214/1157); indeed, it seems to me that we will never be done with this word "sens" or "*Sinn*" or "sense," with all its ambiguities. In any case Bergson compares this unity of sense to a "point" (*TS* 1191/253) and to a star (*un astre*) or a "planet" (*TS* 308/1238). We know what is implied with this image. A "planet," a shiny point up in the nighttime sky, is during the day occluded by the bright light of the sun; yet the planet is still there. But the image of the planet suggests something else. Like our moon, a planet revolves, showing us at one time one side and at another time the other side. For Bergson, this revolving moon is an image of what he calls the "Christian ideal," and indeed he even uses Nietzsche's phrase and speaks of "the ascetic ideal." What Bergson is implying in *Two Sources* is that the ascetic ideal itself at one moment shows the side of the frenzy of asceticism and at other times the frenzy of industrialism. The connection is that asceticism, for Bergson, is about mysticism and therefore the love of all things and industrialism is about improving the life of all things, that is, humans, so that industrialism too is an extension of love. As we have seen, this frenzy of industrialism can go in the direction of luxuries and thus towards sexual pleasure. We return again to the aphrodisiacal nature of contemporary culture. And the aphrodisiacal nature of contemporary culture brings us to "cheating nature."

CHEATING NATURE

I am not artificially introducing the question of sexuality into Bergson. Since *Two Sources* is published quite late, it relies on the evolutionary theory that Bergson developed earlier in *Creative Evolution*. Thus all species have an instinct to reproduce and preserve the species. This instinct, according to Bergson, produces in all the species including us a "procreative sense." Bergson says, and we all know this, "The demands of the procreative sense are imperious" (TS 302/1232). The demands must be satisfied and when they are, we experience pleasure. But the purpose or end of the sense and its satisfaction and its pleasure is reproduction. Now, Bergson thinks that "we would finish with these demands [of the procreative sense] quickly if we held ourselves to nature" (TS 302/1232); in other words, if we restricted ourselves to the natural function of procreation like other animal species, humans would engage in the sexual act and be done with it. If we restricted ourselves in this way, the sexual act would be a means to an end, the end being the multiplication of individuals in order to conserve the species. But since, for us, today, everything is about sex, something has happened to this means-end relation. The direction (*sens*) of sexuality has been displaced from its natural direction.

How is it possible to go in the opposite direction from nature, to misdirect nature, to be counter-natural? In chapter 1 of *Two Sources*, Bergson describes the transition from closed morality to open morality in the following way: "there are numerous cases where humanity has *cheated* [*a trompé*: also, more literally, "has triumphed over," "has trumped"] nature, which is so knowing and yet so naïve. Surely, nature intended that humans should procreate endlessly, like all the other living beings. Nature has taken the minutest precautions in order to ensure the conservation of the species through the multiplication of individuals. It has not therefore foreseen that, by giving us intelligence, intelligence would discover immediately the means of cutting the sexual act off from its consequences, and that humans could abstain from reaping without renouncing the pleasure of sowing" (TS 56–57/1022–23; emphasis added). The "cheating" (*la tromperie*) that intelligence plays on nature allows us to enjoy the pleasure of sex without producing children. In other words, intelligence has found a way of "cutting off" the means—the sexual act and its pleasure—from its natural goal. It has found a way of turning "Venus' love"— this is how Bergson talks—into an end in itself. Love becomes the love of pleasure in and of itself. Bergson describes the sexual sensation as "impoverished." We can understand the impoverishment in the following way: Since the "cheating" that intelligence plays on nature separates the sexual act from its natural goal, the pleasure creates nothing. *Pleasure has no goal; pleasure has no direction; pleasure is not used.* We could say that this side of the deception is a superficial repetition of the same. Bergson, however, continues the above quote:

> It is in a *wholly other direction* [sens] that humans *cheat* [trompe] nature when they extend social solidarity into human fraternity, but humans cheat nature nevertheless. Those societies whose design was pre-formed in the original structure of the human soul, and of which we can still perceive the plan in the innate and fundamental tendencies of modern humanity, required that the group be closely united, but that between group and group, there should be virtual hostility; we were always to be prepared for attack or defense. Not of course that nature designed war for war's sake. Those great leaders of humanity drawing humans after them, who have broken down the gates of the city, seemed indeed thereby to have placed themselves again in the current of the vital impetus ... [and] re-open what was closed. (TS 57/1023; emphasis added)

Nature aims only at the closed. The very same "cheating" allows humanity to open and go against nature by going either in the direction (sens) of pleasure for its own sake or in the direction (sens) of the love of all beings, of everything.[10] The love that I have for one person can be repeated to everything. This would be a repetition not of the same, not a superficial repetition, but a deep repetition of difference. These two "cheating" senses become, for Bergson, the two frenzies of sexuality and asceticism.

But we can see already the point from which these two frenzies are suspended: the repeatability of the form. The form of love can be repeated. Intelligence cheats, trumps, or triumphs over nature, since its function, according to Bergson in *Two Sources* but also in *Creative Evolution*, is to manufacture tools. Because intelligence has this function, it must be able to reflect (*TS* 210/1158). And as soon as I reflect, as soon as I think, as Bergson says, I think of myself. The point suspending the pendulum of the two frenzies is auto-affection.[11] It is self-imitation (see *TS* 149/1102, 168/1118). If self-imitation is fundamental, then the self is always already doubled. Here we have what must be called "the paradox of the double." The paradox is that, if the self can be imitated, it must be possible to be imitated and that *necessary possibility* means that the self is always already imitated, memorized, formalized, or "imaged." We might even say that the self is always already art, artifice, and artificial. Reflection (and not a reflex), this fold—"pli," as in "im-pli-cation," "com-pli-cation," and "sim-pli-fication"—puts an interval between the stimulus and reaction; there is a hesitation (see *TS* 19/990). Thanks to the hesitation, the past returns and the future is already seen. Although the derivation is unclear, the word "trompe" is associated with infidelity, perfidy; there is a loss of confidence (as we have seen) in self-reflection. This is a "deficit" (*TS* 1159/210), a "lack" (*TS* 211/1155), de-pression. One is no longer confident that what returns from the past into the present will go in the right direction (*sens*); perhaps we are in the madness of error, errancy, wandering. There is an "interval" (*TS* 37/1005) between the present and the future. Or, there is a kind of imbalance or disequilibrium between the past and the future. But this disequilibrium means that the returning form is freed from the present. Thus the form of what returns is iterable or, as Bergson would say, "transformable," "transfigurable," or "transferable" from one object to another, even to unnatural or irrational objects. We cannot but think of Nietzsche: "the form is fluid, but the sense [Sinn] is even more so."[12] The form and sense can be hooked or unhooked, folded, refolded, defolded. Yet, with Nietzsche in mind, we must ask: what does the hooking and unhooking? In Bergson, "we have no choice" (*TS* 39/1008). There are always and only two forces: the force of nature or instinct or habit—the procreative sense is imperious—or the force of religion or intuition or emotion—what Bergson calls "creative emotion." But these two forces, like the two frenzies, are reciprocally implicated in the *élan vital*. Unlike the abstract concept of the will to live, the power of the vital impetus, as Bergson stresses, is empirical, meaning that it can be experienced (*TS* 115/1073).

Now it would be necessary to investigate the concept of mystical experience in Bergson. Such an investigation, however, goes beyond the scope of this chapter.[13] Yet we have seen already that mystical experience in Bergson is an experience of disequilibrium. Mystical experience in Bergson is the experience of the élan vital, which means that there is a fundamental disequilibrium within life itself. The doubling—the trumpery and cheating—means that life is always out of joint (anachronistic) and thus always fundamentally unjust. Thus, to conclude, I would like only to speak of justice in *Two Sources*. In the first chapter of *Two Sources*, Bergson differentiates between relative justice and absolute justice. In a very general way, the difference between relative justice and absolute justice defines, for Bergson, the difference between closed morality and open morality. Relative justice is determined by the idea of compensation, weighing. Sounding very much like Nietzsche, Bergson claims that this relative justice has a mercantile origin. Everything can be measured, everything has its price. But this principle of relative justice is really a principle of revenge: an eye for an eye. For Bergson, it is only absolute justice, whose other name is charity, which truly overcomes revenge. Absolute justice is determined by the absolute worth of every individual; the value of each is beyond measurement, compensation, and price. But insofar as each is beyond compensation, the cry for justice is infinite, even relentless. In the discussion of Christian mysticism in *Two Sources*, Bergson emphasizes that "the Christ of the Gospels" was "the continuator of the prophets of Israel" (*TS* 240/1179). Bergson says, "When a great injustice has been committed and admitted, it is the voice of the prophets of Israel that we hear" (*TS* 76/1038). Now I have been drawn to this passage about the prophets of Israel in *Two Sources* because of Jankélévitch. Thus my inspiration in this text not only comes from Foucault but also from Jankélévitch. In the appendix to his book on Bergson in 1959—the appendix, by the way, is called "Bergson and Judaism"—Jankélévitch says, "The infinity of forgiveness and the supernatural asymmetry of grace shatter the cycle of vindictive expiation: the unjust love that paradoxically commands us to return good for evil." What Jankélévitch seems to be implying here is that only an "unjust charity" can respond to the paradox of the double, to the fundamental disequilibrium, to the fundamental injustice within life itself.

We can go one step further. It is clear that the cry for justice requires that one can hear. In order to do that, one must exert the effort to listen. Although it suggests passivity, unjust charity therefore is first and foremost an activity, perhaps, the hardest activity (the activity of making oneself deaf to oneself). If one can hear, then the cry for justice, being infinite, is relentless. Even when it is reduced to silence, it never stops haunting. Then the cry for justice (for absolute justice) demands a hyperbolization. Perhaps hyperbolizing the command for justice is what is most unnatural, most cheats nature, what is least naturalistic. It commands a change for the whole world. Unconditionally, it commands justice for everyone. It commands those who can hear to be just not only to the friends but also to the enemies, not only to the children but also to the beasts. Yet, this hyperbolic rendering of justice is impossible. The impossibility does not result in pessimism and paralysis. Made unconditional, the commandment then demands constant frenzy. Yes, this is a mad justice, a mad justice to set free. (1) Unjust charity consists in the constant passivity of letting all the others go. (2) Unjust charity consists in the constant activity of loosening our (abstract and concrete, concepts and walls) grip on others. (3) And unjust charity consists in the constant search for ways out. Perhaps these formulas can be summarized in the simple commandment, "Let others pass!" As Bergson would advise, we must not remain bound by these three or four simple formulas; instead, we must remain open to the senses (all the senses) that they imply.

NOTES

This chapter is an updated and revised version of my "Asceticism and Sexuality: 'The Trumpery of Nature' in Bergson's *The Two Sources of Morality and Religion*," *Philosophy Today* 46 (2002): 92–101.

1 I have frequently modified and retranslated the passages cited from *Two Sources*.

2 Foucault, *The History of Sexuality, Volume Two*, 8 (translation modified).

3 Indeed, what is at stake in *The History of Sexuality, Volume Two*, is freedom, the freedom of thought. The idea of freedom seen late in Foucault's career refers back to his first great work, *History of Madness*. It is possible to argue that the entire *History of Madness* concerns freedom, but this is a freedom that also "cheats nature," insofar as Foucault calls it an "animal freedom," an "absolute freedom," that is "counter-natural" (see *The History of Madness*, 148, 151, 156–57). Insofar as the *History of Madness* rejects to consider history "retrospectively," that is, to interpret the past as an anticipation of the present truth (in which case there would be no events and no creativity), it looks to be quite close to Bergson's view of evolution. On the rejection of retrospection, see *The History of Madness*, 105.

4 See for example, Jankélévitch's chapter in this edited volume; Vieillard-Baron, *Bergson*, 83–100; Soulez, *Bergson politique*; Cariou, *Bergson et le fait mystique*; Gouhier, *Bergson et le Christ des évangiles*; and Lalande, "Philosophy in France, 1932."

5 Mullarkey's *Bergson and Philosophy* is the best book on Bergson produced in the English language recently. The best book now in French is Riquier, *Archéologie de Bergson*. Goddard's *Mysticisme et folie* is also an excellent book on *Two Sources*.

6 Cariou, *Bergson et le fait mystique*, 228–29.

7 See Gouhier, *Bergson et le Christ des évangiles*, 154.

8 Strictly, for Bergson, before its indefinite extension, magic is rational and not madness (see TS 136/1090). At the beginning, magic apparently worked (TS 166/1116), and this efficacy is why magic contributed at times to the progress of science. Magic becomes irrational when it extends itself in the direction of evil spirits and the mechanical repetition of incantations (TS 168–69/1117–18).

9 See Worms, "L'intelligence gagnée par l'intuition?" It is clear that Bergson's thought always amounts to a criticism of Kant's thought. This direct opposition is seen most clearly in Bergson's "Introduction to Metaphysics" of 1903. I have produced a new interpretation of this important Bergson text in my *Early Twentieth-Century Continental Philosophy*.

10 This love is perhaps the model for what Deleuze and Guattari call "devenir tout le monde" (becoming-everyone or becoming-the-whole-world, that is, making the whole world and everyone become). See Deleuze and Guattari, *A Thousand Plateaus*, 199–200.

11 I have investigated the experience of auto-affection elsewhere. See Lawlor, "Auto-affection and Becoming (Part I)" and "Becoming and Auto-affection (Part II)."

12 Nietzsche, *On the Genealogy of Morality*, second essay, §12.

13 See Lawlor, *The Challenge of Bergsonism*, in particular appendix 1.

EIGHT

Creative Freedom

HENRI BERGSON AND
DEMOCRATIC THEORY

Paulina Ochoa Espejo

Bergson conceives of his method as relief from false problems. In this chapter I will use Bergson's method to dissolve a major problem of contemporary political theory: "the problem of the people." This is a problem of self-reference that arises because the demos seems to be both cause and consequence of the democratic process. This problem is at issue whenever there is a tension between a concrete people and the universal democratic ideals of freedom and equality: it spans debates on cosmopolitanism, democracy without a state, and the criteria for exclusion from the demos.

I claim that "the problem of the people" is a false problem, and Bergson's philosophy, specifically the argument he advances in *The Two Sources of Morality and Religion,* can help us dissolve this problem. I argue that the democratic people is an ongoing process that evolves under the aegis of a self-creative drive derived from the lived experience of time and the indeterminacy of nature, a drive I call *creative freedom.* This conception of the people dissolves the problem of self-reference. It also prepares the ground for a democratic theory that acknowledges critical views but is not buried under them. Thus, a Bergsonian solution to the problem of the people navigates two poles in contemporary democratic theory. On the one hand, it avoids the problem of self-reference in liberal democratic theory grounded in the social contract tradition.[1] On the other hand, it steers clear of the radical criticism of liberal democracy that holds there cannot be a political project based simultaneously on a people and on the ideals of universal human freedom and equality.[2]

I develop this argument in four sections. The first section describes the problem of the people in detail, while the second describes Bergson's insight in *Two Sources* and its genesis in prior works. The third section then brings this insight to bear on the problem and describes its dissolution. Finally, the fourth section responds to an objection: if a Bergsonian solution legitimizes democracy by relying on a mystical intuition rather than on rational agreement, can it really offer a practical political solution to the problem? My answer that "yes, it can" is developed by the notion of creative freedom.

THE PROBLEM OF THE PEOPLE

The problem of the people is that the liberal democratic requirement of a self-governing group of free and equal individuals is both incoherent and also makes democratic legitimacy impossible.[3] The problem becomes evident when the three main requirements for democratic legitimacy are made explicit:

1 A democratic government requires a people. This is a definitional truth: in a democracy the people rule and are ruled.
2 According to liberal democratic theory, legitimacy requires that all individuals composing the people be treated as free and equal.
3 In a liberal democracy all individuals should be able to agree to the principles of democracy and to give their consent to be governed (that is, they must have the option to join the group, or at least have the possibility of leaving it).

In sum, democratic legitimacy requires both a people and the freedom and equality of the individuals composing the people.

Why, then, do these requirements make legitimacy impossible? Because any argument for legitimacy that fulfills these conditions either leads to a *vicious circle* or to an *infinite regress*.

A vicious circle arises because in order to fulfill the requirements of democratic legitimacy, democratic institutions must be created by the governed through their consent. But in order for individuals to voice their consent, legitimate democratic institutions such as citizenship and an electorate must already exist. So there is a problem of self-reference. This vicious circle between democratic institutions and citizens is known in the literature as "the paradox of democratic politics."[4] Moreover, given that both geographic borders and the limits of the demos are democratic institutions, the requirement of freedom and equality prevents one from defining a people. This occurs because the existence of a people depends on the borders and the limits of the demos, but in order to be legitimate the limits of the demos must be determined by the people. So the vicious circle arises here too.

To escape the circle, democratic theory must give up on creating a people by consent. So instead, much contemporary democratic theory relies on a preexistent group of individuals brought together by chance. Contemporary democrats thus rely on a nation or on preexistent geographical barriers to define a population. In much mainstream democratic theory this preexistent group gets together to create institutions on the basis of a contract drawn under the principles of freedom and equality. However, although this solution escapes the vicious circle, it instantly generates an infinite regress. In order to treat equally those individuals who voice their consent to be governed, it is necessary that they all participate in the decision that settles the terms of the political agreement. But to fulfill this last requirement, any agreement among a group of individuals requires a prior agreement on the terms of agreement, and this agreement requires a prior agreement, and so on. Given that this infinite regress is impossible, attaining a legitimate democracy or self-governing people on this basis is also impossible. This problem is known as the problem of "constituting the demos."[5]

Although the vicious circle and the infinite regress are the consequences of logical problems, they engender a problem of political morality. Liberal democracy must be grounded on the moral principle of universal freedom and equality, but if you cannot constitute a demos on the basis of consent, then it seems that liberal democracy must rely instead on morally irrelevant criteria, like ethnicity or geographical location. It would appear, therefore, that democratic legitimacy as conceived by liberals is impossible because a self-governing people is not compatible with universal freedom and equality.

And with this theoretical problem comes a host of practical implications: democratic theory cannot find the proper subject of global governance, nor can states justify the existence of borders, nor can they justify the exclusion of individuals from the demos on the basis of democratic principles. More importantly, without a solution to the problem, political theory cannot explain why democracy is legitimate or desirable. As I will discuss in the third section, Bergson can help us to deal with the problem of political morality by dissolving the false problem that underpins this paradox. So, let us first examine the philosophical path he follows to deal with false problems.

BERGSON'S INSIGHT: THE DISTINCTION
BETWEEN THE TWO SOURCES

Bergson's philosophy can help us reject the conclusion that there is an intractable paradox at the heart of liberal legitimacy. His work fixates on just such paradoxes: problems that appear to be logically impossible to solve but are instead dissolved when tackled at their metaphysical root (see TFW xix/3; MM 16/168; CE xi/491).[6] Thus, Bergson's work can serve as a model for dealing with the problem of the people.

Bergson deals with intractable logical problems by reconsidering their metaphysical presuppositions. His method allows us to see that, "the problems we considered insoluble will resolve themselves, or rather, be dissolved, either to disappear definitively, or to present themselves in some other way" (CM 36/1276). Bergson uses this method in his first book and employs it in each subsequent work. In each case he takes an apparently insoluble paradox, gives a fresh analysis of its terms, and then dissolves it by showing that the premises muddle assumptions about time and space. Once the premises are shown to rest on inadequate metaphysical grounds, the paradox dissolves. In each case he illustrates the problem by analogy with Zeno's paradoxes of movement.[7] His procedure in *Time and Free Will* exemplifies this.

Bergson tackles the problem of free will and determinism and uses a novel analysis of the paradox of Achilles and the tortoise to illustrate how to dissolve the problem (TFW 113–14/75–76). For Bergson, the Eleatic "proof" that movement is impossible is in fact a sophism arising from a false premise: the perfect divisibility of movement. This divisibility depends on describing movement in terms of space, and in Bergson's view movement always occurs in temporal duration, which is not reducible to space. Hence the paradox of Achilles and the tortoise arises when Zeno reduces heterogeneous movements interpenetrating each other in lived time to homogenous successive points in space.[8] Analogously, Bergson claims that the determinist argument that ostensibly proves that choice is impossible also depends on a premise that reduces heterogeneous movements in the duration of consciousness to homogeneous points in space that resemble a fork in the road. But this premise is untenable. In Bergson's words, "we cannot make movement out of immobilities, nor time out of space" (TFW 115/77). In sum, Bergson analyzes the premises of the problematic argument and exposes its roots: time and space. Then, he shows that when the problem reduces one of the elements to the other—or, more specifically, when it reduces time to space—it produces a logical paradox. As Bergson argues, this is not surprising: "When an illegitimate translation of the unextended, of quality into quantity, has introduced a contradiction into the very heart of the question, contradiction must, of course, recur in the answer" (TFW xix/3). The way out, he claims, is to avoid these reductions.[9]

Bergson uses the same strategy to tackle intractable logical problems in moral and social philosophy. In these fields difficulties also arise due to the muddling of two different kinds of moral motivation that are not reducible to one another: these are the two sources of morality and religion. The first source is *social pressure* that generates individual obligation through entrenched habits and institutions. Pressure, Bergson argues, is both natural and universal: it underlies all societies and their quest for security, cohesion, and survival. The second source is an *aspiration* that takes the form of *creative emotion*. It leads to novelty, hence to social change and transformation. In its pure form it is embodied in a mystical intuition, which appears only rarely and in exceptional individuals. The first source is a tendency to create determinate or closed societies: "The closed society is that whose members hold together, caring nothing for the rest of humanity, on alert for attack or defense, bound, in fact, to a perpetual readiness for battle" (TS 266/1201). The second source generates an aspiration toward an indeterminate society encompassing all humankind (TS 267/1202). These two sources of morality are irreducible to one another, and philosophical problems arise when one postulates the possibility of a gradual transition from the first to the second. That is, we encounter problems when we assume that the obligations or laws of a society apply to all humankind (as in a certain vision of human rights) or that the aspirations of universal morality can be reduced to rules or obligations in a determinate society (as when one seeks to legislate charity or love).

In Bergson's discussion of social pressure and creative emotion in *Two Sources*, we see a deep continuity with his treatment of Zeno's paradox in his earliest work. As in the paradox, arguments that muddle the two sources conceive of moral progress as the diminution of the distance that separates morality in the present from the ideal to be attained. But the trouble is that once moral progress is depicted as a path, it becomes a distance consisting in an infinite number of finite intervals. In other words, the depiction spatializes real duration, or the lived experience of moral agents, and thus creates philosophical and practical problems like those described above. And yet, as before, these "artificial difficulties," as Bergson calls them, "vanish when we analyze the terms in which they are expressed" (*TS* 20/991). Could this type of analysis then help to solve the problem of the people?

USING BERGSON'S INSIGHT TO DISSOLVE THE PROBLEM

The problem of the people arises from the apparent incompatibility between the two requirements for democratic legitimacy: on one hand, a self-governing people and, on the other, universal freedom and equality. Bergson tells us that social pressure engenders the tendency toward closure in every people, and that creative emotion engenders political arrangements with universal moral aspirations. We may thus be tempted to conclude that the conflicting terms of the problem of the people correspond to the two sources of morality and thus straightaway use Bergson's insight to dissolve it. However, the correspondence is not perfect: to dissolve the problem we first have to understand and analyze the problem in Bergson's terms.

The traditional concept of the people muddles the two sources because it requires particular and universal standards at the same time. First, democracy requires self-government. Hence it requires a determinate group of people to govern and be governed. At the same time, democracy requires the freedom and equality of all individuals ruled. But if democracy is to sustain freedom and equality, the group cannot rely on a clear rule to determine the people's limits. The difficulty here is that a limit, or exclusion rule, is incompatible with freedom and equality inasmuch as the rule must be prior to the group it defines. This means that at least some of the individuals in the group will not get to choose the rule that defines their group, while other members will have a say in this decision. In this case the equality requirement is not satisfied. But if instead the rule treats all equally (that is, if nobody in the group had a say in choosing the rule), then the externally imposed rule makes it impossible to satisfy the requirement of self-government and eventually the requisite of freedom, where this is understood as autonomy. Thus, in order to satisfy the requirement of freedom and equality the group must be indefinite, but this makes it incapable of self-rule. In sum, a democratic people would have to be definite and indefinite, completely open and absolutely closed at a given moment. This absurd conclusion shows that the requirements for a democratic people are incompatible. The normative ideal embodied in the traditional concept of the democratic people requires both sources of morality in their pure form.

One could argue that the absurdity arises only because these requirements are too strict. Freedom need not be conceived as autonomy, and the criterion for self-rule could be less stringent. Moreover, even in Bergsonian terms, to attenuate the rigor of the requirements does not seem to be a problem: every living thing or idea is a composite of opposing tendencies. However, even if we granted these objections, there is another aspect of the muddling that is truly problematic: the concept of the people, in its traditional formulation, considers popular self-rule and universal freedom and equality as aspects of *the same* moral source. (Or rather, it does not even consider that self-rule, and universal freedom and equality, draw their strength and inspiration from different places.) And so, the traditional concept of the people requires that we posit the possibility of a smooth transition between particular and universal standards of morality. But, according to Bergson, it is impossible to progressively expand the political morality of a specific people into the morality of a worldwide community (TS 32/1001). This claim is controversial because most democratic theorists hold that there is no contradiction between particular and general interests in a people (no matter how large the group may be).[10] In their view ideal rational behavior brings together self-regard and general well-being,[11] such that even if a democratic people do not exist now, particular and universal forms of democracy are compatible at an ideal limit. In this view universal democracy is a normative ideal that societies gradually approach by adhering to rules that any reasonable individual could agree to. Bergson, however, disagrees: "Never shall we pass from the closed society to the open society, from the city to humanity, by any broadening out. The two things are not of the same essence" (TS 267/1202).

Liberal political theory insists that the progressive expansion of local democracies is possible. However, according to Bergson, the expansion of the morality of a particular society into a universal moral order produces absurd conclusions because this idea of progress depends on the invalid juxtaposition of two moralities that differ in kind (TS 233–34/1173–74). Like other cases of theories muddling differences in kind, liberal democratic theory conceives of progress as a continuum between the present situation and the goal. Thus, among democratic theorists, ideal or universal democracy is often seen as a finish line. In this view a particular demos progresses toward democracy by embracing the universal principles required to treat everybody equally while respecting their freedom. Such progress would allow this demos to approach equality gradually, as a journey down the path of moral development. All democratic peoples would eventually meet at the goal, creating a universal democracy. However, as in the other cases of juxtaposition of space and duration, these theorists represent the continuum as spatialized time, as a timeline consisting of discrete points: "You substitute the path for the journey and because the journey is subtended by the path, you think that the two coincide" (MM 190/325). The gradual approach thus produces absurd results similar to those of Zeno's dichotomy paradox (TS 73/1036). In the dichotomy a traveler must arrive halfway to the goal in order to get there, and there are always an infinite number of points in any given interval. Given that going through the infinite number of halfway intervals should take an infinite time, he can never arrive. So, just as getting halfway to the goal makes a traveler get lost in infinity, getting halfway to universal freedom and equality prevents one from getting all the way there. This occurs because approaching democracy, the form of government that actualizes these principles requires that a developing society *already* espouse liberal principles and procedures; for only a liberal democratic society can democratically choose the rules that allow it to approach the goal. So the gradual approach to democracy is doomed never to reach its destination. This impasse shows that the two sources are muddled in the idea of a democratic people. It also shows that the proposed continuum between the morality of a concrete people with definite limits and an abstract humanity with indefinite edges cannot be traversed. Morality for all mankind does not grow out of the womb of a closed society: democracy must make a jump-start or a "leap" (TS 73/1036).

An objector might disagree with the previous conclusion. For after all, *there has been* moral change converging toward democracy in the last two centuries. But there is a ready answer to this objection: the appearance of progress is the backward projection of that which exists now. This is what Bergson calls the illusion of the "preexistence of the possible in the real" (TS 73/1036; see also CM 91–106/1331–45). We observe democratic organizations and principles as they exist in the present and become convinced that the possibility of democracy already existed before societies developed this form of government. Hence we imagine that "the possibility of things precedes their existence" (CM 99/1339). This projection creates the illusion that there was a gradual development toward an ideal, whereas in fact there is only novelty and creation without precedent. It is this illusion that causes some democratic theorists to believe that a more refined form of democracy than the one now extant could develop through a path of gradual development in democratic countries.[12] They also hold that nondemocratic societies could (sometimes should and sometimes must) traverse the same path of development that other societies traveled in the past. It is, however, obvious that gradual development toward the future is impossible. As Bergson puts it, great democratic reforms cannot occur because "they could be carried out only in a society whose state of mind was already such as their realization was bound to bring about" (TS 74/1038). This is another form of the dreaded vicious circle between democratic citizens and institutions. Thus, the return of the paradox reveals that the forward projection is a mistake. Either in the present or in the future, the idea of a determinate democratic people and the ideal of democratic progress produce absurd results.

In order to dissolve the problem of the people, then, one must begin by understanding that actually existing peoples are always a composite of the two sources, but these two sources in their pure form are distinct normative tendencies that should be kept apart. On the one hand, the moral and legal obligations of a people are natural or biological phenomena: obligation, discipline, and social organization are always the result of a natural or instinctual social pressure that seeks social cohesion. On the other hand, the search for universalization is the fruit of a supraintellectual intuition felt by a few individuals and spread to others by example. Two key conclusions follow from this separation of the sources. First, the idea of popular rule must be independent of ideals of universality in arguments justifying the state. And second, democratic theory should give up the ideal of a people conceived as a collection of individuals brought together by the ideals of freedom and equality. In short, Bergson's insight allows us to dissolve the problem of the people by parting with the ideals of a social contract and of legitimacy premised on popular sovereignty alone.

Bergson's insight shows that popular sovereignty or self-foundation based on legal rules cannot explain progress toward liberal democracy because any such explanation will end in paradox. Instead, the open people to which liberal democracy aspires must be conceived as an open community bound together by fraternity rather than contract (TS 282/1215). This fraternal feeling is not the fruit of a gradual development according to rational rules; rather, it is the result of sudden social transformations, which are brought about by the diffusion of new emotions. These emotions are not fully expressed in the ideals of freedom and equality as they are understood in the social contract tradition. For freedom and equality *within* a people, or freedom and equality as the ground of legal obligation, lead toward a closed society. Rather, the emotions in question are always new, thus breaking with existing practices and seeking to open established boundaries. These emotions, it is true, eventually congeal into social practices, rules, or habitual doings; but the change toward wider inclusion in democratic governance is only possible if preceded by an initial change of disposition in a society. This latter kind of change occurs suddenly and unexpectedly, even when it seemed impossible before it occurred (TS 78/1041).

One can understand and explain the origin of democratic practices on the basis of an intuition that thrusts some individuals toward change in the direction of universalization. Their example may inspire other individuals to follow, and the intuited emotion may spread across a society, which turns the intuition into improved practices of rule. In this view democracy is the form of rule that aims at freedom and equality and incorporates a thrust toward universalization by leaving space for change and novelty in practices and institutions. Thus, Bergson's insight shows that democratic legitimacy arises from not one but two sources. He also shows that while in practice these sources inevitably mingle (or, in his language, become composite), they must be kept analytically distinct if we are to understand democracy. The first source standardizes rules and obligations; the second source breaks through them by seeking universalization. This means that the synthesis of rule-based obligation and universal freedom and equality in an original contract is not required to explain or justify a democratic state. And if you do not require a contract or agreement, then there is no vicious circle or infinite regress. In sum, if you keep the sources apart, then the problem of the people does not arise.

A GENUINE SOLUTION? CREATIVE FREEDOM

To dissolve the problem of the people using Bergson's insight requires that we abandon the idea of the sovereign people understood as a community of free and equal individuals joining together on the basis of rational consensus. It requires, instead, that we conceive the people as primarily held together by habits and rules. It is, in this view, a closed society that, may transform itself when opened up by an aspiration toward universality. Hence there is no need to explain democratic legitimacy by appeal to a legislating popular will, and there is no regress of original contracts or circularity between citizens and institutions. In a way Bergson does to democratic theory what Pythagoras did to Zeno: in order to demonstrate the possibility of movement he did not give an argument. He simply stood up and walked.

This dissolution may, however, seem insufficient to democratic theorists, particularly to those who accept the traditional view of democracy as based on rationality and consent. This is not surprising, given that Bergson dissolves problems relying on a mystical intuition, rather than by solving them through rational discourse. A Bergsonian approach to the problem of the people rejects the premise of the paradox instead of finding a better argument to accommodate it. Is this a genuine solution to the problem?

To formulate a response, let us examine the objection in detail. The objector could grant that Bergson's position explains how democratic change has actually come about, but it does not seem to help legitimize democratic rule. In traditional democratic theory, the state is legitimate if there is a political arrangement to which everybody could rationally agree. The principles of popular self-rule and the principle of freedom and equality together satisfy this demand. But these are normative standards, not extant states of affairs. So in order to successfully deal with the problem of the people, it is not sufficient to claim that the premises are factually wrong or that they are difficult to attain. A real solution to the problem of the people, the objector might say, should retain the premises of popular self-rule and freedom and equality, while avoiding the conclusion that a democratic people is an absurd expectation. Yet the solution based on Bergson's insight seems rather to dismiss the ideal of legitimacy premised on rational standards that any reasonable individual could accept, and replaces it with a mystical intuition that individuals may or may not have. Given that the original argument of popular self-rule was intended to provide a rational justification for democracy, this "solution," we might say, is worse than the problem. The mystical root of the second source cannot really solve the problem of the people because it dismisses the need for rational justification. But the need for such a justification is precisely what gave rise to the problem in the first place.

To respond to this objection we must further examine Bergson's second source. At first it may seem that Bergson grounds democracy on the irrational demagoguery of a charismatic leader. However, a careful reading of *Two Sources* shows that the second source is not a specific moral doctrine that such a leader could use. Each source, considered in and of itself, has no particular moral content. In the second source this can be seen in the fact that any particular formulation of a moral doctrine is already a mixture of the two sources. For example, the second source cannot be solely an aspiration toward universal freedom and equality, because those concepts are always already embedded in legal and social practices. The concepts of "freedom" and "equality" are composites of the two sources: they include an aspiration to universality, but they are also the fruit of particular social practices and institutions and thus have a tendency toward closure. Freedom can be seen as the indeterminacy inherent in nature and all human action, but it can also be an individual capacity that is determined and enabled by interactions within a particular social group. Equality can be seen as a universal human trait expressed in individual differences, but it can also be seen as sameness between members of a group or a class. In short the moral ideals that motivate current conceptions of democracy cannot solely embody the second source because they are composites of the two sources. The same would happen to any particular moral doctrine that claimed to exhaust the second source. The second source always resists such exhaustion, because it is an intuited emotion rather than a rationally constructed discourse. For this reason, the source cannot be reduced to an ideology appropriated by a leader.

The second source, instead, should be seen as the condition of possibility for creative change and the capacity for moral improvement: it is the condition for the emergence of new moral doctrines. A moral intuition from the second source seeks to turn humankind into a "creative effort," such that humans can change and evolve, and "turn into movement what was, by definition, a stop" (TS 235/1174). From the indeterminacy of nature and the lived experience of time, humans may bring forth intuitions about the basic structure of the world, including the tenet that creativity is possible. Seen in this light the second source does not have a specific moral content: it is just a tendency to generate and perceive novelty in the world. It is a *source* from which something flows, rather than the flow itself.

This interpretation of the second source may be contested. Is it really true that the second source does not have moral content? After all, according to Bergson, love is at the heart of the tendency toward openness (TS 38/1006). But the love in the second source is not filial or romantic in origin. It is mystical. As such, the second source is a creative emotion that does not have a specific content: it can be equated to the indetermination that is prior to all creation and that sustains it without giving it form.[13] This means that the second source is "more metaphysical than moral in its essence" (TS 234/1174).

Let us call this source, when it deals exclusively with political morality, *creative freedom*. Creative freedom is not incompatible with a rational justification of rule. In fact it is its condition of possibility. Any rational justification presupposes creative freedom because the second source is "at the very root of feeling and reason, as of all other things" (TS 234/1174). Given that it does not have any specific moral content, this source is a less demanding metaphysical requirement than other fundamental assumptions of traditional democratic theory, such as the dignity of persons or the idea of sovereignty. Yet, for the same reasons, creative freedom cannot tell you what to do or what is right: it simply opens the possibility of freedom and other kinds of indetermination in the world. In short, because it is at the root of reason, acknowledging creative freedom is a necessary part of any rational justification for government, and it is also necessary for contesting any such justification and for proposing new justifications. Hence it is compatible with traditional democratic legitimacy and does not make the problem of justification worse.

Once this objection is rebutted, we can see why Bergson's *dissolution* of the problem of the people can be the basis of a genuine *solution* to the problem of legitimacy in democratic theory. On the basis of creative freedom, we can conceive the people as an entity capable of change and invention. The people endure: they are not a thing but a process (or, to use Bergson's terms, a progress). In this view a democratic people can be—at least at times—compatible with indetermination. This trait allows democracy to give up the requirement of a people founded by a social contract without giving up the principle of popular self-rule. So rather than propose a society constructed on the grounds of a specific moral or religious doctrine, democratic theory can conceive of a democratic people—an *open* people, or better, an *opening* people—by appeal to the notion of creative freedom.

The idea of an opening people offers a genuine solution to the paradox of the people because it can retain the premises associated with a rational justification of the state (popular self-government and freedom and equality), while at the same time dealing with the logical problem of the people. This conception of the people does not fall into logical problems because it is self-creative. That is, due to its dynamism, an opening people is both its own cause and consequence. A people creates itself, for it develops over time rather than arising out of nothing. *Pari passu*, it can be the consequence of itself because it determines its own path of development as it unfolds in time. As it unfolds, the group changes. Thus the people emerges from an entity that was not yet the fully formed people, even if in retrospect we can see that crucial elements of the people already existed. This retrospective vision allows us to explain how, in a way, the people is indeed a *product* of democratic processes and aspirations. In sum, given that the opening people is never fully formed, it can solve the vicious circle of self-foundation. This same move can also help solve the infinite regress of foundations because an opening people does not require an original agreement to legitimize the state in order to sustain the requirement of freedom and equality. These two requisites are satisfied to the extent that all individuals related by habits fully participate in the people's creation; and they can do so because the rules and the institutions are never completely settled. It is without regress, therefore, that we can say that the democratic people is the *condition* of democratic rule. In sum, you can solve the problem of the people by arguing that the opening people is both the condition and the product of democratic conditions of rule. As Bergson says, "action on the move creates its own route" (TS 296/1227).

NOTES

1 See Habermas, *Between Facts and Norms*; and Rawls, *A Theory of Justice*.
2 See Schmitt, *The Crisis of Parliamentary Democracy*; and Mouffe, *The Democratic Paradox*.
3 In *The Time of Popular Sovereignty*, I call this problem "the indeterminacy of popular unification."
4 For elaborations on this problem, see Honig, "Between Decision and Deliberation"; and Olson, "Paradoxes of Constitutional Democracy." The problem is also called "the paradox of founding": see Arendt, *On Revolution*; Connolly, *The Ethos of Pluralization*; and Michelman, "Constitutional Authorship."
5 It is also known as "the boundary problem." See Goodin, "Enfranchising All Affected Interests, and Its Alternatives"; and Whelan, "Democratic Theory and the Boundary Problem."
6 See Deleuze's formulation of the "complementary rule" in his rendition of Bergson's method, *Bergsonism*, 17. Jankélévitch makes a similar point in *Henri Bergson*, 23.
7 Due to space constraints, I must assume that the reader is familiar with the Eleatic paradoxes. For a summary, see Salmon, *Zeno's Paradoxes*, 8–15.
8 In this view the paradox of Achilles or the arrow would be equal to the dichotomy, even though the first divides a movement and the second divides a thing.
9 Bergson proceeds in the same manner when he dissolves intractable problems in his other works; in each case he draws a parallel to one or more of Zeno's paradoxes (CE 308–13/775–80; MM 191–93/327–28).
10 This claim is at the core of social contract theory in the tradition of Rousseau and Kant, as well as its contemporary instantiation in the work of Rawls and Habermas and their followers.
11 "Such is democracy in theory," according to Rousseau and Kant (TS 282/1215).
12 See, for example, Habermas's response to the problem of self-foundation in "Constitutional Democracy."
13 Given that this love coincides with "God's love for His handiwork" (TS 234/1174), one could make the case that the second source is identical to Bergson's *élan vital* as formulated in *Creative Evolution* and the idea of "the virtual" in *Matter and Memory*. However, due to space constraints, I cannot make the full case in these pages.

NINE

Bergson's Critique of
Practical Reason

Carl Power

For such a controversial philosopher, Bergson had a remarkable lack of interest in intellectual polemics. He readily confessed to the "striking inferiority" of his own philosophy when it came to the cut and thrust of academic debate, but he did not consider this much of a defect (CM 37/1277). On the contrary, he thought that those skilled in the art of debating—those "clever in speaking, prompt to criticize" (CM 83–84/1323–24)—had merely achieved mastery of ready-made ideas and did not appreciate how far reality resists intellectual analysis.

In Bergson's view, the best way to refute a theory is to present an alternative hypothesis that cleaves closer to the facts under consideration or, more radically, to demonstrate that, in view of these facts, the problems that one's rival seeks to solve are entirely false. *The Two Sources of Morality and Religion* provides a good example of this strategy. Bergson thought that his investigation into the origin and structure of morality (an investigation combining the evidence of phenomenology, sociology, anthropology, and biology), swept away many of the defining problems of moral philosophy, including the search for a justification of morality. This is why he spared only a handful of pages to demonstrate the futility of what most moral philosophers have spent most of their time arguing about (TS 85–96,

267–70/1047–57, 1203–6). What I have called (somewhat hyperboli-cally) Bergson's "critique of practical reason" concerns these pages. By focusing on this minor part of *Two Sources*, I hope to bring into relief Bergson's unique contribution to practical philosophy and highlight its importance today.

I will begin by explaining, in general terms, why Bergson rejected the whole philosophical project of justifying morality. Then I will look more closely at what he thought was wrong with the three main schools of moral philosophy: Kantian deontology, empiricism, and rational intui-tionism. Finally, I will examine Bergson's philosophical alternative which, to my mind, anticipates a distinctly poststructuralist ethics. Doing so not only helps us understand the practical implications of poststructuralism, it suggests a new direction for moral and political thought.

INTELLECTUALISM AND ITS DISCONTENTS

One of the central tasks of traditional moral philosophy—a task that Bergson rejects—is to find an answer to what Christine Korsgaard calls the "normative question": Why should I act morally?[1] All philosophical attempts to justify morality are attempts to give a systematic answer to this question. As Korsgaard explains it, the normative question first arises in our everyday lives. We begin with an unreflective awareness of obliga-tion, an unquestioned *tendency* to act according to moral norms. How-ever, we become aware of a resistance, perhaps the contrary pull of desire or personal interest, and so hesitate to do our duty. Now *reflecting* on our situation, we ask the normative question and, in so doing, seek an explicit reason why we should act morally. All going well, the reason we receive will satisfy us and we will consciously reapply ourselves to the norms we otherwise would have followed automatically. People have always looked to religion for definite answers to the normative question, but philosophy also claims authority in this matter.

Bergson would no doubt agree with this account of how the normative question arises. However, he would add that, just because the normative question makes good sense in everyday life, it doesn't necessarily make for a good philosophical question. In fact, he would regard it as a *badly stated* question, that is, one that tends to obscure a real difference.[2] The following passage highlights such a difference:

In order to resist resistance, to keep to the right paths, when desire, passion or interest tempt us aside, we must necessarily give ourselves reasons. Even if we have opposed the unlawful desire by another, the latter, conjured up by the will, could arise only at the call of an idea. In a word, an intelligent being generally exerts his influence on himself through the medium of intelligence. But from the fact that we get back to obligation by rational ways it does not follow that obligation was of a rational order . . . [A] tendency, natural or acquired, is one thing, another thing the necessarily rational method which a reasonable being will use to restore to it its force and to combat what is opposing it. (TS 22/992–93)

When philosophers attempt to construct a systematic proof for obligation in general, they effectively assume that practical reason is the ultimate ground or source of morality. What they fail to appreciate is the difference in *kind* between our habitual, pre-reflective obedience to moral norms, and our attempts to find good reasons to perform our duty. So profound is this difference that our tendency to act morally is not reducible to, or reconstructable by, any system of reasons.

None of this is to deny the importance of practical reason: "It is on the plane of intelligence, and on that plane alone, that discussion is possible, and there is no complete morality without reflection, analysis and argument with others as well as with oneself" (TS 97/1057). For the individual, rational instruction is indispensable to give "confidence and delicacy to the moral sense" (TS 97/1057). It helps us to determine our duty in this or that situation, to compare different lines of conduct, and to achieve some measure of self-consistency in our actions. Yet it always *presupposes* that our intentions are good, that we already feel the pressure of obligation or the pull of a moral ideal.

What Bergson insists upon is that, in the first instance, morality is spontaneously enacted or embodied rather than explicitly represented. No doubt, in societies like ours, much of morality has been rationally organized, and we tend to think of it in terms of explicit prescriptions and prohibitions, commandments and laws. Yet this codification depends upon a background of shared practices that resists articulation. Morality is primarily a "know-how" and only secondarily an explicit "knowing-that." I might well be able to justify my actions as moral but, if pressed to back up my reasons, I am liable to hit a brick wall. Yet, as Wittgenstein points out (and Bergson would surely agree), we often follow rules without being able to fully explain what we are doing and why: "My reasons will soon give out. And then I shall act, without reasons."[3] This is an important *first-person fact* about morality, and about rule-following more generally, a fact that philosophers often fail to properly grasp. They assume that my inability to find ultimate reasons says something about *me*, my finitude, my lack of time, energy, and intellectual rigor. For Bergson, on the contrary, the limits of reason are at stake. It is not possible to translate, without loss, our moral know-how into an explicit knowing-that.

According to Bergson, the basic error of traditional moral theory is *intellectualism*: our lived reality is confused with the means by which we symbolize it (*TS* 269/1204). Throughout his philosophical career, Bergson identified numerous versions of intellectualism. In *Time and Free Will*, his first book, he challenges the way we commonly confuse our concrete experience of duration with our spatialized representations of it. In *Two Sources*, his last book, Bergson finds a comparable error in the assumption that morality is primarily a matter of judgment rather than intuition, the ability to act on the basis of concepts and principles rather than to respond spontaneously to the situation at hand. This mistake can be traced back at least as far as Socrates. By treating virtue as a kind of science, Socrates "identifies the practice of good with our knowledge of it; he thus paves the way for the doctrine which will absorb all moral life in the rational function of thought" (*TS* 61/1027).

Breaking with this Platonic paradigm, Bergson might be said to join a counter-tradition that begins with Aristotle and includes more recent names such as Dewey, Heidegger, Wittgenstein, Bourdieu, and Taylor. What these disparate figures share is a propensity to see the human agent, not as a locus of representations, but as a being who is immediately engaged in the world and whose understanding of self and other is first and foremost expressed in practice.

In other respects Bergson stands apart. Unlike those allies I have just mentioned, he explains morality in terms that are essentially biological. He does more than just place morality in the context of evolution (arguing, for instance, that the survival of our species depends on our possession of a moral sense); he insists that biological forces directly constitute morality. This suggests an obvious criticism: like anyone who explains morality naturalistically, Bergson must approach his object from the *outside*, that is, from the third-person perspective of the scientist; but this is to ignore or falsify the most basic fact about morality, that it belongs essentially to our lived experience and makes first-person demands on us. No wonder, then, that Bergson can reject the normative question. In explaining morality, he has simply explained it away.[4] This judgment, I think, is unjust. For Bergson's brand of naturalism is radically *non-reductive*. To an extraordinary degree, his theory of life unites the perspectives of science and lived experience. In *Creative Evolution*, he develops his famous notion of the *élan vital* by cross-pollinating the evidence of evolution with his phenomenology of time. And in *Two Sources*, he stretches his notion of biology still further to accommodate moral experience.

Another thing that makes Bergson unique is the way he splits morality into two halves: obligation and aspiration. Or, rather, he identifies two fundamentally different kinds of morality and claims that every given society presents us with a specific mixture of both. This is a second qualitative distinction that, in his view, moral philosophers have failed to appreciate. Each morality has its own psychological faculty and biological source, and each outstrips our rational capacities. That is why, for Bergson, there are two quite different ways we can run out of reasons for acting morally.

On the one hand, obligation depends on an infra-intellectual force. Should you press me to provide you with reasons for obedience, I will ultimately come up with a bare tautology: "You must because you must" (TS 25/995). With this tautology, Bergson reduces obligation to its barest minimum, its lowest limit, the point at which it almost (but not quite) achieves the blind compulsion of instinct. This morality is what belongs to us as members of the human species; it is a fundamental ingredient of each and every society, whether ancient or modern, insofar as it forms a relatively closed and self-preserving whole—what Bergson calls a *closed society*. If obligation is "not quite" instinct this is because it remains a "necessity with which one can argue" (TS 92/1053). We hesitate in the face of duty, asking ourselves why we must do as we are told, deciding whether to resist or obey morality's command.

How, in more positive terms, are we to understand this pseudo-instinct? For Bergson, obligations are collective habits, habits of command and of obedience. The closed society is a "system of more or less deeply-rooted habits" that all "hang together" to form a "solid block," each one drawing upon the force of the whole (TS 10/982). As habits, individual obligations are acquired and vary from society to society. Yet they presuppose an innate capacity necessary for social cohesion and order: the "habit of contracting habits" (TS 26/996–97). Bergson goes further, linking obligation not just to human nature but to a general biological principle. All vital organizations—whether organs, organisms, societies, or ecosystems—*tend* to form closed and durable totalities. The closed society is a particular expression of this *tendency*.

On the other hand, Bergson insists that something more than reason has driven all major historical advances towards a properly universal morality. From the birth of Christianity to the French Revolution and beyond, a kind of mystical impulse has been at work. The love of humanity has propelled exceptional individuals to unplug themselves from the closed society and call for a new and more inclusive social order, the ideal of which—or, rather, the direction in which this movement tends—Bergson calls the *open society*. When we follow the lead of these moral heroes, we experience something of the universal love that inspired them, a supra-intellectual force that "seems to baffle expression, and yet which had to express itself" (TS 46/1013). This is why the words of great moral innovators are often paradoxical (e.g., the Sermon on the Mount) and why their deeds often defy common sense.

Again, Bergson finds a way to fit this moral experience into his theory of life. The demand for a new and universal morality has, he argues, a biological principle. More precisely, the creative emotion that drives this demand expresses, at the level of human psychology and history, the creative movement of life itself, a movement that passes through all vital organizations, opening them to change and gathering them into an open whole. That is to say, in the love of humanity we experience the *élan vital* firsthand. This shows just how far Bergson is willing to stretch his notion of biology.

We can now see, in very general terms, what Bergson thinks is fundamentally wrong with most moral theories. In his view morality is immediately constituted by infra- and supra-intellectual forces that express the two biological tendencies toward closure and openness. Rational reflection on moral questions is useful, but it cannot grasp these primary processes. Once we realize this, all attempts to rationally reconstruct and justify morality become both unnecessary and futile.

This brings us to Bergson's complaints against particular brands of moral intellectualism. He divides the domain of moral philosophy into three main camps. First, the Kantians, who base morality on *pure* reason, empty of content, and who see in obligation "the necessity, pure and simple, of [reason] remaining logically in agreement with itself" (TS 86/1047). Opposite them stand the empiricists, a rather heterogeneous bunch that includes Hume, Hobbes, and Mill. They base morality on *prudential* reason and see in obligation "an invitation logically to pursue a certain end" (TS 86/104), an end approved by reason but set by our desires, interests or sentiments. Between the Kantians and empiricists are the rational intuitionists, those who, from Plato to Moore, "explain moral obligation by the fact that the idea of the Good forces itself upon us" (TS 87/1049).

Against these three schools of moral philosophy, Bergson mounts a two-pronged attack. To better understand this strategy, I will analyze each prong separately. This means examining Bergson's critique of Kantianism, empiricism, and intuitionism *twice*, each time from a different point of view.

THE IMPOTENCE OF PRACTICAL REASON

When philosophers make practical reason the source of morality they fail to comprehend the real *forces* animating morality. This is Bergson's first line of attack. Let us start with his reproach of Kantian deontology. According to Bergson, when Kant explains moral obligation in terms of the bare imperative of not contradicting oneself, he is quite simply mistaking a vital necessity for a logical necessity, a pseudo-instinctive force for the force of an argument. Contrary to what Kant might think, the intellect cannot, by itself, bind the will to an obligation: "Never, in our hours of temptation, should we sacrifice to the mere need for logical consistency our interest, our passion, our vanity" (TS 23/994). To those who think that pure reason "should be sufficient to silence selfishness and passion," Bergson congratulates them for having "never heard the voice of the one or the other very loud within themselves" (TS 87/1048–49).

It must be admitted that Bergson is not being entirely fair to Kantians. As Kant formulates it, the categorical imperative is more than just a bare logical necessity; it involves the a priori insight that all humans, as "ends in themselves," are worthy of respect. Nevertheless, Bergson's criticism still carries weight. Indeed, it echoes a complaint made by Hegel that contemporary Kantians still struggle with. Habermas, for instance, admits that practical reason suffers from a serious motivational deficit.[5] When we subject our actions to the requirements of practical discourse, we discover good reasons to act morally, but these bear only a weak motivational force. We may know what we ought to do without feeling compelled to do it. Habermas tries to make up for this deficiency by taking into account supplementary sources of motivation, including the concrete forms of social life that embody moral norms and the processes of socialization that shape moral individuals. However, such amendments would hardly satisfy Bergson. He insists that no amount of intellectual speculation can determine an "ought" in the first place. When Habermas supplements the weak force of practical reason with the stronger (but essentially nonmoral) forces of social solidarity, he simply misrepresents our lived experience. Bergson's phenomenological investigation reveals that it is obligation itself that binds us together into a (closed) society. Obligation is a necessity with which we can argue; it is not an argument to which we can add motivational force.

In one respect at least, Bergson prefers empiricists to Kantians. Like Hume (and unlike Kant), Bergson thinks that there is no great conflict between reason and our inclinations, chiefly because the former is power-less against the latter. At best, reason gives direction to the desires we already possess, helping us to determine how best to achieve our ends. Yet Bergson is unhappy with empiricists, and for much the same reason that Kant is. An empiricist generally begins with a disposition that is supposed to belong to human nature (e.g., self-interest, pride, sympathy, benev-olence) and then attempts to show that not only is its aim in conformity with reason but its accomplishment is best pursued in a rational manner. Morality is the system of means that reason determines for the optimum satisfaction of our fundamental ends. An ethical egoist might argue that we are most likely to achieve our own happiness by behaving in a moral way, thus promoting the happiness of others. Hume, by contrast, ration-ally reconstructs morality on the basis not of self-interest, but of feelings such as sympathy and antipathy. These feelings provide us with reasons for acting and form the moral bonds that unite a community. There are innumerable versions of moral empiricism but, in Bergson's view, they all share a certain basic defect, one that Kant saw very clearly, prudential reason determines only *hypothetical* imperatives: "For we may be obliged to adopt certain means in order to attain such and such ends; but if we choose to renounce the end, how can the means be forced upon us?" (TS 90–91/1052). If we have the feelings and aims that empiricists assume we do, their arguments may persuade us to behave morally. But they have nothing to say to those who, for instance, lack sympathy for others or else have little regard for their own best interests. According to Bergson, the empiricist approach misses one of the most basic features of moral experience: obligation addresses us in the form of a *command*. This is why Bergson allows that at the core of obligation there is a kind of categorical imperative, *albeit* a radically non-Kantian one. It is a pseudo-instinct we spontaneously enact rather than a rule we reflectively apply (TS 24–25/995–96).

Bergson locates rational intuitionism between the other two camps as though it combines something of each. With empiricism, it provides a teleological account of morality; with Kantianism, it affirms reason's capacity to determine, by itself, what is moral. The majority of intuitionists are *cognitivists*. Typically, they claim that careful reflection reveals, a priori, a number of substantial moral truths that are self-evident, universal, and mutually consistent. Like Hume before him and J. L. Mackie after him, Bergson takes issue with this view on the grounds that, even if we do somehow perceive objective ethical values and can measure our actions against them, it is extremely unclear how such knowledge could motivate us. According to Bergson, there is no saying why anyone *ought* to strive towards this or that idea of the good: "You can invoke in its favor only aesthetic reasons, allege that a certain line of conduct is 'finer' than another, that it sets us more or less high up in the ranks of living beings: but what could you reply to the man who declared that he places his own interest before all other considerations?" (TS 88/1049–50). By an "aesthetic reason," Bergson means something we can appreciate in a detached, speculative way, much as we admire, say, the beauty of nature. Such reasons cannot explain the compulsive force of our obligations or the attractive force of our highest ideals.[6]

For Bergson, the "good" is merely the name or label we give to that which moves us (TS 87–88/1049). We desire something not because we recognize it to be good; rather, we call something good because we desire it (a view made famous by Spinoza and Nietzsche). However, when intuitionists treat the good as, first and foremost, an object of knowledge, they make morality depend on a representation and render its motivational forces inexplicable: "The truth is that an ideal cannot become obligatory unless it is already active, in which case it is made obligatory, not by the idea contained in it, but by its action" (TS 270/1205).

If we look for what is common to the theories that Bergson rejects, we can see that all of them understand moral behavior on the model of intentionality. Our tendency to act is always mapped onto our reasons for acting—whether this is an idea we are pursuing, a need we are seeking to satisfy, or a rule we are applying. Against this assumption, Bergson asserts a double disjunction between action and intention. This is something he proposes in *Time and Free Will* when he demonstrates that consciousness is, by its very nature, stretched between the poles of automatism and creative freedom. In both directions our consciousness outstrips our intellect, and we find ourselves performing acts for which we can, only in retrospect, assign a plausible motive. With *Two Sources*, Bergson provides a moral theory that accommodates this double disjunction. The twin sources of morality are obligation and aspiration understood as infra- and supra-intellectual forces. They constitute the opposite poles of a force field within which our representations about morality emerge, make sense, and have the capacity to move us. We may certainly seek to identify and explain the sources of normativity, but we should not imagine that morality itself depends on such intellectual endeavors. This is why Bergson thinks that *all* theories of morality—even his own—are *impotent*. By themselves, they cannot empower us to act morally.[7]

THE REDUNDANCY OF PRACTICAL REASON

Bergson's second complaint against moral intellectualism is that it always *presupposes* the morality it attempts to explain or justify. Empiricism is an obvious target for this attack. It has often been said that when philosophers such as Hume and Hobbes ground morality on human nature, they in fact smuggle in the values and standards of their own society. Bergson develops this familiar criticism in a unique way. In his view, a society is a vital organization whose elements are internally related and posited together as a whole, such that no element can be abstracted out and considered the cause of all the others. But empiricists try to do just that. What they regard as the essential characteristics of human nature—whether self-interest, sympathy, benevolence, etc.—they have selected from those that social life offers. Each carries with it something of the social whole to which it belongs. And each is already adapted to the existing moral order.

Since empiricists start with an already socialized end, it is easy for them to construct a system of means (to attain that end) that more or less resembles the current morality. Says Bergson,

> Even if we set up personal interest as the moral principle, we shall find no great difficulty in building up a rational morality sufficiently resembling current morality, as is proved by the relative success of utilitarian ethics. Selfishness, indeed, for the man living among his fellow-men, comprises legitimate pride, the craving for praise, etc., with the result that purely personal interest has become impossible to define, so large is the element of public interest it contains, so hard is it to keep them separate . . . Still easier will it be, then, to draw all moral maxims, or nearly all, from feelings such as honor, or sympathy, or pity. Each of these tendencies, in a man living in society, is laden with all that social morality has deposited in it; and we should have to unload it first, at the risk of reducing it to very little indeed, if we wished to avoid begging the question in using it to explain morality. (ᴛꜱ 90/1051)

One would expect Kant to avoid this error. After all, he entirely rejects the idea that morality's source can be found amongst the interests and predispositions attributable to human nature. He and his followers instead derive morality from a bare rational procedure that is supposed to be free of all empirical content and thus detached from the substantive values of any given community. Bergson, however, doubts the purity of pure practical reason. In fact, he regards the mainspring of Kant's categorical imperative—the demand for "logical consistency" in action—to be just another aim or end extracted from social life (ᴛꜱ 269–70/1204). And like any of the ends that an empiricist might select, it already bears the stamp of the existing morality.

Bergson illustrates this point with Kant's famous example of repaying a loan.[8] To insist, as Kant does, that it is self-contradictory to accept a loan without intending to give it back only makes sense within a moral context where the practice of "giving one's word" is already established, where the "right to property" is already respected, and where "entrusting" something to someone already entails an obligation that should not be betrayed. If we don't presuppose such a context, the loan was not a loan to begin with, no promise was made, and there is no contradiction in holding onto the money even if you said you would return it. But, according to Bergson, if we do presuppose this context, the moral obligation would no longer pertain to the bare and empty necessity of not "contradicting one-self, since the contradiction in this case would simply consist in rejecting, after having accepted it, a moral obligation which for this very reason was already there" (TS 86/1048).

Although again Bergson reduces Kant's argument to a kind of carica-ture, his complaint remains cogent. In recent times, for instance, David Wiggins has made a similar diagnosis of Kantianism. Like Bergson, he allows that it is worthwhile reflecting on whether we can consistently universalize our actions. But such a procedure can only *remind* us of what we should do, helping us correct and organize our moral intuitions; it does not provide morality's foundation: "Universalization is no longer a method or any part of a method for the initial generation of moral ideas and principles. It works on what is already fully moralized."[9]

What of rational intuitionism? As we know, Bergson thinks that the "good" is little more than the name we give to that which moves us, the heading under which we classify actions we already judge to be moral. These actions are already organized, within our ethical community, into a hierarchy of conduct. Those who think that the idea of the good provides the ground of morality merely reify an empirical generality, converting a product of social life into its principle: "We fail to see how it [the good] can be defined without assuming a hierarchy . . . of actions, of varying elevation: but if the hierarchy exists by itself, there is no need to call upon the idea of the Good to establish it" (TS 88/1049). For Bergson, this is more than just the intuitionist version of a common philosophical mis-take; it is the very archetype or model of this mistake. Kantians and empiricists follow the lead of rational intuitionists when they assume that the motive or end they have "taken up as a principle is 'preferable' to the others, that there is a difference of value between motives, and that there exists a general ideal by reference to which the real is to be estimated" (TS 270/1205). In a sense, they all take "refuge in the Platonic theory, with the Idea of the Good dominating all others" (TS 270/1205).[10]

According to Bergson, moral intellectualism can be avoided only by proceeding in the opposite direction. One must dig beneath the level of social facts and representations, beneath the ready-made institutions, belief-systems, and motives that social life supplies, to find the twin bio-logical forces on which these all depend. Most philosophers only ever deal with the *products* of these biological processes. The moral theories they devise, however speculative, are little more than reconstructions of what is already given.[11] As a result, they cannot grasp the original basis for morality, the prehistoric-yet-active tendency to preserve the existing (closed) moral order. Nor can they appreciate the world-historical events —so unexpected, they defy a simple linear account of history—in which moral and political universalism emerges. Blind to the profound hetero-geneity at the heart of morality, philosophers typically speak of moral progress in homogenizing terms. They imagine it as the diminution of an interval separating us from an already-given endpoint, the ideal towards which we are striving. This is a particular instance of a very general error that Bergson never tires of exposing: the confusion of a movement with the series of positions it traverses, of a process of becoming with what has already become, of duration with space (TS 270–71/1205).

A BERGSONIAN ETHICS

Earlier I gestured towards a philosophical counter-tradition to which Bergson belongs, one that regards the moral agent not as a locus of representations but as a being who is immediately and intuitively en-gaged in the world. Here I want to be more specific. To my mind, some of Bergson's closest allies are poststructuralists, such as Deleuze, Guattari, Foucault, and their precursors, especially Spinoza and Nietzsche. There are some obvious commonalities. For instance, they all recognize that our explicit motives and reasons for action are secondary in relation to the play of largely unconscious forces that constitute us as living beings. This involves making the *body*, rather than consciousness, the model of practi-cal philosophy. In addition, they all eschew problems of justification and rational reconstruction and set themselves instead problems of diagnosis and evaluation. Borrowing Deleuze's terminology, we might call this a shift from "morality" to "ethics." A morality is a system of judgments that, whether it is based on God's commandments or reason's dictates, "always refers existence to transcendent values." By contrast, an ethics is "a typol-ogy of immanent modes of existence. It compares different forms of life and evaluates their intrinsic qualities, forces and tendencies."[12] This is just what Bergson does when he distinguishes open and closed moralities. Rather than measuring life against moral values that are supposed to stand over and above it, he measures the value *for life* of different kinds of morality.[13]

Like his poststructuralist heirs, Bergson has been criticized for leaving no place outside the push and pull of conflicting forces from which to view things impartially and establish universal and apodictic moral standards. While this is true, it does not mean that Bergson leads us into moral relativism. On the contrary, he acknowledges our capacity to intuit the difference between superior and inferior forms of life, open and closed moralities. One might reply that he merely sets out different modes of existence without giving us any reason to prefer one to the other.[14] But, for Bergson, the superiority of the open over the closed is lived before it is represented, felt before it is explicitly thought. Our moral and political decisions outstrip the reasons we give ourselves for making them. The best a philosopher can do is to invent concepts that clarify the choices we face, outlining the critical differences at stake.

Here we should mark an obvious disagreement between Bergson and those poststructuralists—amongst them, Deleuze, Guattari, and Foucault—who have rejected all moral universals, a gesture that owes much to Nietzsche's influence.[15] Bergson, by contrast, regards the "rights of man" as a major moral accomplishment, a triumph for what he calls "absolute justice." It is tempting to treat his commitment to universal values as a kind of historical residue that can be stripped away (along with his humanism, his liberalism, and his enthusiasm for Christianity) to reveal a thoroughly "new Bergson." I would suggest a different strategy. We should consider the possibility that such apparently outdated aspects of Bergson's work might indicate a way to extend the poststructuralist project.

To give a single example of this, I want to compare Bergson and Alain Badiou on the question of human rights. Badiou, in his book, *Ethics*, first published in 1998, seeks to defend the legacy of poststructuralism while nevertheless asserting a version of ethical universalism.[16] He complains of a reactionary tide that has swept though Europe, reversing the intellectual and political gains of the sixties and reinstating a bankrupt humanism. Invoking the spirits of Foucault, Althusser, Lacan, and, above all, Nietzsche, he declares once more the "death of Man" and stages a trenchant critique of human rights.[17] According to Badiou, the discourse of human rights relies on empty ahistorical abstractions that prevent us from thinking the singularity of concrete situations. It offers no positive vision of the good but merely rejects or negates a series of evils that it claims to recognize a priori. More profoundly, the discourse of human rights comprehends only the basest part of our existence, defining "Man" as an animal capable of suffering (and of reflecting on this fact), an animal whose life, however pitiful, must be preserved. Thus, its talk of human dignity actually hides a terrible contempt for humanity. Against what he sees as the hypocrisy and nihilism of human rights, Badiou calls for a new "ethics of truth." In such an ethics, we are not merely animals seeking to preserve our lives and happiness, but beings able to invent eternal and universal truths and, by our fidelity to such truths, able to achieve a measure of immortality.

Integral to Badiou's critique is a contrast between two modes of existence: on the one hand, human rights address our subhuman selves, our animalistic substrate, while on the other hand, an "ethics of truth" demands from us something superhuman. Bergson makes a not-dissimilar distinction between the morality we have as intelligent animals and the one we invent as near-gods, yet he claims that human rights belong to the latter. How are we to understand this tension? As I will attempt to show, Bergson's account of human rights answers Badiou's critique, revealing it to be, if not entirely wrong, then extremely one-sided. I have three main points in mind.

1 Badiou thinks that when Foucault and others announced the "death of Man," that is, when they contested the idea that "Man" has an innate and essential identity, they also effectively undermined the foundations of human rights. That claim makes no sense from Bergson's perspective. For he regards human rights not as something derived from human nature, but as an invention, the result of a collective experiment made by particular individuals at a particular place and time. The singularity of this event, however, does not contradict its world-historical significance (TS 74–75/1037–38). The French revolutionaries who, in 1791, declared the "Rights of Man and Citizen" did more than just transform their own lives. They established for everyone thereafter new possibilities for social and political life, new expectations and demands, new coordinates for thought and action.

2 Badiou thinks that human rights are reactive and life denying because, instead of offering a positive vision of the good, they merely reject or negate a series of evils. Bergson is well aware that human rights are framed negatively; together they express a principle of non-discrimination and non-coercion: "Every sentence of the Declaration of the Rights of Man is a challenge to some abuse. The main thing is to put an end to intolerable suffering" (TS 283/1216). However, behind the repeated protests against

injustice, Bergson finds a pure positivity at work, a love of humanity affirming itself. This love is expressed quite openly in the democratic formula: liberty, equality, and fraternity. No doubt, this formula is far too vague to constitute a "positive vision of the good," but this is simply because it stands not as a determinate end but as a signpost indicating the direction in which to proceed. Or rather it expresses a creative impulse—a becoming—still in the process of actualizing itself.[18]

3 Badiou thinks that human rights are degrading because they define "Man" as little more than an animal that seeks, individually and collectively, to preserve its life and well-being. In effect this reduces us to that frail and rapacious part of ourselves that is ultimately destined to die. Bergson grants that there is a morality belonging to us naturally as intelligent animals, and that its primary function is to preserve, one within the other, the life of the individual and that of (the closed) society. However, he links human rights to an altogether different form of morality. In his view human rights express an "absolute justice" that soars above our heads, "categorical and transcendent" (TS 76/1039).[19] They articulate an irrepressible, all-or-nothing demand for justice that cannot be relativized according to historical or cultural conditions, a demand that may be revived again and again in different social contexts and historical periods. Those who first declared those rights made a break with the existing social and political order, a break with history (at least if history is understood as a linear development), a break too with their species' nature. In so doing, they leapt into the element of creation—which Bergson identifies with God.

For Bergson, true creation hovers between history and eternity. Though the emergence of the new can always be dated, the essence of this event endures as long as the possibilities for life it opens remain open possibilities. Those who invented human rights gained for themselves a measure of immortality, and so do those who follow their example. This helps explain Bergson's enigmatic claim that "the great moral figures that have made their mark on history join hands across the centuries, above our human cities; they unite into a divine city which they bid us to enter" (TS 68/1032).

It should be clear that Bergson's account of human rights resembles Badiou's alternative "ethics of truth." There is, I think, a good reason for this resemblance. Bergson and Badiou both find the foundation of ethical universalism in the same place: Christianity.[20] Not the established Christianity of popes and churches, of fixed hierarchy and obedience to dogma, but the first Christianity, an emancipatory social movement inspired by a universal love. Bergson parts company with Badiou by regarding the "rights of man" to be the result of a marvellous reactivation of Christian love (TS 282/1216). Because Badiou fails to make this connection, he cannot see how similar his own ethics is to that which he rejects. As Peter Dews has noted, there is little real difference between the notion of "Man" implicit in human rights and the one that Badiou propounds: "Both conceptions are clearly secularized offshoots of the Judeo-Christian tradition. . . . Indeed, if anything, Badiou's unabashed rhetoric of 'eternity,' 'immortality,' and 'fidelity' displays its religious origins more openly."[21]

How is it that Bergson finds in the ethics of human rights the very thing Badiou claims it lacks? It seems to me that they have adopted different temporal perspectives. Bergson focuses on human rights at the moment of their emergence, an eternal moment that continues to resonate. Badiou focuses instead on human rights as those in positions of authority often invoke them today. He is particularly incensed by the way these rights are used to justify tyranny at home (e.g., the bureaucratic administration of life) and imperialism abroad (e.g., "humanitarian interventions"). Badiou's polemic is incisive but one-sided. He does not acknowledge the obvious: that the meaning and value of human rights are contested, and that they inspire as much emancipatory activism as cynical moralism.

In *Two Sources* I think we find a corrective for Badiou's error. Bergson not only brings into view the positive potential that human rights have for emancipatory politics, he provides us with a way of understanding their troubling duplicity. Like any instance of what Bergson describes as moral progress, human rights are caught up in a double movement. On the one hand, they were born from a collective leap into the absolute that posed, and continues to pose, the promise of an open society. On the other hand, they have been captured (without being entirely contained) by the forces of a closed society that has adapted itself to this alien element. From a Bergsonian perspective, every leap forward is followed by a fall; every revolution is betrayed to some extent by the social and political order meant to preserve its achievements; every emancipatory ideal can also serve as an instrument of oppression.[22] It is no surprise that human rights are Janus-faced. The important thing is to approach them from the right side.

For practical philosophy today, *Two Sources* has a negative and a positive relevance. Much of this chapter has been concerned with its negative value. I have tried to explain why Bergson rejects the central problems of traditional moral theory, problems that either have no solution or have innumerable conflicting ones (which is much the same thing). By demonstrating that the sources of morality cannot be reduced to—or reconstructed by—reason, he helps clear the way for a very different style of ethical thought. But Bergson also provides positive indications of how to proceed. His distinction between the closed and the open is an especially useful tool for understanding and analyzing moral and political phenomena. That is what I hoped to show by comparing his views on human rights with those of Badiou. An important precursor of poststructuralism, Bergson can help us reorient practical philosophy in its wake.

NOTES

1 Korsgaard, *The Sources of Normativity*, ch. 1.

2 On badly stated questions for Bergson, see Deleuze, *Bergsonism*, 17.

3 Wittgenstein, *Philosophical Investigations*, 211.

4 For an example of this kind of criticism, see Copleston, "Bergson on Morality," 247–66.

5 Habermas, *Moral Consciousness and Communicative Action*, 207–8.

6 Recognizing that knowledge of the good provides little motivational force, some intuitionists supplement it with stronger, extra-moral sources of motivation. This "externalism" involves the same basic error we found in Habermas's theory.

7 Earlier I mentioned similarities between the views of Bergson and Taylor. Here I want to stress their difference. Though Taylor acknowledges that our ethical values are primarily expressed in a practical know-how, he nevertheless thinks that the force of morality depends on our possessing appropriate ideas or theories of the good. For Taylor, a constitutive good is a belief that motivates us; for Bergson, morality is immediately constituted by motivational forces that condition our beliefs.

8 Kant, *Critique of Practical Reason*, ch. 1, 4.

9 Wiggins, *Needs, Values, Truth*, 78–79.

10 Bergson is not alone in identifying a Platonic defect at the origin of most moral theories. Taylor also claims that philosophers, both ancient and modern, have unwittingly followed Plato's lead by organizing their moral theories around some single overriding aim—in his terminology, a "hypergood"—which they have selected from their social milieu. Whether happiness, authenticity, benevolence, solidarity, respect for others, logical consistency, or whatever else, this hypergood is segregated from other goods, raised up, and made the standard against which moral action is measured. See Taylor, *Sources of the Self*, 62–66.

11 As Bergson says in another context: "It is of the essence of reasoning to shut us up in the circle of the given" (CE 211/658).

12 See Deleuze, *Spinoza*, 17–29.

13 These commonalities could be explored further. Of particular interest is the structural resemblance between the social typology of *Two Sources* and that of Deleuze and Guattari's *A Thousand Plateaus*.

14 According to Jacques Maritain, "Bergson does not leave us any means of choosing between the service of society and the call of the hero" (*Bergsonian Philosophy and Thomism*, 331).

15 Some doubt the coherence of this gesture, arguing that these poststructuralists *implicitly* affirm certain moral universals: opposition to oppressive social relations, the promotion of difference, and so on. Habermas thinks that poststructuralists are contradicted by their own moral commitments, while Todd May attempts to justify these commitments on their behalf. See Habermas, *The Philosophical Discourse of Modernity*, especially 336–37; and May, *The Moral Theory of Poststructuralism*.

16 Obviously Badiou is not alone in trying to bring ethical universalism back within the poststructuralist fold. Others, like Žižek, Balibar, and Derrida, have also done so.

17 Badiou, *Ethics*, ch. 1.

18 Etienne Balibar characterizes the democratic ideal as a demand for "equal liberty" and links its essential indeterminacy to the Hegelian notion of "negative universality." Equal liberty realizes itself only by negating a potentially infinite series of determinate situations of injustice. See Balibar, "'Rights of Man.'" From a Bergsonian perspective, Balibar fails to see the positivity—the universal love—expressed in the work of the negative. Indicative of this failure is the absence of "fraternity" from Balibar's equation: equality = liberty. For Bergson, however, fraternity is everything; it is the genetic element from which liberty and equality derive (TS 282/1215).

19 Note that it is quite possible for an immanent typology to admit an "absolute" or "transcendent" element. Spinoza does so by equating God and Nature. For him, what transcends the created order of nature (*Natura naturata*) is God understood as the creative principle immanent to nature (*Natura naturans*). In a similar way, Bergson equates God and the *élan vital*—though he does so with some reservations (TS 220–21/1162).

20 Badiou, *Saint Paul*.

21 Dews, "Uncategorical Imperatives," 36.

22 This is not to suggest that the incorporation of the open by the closed is, in all respects, a bad thing. On the contrary, Bergson insists that bursts of moral and political creativity—and with them the promise of the open society—would vanish without a trace if they did not find at least partial expression in the obligations, institutions, formulas, and rituals characteristic of the closed society (TS 49–50/1016–17).

TEN

Bergson and Human Rights

Alexandre Lefebvre

Henri Bergson is difficult to place with respect to the human rights tradition. In terms of a concrete contribution to international institutions of human rights, he is unique among major philosophers. As the French emissary to the United States during the First World War, Bergson was instrumental in persuading Woodrow Wilson to enter the war and worked with the Wilson government to establish the League of Nations. Later, he was appointed president of the League's International Commission for Intellectual Cooperation (the precursor to UNESCO).[1] And not least important, Bergson had a profound intellectual influence on John Humphrey who was the principal drafter of the *Universal Declaration of Human Rights* (1948). As one historian puts it, "Humphrey kept a journal of his private thoughts during his early tenure at the United Nations. From these journals, it is apparent that he came to view the *Universal Declaration* in terms of Bergson's book *The Two Sources of Morality and Religion*."[2]

In terms of his contribution to the philosophy of human rights though, Bergson's impact would seem to be negligible. On the one hand, he is virtually unknown in contemporary human rights discourse. And on the other hand, as if to justify this neglect, he dedicates only two short sets of pages to human rights, both of which are in *Two Sources* (TS 74–81/1037–46, 281–83/1214–16).

Let's start with the second point. A major goal of this chapter is to show that human rights are not a subject of particular or local interest in *Two Sources*. They are not one topic among others, as if their importance for Bergson corresponded to the direct attention he gives them. Instead, human rights are the organizing center of his political philosophy. By this I mean that Bergson's political philosophy can be unlocked by a focus on human rights; and that he brings his entire metaphysical project to bear on them. More specifically, in *Two Sources* human rights serve as a perspective from which to evaluate institutions, types of government, and what we might generally call political phenomena. In this sense I suggest that human rights in *Two Sources* have the same importance as the republic in Plato's *Republic* or democracy in Spinoza's *Theological Political Treatise*: human rights are at once a specific institution (hence the dedicated pages), but, much more importantly, they are also the means to judge the sense, value, and orientation of all other political forms.

But if I'm right, why is Bergson not more widely read on human rights? Why has he been ignored by mainstream discourses of human rights?

A main reason, no doubt, is that *Two Sources* (1932) is written prior to the Holocaust. Consider how Hannah Arendt opens her essay critical of human rights: "It is almost impossible even now to describe what actually happened in Europe on August 4, 1914. The days before and after the First World War are separated not like the end of an old and the beginning of a new period, but like the day before and the day after an explosion."[3] What the First World War was to a generalized European consciousness, the Holocaust is to the philosophy and practice of human rights. It is a rupture that redefines everything: it shows the theoretical and practical inadequacy of existing human rights institutions (notably, the League of Nations);[4] it reveals a new depth of evil against which human rights must brace themselves;[5] and it precipitates the creation of our present-day human rights institutions, such as the United Nations and the *Universal Declaration*.[6] Seen through the historical index of the Holocaust, Bergson's theory of human rights is likely to seem quaint, of period interest only, and unequipped to deal with the challenges of the present moment. And if we also we note Bergson's enthusiasm for the failed League of Nations, and his reliance on theories of vitalism and pantheism that certain critics, such as Adorno,[7] hold to be blasphemous in light of the

Holocaust, it is unsurprising that Bergson has been forgotten in the world of human rights.

But perhaps it is not just obscurity that keeps Bergson at a distance from human rights discourse. It could also be principled opposition. I mean that while there has been no direct encounter between Bergson and the contemporary "postmetaphysical" liberal tradition in human rights, I suspect that if this tradition did have occasion to turn to *Two Sources*, it would have special reasons to reject it. I have in mind the argument made by John Rawls, Michael Ignatieff, and Martha Nussbaum among others that it is both unnecessary and undesirable to search for the grounds of human rights. In this view human rights are a strictly political instrument designed to protect individuals, and attempts to find a foundation for them are divisive, violent, and ultimately ineffective.[8] Bergson's *The Two Sources of Morality and Religion*—indeed, its very title—is in direct contradiction to this line of argument. Here, to start, I list Bergson's three major theses on human rights.

1 Human rights are biologically grounded. They do not merely protect life; they are an expression of life.
2 Human rights are religious. They are not merely a secularized theological concept. Instead, they *are* religious and enjoy the same relationship to the divine as does, for example, the Christian Church.
3 The primary purpose of human rights is to transform the human species rather than merely protect it.

Put starkly like this, of course, Bergson is bound to seem far-out. The plan of this chapter is to work backward and reconstruct each thesis in order to show Bergson's pertinence for human rights today. But to do that, we must first define human rights.

A DEFINITION OF HUMAN RIGHTS

Whenever Bergson is confronted with a phenomenon to define, he proceeds pragmatically. His first move—whether faced, for example, with intelligence, instinct, or religion—is always to ask "how does x enhance action and secure survival?" Accordingly, the phenomenon in question is defined by the action it makes possible: human intelligence is the ability to "think matter" (CE ix/489); instinct is the faculty of using "organized instruments" (CE 143/616); and (static) religion is a reaction against the "dissolvent power of intelligence" (TS 122/1078). In essence, *a thing is defined by what it does to ensure survival.* We can readily adapt this form of definition to human rights: how do human rights enhance the action and secure the survival of the human species?

Writing on the eve of the Second World War, survival is very much on Bergson's mind. As he puts it in the penultimate sentence of *Two Sources,* "[Ours] is the task of determining first of all whether [we] want to go on living or not [*continuer à vivre*]" (TS 317/1245). I propose that for Bergson, human rights are *the* institution that determines both whether we *shall* go on living and, incredibly, whether we will *want to* go on living. To these two goals—shall and want—correspond the two functions of human rights in *Two Sources:*

1 To protect human beings against our natural tendency toward closure, hatred, and war.
2 To initiate human beings into a new and open form of relationship, which Bergson calls love.

These are the two simultaneous functions of human rights. The first protects: human rights are an institution with the force of law designed to ensure survival. And the second converts: human rights are an institution to initiate people into a way of life (i.e., love) that makes us want to survive. Put in the form of a schematic definition, *human rights are the institution that protects us from hate and converts us to love.*

CRITIQUE OF HUMAN RIGHTS

I have defined Bergson's idea of human rights with concepts of emotion (*sentiment*, in French) to bring us to his critique of the human rights tradition. It is this: if human rights are understood rationalistically, that is, if the source and motivation behind human rights is seen to be reason and not emotion, human rights become ineffective and moralistic. Or, phrased in pragmatic terms, a rationalistic approach to human rights vitiates what they can do.

Here is a key place to connect Bergson with the human rights tradition. We'll begin with Bergson's confrontation with his own contemporaries before moving to our own.

Emile Durkheim, the founder of the discipline of sociology, is Bergson's main interlocutor in the first chapter of *Two Sources,* "Moral Obligation." This fact often goes unrecognized because Durkheim is named only twice in *Two Sources* (TS 104/1063, 134/1089) and not at all in chapter 1. Nevertheless, his presence is undeniable: the beginning and end of that chapter insistently and critically deploys Durkheimian terms ("pressure," "obligation," "society," "constraint," "[social life] as a fact," and so on); and, moreover in his correspondence, Bergson explicitly names the "Durkheimian school" as his object of criticism in chapter 1.[9] Although by now it is established that Bergson's concept of moral obligation is formed in response to Durkheim,[10] I want to argue a narrower point: Bergson's concept of human rights emerges from within the context of his critical engagement with Durkheim and, as such, is only understood when viewed within this broader framework.

So what is Bergson's objection to Durkheim? It is a curious critique because *Two Sources* appears to open with widespread agreement. Durkheim, Bergson seems to say, gets everything right about society: he rightly conceives of society as held together by pressure (TS 23/993–94); he richly describes a phenomenology of social obligation (TS 9/981); he appreciates that obligation is rooted in durable practices and habits (TS 26/996); and he sees that social pressure checks egoism while simultaneously shaping the self (TS 14–15/986). But there is one all-important shortcoming. It is that Durkheim fails to see that the source of society—and hence the source of pressure, obligation, habit, and all the rest—is biological. And this, for Bergson, is decisive: "Everything is obscure if we keep ourselves to mere manifestations, whether they are all indiscriminately called social, or whether one examines, in social man, more particularly the feature of intelligence. All becomes clear, on the contrary, if we go and search beyond these manifestations for life itself. Let us then give to the word biology the very wide [*compréhensif*] meaning it should have, and will perhaps have one day, and let us say in conclusion that all morality, be it pressure or aspiration, is in essence biological" (TS 100–101/1060–61; translation modified). These closing lines of chapter 1 are the definitive statement of Bergson's critique of Durkheim. His reproach, quite literally, is that Durkheim's theory of society is *superficial*—it adequately describes the "manifestations" of the social but misses their biological source.[11] This results in two shortcomings. On the one hand, Bergson charges Durkheim with theoretical confusion: by failing to relate social phenomena to their biological source they remain obscure. And on the other hand, we will see that Bergson charges Durkheim with political confusion: by failing to relate social phenomena to their biological source, he is blind to their limited sphere of application.

"Everything is obscure," says Bergson. Maybe so; but in *Two Sources* one phenomenon exemplifies this confusion: human rights, or rather, a certain conception of human rights. In particular, Bergson addresses a widespread and pernicious illusion—that human rights are simply the extension of political rights to a universal community: "We are fond of saying [*on se plaît à dire*] that the apprenticeship to civic virtue is served in the family, and that in the same way, from holding our country dear, we learn to love mankind [*le genre humain*]. Our sympathies are supposed to broaden out [*s'élargirait*] in an unbroken progression, to expand while remaining identical, and to end by embracing all humanity" (*TS* 32/1001). We are tempted to think of human rights as the outermost ripple of a pond: because love and obligation do in fact extend from family to nation, we believe it takes only one more concentric circle to cover all of mankind. In this view love of nation (but really, love of any determinate group) and love of mankind are continuous. Or, in Bergson's terms, this picture of human rights holds that between nation and humankind lies a quantitative difference in degree, not a qualitative difference in kind.

Now this picture of human rights can't be confined to a singular interlocutor. It is widespread, just the sort of thing Wittgenstein would say naturally inhabits language: we simply project our idea of love onto one group and then another.[12] One particularly striking version is given by W. E. H. Lecky in his *History of European Morals*: "At one time the benevolent affections embrace merely the family, soon the circle expanding includes first a class, then a nation, then a coalition of nations, then all humanity, and finally, its influence is felt in the dealings of man with the animal world."[13] Nevertheless, it seems to me that seeing Durkheim as the source, heuristically at least, of such a position brings out the full force of Bergson's criticism of human rights. Why? Because Bergson submits this picture of human rights—that is, that the affections and obligations characteristic of national solidarity can be universally extended—to the same criticism he makes of Durkheim: we come to it only by ignoring the biological source of human rights. It should come as no surprise, therefore, that Durkheim repeatedly articulates this position: "Man always lives in the midst of many *groups*. . . . Despite certain simplistic statements that have been made, *there is no necessary antagonism between* these three *loyalties*. . . . Family, nation, and humanity represent different *phases* of our social and moral evolution, *stages* that prepare for, and build upon, one another. Consequently, these groups may be *superimposed* without excluding one another. . . . It is not a matter then of making an exclusive choice among them. Man is morally complete only when governed by the threefold force they exercise on him."[14] And, in another work: "As we advance in evolution, we see the ideals men pursue breaking free of the local or ethnic conditions . . . and rising above all that is particular and so approaching the universal. We might say that the moral forces rank themselves [*se hiérarchisent*] according to their degree of generality! Thus, everything justifies our belief that national aims do not lie at *the summit* of this hierarchy—it is human aims that are destined to be supreme."[15]

Just look at the different registers in which Durkheim establishes continuity and compatibility between national and universal morality: mathematical (both are sets, "groups"), affective (loyalty attaches us to both groups), moral (both represent stages on a moral continuum), developmental (both are phases of evolution), and ontological (the two can coexist). But behind all of these registers is a single driving point: in principle, the idea of a *human society* is not paradoxical or contradictory. While the realization of human society may be remote, it is fundamental to Durkheim that morality—which is always already social and includes legal as well as more strictly "moral" obligations[16]—can indefinitely expand to include all mankind. In this sense universal morality has two roles: it is a regulative ideal to guide nations, and, through institutions such as human rights, it is a fact working to establish itself. In other words the morality of nations is tractable and can be guided by a universal aspiration, and the morality of nations can ground and support human rights.[17]

Turning back to *Two Sources*, Bergson paraphrases the kind of schema held by Durkheim: "We observe that the three groups [family, nation, and humanity] to which we can attach ourselves comprise an increasing number of people, and we conclude that a progressive expansion of feeling [*une dilatation progressive du sentiment*] keeps pace with the increasing size of the object we love" (*TS* 32/1001–2). But here Bergson pauses and raises the problem of a brutal fact that does not seem to fit with Durkheim's picture of human rights—what about war? If the feelings and duties of a particular society can naturally extend to mankind—or better, if some nations do in fact profess respect for humanity and have mature human rights institutions—how is war possible? In other words, if Durkheim's picture of love, obligation, and human rights is adequate, how do we explain the omnipresence of war? Where do we place it?

It is a commonplace, especially in liberal political thought, to treat war as exceptional. Or, as Bergson puts it from another angle, the suspension of human rights in war is assumed to be temporary and abnormal: "[Society says] that the duties it defines are indeed, in principle, duties toward humanity, but that under exceptional circumstances, regrettably unavoidable, they are for the time being suspended" (TS 31/1001; translation modified).[18] But this explanation is unsatisfying. Indeed, it begs the question: why would any society that acknowledges duties toward all others go to war? For Bergson, it doesn't make sense: if we see peace (underwritten by universal sympathy and duty) as the norm and war as the exception, the latter becomes inexplicable. But if, by contrast, we acknowledge that war is the norm and peace the exception, they both make perfect sense. And this is his position: "Peace has always been a preparation for defense or even attack, at any rate for war" (TS 31/1001). Peace, however long, is a suspension of hostilities. A stable peace will stay war but can never hope to eradicate it. To borrow Durkheimian terms—which, incidentally, Bergson does (TS 31/1001)—preparation for war is a normal and not pathological state of society.

Perhaps this sounds extreme.[19] But consider it from the perspective of Bergson's evolutionary pragmatism. Grant his premise—uncontroversial for most of us—that war is natural and ineradicable. The question becomes: how has the human species survived itself? Bergson's answer is unequivocal: we have formed societies; or rather, we have evolved as social beings. Natural aggressiveness and natural sociability are co-original: the protection and security of society is the evolutionary solution to the problem of war.[20] (No doubt society also organizes and channels aggression, but that only makes the need for security all the more basic.) And not just any kind of society, of course, but one defined by preparation for war.[21] Obviously, Bergson does not mean that the everyday state of society is armament, tension, and suspicion. Instead he means that everyday social life is geared toward fellowship, stability, and security. As he puts it, "who can help seeing that social cohesion is largely due to the necessity for a community to protect itself against others" (TS 32–33/1002)?

A host of implications follow for human rights from this connection between biology, society, and security. Bergson sums them up with his concept of the *closed society*, which, in fact, designates a tendency toward closure on the part of all societies. This concept has several different dimensions, such that society is closed in all of the following ways:

- Political: "[The] essential characteristic of the [closed society is to] include at any moment a certain number of individuals, and exclude others" (TS 30/1000).
- Moral: "Obligation always has in view . . . a closed society, however large" (TS 32/1001).
- Affective: "It is primarily as against all other men that we love the men with whom we live" (TS 33/1002).

We can now bring Bergson's criticism to a point: the purpose of the rights, duties, and fellowship of a society is to secure and promote *that* society (i.e., that determinate group). It is, therefore, both theoretically incorrect and politically disastrous to believe that the obligation and love characteristic of the closed tendency of society can simply extend beyond its borders to include all human beings. That is Durkheim's mistake, according to Bergson. More particularly, if we fail to see the biological source of morality—that is, if we fail to see that social morality is a constitutively closed morality—human rights do in fact become what certain critics have always suspected them to be: rationalistic and moralistic. On the one hand, they appear as they did to Edmund Burke: an abstract extension of the real rights of a community. As Bergson puts it, the smooth steps from family to nation to humanity are nothing but the product of "*a priori reasoning*, the result of a purely intellectualist conception of the soul" (TS 32/1001). And on the other hand, human rights appear as a mere piety that folds at the slightest threat to the nation. They become, as in Arendt's cruel phrase, "the uncertain sentiments of professional idealists": at once sanctimonious and scolding, human rights draw imaginary strength from a closed source that will not back them when it counts.[22]

FIRST FUNCTION OF HUMAN RIGHTS: PROTECTION

As severe as Bergson's criticism of human rights is, he does not, of course, give up on them. In the following two sections, we turn to their unique and indispensable functions: protection and conversion.

By focusing on Bergson's positive concept of human rights, we have a chance to develop an underappreciated element of his philosophy: what Gilles Deleuze calls his "superior empiricism."[23] Consider Bergson's opening line in *Creative Mind*: "What philosophy has lacked most of all is precision." "The only explanation," he elaborates, "that we should consider satisfactory is one glued to its object, with no gap between them . . . one which fits the object only and to which alone the object lends itself [*elle ne convient qu'à lui, il ne se prête qu'à elle*]" (CM 11/1253; translation modified). We've already seen this criticism in action: Bergson's objection to Durkheim is that *human* rights cannot extend the obligation and solidarity characteristic of *political* rights. A major ambition of *Two Sources*—its superior empiricism, if you will—is to create a concept of human rights that acknowledges the singularity of this institution.

How? Bergson tackles human rights with a method tried and tested throughout his oeuvre. It is this: for Bergson, all phenomena—each experience, every life form, and all societies—are composed of two distinct tendencies. His different books give these tendencies different names: most often, they are "time" and "space"; in *Two Sources*, they are "open" and "closed." Society, politics, religion, morality, and, of course, human rights, are all "composite" for Bergson, that is, mixtures of open and closed tendencies. Bergson's central methodological claim is that we cannot properly see a phenomenon until we recognize that it is composed of two distinct tendencies. And to do that, he proposes a two-step procedure: *divide* the composite into pure tendencies and *reassemble* the tendencies back into the object. He repeats this operation so often that Deleuze goes so far as to call it a rule and its complement:

1 Divide. "SECOND RULE: Struggle against illusion, rediscover the true differences in kind or articulations of the real."
2 Reassemble. "[A] COMPLEMENTARY RULE to the second rule: The real is not only that which is cut out . . . [*se découpe*—i.e., divides] according to natural articulations or differences in kind; it is also that which intersects again . . . (*se récoupe*—i.e., reassembles] along paths converging toward the same ideal or virtual point."[24]

Or, in plainer terms: (1) Everything is a mix of two tendencies. (2) The fact of mixture makes it difficult to see a phenomenon with any precision. (3) We divide the phenomenon into its pure tendencies in order to isolate and analyze them. (4) Equipped with a new awareness of the tendencies, we reassemble the tendencies back into the object and achieve a precise view of its actual mixed reality.

It is crucial to emphasize that this procedure must always involve both steps: to stop at division would wrongly imply that a purely open or closed phenomenon exists. It does not. For example, there is no such thing as *a* closed or *an* open human society: the former would amount to a society of ants (TS 25/995), the latter to a society of Christs (TS 59/1024, 240/1179). And neither are open and closed regulative ideals to be achieved: they are not something toward which we might make infinite progress (TS 84/1046). Rather, pure tendencies are strictly heuristic and intended to provide concepts with a better—that is, accurate, closer fitting—hold on the world. A Bergsonian study of human rights, therefore, must stress both moments of the method: division into their pure tendencies and reassembly into their composite reality. It must start with the composite and end with the composite.

Let's return to Bergson's problem. Our everyday idea of human rights is confused: love of family → love of nation → love of mankind. In particular, our idea of love is confused: it indifferently groups different kinds of love under the same word, such that we think it can be extended without modification. (In Deleuze's language, our everyday idea of love is a false composite that entails sterile repetition.) In the face of this confusion, we should practice Bergson's division into purely closed and open tendencies. Late in *Two Sources* he distills the closed society and open society into two formulas (TS 282/1215). This is how they look in their pure state:

- ᐧ Closed society: Authority, hierarchy, and immobility.
- ᐧ Open society: Liberty, equality, and fraternity.

Bergson intends for these mottos "to tally, word for word" (TS 282/1215). But while the oppositions between (1) authority and liberty and (2) hierarchy and equality strike us as intuitive, the opposition between immobility and fraternity might seem strange. Immobility and movement, certainly; fraternity and clan, possibly; but why immobility and fraternity? To make sense of this opposition, we must see that in *Two Sources* the words "open" and "closed" take on a double sense, one that corresponds to ordinary usage.[25] On the one hand, "open" means open-ended, unsettled, and up in the air. And on the other hand, "open" means inclusive and welcoming. It is this double sense of "open" that Bergson exploits in his formula. Here, "fraternity" stands not only for inclusiveness but also for movement, creation, and indetermination. This snaps "frater-nity's" opposition to "immobility" into focus: the closed society excludes and immobilizes, whereas the open society includes and moves.

But here we should pause to remember that every society realizes both of these tendencies. While in some societies—for example, tyrannies—the closed tendency predominates, whereas in others—for example, de-mocracies—the open prevails, every society, along with each of its institu-tions, stands for a unique and simultaneous actualization of both open *and* closed tendencies. It follows, therefore, that for Bergson human rights are *at once* exclusive and inclusive, immobilizing and creative. What could this mean? Or, to get a handle on this question, what could it mean for any institution to express all of these qualities?

Although Bergson gives us little indication of how human rights simul-taneously express both tendencies, he provides a pertinent model in the case of religion. The crucial point for our investigation is his discussion of the origin and function of religion. For Bergson, the genesis of any reli-gion is roughly the same: it codifies and disseminates the teachings of an individual (a "mystic," in his terms) who strongly embodies the open tendency. (Christ is, of course, the preeminent example, but Bergson discusses other mystical figures such as Socrates, Moses, and Buddha.) Religion is the translation (or crystallization) of mysticism into an in-stitution: "We represent religion, then, as the crystallization, brought about by a scientific process of cooling, of what mysticism had poured, white hot, into the soul of man" (TS 238/1177; translation modified). Or again, "since [mystics] cannot communicate to the world at large the deepest elements of their spiritual condition, they transpose it super-ficially; they seek a translation of the dynamic into the static which society may accept and stabilize [*rendre définitive*] by education" (TS 274/1208). All religion, therefore, is animated by an open intuition that it converts into a doctrine (which immobilizes the meaning of mysticism) and shapes into a congregation (which excludes nonbelievers). Doctrine and congregation are not, for Bergson, things to condemn: all he shows is the necessity for the open tendency to transform and anchor itself in a stable composite institution.

But if this is the genesis and role of religion, could we not say the same for human rights? More strongly, can we not say that human rights are, in the strictest sense, religious?[26] *They institutionalize the heart of the open tendency*: universal love, that is, love without preference, exclusion, or hatred. Just like religion—or rather, in exactly the same way as religion (which, given Bergson's pragmatism, means religiously)—human rights take a dynamic tendency and transform it into a series of rules backed by social pressure *and* expose great numbers of people to that tendency. I can thus restate the two functions of human rights in light of the open tendency they translate.

1 Conversion. Human rights seek to expose and initiate people into a mode of love that is different from the partial or preferential love of the closed society. The aim is that norms of human rights will instill (or rather, awaken) the open tendency in each and every human being. I will focus on this aspect in the next section.

2 Protection. Human rights seek to prevent and check the dangerous aspects of the closed tendency. Here, the aim is not to convert but to protect, and, to this end, human rights intervene with legal or even military pressure if necessary. I will conclude the section with this point.

That human rights have a closed tendency at all may strike us as paradoxical. For isn't their entire purpose to counteract the dangers of the closed tendency such as exclusion, xenophobia, and persecution? Yes it is, and, to that end, I take Bergson to affirm that human rights attempt to turn the closed tendency against itself. In this sense they perform a classic dialectical operation: they negate and preserve central features of the closed tendency. Below are three instances of the closed tendency, each of which characterizes a different part of the human rights machinery.

➤ *Declarations and Conventions.* "Every sentence of the Declaration of the Rights of Man is a challenge to some abuse. . . . Above all, they are applicable only if transposed, absolute and semi-evangelical, into terms of purely relative morality or rather of general utility" (TS 283/1216; translation modified). Bergson is explicit that human rights actualize absolute justice through the medium of laws. As such, they prosecute justice by means of prohibitions and obligations (see TS 74/1037).

➤ *International Interventions.* A central purpose of bodies like the United Nations is to alleviate the causes of war and intervene in desperate situations. Should nations prove recalcitrant to these aims, Bergson argues that they must be compelled: "it is a dangerous mistake to think that an international institution [*organisme international*] can obtain permanent peace without having the authority to intervene in the legislation of the various countries, and even perhaps in their governments" (TS 290/1222). Let us put to the side the massive practical difficulties and theoretical problems raised by downplaying state sovereignty this way. The point I wish to stress is that in the same way that social pressure curbs the egoism of individuals, Bergson argues that so too must international pressure—for example, opprobrium, sanctions, even intervention—curb the egoism of nations.

➤ *International Criminal Courts.* In the open tendency love is all-inclusive. But the same cannot be said of human rights. They establish an outsider within the idea of humanity itself: the war criminal, that is, the individual whose acts place himself outside the human community. Bergson too acknowledges this figure (though his language hides the point): "Some people are doubtless utterly closed [*totalement fermés*] to the mystic experience, incapable of feeling or imagining anything of it" (TS 246/1184; translation modified). In Bergson's terms, the war criminal and the (complete, or nearly complete) non-mystic are coextensive: they designate an individual in whom—whether by constitution or custom—the open tendency is negligible. Thus, if the open tendency cannot move certain people, it is necessary to have an institution that punishes and deters them.

As we can see, Bergson acknowledges and, within limits, affirms a closed tendency in human rights. But where does that leave us? Doesn't this argument make human rights vulnerable to his original criticism of Durkheim: that they problematically borrow the social pressure characteristic of moral and legal obligation? Yes it does, and Bergson knows it: "The difficulty of abolishing war is greater even than is generally realized by most people who have no faith in its abolition. . . . Even if the League of Nations had at its disposal a seemingly adequate armed force . . . it would come up against the deep-rooted war-instinct underlying civilization" (TS 287/1219–20). To say that Bergson's faith in the League of Nations— and its vision of human rights—is faint puts the point generously. Then, as now, national priorities trump international obligations, such that when national interests are threatened, support for international pressure evaporates. In other words, insofar as we concentrate on the closed tendency of human rights, Bergson turns his original criticism of Durkheim on himself: human rights are practicable only when remote from the interests of those societies that maintain them. What hope then does he have for them?

But this is the wrong question. The better question is—and the one that allows us to assess his hope—what is the purpose of his critique of human rights? This purpose comes into view once we place it within his critique of Durkheim.

Recall Bergson's conclusion: Durkheim accurately describes the features of social life but misses their source in biology. He does not, for example, contradict Durkheim by saying that society is *not* held together by pressure and obligation; instead, he grants their place as the actualization of the closed tendency. In other words Bergson performs an exemplary Kantian critique: he confines pressure to one part of the social and, in so doing, clears room for the open tendency. In short he limits the closed tendency to its proper place and, in so doing, introduces the open tendency as necessary to both describe and direct our institutions.

It is from within this context that we can appreciate Bergson's critique of human rights. Its purpose is to create a *multifaceted* concept of human rights, one that can acknowledge the place and purpose of *both* the closed and open tendency. As we have seen, human rights problematically actualize elements of the closed tendencies as protection from the closed society. At once necessary and flawed, Bergson affirms this facet of human rights all the while sharply noting its defects. But, just as in his critique of Durkheim, *Bergson confines the closed tendency of human rights to a limited sphere of application.* His goal is to show us that the closed tendency does not exhaust the function or ambition of human rights. And so, to answer the question of what hope Bergson has for human rights we must pass to the other, open, and primary purpose of human rights: conversion.

SECOND FUNCTION OF HUMAN RIGHTS: CONVERSION

Earlier I said that for Bergson rationalism vitiates a theory of human rights. We've encountered one aspect of this argument: it is an intellectualistic error to think we can quantitatively expand the love characteristic of the closed tendency to include all humanity. But Bergson also makes another, more trenchant criticism of rationalism: reason (i.e., concepts and representations) is powerless to affect the will.[27] Here is a picturesque version of the argument: "Never, in our hours of temptation, should we sacrifice to the mere need for logical consistency our interest, our passion, our vanity" (*TS* 23/994). And again, this time chiding his fellow philosophers: "Our admiration for the speculative function of the mind may be great; but when philosophers maintain that it should be sufficient to silence selfishness and passion, they prove to us—and this is a matter for congratulation—that they have never heard the voice of the one or the other very loud within themselves" (TS 87/1048–49).

In a nutshell, Bergson's argument is that emotion and not reason primarily motivates conduct. Once again, this claim is grounded in an evolutionary perspective. In *Two Sources* two emotions are basic: social pressure and aspiration. Pressure is the emotion associated with the closed tendency of life; it preserves social discipline by keeping egoism in check. Aspiration is the emotion associated with the open tendency of life; it introduces into society the dynamism that for Bergson characterizes life itself (the *élan vital*). For the moment, the details of pressure and aspiration are secondary. The thing to consider is that for Bergson, conduct is primarily informed by these two emotions. This argument has a theoretical and practical dimension. Theoretically speaking, Bergson invokes a kind of parallelism: in this scheme, an idea can only primarily affect another idea, and only an emotion can primarily affect another emotion.[28] Ideas and representations are not without importance—for example, they introduce consistency into a line of conduct and also validate certain emotional responses (TS 22/993)—but Bergson is explicit that the forces that animate our will are extrarational: the pressure of the closed society is "sub-rational," whereas the love of the open tendency is "supra-rational" (TS 84/1046). Practically speaking, Bergson insists that a line of conduct will only change if one emotion checks another. If, therefore, the conduct and morality of a society change, the cause will not be found in a new moral theory but rather in a new actualization of the closed (pressure) and open (aspiration) tendencies of life.

The implications for Bergson's theory of human rights are immediate. If the purpose of human rights is to preserve us from the destructive emotions of the closed tendency, and if only an emotion is able to check another emotion, then at the core of human rights we should expect to find emotion. And this is precisely Bergson's thesis: *the essence of human rights is love*. We can restate the point. The closed tendency of society is dangerous because it confines love to fellow citizens and regards outsiders with hatred and alienation (TS 286/1219). The purpose of human rights, therefore, is to meet this closed conception of love with one that is open: that is, to fight love with love. We will expand this concept of love in a moment, but, for now, the essential point for Bergson is to acknowledge human rights as first and foremost an emotional force: only then will they be able to do their job and counteract the closed tendency.

Bergson is not alone in arguing that emotion is central for human rights. Indeed, Michael Ignatieff, a contemporary liberal theorist of human rights, has made a case for it:

> A secular defense of human rights depends on the idea of moral reciprocity: that we judge human actions by the simple test of whether we would wish to be on the receiving end. And since we cannot conceive of any circumstances in which we or anyone we know would wish to be abused in mind or body, we have good reasons to believe that such practices should be outlawed. That we are capable of this thought experiment— that is, that we possess the faculty of imagining the pain and degradation done to other human beings as if it were our own—is simply a fact about us as a species. Because we are all capable of this form of limited empathy, we all possess a conscience.[29]

This passage is an excellent occasion to bring out Bergson's originality: it blends emotional and rational elements in precisely the way he finds objectionable. Ignatieff's argument, I take it, elaborates the Golden Rule: human rights proscribe harmful practices that we ourselves wish to avoid. To reach this conclusion, he takes the following steps: 1. We wish to avoid pain. 2. We can imagine the pain of others. 3. The idea of moral reciprocity leads us outlaw practices (1) that we would wish to avoid and (2) that we know cause pain to others. It is with respect to the third step that Bergson makes a decisive intervention. On his terms, it is either deluded (if it means that practical reason can by itself outlaw practices) or else it presupposes the essential (if it means that practical reason is imbued with love).

We can put the criticism this way. Ignatieff appears to identify our capacity to imagine the pain of others with conscience. But this is an unwarranted and dangerous leap. Our ability to imagine the pain of others is a morally neutral capacity: it can be both the reason why we harm and the reason why we protect other beings. Think of a child engrossed in torturing an insect: obviously, this action depends on the capacity to imagine the pain of the creature, on knowing that it is being made to writhe rather than just move. (Or the reverse: if in our minds we substitute a leaf for the insect, it becomes difficult to picture the same absorption and delight in the child.) The point is that the capacity to imagine the pain of others cannot ground human rights because it can equally serve as the foundation for human rights *or* very the reason for why we need them. In short, Ignatieff rides roughshod over Bergson's very real insight that the empathy, conscience, and love of the closed tendency can motivate atrocity. Or, to restate the opposition, for Ignatieff we need human rights because individuals ignore their conscience, whereas for Bergson we need human rights because atrocity is most often committed in the name of conscience.

The ability to imagine the pain of others, therefore, needs a tutor. But Bergson would object to both options proposed by Ignatieff: on the one hand, to identify this ability with conscience is dangerous because it can serve either closed or open morality, and, on the other hand, to believe it will simply be guided by reason ("moral reciprocity") is fantastic. In light of this criticism, we can state Bergson's positive contribution: human rights are not based on the ability to imagine the pain of others; rather, they are a way to manage and shape that ability. And the way they do that is by initiating human beings into the definitive emotion of the open tendency, love.[30] This is the second and key function of human rights.

Let us proceed directly to love. What is the hallmark of human rights? Universality: they apply to all human beings as human beings. For Bergson, this inclusiveness derives directly from the open tendency and love: "[What] is allowed in? Suppose we say that [the open soul] embraces all humanity: we should not be going too far . . . since its love may extend to animals, to plants, to all nature. And yet no one of these things which would thus fill it would suffice to define the attitude taken by the soul, for it could, strictly speaking, do without all of them. *Its form is not dependent on its content.* We have just filled it; we could as easily empty it again" (*TS* 38/1006–7; emphasis added). No doubt, it is difficult to wrap one's head around this kind of pure objectless love. It outstrips even Christian love, directed as it is to the universal neighbor. But for our purposes, we needn't go into it. All that is necessary to show is that for Bergson human rights institutionalize a (mystical or open) love that is without preference or attachment. Certainly, human rights limit this love to human beings (and mark an exclusion with nonhuman animals and the environment); nevertheless, the ambition to preserve all human beings without attention to group attachment is inconceivable within the logic of the closed tendency.

At the start of this chapter, I claimed that human rights are the organizing center of Bergson's political philosophy. We now see why: *they are the political institution that most purely embodies the open tendency.*

- ► Human rights are the unique political institution that endeavors to care for all human beings equally.
- ► Human rights introduce the criterion of the open to political judgment, which provides a new standard of assessment of governments and institutions.
- ► Human rights proselytize and have become the most widely shared bearer of the open tendency.

I will conclude with this last point on the proselytizing nature of human rights. In *Two Sources* Bergson explicitly makes the connection between human rights and dynamic religion: "Humanity had to wait until Christianity for the idea of universal brotherhood, with its implication of equality of rights and the inviolability of the person, to become operative. Some may say that it has been rather a slow process; indeed eighteen centuries elapsed before the rights of man were proclaimed by the Puritans of America, soon followed by the men of the French Revolution. It began, nevertheless, with the teachings of the Gospels" (*TS* 78/1040–41; translation modified). I take it Bergson makes an observation most often associated with the later Wittgenstein: for an utterance or question (or institution) to be so much as possible, the necessary forms of life must be in place to motivate and sustain it.[31] Human rights do not come out of the blue but require centuries of preparation and the slow spread of universal love. Only once this new kind of love becomes a widespread form of life is the leap to human rights imaginable: "The method [of the mystics] consisted in supposing possible what is actually impossible in a given society, in imagining what would be its effect on the soul of society, and then inducing some such psychic condition by propaganda and example: the effect, once obtained, would retrospectively complete its cause; new feelings, evanescent indeed, would *call forth the new legislation seemingly indispensable to their appearance, and which would then serve to consolidate them*" (*TS* 78/1041; emphasis added).

Earlier I cited Bergson to the effect that the relationship between mysticism and religion is one-way: religion was simply the effect or "crystallization" of mysticism (*TS* 238/1177). I then concluded that because human rights perform this same crystallizing function, they are properly called religious. In this above passage, however, the relationship between mysticism and human rights is reciprocal. It takes the form of stages. First, the mystic (i.e., any human being inspired by the open tendency, whether saint or statesman)[32] presumes the condition for the declaration of human rights: that the open tendency is widespread and well anchored in society. Second, "the new legislation," that is, human rights, is declared. Third, human rights—as the institutional embodiment of the open tendency—disseminate the open tendency and thereby retrospectively achieve their condition of existence: the widespread presence of love. To put it in religious terms, the last step performs the conversion presupposed in the first step: hence, the proselytizing function of human rights.

Throughout this chapter I have tried to present Bergson's superior empiricism. The virtue of his concept of human rights is that it is multifaceted: it acknowledges their closed and open face. On the one hand, he affirms the traditional vision of human rights as an institution backed by legal, social, and economic pressure. And although Bergson concedes that this function is fated to fail in the most serious situations, he nevertheless insists on the need for an institution that can turn the closed tendency against itself. But, on the other hand, Bergson brings to light a lesser known but perhaps more fundamental function of human rights: conversion to love, that is, to initiate all human beings into a universal love irreducible to the closed tendency.

These are the two sides of human rights. Certainly, human rights documents contain a list of articles that represent international agreement on how human beings must be treated. And hopefully, these documents include enforcement mechanisms to put pressure on compliance. But, with a slight shift in perspective, these same documents are also *the* contemporary bearer of an open tendency. Each article is, therefore, both a rule to guide conduct *and* a message "to bring about a certain state of the soul" (TS 59/1025; translation modified). Hence, the two incredible ambitions Bergson sets for human rights. First, not just to ensure our survival but also, by initiating us into the open tendency, to make us not simply want to survive but to be worthy of survival. And second, not to just to preserve the human species but, quite literally, to overcome it by turning us away from the closed tendency.

NOTES

Thanks to Melanie White, Carl Power, and Danielle Celermajer for their valuable comments.

1 For more on Bergson's wartime political responsibilities, see Soulez, *Bergson politique*, 89–126; and Soulez and Worms, *Bergson*, 153–70.

2 Curle, *Humanité*, 6.

3 Arendt, *The Origins of Totalitarianism*, 267.

4 Ibid., 267–302.

5 See Badiou, *Ethics*, 8–9. A central criticism of human rights by Badiou is that they reduce the field of politics to a negative goal: the identification and elimination of evil.

6 See Ishay, *The History of Human Rights*, 173–244.

7 See Adorno, *Metaphysics*, 121.

8 See Rawls, *The Law of Peoples*, 15; Ignatieff, *Human Rights as Politics and Idolatry*, 54; and Nussbaum, *Women and Human Development*, 83.

9 See the recently discovered text by Bergson in de Belloy, "Inédit," 133, 133n2. Also see Bergson's *Correspondances*, where he states, "I consider my last book [i.e., *Two Sources*] to be a sociological book" (c 1387). And in another letter Bergson voices mixed praise for Durkheim when he expresses his dissatisfaction with standing theories of obligation: "No philosopher, in my opinion, has adequately accounted for the presence of obligation, except perhaps for fundamental social duties" (c 1429).

10 See Lefebvre and White, "Bergson on Durkheim."

11 See ibid., 11–12.

12 See Wittgenstein, *Philosophical Investigations*, 115.

13 Lecky, *History of European Morals from Augustus to Charlemagne*, part 1, 100–101.

14 Durkheim, *Moral Education*, 73–74 (emphasis added).

15 Durkheim, *Professional Ethics and Civic Morals*, 72–73 (emphasis added, translation modified).

16 See Durkheim, *Division of Labor*, xx, 221, 331.

17 Or, more precisely, Durkheim holds that the human ideal can only be realized through the most highly developed group we know: nations. That is, although national and human goals must not be conflated, human ideals will only be realized "through the efforts of specific nations." See *Moral Education*, 76–77, as well as Guerlac's contribution to this volume.

18 This quotation is interesting from the point of view of the post–Second World War development of human rights. I take Bergson to say that if nations were to recognize the rights of all human beings, they would refrain from war. And logically, this is no doubt true. Nevertheless human rights have developed into an institution designed primarily to protect individuals from their *own* states, that is, abuses that states commit against their own nationals. This direction in human rights is perhaps most evident in the status of economic and social rights: for example, while there is a weak reference in the *International Covenant on Economic, Social, and Cultural Rights* (1976) for the international community to provide support for states, the primary obligation rests with the states themselves. And so while I do not take this history to contradict Bergson's argument—human rights apply, of course, at an intranational and international level, and abused national citizens are in some sense treated as outsiders—it is noteworthy that the trajectory of human rights is different from the one Bergson had anticipated.

19 This formulation, however, is tame compared to Bergson's later argument that the smaller, almost genteel bygone wars were only a warm-up for the real thing: "if we put side by side with these occasional scraps those *decisive wars which led to the annihilation of a whole people,* we realize that the second account for the first . . . [which occur] simply to keep the sword from rusting" (*TS* 285/1217; emphasis added, translation modified). In other words, genocide is natural: it is not an excess of the war instinct but is its consummation.

20 This view continues to be held in evolutionary biology: "The profound irony is that our noblest achievement—morality—has evolutionary ties to our basest behavior— warfare. The sense of community required by the former was provided by the latter" (Waal, "Morally Evolved," 55).

21 In a summary of chapter 1, Bergson does not mince words: "Such is human society fresh from the hands of nature. . . . Members hold together, caring nothing for the rest of humanity, on the alert for attack or defense, bound, in fact, to a perpetual readiness for battle [*attitude de combat*]" (*TS* 266/1201). This is not an anthropological claim. Bergson is not dreaming up what a *chronologically* original society looks like. Instead, he means to demystify the perception of our own society: if the war instinct is natural and ineradicable, then all societies, no matter how "advanced," are fresh from the hands of nature and battle ready; it is the starting point of every society and one we never move beyond (see *TS* 271/1205–6).

22 Arendt, *The Origins of Totalitarianism,* 292. In many respects Arendt and Bergson's criticisms of human rights dovetail. Her point is that human rights cannot be modeled on an extension of national rights; his point is that human rights cannot be modeled on an extension of national obligations and solidarity.

23 Deleuze, *Bergsonism,* 30.

24 Ibid., 21, 29.

25 See Worms, *Bergson ou les deux sens de la vie,* 271.

26 In this chapter I do not discuss the mythmaking function (*fonction fabulatrice*) of religion with respect to human rights. I take it, however, that nothing excludes the possibility that ideas of intrinsic human dignity and worth—that is, the cornerstone of the human rights imagination—might be mythological, in the robust sense Bergson gives that term: a fiction designed to counteract demoralizing insights of insignificance and meaninglessness.

27 See Carl Power's chapter in this collection.

28 I develop the idea of Bergson's parallelism further in my "Human Rights in the Later Philosophy of Deleuze and Bergson."

29 Ignatieff, *Human Rights as Politics and Idolatry,* 88–89.

30 This idea of initiation is strongly indebted to Cavell's *Claim of Reason,* 169–80.

31 See Wittgenstein, *Philosophical Investigations,* 31.

32 For Bergson's characterization of Woodrow Wilson as a mystic, see Soulez and Worms, *Bergson,* 165.

PART III

Religion and Mysticism

ELEVEN

Bergson and Judaism

Vladimir Jankélévitch
Translated by Melissa McMahon

The problem of the relationship between Bergson and Judaism lies entirely in the conjunction
"and." Moreover, for our problem to be clear in itself, Judaism
would need to have a univocal meaning. But this religion
seems to be at the same time and paradoxically traditionalist
and messianic, formalist in some respects, emotionalist in
others. Judaism is the Law, but it is also Prophecy, and within
the Law itself there is both a juridical and a mystical aspect.
Judaism is Talmudism, but it is also the Hasidic spiritualism
so profoundly examined by Martin Buber. To the problem of
evil, for example, Judaism provides contradictory responses,
the rationalists treating it as privative, some Kabbalists, in
contrast, acknowledging a form of positivity in it. This contradiction is not for that matter absent from Bergsonism
itself, which oscillates between two contradictory definitions
of evil, and there is also a Bergson who is turned toward the
past, in *Time and Free Will*, for example, and a Bergson who,
in *Creative Evolution* and *The Two Sources of Morality and
Religion*, looks rather toward the future.

If there are several Judaisms and if Bergsonism itself is a
complex philosophy, able to justify both a conservative attachment to the past and a form of futurism, both tradition
and messianism, our comparison is in danger of becoming
quite confused. Moreover, certain themes in Bergson that

effectively appear to be biblical, such as the idea of creation or the idea of freedom, can just as well be derived from his reading of the Christian mystics.[1] Conversely, to the extent that the doctrine of creative evolution excludes traditional dogmatism and the idea of the transcendent Creator, Bergson is no less opposed to Christianity than to Judaism. We are thus on an uncomfortable footing in a difficult subject area.

Before discovering the deep affinities, if there are any, let's define what, at first glance, opposes Bergson to Judaism. Those who deny any creative talent in the dilettante of duration and the inner melody accuse Bergson of dragging substance into the flux of becoming. Becoming, the solvent of being, would prevent Bergson from building a genuine architectonic system. We can recognize the same inability to provide grounds for the Absolute in two other great contemporaries of Bergson: Einstein's physical relativism and Georg Simmel's philosophical relativism, which alike dismiss any system of reference, would effectively fall victim to the same reproach. We should firstly respond to this that while Georg Simmel, in *The View of Life* (1918), was in effect influenced by Bergson, Bergson by contrast, in *Duration and Simultaneity*, conducted a lively polemic against Einstein in the name of the duration of common sense.

But even if we suppose Bergson to be a relativist, are we to think that renouncing a system of reference, mobilizing substance, involving the observer and instruments of measure in movement are symptoms of Judaism? In that case there would be nothing Jewish about Hebrew monotheism and Spinoza, who subtracts substance from time and gives reason the privilege of being able to consider things "under a certain aspect of eternity"; Spinoza, who affirms everything that Bergson denies, would be the opposite of a Jew. It will be said that Spinoza was precisely excluded from the synagogue. But it wasn't for his eternitarian and static monism that he was excommunicated! And for that matter, Bergson, who professes diametrically opposed ideas, went right to the very edge of apostasy. In fact we don't see why "Heraclitism" would be, rather than Eleatism, a Jewish specialty: if that were the case we would have to believe that all of the dynamism, historicism, and evolutionism of the nineteenth century was a product of Judaism. The incoherent, arbitrary, and contradictory nature of these reproaches and journalistic generalizations is thus glaringly obvious.

There is a form of temporalism in the Bible that, at first glance, may appear specious. *Creative Evolution*, for the first time, reversed the immemorial pronouncement of Plato's *Timaeus*, taken up again by Plotinus: "time is a moving image of eternity," a pronouncement according to which eternity is the model and time is the inconsistent and quasi-nonexistent image. André Neher radically opposes Hebrew historicism or temporalism and Greek eternalism: the Bible presents itself as a story—first of all the six days of Creation, a series of grandiose events staggered over a week, then the event of sin and finally the historical chronicles. These are three distinct forms of temporality:

1. The *fiat* of the absolute Beginning and the nameless cosmogonic events that follow it are gathered together in a nicely filled Hexameron. These catastrophes, cataclysms, and cataboles, hanging on an initiative more radical than any "clinamen," are expressed in the Scripture in a tense that would be our *passé simple* (simple past or preterite): "*Dieu dit*" (God said), "*Dieu fit l'espace*" (God made space), "*Il fut soir, il fut matin*" (There was evening, there was morning) (Genesis 1:6, 1:5, 1:7). The perfective or semelfactive form of the preterite tense is applied to events that happen once. Is there not as great a distance between the story of Genesis and the Greek cosmogonies,[2] as between the Creator and the Demiurge, between the God of Abraham and the "author of mathematical truths" or "of the order of the elements"?[3] The high temporal drama of Genesis is no less distinct from the "eternal events" and monstrous ahistorical convulsions recounted in Hesiod's *Theogony*, and it is quite the opposite of a "procession," because what is more opposed to an intemporal Emanation than a succession of decrees?

2. Creation is the absolutely radical origin of all created things, but the free sin of the creature is the relatively radical origin of history. After the cosmogonic ephemerides, the moral event called sin—a sin of disobedience, betrayal, and curiosity—is an accident that is if not absolutely primordial then at least relatively so, occurring at a given moment not at the heart of nonbeing, like the original being, but during the intemporal existence of an already-created creature. This contingent fault disturbs the eternal, ahistorical paradise that was supposed to be established in the Garden of Eden. The evil suggestion of the snake, the temptation of woman, and the sin of man are the three moral events of this ill-fated series. If Adam hadn't given in to his companion and she to the snake, if the keeper of the Garden of Felicity had not partaken of the forbidden

fruit, there would be no reason for anything ever to come to pass—
because bliss has no history. Just as if the atoms had fallen through the
Epicurean void in a perpetual free-fall, if the minimal event required for
there to be a world had never happened, namely the arbitrary deviation
of an atom, the physical universe in its various arrangements, its aggre-
gates of all kinds and its bodies of many shapes, could not have formed:
the monotonous fall would have continued *usque ad saecula saeculorum*
(continually for all eternity) without anything ever coming to pass. Everything became possible from the moment a single atom, for no reason,
veered off its course. You have to start somewhere! Give me this bare
minimum that is the clinamen, and I will give you the whole of nature
with its minerals, its rocks, its mountain ranges. Give me the first sin of
the first man, and I will give you the whole of history with its curious tales
and its massacres. Adam's sin is the first crazy idea, the first inflection or
deviation of a free will that suddenly stops willing with God, and just as
the clinamen produces ricochets and collisions, so the guilty decision
engenders the lumps and nodules that result in the tumultuous conflicts
of History.

The initial alteration called sin gets historical time underway: the
sinner instigates history and with history are unleashed the vicissitudes,
ups and downs, mishaps, eras and episodes that diversify this great adventure. The first complication, which is to say the first kink in the un-
disturbed eternity of Edenic bliss, will effectively make all the subsequent
complications easier; the first free step (the first step is the only one that
counts) will produce, in a sort of dizzying bidding war, a string of disas-
ters, a cascade of misfortunes, a cataract of cataclysms: "And the Lord saw
the sin of man multiplied over the earth" (Genesis 6:5).[4] After the expulsion from Paradise we have the crime of Cain, then the Flood and the
confusion of Babel. The sins become more and more serious: Cain's
fratricide ups the ante on Adam's disobedience, acts of violence and
murders multiply with the speed of an avalanche. The hurried pace of the
genealogies goes hand in hand with the frantically accelerated tempo of
the chronology. This deterioration constitutes the very historicity of the
drama whose sequence was set in motion by the first man, thereby inau-
gurating a becoming.

3. After the cosmogonic chronicle and the ante-historical, immemorial
act of sin, there is the historical record proper, in this case the annals and
res gestae of the Israelite nation. It is true that this nation is a privileged

people, that its story is a "holy" one, and that the vicissitudes of this supernatural destiny sheds light on human destiny in general. And yet a fallen humanity can't skip any steps, miss any stations, or skimp on the successive moments in the theological drama of its destiny; this duration cannot be compressed. "A whole world born in a day!," exclaims the prophet Isaiah (66:8),[5] because only an unprecedented miracle can save us from proceeding *per gradus debitos*; no magic can reduce to a duration-less instant the biological time of gestation. Just as Bergson (CE 9/502) must wait for the sugar to melt in his glass (because no one can compress the time of fusion, nor in general the duration of changes in state, and physical time is as incompressible as the biological time of a fever), so Israel must await the coming of its Messiah. Let us give up, with the *Philebus*, the adialectical εὐθύς ("immediately") of the impatient. The temporality that comes to light in the cosmogonic Hexameron, in this initial contingency that is the παρέγγλισις ("summons" or "exhortation") of the first will and in the annals of the people of Israel, is it a time in the Bergsonian sense of the word? At first glance one is tempted to say no.

1. Time begins with the fall: history is the child of shame, since it is the child of sin; theologically it is akin to the reflection, shadow, and lesser being, like the Platonic time the *Timaeus* called a moving image of eternity. This explains the shifting transience and artificial character of becoming. In Ecclesiastes the pathos of disillusionment further accentuates the depreciation of time: historical time is a lost time and the vainest of vanities, sterile and monotonous, a perpetual and pointless repetition where beginning and end meet. The curse cast by the Lord on the first offender—you shall return to the earth from whence you came, dust you were, to dust you shall return[6]—weighs heavily on the accursed of Ecclesiastes: it is written in the arc of the sun, in the course of the wind, and the cycle of water. But what is a movement where the end point is the starting point, where the *quo* and *unde* coincide, if not an infernal wheel and a Sisyphean torture? What is a time where what will be is what was and what is already done, where the future leads to the past and the omega to the alpha, where the future is a past in reverse, if not a bewitched time, a cursed time? Death acts as a counterweight to birth, war to peace, "catagenesis" to "anagenesis" and every positive action (building, planting, finding, keeping, loving, and so on) has its symmetrical negative one (destruction, uprooting, losing, dissipation, hating) that balances and cancels it out; the Deed finds its heartbreaking counterpart in the Undo-

ing, "There is nothing new under the sun." What could be more opposed to a "creative evolution"? The time of Ecclesiastes is not the fertile, irreversible, progressive time of ripening and gestation but a stationary or circular time and an absurd detour. "What's the use?," asks Ecclesiastes (2:15).[7] How better to question the purpose of a becoming that becomes nothing and consequently contradicts its vocation as becoming and gives the lie to its promises. It is a form of alteration that instead of engendering the other, instead of placing its temporal stress on the other, amounts to the same thing and goes round in circles—that is the monster of cursed time!

This circle excludes not only innovation but memory: the past of *Time and Free Will* is as foreign to it as the future of *Creative Evolution*. It is not a dimension where treasures can be acquired and piled up, where property can be capitalized, where the fruits of one's labor are amassed and one's works preserved over time but rather the realm of oblivion and dissipation. It is neither conservation nor permanence but rather waste, sterile loss, and pure insubstantiality. Here we think less of a Sisyphus without a future than of the wastefulness of the Danaides. "Our days on earth are like a shadow," we read in the book of Job (8:9), and in the Chronicles (39:15) man is only a guest here below. This image of an image, reflection of a reflection, obviously looks less like Bergson's duration than Plato's εἰκὼν κινητή ("moving image") or even Heraclitus' ποταμοῦ ῥοή ("river flow"). Is not man's volatility, the disavowals of a creature unfaithful to the Covenant and the legacy handed down to him, the natural consequence of this lack of substance?

2. Biblical time resembles a large-scale fresco or a long tapestry fully laid out along a wall: its moments are, so to speak, given in space. Bergson would no doubt have said that this time is not evolution in the making but an already-evolved and thus spatialized evolution. Edmond Fleg notes that for many Talmudists the moments of this time could be reversed and that their chronology is ultimately an indifferent matter. The holy story is like a text where you can dip into any section at will, reverse the order, retrospectively freeze an episode, recapitulate its development. An already-developed development, an already-elapsed becoming, biblical time is the opposite of the Bergsonian "in-the-making." Biblical time is not the time of its own contemporaries, a time lived as it unfolds, but rather the panoramic and posthumous time of a theological history where the theologian is both a super-consciousness and a retro-consciousness: an "over-

consciousness" looking down on Israel's trajectory and the historical field of its destiny, a retrospective consciousness comparing the different events of this trajectory after the fact. The spectacular and terrible events that punctuate the career of the chosen people, while not eternal events like those of the *Theogony*, are nevertheless normative and somewhat detemporalized: the crossing of the Red Sea, the breaking of the Tablets of Stone, the victory of David over the Amalekites resemble in this respect the events of Christ's life, whose anniversaries we commemorate with holidays. These events, immortalized in painting and poetry, celebrated on fixed dates of the calendar, periodically recur according to a uniform rhythm, and have thus lost any unpredictable character.

3. History is not only a fallen, stretched out, degenerate form of eternity, or a fully elapsed duration: its outcome also seems to be stripped of any element of chance. The result doesn't seem to be subject to any doubt, and we can place our bets safely: the direction of human destiny is as predictable as that of a metaphysical drama whose successive stages we know in advance. In this case biblical time would be lacking the only feature that, according to Bergson, can temporalize time: unpredictability. Unpredictability is the untamed and intractable element, disturbing and exciting, the random element, in a word, that constitutes the risk of temporal being. When we do not know what tomorrow will bring, it is time to tremble and the heart beats faster. In the vast panorama of the holy story the element of adventure and risk of the gamble seem reduced to a minimum. This story that excludes the novelty inherent to a genuine "futurition" seems rather an easy adventure. The protagonist of this chanceless adventure may not experience the hope that an open future inspires in man, and which is danger's reward, but he does have trust and patience. Even the aimless becoming of Ecclesiastes, though it implies discouragement and pessimism, seems to exclude any genuine anxiety. The trust of the faithful must find a counterpart in the promise of the prophets. "Yes, there is hope for your future," says the Lord to Israel, speaking through Jeremiah (32:17). By a sort of unspoken contract, the prophetic words act as a guarantee to the people that, certain conditions being met, certain commitments will be fulfilled: provided that Israel makes good use of its freedom, the salvation of each shall be assured.

Prophecy appears in this respect as a moral and relatively reasonable form of assurance against the evil genius of time, namely the unexpected in time that could be lying in wait in the moment to come and that makes any "advent" an adventure and turns any imminent transformation into a risk of death. The prophetic word dispels this wariness, it soothes and consoles: "Every valley shall be exalted, every mountain lowered, the crooked paths will be straightened," Isaiah promises to his people, "I shall convert the darkness into light and the rough terrain into smooth" (42:16). And Jeremiah: "I will turn their mourning into gladness and consolation, I will give them comfort and joy instead of sorrow . . . for your work will be rewarded." (31:13 and 31:16). This prophesied future is the security offered by a providential finality that keeps history on the right track. But for *Creative Evolution*, the prophetic teleology would instead be proof of the predestined or predetermined nature of this time: everything is said, everything is done, everything is already played out!

The prophets, as we know, speak in the future tense: the Lord will ride on a cloud, the rivers will dry up, the nations will tremble, and so on. Certainly there is a world of difference between the prophet and the seer; and in fact the Law itself justifies this opposition indirectly by accusing divination of imposture. Leviticus (19:31) and Deuteronomy (13:2)[8] effectively condemn as pagans those who consult magicians in order to know the secrets of the future. It is the soothsayer, not the prophet, who neutralizes time and annuls futurity by removing the future's exciting and adventurous uncertainty. It is the oracle and soothsayer who see the future using foresight, who have foreknowledge of the future, read the future in advance, and detemporalize time by treating tomorrow as today. The Bergsonian critique of spatialized time doesn't affect Jewish prophecy but rather the pagan seer and, behind the seer, the eternalism of the Greeks. This vision of a future given in advance, this prereading that reads before the fact, this foreknowledge that knows ahead of time effectively annuls the historicity of history and substitutes what is becoming with what has become. The impostor who foresees and predicts the future in a timeless way turns this future into a present and abolishes time with a magical flourish.

The prophet who has a premonition of the future, on the other hand, does not annul time but on the contrary passes through all of its thickness in full flight. He senses the future within duration and coincides with it in an act that is quite similar to Bergsonian intuition, but what duration gradually discloses in a process of unveiling prophecy, a concentrated form of duration, discloses all at once in an instantaneous revelation. The professional oracle claims to literally know God, but the prophet, for his part, glimpses a pneumatic mystery: this mystery appears to him in an ambiguous and even contradictory form, and this is why he expresses himself, like Ezekiel, in parables, figures, and allegories. Prophetic amphiboly, it should be noted, is not at all like the prudence of those charlatans who use equivocal formulas to avoid committing themselves; it is rather the esoteric and ineffable nature of the message that makes metaphors and myths necessary. The prophet himself does not have a clear grasp of the situation: something is expressed within him, he does not himself know what or why. Prophecy, in this way, is more like the poetic inspiration discussed in Plato's *Ion*, or the mystical enthusiasm, the "divine madness" in the *Phaedrus*, than pagan divination properly speaking. The distance between the foresight or clairvoyance of visionaries and the half-sight or *glimpse* (*entrevision*) of the inspired is as wide as between earth and heaven. The opposite of any "grammatic" or literal anticipation, isn't the glimpse of the prophet a vision across time?

It remains that the prophet, while not annulling futurity, nevertheless foretells the future and, in a certain way, renders it less adventurous: the surprise of novelty is thereby forestalled. And what does it matter if this spokesman of God suffers with his brothers, lives the drama of history alongside them! Time momentarily ceases to be an obstacle for the one God speaks to. "New things I declare; before they spring into being I announce them to you," says the book of Isaiah (42:9, 46:10).[9] Not that the prophet knows the future in advance, but prophetic time is nevertheless deprived of the irreducible element of its temporality: there is no more emergence. The messianic promise has suppressed the disturbing and unpredictable upsurge of novelty.

We cannot therefore identify Bergsonian time with biblical time. But another divergence, more serious perhaps, seems to separate Bergson (or at least the first Bergsonism) from messianic prophecy. What apparently makes Bergson's philosophy of experience the antipodes of Judaism is its decided rejection of any reflections on the beginning and the end, any speculation on the two extreme terms. Bergsonism is, at least initially, a philosophy of empirical fullness and continuity: in agreement with Spinoza, with English empiricism, and (on this point only) with criticism, Bergson refrained for a very long time from asking any questions concerning the first beginning or final end: "I, the Eternal, am the first and last" (Isaiah 41:4, 44:6, 48:12).[10] The first and the last! Bergsonian empiricism would have considered this protology and this eschatology to be pseudoproblems and rejected, in the name of perceived or perceptible facts, any metaphysical or apocalyptic speculation about the Alpha and the Omega. God "has nothing of the already made," the Absolute "endures" (CE 248/706, 299/747; and TS chapter 3)—we know what a scandal *Creative Evolution* provoked among the dogmatic Christian theologians with these assertions. Bergson was naturally suspected of pantheism. Did Bergson mean that God is cause of himself, in the sense of Jacob Boehme and mystics? The Bergsonian God is not *causa sui* in this sense, but it is all activity and continual outpouring: the divine is the actual continuation of the élan that causes the spread of organisms and species to blossom before our eyes.

The problem of the radical origin would thus have been for Bergson an ideological mirage and delusional representation: the idea of a creator God positing heaven and earth in the void of all preexistence is for *Creative Evolution* as unintelligible as, for *Time and Free Will*, the myth of a freedom of indifference at the fork between two paths, where the decision of how to proceed is made in a vacuum of any determination. And just as free will is the will of a consciousness supported by its deep past, a psyche pushed by its personal traditions and by the lessons of experience, so the divine act is a creation in the midst of continuation. God no more operates in the spiritual bell jar of absolute nonbeing than free will does. The nominalist philosophy of plenitude, criticizing the ideas of disorder and nothingness, depreciates both the yawning chaos of Hesiod's *Theogony* and the nothingness of creation *ex nihilo*. Nothingness is a frightening representation the mind uses to scare itself, to make itself dizzy and play at teetering over the abyss. Just as we like to skirt along the edge of a precipice, and especially when there is a parapet, so the metaphysician gives himself the thrill of skirting the precipice of the abyssal *nihil* from which the first being would emerge. So it is that Leibniz takes his turn at examining the void by writing his treatise on the *The Radical Origin of Things* and for a few moments savors the delicious vertigo, but he quickly fills in the abyss and shows that ultimately God does everything in a very reasonable way and that eternal truths preexisted his benevolent will. There is thus a parapet that prevents the mind from falling into the precipice. The author of *Creative Evolution* could not understand this beginning of all beginnings, this radical Berechit that, in the first verse of the first chapter of Genesis, remains enveloped in an ineffable mystery, because absolutely nothing existed before the benevolent act that creates heaven and earth, and the *fiat lux* itself comes after this first making of being.

The philosophy of temporal positivity is, in this sense at least, resolutely anticreationist. Over the absolute nothingness, Bergson would no doubt have preferred the mystical nothingness of the Kabbalah and Dionysius the Areopagite, because that nothingness is richness and plenitude, inexhaustible infinity (En-Soph) or, as Angelus Silesius says, "Super-Nothing";[11] that nothingness is not the void where the spectacular magic of creation is wrought in a *coup de théâtre*, but rather like the dynamic schema that is the germ of poetic improvisation: it is the unfathomable abyss and fertile night referred to in negative theology. If creation is an event that happened all at once at the beginning of time, Bergson is indeed an anticreationist, but on the other hand he is a creationist and more than a creationist if it is true that for him continuation is itself creation, continual and temporal creation. Is this not precisely the paradox of a "creative" evolution, which begins by continuing?

Just as Bergson rejects the problem of the radical origin, he also rejects the insoluble aporia concerning "ultimacy" and dismisses any eschatology. The anguish of the Last Judgment, the millenarian speculations about the End of History, the end of the world, the "end times" do not exist for him. Duration will never stop enduring—because it is spirituality itself. The idea of a time that is fully achieved, unfurled, unwound, is an absurd fantasy, one that generates imaginary problems, maddening aporia, and metaphysical phobias. Time, for this philosophy that is both creationist and "continuationist," is not a finite quantum that would gradually run out until the fifty-ninth minute of its eleventh hour, using up moments until the penultimate one, and finally stopping like an unwound clock when the last stroke of its last hour has struck, and similarly the history of the world does not culminate in a general conflagration when humanity has reached the end of its rope. Humanity, on the way to salvation, does not have a finite gap to fill in, a certain discrepancy to compensate, a certain distance to catch up. These anthropomorphic myths are only metaphysical by pretention, because time, like duty itself, is inexhaustible. The bogeyman of "chiliasm" is thus as foreign to *Creative Evolution* as the vertigo of the Beginning. If nothingness is a false problem, the annihilation that would result in this nothingness, the extermination that makes possible this annihilation, are also concepts made for the empirical world of quantity. *In nihilum* is as empty, as "verbal" a phrase, as *ex nihilo*.

We can thus understand the infinite precautions Bergson takes when approaching the problem of transcendence: the pluralist immanentism of *Matter and Memory* and *Creative Evolution* doesn't lend itself well to the idea of a monotheistic transcendence. Transcendence effectively leaves gaping a vertiginous hiatus between the Creature and the Absolute: this yawning void is, for a philosopher of plenitude, the fantasy of fantasies. Bergson's distaste for the void that opens up between God and man in creationism could have very easily pushed the doctrine of *Creative Evolution* toward pantheism. We know how Rauh, relaunching against Bergson the objections raised in the *Theaetetus* to the mobilism of Heraclitus and Cratylus, regrets the absence of a transcendent consciousness of becoming that would have allowed Bergson to distinguish past and future.[12]

Does a doctrine that is temporalist, continuationist, immanentist, and on top of all that pluralist have anything in common with Hebrew monotheism? The reason for these fundamental differences between Bergsonism and Judaism, some concerning time and others concerning eschatology and transcendence, lies in the fact that Bergsonism was not at the outset a philosophy with ethical aspirations. It is the moral agent who has a relationship with a transcendent Absolute; it is the bearer of values who feels ruled by a transcendent Good, who is drawn to a transcendent duty, and who wills across the void. The great moral philosophies, like those of Renouvier and Lequier, were both arguments for free will and defenses of divine transcendence and divine unity. In *Time and Free Will*, by contrast, freedom is not so much a practical responsibility and an opportunity to do this or that as a demand for depth: it is about being wholly oneself, not at all about achieving a transcendent ideal. What does the Decalogue and the Tables of the Law have to say to us? At the time of *Time and Free Will*, the Bergsonian individual has nothing special to do: to act freely means to act deeply, which is to say, sincerely. Bergson does not tell us what man's task is, he tells us rather: be yourself, put yourself wholly into your actions, become what you already are,[13] whoever you are. This is what we could call immanence: to ask a will to put itself wholly into its decision, to become deeper, to totalize itself, is not telling it what to do. The Bergsonian problem, at this time, is thus an aesthetic problem concerning personal development and inner life: man acts in the fullness of duration, human freedom is a freedom within immanence and plenitude, and the only real imperative is that of private reflection and energy! Freedom is not the arbitrary, autocratic, unpredictable decree that decides or initiates, but rather it is the expression of a personality. It does not introduce a revolutionary discontinuity in our personal biography but rather emanates from the past like a perfume. The lived duration of *Time and Free Will*, strongly imbued with emotional and descriptive experiences where the body, as in Maine de Biran, plays a large role, appears to be a vehicle for content that is too involved and too concrete and whose pathic mood is too strong for the problem of transcendence to establish itself there: qualitative subjectivism seems, in this period, to prevail over ethics! It has to be said: the writer who recognized freedom in the way of breathing the perfume of a rose (TFW 161/107) was more closely related to Marcel Proust than the prophet Isaiah.

Bergson, for that matter, unlike the prophets, neither thunders nor castigates. The mystical and passionate indignation of Isaiah and Jeremiah are foreign to him, since there is no ethico-religious contract between man and Creator, and Bergsonism is not a philosophy of salvation. It is with *Two Sources of Morality and Religion* that Bergsonian freedom rediscovers a calling.

In fact it is paradoxically in plenitude and positivity that we will recognize Bergsonism's most deeply biblical trait. This plenitude is not, as in Spinoza, the plenitude of being but the plenitude of becoming. For just as Spinoza turned around the Platonic meditation on death into a meditation on life, so Bergson intentionally reverses Spinoza's *sub specie aeternitas* into a *sub specie durationis* (see CM 129/1365). It is the opposite and perhaps the same thing! The eternity of life, which is an infinite becoming, supplants the eternity of death, which is timeless negativity. Hellenism (and Aristotle is in agreement with Plato on this point) was in the habit of considering becoming as a lesser perfection, as an insubstantial form of being riddled with nonbeing. Bergson, reversing the accepted wisdom, dethrones eternity from its hegemonic precedence and paradoxically recognizes being as a deficit of becoming, stillness as a privation of movement: the negative and the positive terms exchange their signs. Bergson, who establishes us firmly within the immanence of becoming, thereby roots us in our condition here below. Is not this unhesitating implantation a profound trait of the Jewish soul? Becoming is no longer the vale of tears from which man, the perpetual pilgrim, thinks only of escaping; man is no longer in exile here below.

In the first Oxford lecture on "The Perception of Change" (cm 138–39/1374), Bergson, accusing Plotinus of preferring contemplation to action, denounces the pathos of flight and desertion that not only fills the Catharism of the *Phaedo* but all of Neoplatonism and up to modern romanticism: "φεύγειν δεῖ πρὸς τὸ ἄνω φεύγωμεν δὴ φίλην ἐς πατρίδα" (Let us flee, let us flee then to the beloved Fatherland).[14] Let us flee from here, flee toward heavenly Jerusalem, *in civitatem sanctam* Jerusalem (to the holy city of Jerusalem), let us flee to our dear homeland. Flee, always flee! And why, if you please, would our homeland not be here below? Why would our holy Jerusalem not be the Jerusalem here below? The Jerusalem of this world? In his affirmative attitude toward human actions, and even in his marked preference for the activist mystics, Bergson is connected to the ethics of the prophets, even to that of the Law. What contemplationist metaphysics considered to be pure negativity is on the contrary the height of positivity; pessimism is thus turned into optimism. It is because he considered becoming as an imperfect mode of being that Schopenhauer spoke of the misery of existence—man is under house arrest within becoming, man is the slave of the forced labor of temporality —it is thus our eternitarian and ontological prejudices that are the reason for our nostalgia and our languor. On the other hand distress turns to joy if being is a negation of becoming, if there is no other way of being for man than becoming. Becoming, namely being while not being, or not being while being, both being and not being (is this not the way it is conceived in Aristotle's *Physics*?)—this is the only way man has of being a being! Man, turning his gaze away from the mirage of the timeless, put down roots in the joyful plenitude. Is not this idea of an earthly or intraworldly beatitude shared by Bergson and Tolstoy?

There is thus no place in Bergsonian duration for the tragic and intractable conflicts so beloved of modern philosophers, popular in particular with philosophers who have never experienced our tragedies: is this not one of the reasons why the pseudo-tragic youth of today show no interest in Bergsonism? Because the absurd, in Bergson, is still an instrument of progress; the obstacle itself, in *Creative Evolution*, is still an organ! Thus it is that the presence of matter, although unexplained in its radical origin, does indeed seem to come from the same source as life and mind. What, in one sense, weighs down and hypnotizes this mind, brings down and slows the élan of this life, in another sense is the instrument of its positive achievements. Matter is necessary to life as the springboard for the élan: the divine élan, however divine, needs something as leverage. Matter is thus a blessing and not a curse; the reverse tendency of the élan vital provides the necessary counterbalance to the upward tendency of life.

Nor is there any room in Bergson for that extra element in the general economy of being, that absolutely irreducible element that must be considered separately, in short for that irrational element that doesn't fit into any category and is called Evil. No theodicy is necessary therefore in order to justify something that is neither a principle nor a moment, and that is not in any way a substance (hypostasis) or a demon. If Bergson had posed such a problem, it would no doubt have been in the spirit of Spinoza, in order to recognize evil as a Manichean fantasy, a myth,[15] analogous to nothingness, a mirage comparable to chaos, the pseudo-problem par excellence. But while the hypostatized nothing (void or *tabula rasa*) is a myth invented by our fabricating intelligence in order to explain creation and knowledge, evil is rather an anthropomorphic myth of symmetry, originating in what we would like to call the obsession of the "garniture de cheminée."[16] From time immemorial it has been necessary, says the *Theaetetus*, for evil to be the counterpart of the good, to act as a foil to the good. The pairs of opposites in dramatic dualism, the hypostasized zero in the doctrines of nothingness, are verbal abstractions. Just as space and time are in no way parallel, just as the future is in no sense the past turned around the other way, so evil is not an upside-down good: for everything is right way up to a philosophy of the irreversible.

Matter is a not a real obstacle, nor is evil a real principle, and likewise death doesn't have, for Bergson, any tragic significance. In this respect Bergson is very far removed from the Russian Lev Shestov, who reflected on Tolstoy's anguish and had a particularly acute and profound sense of death and the revelations of death. Even more, Bergson was not even obliged, as Tolstoy's pantheism was, to drive back a constantly reemerging anxiety. At the end of the third chapter of *Creative Evolution*, Bergson offers us a hyperbolic, progressive, apocalyptic hope of victory over death. Is not Bergson's immortalization of the death of death already announced by Isaiah (25:8)?[17] "Death will die," Edmond Fleg has Bergson say. Foreign to any form of tragic pathos, Bergson does not see in death the absurdity of nonbeing to which the individual ipseity is incomprehensibly doomed, death is not an encounter between a super-natural destiny and a trivial physical contingency that abruptly ends our career. Death is nonbeing, and the philosophy of plenitude, extinguishing this nothing like it extinguishes the Eleatic aporia, shows in its own way that death is οὐδὲν πρὸς ἡμᾶς ("nothing to us").[18] Bergsonian thought is certainly without any blend of necromania or necrophilia: the love of death, the taste for the cadaverous, thanatophilia, the morbid attraction of the funereal, all of these complexes whose formation at the dawn of modern times has been described in such depth by Huizinga,[19] all those as well that developed in the Romantic period, these are all pessimistic and ambivalent complexes where an indulgent attitude toward death is bizarrely combined with anguish about death. These very modern complexes are as far removed from Bergson's spirit as the taste for nothing-ness. "Love," says the Song of Songs, "is as strong as death" (8:6). But life, for its part, is infinitely stronger than the nothing of death! It is not much to say that life is the set of forces that resist death, given that being is in general the continuing victory over nonbeing, namely negation denied, just as movement is at all times the refusal of immobility, immobility mobilized, resuscitated. Resurrection or rebirth is not only the spring-time miracle that happens once a year in the season of renewal but the continuing miracle of each moment; for each instant is springlike in its way. One could say, in this sense, that duration is a continuous spring-time. Maybe we should understand in this way the living God of Psalms, Isaiah, and Exodus, that is to say, the idea of a God that is perpetual spring and renewal. Is not the Bergsonian god itself the élan of a continuous creation,[20] the wonder of every minute? Blessed be the God who allows each minute to follow the preceding one! Blessed be the God who allows the systole to follow the diastole and the diastole the systole! Who allows each beat of my pulse to follow the preceding one! Blessed be the God who allowed me to see this new dawn and this new spring! But the annual renewal and the renewal of each morning are no more miraculous than the infinitesimal recommencement of a duration that continues from moment to moment: our trust in the perpetuation of each moment, justified by the affirmative God of David and Abraham, chases away the bogeyman of the evil genius, just as it dispels the scruples of Zeno. The doubts, nightmares, and trembling are no more. Does not the Hasidic prayer thank God for the inexhaustible grace of each dawn? The élan vital is this grace itself, this perpetual blessing. God is life, the supreme positiv-

ity, the vital *Yes*, and, in this sense, as Edmond Fleg recalls in relation to
Moses Maimonides, God is indeed the negation of negation.

And not only is the God of Abraham, Isaac, and Jacob the living God,
this God is moreover the God for the living, as Jesus himself says, recall-
ing the appearance of the burning bush (Exodus 3:6).[21] "The living, the
living," cries Isaiah, "they praise you!" (38:19). And in the Book of Wisdom (1:12–14) we read this: "Stop seeking death so keenly in the errors of
life!" And a little further on: "for God made not death . . . he created all
things, that they might have their being." The ascetic radicalism of a Saint
Bernard, nihilistic spirituality, and necrophilia all seem to be condemned
in advance here. There will be no sleeplessness or anxiety, "your sleep will
be sweet," King Solomon promises us (Proverbs 3:24–25). And Isaiah's
God: "Do not be afraid, for I am with you" (43:1, 43:5). Let us not be
afraid of anything, because even the most atrocious humiliations, even
the undeserved sufferings, are just a test, and the unjust trials of Job in
turn stop at the edge of the absurd and on this side of absurdity. The
tempted man is stretched *usque ad mortem*, to the point of death, excluding death. Abraham as well was tested to the limit: at the next to the last
instant of the final moment, at the penultimate second of the final minute,
the angel stops the arm of Abraham before it accomplishes the irreparable
absurdity of *hyothysia* and the rights of reason and goodness are restored.
But we were afraid! In the end the impossible supposition was not realized, and the hyperbolic evil of the demon, at the last moment, is driven
back in its nothingness *in extremis*. Thus injustice will have had only the
next to the last word, for if all is lost at the next to the last moment, all is
saved at the last one. So it is that God exterminates all mankind except
Noah, which is to say God safeguards the minimum necessary for the
continuation of being. Here again our trust remains justified! At the
extreme point of tension and at the moment when everything is about to
split apart, everything returns to order; all is lost, all is saved.

Just as Hebrew monotheism can be reconciled with an intraworldly
ethics, so Bergsonian mysticism embeds humanity in the world here
below, in this earthly world where our work as humans lies. Bergsonian
mysticism was born in 1888 in the private reflection of inner life and
meditation on personal becoming, personal development, and personal
depth, but it doesn't remain cloistered, as Marcel Proust's will, in the
intimacy and solipsism of the secret. It shows a more and more definite
orientation toward action and accepts that our freedom is magnetically

charged with values. Bergsonian quality looks less and less like the Ver-
lainian nuance, the muted shades of Proust, the pianissimo of Debussy. In
Two Sources Bergson always gives his preference to mystics who were not
contemplatives but individuals of action and initiative, pioneers, benefac-
tors, organizers: Saint Paul the propagandist and Saint Teresa, founder of
monasteries struggling with secular problems. It is not the time to listen
to one's heart beat, smell the roses, or appreciate the taste of a madeleine
dipped in tea, when war and the industrial age pose so many urgent
problems! Man is thus not an outlaw on earth, and Bergson rejects
everything that would devalue man's duration. "By wisdom the Lord laid
the earth's foundations," say the Proverbs of Solomon (3:19). The wisdom
of man, a reflection of this foundational and edifying wisdom, is not a
form of impressionism busy inhaling perfumes, sounding the vital heart-
beat of becoming, or being lulled by the "melody" of inner life. The sage
has other concerns than the passions and vicissitudes of their emotional
life: the sage makes an effort to transform the human condition. Jewish
mysticism, says Albert Lewkowitz,[22] has no desire to overlook social
relations but rather wishes to sanctify them: it is therefore compatible
with militant action.

    Two Sources goes no further than the somewhat simplified symmetry,
the exemplary diptych, of the two Testaments, the Old and New, which it
opposes to one another. To help us understand the dynamism of the mystical élan, the Bergsonian dichotomy opposes open religion to closed
religion, open morality to closed morality. If the Gospel represents for
Bergson the regime of open consciousness and the Law the regime of
closed consciousness, we have to believe (but Bergson does not put it in
these terms) that the prophets represent, halfway between the closed consciousness and the open consciousness, something like a religion that's
"ajar [*entr'ouverte*]"—a "half-open [*entr'ouverture*]" religion. "An eye for
an eye ... burn for burn," says the justice of retaliation (Exodus 21:24–25),
just as the justice of bartering, when trading, says "an ox for an ox" or "a
sheep for a sheep." This is the Pythagorean justice of ἀντιπεπονθός ("mutual influence" or "reciprocity"), like the reciprocity of Rhadamanthus!
Thus after the closure of the Law comes the half-opening of the prophets,
then in the New Covenant, the openness of evangelical love.

    In fact the moment of opening is already given in the Law itself. It is
true that Jesus declares he has come to *fulfill*, namely to perfect the Law
and complete the work of the prophets. What does this mean? And

should we understand this pleroma or fulfillment as the addition of a supplement that would allow us to totalize the finite but incomplete sum of the truth? Bergson seems to believe that the New Covenant, miraculous and revolutionary in this respect, adds an essential piece to the Law that it was missing: the Law was not full to the brim, Jesus completed it by adding the missing part, "πληρωμα ουν νομου η αγαπη [love is the fullness of the law]" (Romans 13:10). The pleroma of the Law is agape; love is the complementary piece thanks to which the partial Law becomes the Law in full, the Law in its plenitude. But the missing piece was not really missing! Christ himself, responding to the Pharisees who want to embarrass him, sums up the quintessence of his own message in two precepts of the Law, one commanding us to love God with all our heart, the second to love our neighbor as ourselves (Matthew 22:40; see also 7:12). Fulfillment here doesn't consist in simply carrying out but in extracting from the multiple prescriptions of the Law the central or pneumatic precept that brings all the others to life and animates their letter, because without the general idea of love, without the invigorating idea of living love, the detail of the prescriptions is simply a *dead letter*.

This is what happens when there is no heart in it, and this is what Paul means. Christ, himself more modest than some Christians, implies here that the New Covenant exists in embryo in the old one and is therefore not entirely without precedents. It is more like a new form of illumination; it makes explicit a great discovery that could have gone unnoticed in the dense scrub of observances. Thus the abrupt transformation that the Sermon on the Mount represents for Bergson was already anticipated, as Loisy and Guignebert have already suggested,[23] in the prophecy and in the Law. Jesus came, it is said, to open wide onto the infinite a window that was just ajar. A window is either open or closed! But we are precisely able to further specify, and in Bergson's own language, that the only thing that counts is the moment of opening: the moment of opening, namely the qualitative intention, which is an infinite movement and does not depend on the angle of the aperture. Similarly, it is the act of giving that is the conversion to the wholly other order of love, and it is this conversion, this good movement, this intentional dynamism, regardless of the quantitative magnitude of the donation, because the intention to give is not proportional to the size of the contribution! In this paradoxical arithmetic the pauper's penny has the same supernatural value as the banker's check.

Paulinian intentionalism itself thus helps us to understand why all the essentials of Christian "openness" is already implied in the "half"-opening of the prophets. However little the window is opened, everything is already fulfilled! Because from the moment the window is no longer closed, it is already open, consciousness is connected to the infinite plains of the universe and the infinite beaches of heaven, with the ocean air, with the wind that brings messages from the distant horizon, with the smells of the outside world, and for that it is not necessary for the window to be wide open. Wide open or half-open is a matter of numbers and degrees, in other words of more or less, but it is not the big qualitative question of all or nothing. Just as the most fleeting indulgence of temptation is already a great sin, so the infinite movement of love is already wholly given in the moment of the first half-opening. A fledgling love, that of a consciousness that is just starting to open, is immediately an infinite love. The good news of the Gospel is, like Bergsonian novelty in general, a novelty that is already prepared and prefigured in the already wholly positive plenitude of the Law. Is not the Old Covenant itself this continual "plerosis"? Thus in the Proverbs of Solomon, the infinity of forgiveness and the supernatural asymmetry of grace shatter the cycle of vindictive expiation: the unjust love that paradoxically commands us to return good for evil (Proverbs 20:22, 34:29),[24] and to turn the other cheek, transcends the ἀντί (anti; "in return for") of the ἀντιπάσχειν (antipaschein; "suffer in return [for an offence]"). *Vulnus pro vulneris* ("a wound for a wound"): this is what was required in the leveling of action with reaction, the neutralization of the flux of activity with the reflux of passivity. The movement of love, going straight away to the limit, clears away these compensatory reflexes and breaks in one stroke the accursed cycle of retaliation.

Biblical consciousness is already this infinite opening, in space on the one hand and in time on the other, but first in extension. It is certainly not the propagation of a faith that constitutes its universality, and this one was always limited in its spread. But neither is it correct to say that the God of Hebrew monotheism is the God of a single privileged nation and shows a jealous exclusivity. Isaiah speaks for the federation of all humankind, and the peace he heralds is an ecumenical peace (2:4; see also 42:6). The chosen people itself is chosen only as a mouthpiece of an eternally and universally human truth, as a scapegoat or carrier of the great human suffering. God does not reserve any special favors for it. Noé Gottlieb even ventures to say that the "catholicity" of Judaism is even more open than that of Roman Catholicism, as it attaches no denominational conditions to salvation, no specific creed: the Talmud and Maimonides specify that obeying the moral principles contained in the Law is enough to ensure eternal life even to the Gentiles. Judaism only becomes denominational when it imitates Catholicism and closes in on itself in opposition to other faiths. Isaiah is addressed to all men, *whatever their language* (66: 18–20); its message, like that of the Stoics, is a universalist one: philanthropic and philadelphic. But Stoic cosmopolitanism is the rational humanitarianism of a sage who feels sure of their place on earth and in heaven and remains concerned about personal self-sufficiency, whereas prophetic supernationalism is that of an impassioned and ecstatic genius, paradoxically and supernaturally open to all their brothers. The God of Deuteronomy (10:17)[25] is no respecter of nationality, nor of "person," that is to say, this God has no regard for the contingent distinguishing marks that differentiate the individual from the human being. The Talmud affirms the universal nature of this fraternity, founded on the resemblance between God and his creature and on the divine origin of all humans.[26]

The old Law insists at several points, and with a particular care, on the obligation to treat the stranger as a brother.[27] The argument it uses resembles the *as yourself*, the Golden Rule of Leviticus, namely, aiming at the ordinary man, it pulls on the strings of self-interest to turn egoism toward altruism: you yourselves were strangers in Egypt, you know what it is like. Remember then the analogy between the situations and treat the stranger as you would have wished to be treated. This xenophilia, however indirect, is a natural form of universalism in a people whose enemies have always accused it of cosmopolitanism and which itself had an immemorial experience of banishment. The people of the great historical exiles—captivity in Egypt, captivity in Babylon, diaspora, expulsion from Spain, deportations—this people so well specialized in a rootless existence seems condemned to wander among the nations. How could Israel not have a universal vocation? Loving its enemies,[28] the universal people learns the lesson of selflessness twice over: for it loves those who do not love it back, and it loves those who are not worthy of being loved.

After the opening onto space comes the opening onto time and the distant future. Edmond Fleg, a poet of hope, compares in an admirable work the religion of the already come Messiah[29]—where the essential event, despite the anticipation of another order, is in the past—and the religion of the coming Messiah, of the Messiah not yet come and ever awaited, the religion where the essential event and focus in the future: it is the latter religion that is literally messianic. Certainly every possible shade exists in this regard within Christianity itself: Orthodox Christianity, for example, more infused with apocalyptic hope, more eschatological than Catholicism, attaches quite special importance to the return of Christ and the "second coming,"[30] honoring the God who comes (ἐρχομενός ["cometh"]); the sublime legend of the Invisible City of Kitezh is testimony to this. But already in the biblical prophecy consciousness was passionately open to the hope of the future Jerusalem.

In Bergson himself the interval between *Time and Free Will* and *Two Sources* represents the distance between the past and the future. The duration of *Time and Free Will* is above all conservative and past-focused (*passéiste*), its function being to capitalize on memories and build up the past in the present: the weight is on the back foot, and *preterition*, the laying down of events in the past, prevails over *futurition*, positing them in the future.[31] In *Matter and Memory* as well, duration snowballs and has the function of accumulating the past in the present. No doubt *Matter and Memory* is oriented toward action. But *Time and Free Will*, in agreement with Marcel Proust's *In Search of Lost Time*, instigates a cult of the past that implies, if not the retrospection of all memories, then at least their retroversion and retrieval. *Creative Evolution* and especially *Two Sources* look to the future. Is not becoming, which brings about the future, a continual "advent"? Is not becoming to become something else by a constant process of alteration? The focus of becoming—*le devenir*—is no longer memory—*le souvenir*—but the future—*l'avenir*. The "survenir"—what comes up—definitively supplants the "subvenir"—what has gone under the bridge.[32] Becoming rediscovers its true vocation, whose name is futurition or innovation. A vocation is something we feel called by, whereas tradition is something we feel the pressure of. We could say, applying to the past what *Two Sources* says about closed morality, that the emphasis in *Time and Free Will* is still on this pressure, although there is nothing social about this pressure. It is in *Two Sources* that man, responding to the call of dynamic morality, at the same time responds to the lure of the future, which is not a *vis a tergo* (a force acting from behind) but an ideal located ahead. Levitation wins over gravitation. Man thus has a duty, and this duty delimits the scope of things *to be done* or, more precisely, the region of the things *to come* that depend on our work: that part of what should be that will be only if we will it. Duty is a future that is incumbent upon me. Duration is no longer the amassing of memories, or the stockpiling of capital, it is not so much the accumulation of wealth as creation and aspiration, not so much progress as conquest. The stampedes, cavalry charges, and conquering adventures in *Creative Evolution* depreciate the mental nest egg of the solitary consciousness, the very idea of the élan creates the possibility of a *heroic wisdom*!

Thus in the Bible the breach in time cut open by infinite futurity dispels the curse of a circuit that loops back on itself, the Elpidian principle banishes despair. In the Book of Wisdom, as opposed to Ecclesiastes and Job,[33] where time is a shadow, an impasse, a dead end, this pessimism is attributed to the wicked. It is the wicked and the pleasure seekers who, in order to smell the roses and take their voluptuous pleasure from day to day, living from minute to minute, who, in order to enjoy each instant totally carefree, claim that duration has no power and that becoming is not polarized toward the future. "Vanity of vanities!" For the rational optimism of Proverbs and Wisdom, the deep depression of Ecclesiastes looks a little bit like an excuse, a Machiavellian sophism of bad faith, a pretext for ill will, the nihilistic alibi of the perverse. The person who does not intend to work or do anything would like to believe that becoming is the vanity of vanities and absurdity of absurdities, that there is no open futurition but only a closed and cyclical duration, that the end brings us back to the beginning and that all effort is fruitless. Man is not a being born by chance, irreversibly doomed to nothingness and oblivion, a being indistinguishable from nonbeing and who will one day be as if he never were. A world full of meaning and overflowing with intelligibility, a creative wisdom and constructive prudence—this double positivity, cosmological and prudential, is represented in the Bible! Creaturely time is thus valorized as much as it will be in Bergson. In effect, Bergsonian freedom, while it is not, as for Lequier, a dizzying and arbitrary indifference, an initiative without precedents or antecedents, it is also not an aestheticizing totalization or a self-centered deepening of one's personal life. It is not an unprecedented fiat pronounced in a vacuum but neither is it an aimless sincerity. Freedom has a *sense* (sens), which is to say both a meaning and a direction. It is, in a world of plenitude, a serious freedom with the responsibility of transcendent and joyful tasks, the very opposite of an absurd and gratuitous game. "ἔσται γὰρ ὁ οὐρανὸς καινὸς καὶ ἡ γῆ καινή [the heavens will be new and new the earth]," says Isaiah, therefore do not dwell therefore on things of the past (65:17).[34] Just as love breaks open the closure of "a tooth for a tooth," so freedom cures the "vanity of vanities" of the past future and old novelty.

In the Bible as in Bergson the relation of man to time is an affirmative one. Humanity says yes to nature and society, yes to the physical world, yes to brother and sister creatures. This perhaps explains the sacramental spirit of the Psalms; these inspired verses are a hymn of thanksgiving that the psalmist, accompanied on the harp, sings tirelessly to the glory of the Creator and His works. The glory of the Creator is written over all creation—yes, everything speaks of this divine glory, both on earth and in heaven; the splendor of the sun and the trajectory of the stars and the path of the comets all write their praises to the Lord in letters of fire: "Hallelujah! Praise the Lord from the heavens . . . praise the Lord over the whole earth."[35] Humanity says yes to everything seen, to the daisy in the fields, to the blossoming cherry trees, and also celebrates the wonders of the night.

The glorification of the psalms is not, like the theodicy, a laborious justification of the harmony that exists overall: the theodicy of the theologian is the not very convincing pleading of a not very convinced advocate, with little spontaneity. Leibniz reasons too much to truly believe that our world is the best of all possible worlds: his optimism provides us with a scrap of consolation rather than expressing an enthusiastic endorsement of the thing created. David, for his part, needs no indirect arguments, or cosmological proofs, or secondary reasons for believing. God, the splendor that shines, is wholly present in the splendor shined upon; it is thus with an unmediated vision that we can read the glory of God in the visibility of light. The wonderment of the creature before the sacred wonders of creation is above all an expression of trust and gratitude. I bless you, forests, valleys, cornfields, says the poet A. K. Tolstoy. And Psalm 19: "The heavens declare the glory of God and the skies proclaim the work of his hands. The day tells the story to the day, the night passes it on to the night."

Man says yes not only to the universe but to humanity in general. The universal rehabilitation of one's neighbor, the support for one's neighbor, are essentially biblical ideas. Even in the Pentateuch the Law already opens its arms to all the most humble creatures: the long procession of the injured and humiliated—the widow, the orphan, the poor laborer—files through the books of the Law even before the Gospel has announced its Good News. The Good News is announced in the Old Testament, and this news is the general promotion of those who are afflicted in some way. The words "compassion," "mercy," "forgiveness," "pity" appear in every line of the Law. Dare we say that the Torah is "evangelical" in this respect? "I am kind and compassionate," says the Lord in Exodus (22:27; see Psalm 145:9), for all those who are humiliated and injured, according to the prophet Isaiah, are God's friends. The God of Job protects the weak against the strong and the poor against the rich (Isaiah 66:2; Job 5:15). Edmond Fleg has made the observation that love and justice, separate in the modern mind, are merged together in the Bible: "Love thy neighbor as thyself," says Leviticus, as the Apostles will also say (19:18).[36] Not love thyself in thy friend, nor love thy friend as an extension of thyself—because such is the language of Aristotle, namely the philosopher of the "other self" or the alter ego, in that specious form of altruism that is simply a roundabout form of selfishness. The substantial and annexationist ego is given first, and others revolve around this nuclear ego like satellites, added on like annexes or outbuildings rounding out its property—a friend in bronze, a stuffed friend, a piece of furniture or a vase would do just as well. The *as yourself* of Leviticus is not "physicalist" but rather "ecstatic" and properly miraculous. It is *allos autos* (other self) in reverse! "Love your friend as you would your own self" means: I have no other self but my friend; the self has no other self than its loved other—because it is my neighbor who is my own self! Thus the self loves his brother as if he, the lover, did not exist; the self becomes his other in person. The ego is thus in a way enucleated of its egoism; completely dislocated, extroverted into its friend, the self has no more selfhood; the neighbor of the Bible is no longer the "other self" of a shameful form of philautia that dares not speak its name, rather it is really the other *than* myself.

What is Bergsonian is not so much open morality as the spirit of openness, because a completely open morality is already closed up again due to the fact that once morality is opened, if we do not continue to open and reopen it ceaselessly, it goes back to being closed morality. It is the intention to open that matters, which is always *in motu* (in motion). The prophets struggle tirelessly against the complacency of the professionally well-intentioned, the *belles âmes*, and the self-satisfied good conscience, happy to bloom like the rose or parade like the peacock. Strutting about is not to open oneself up, it is rather to wallow in the excellence of a privileged and satisfied self. Could this refusal of any "strutting about," this profound irony with regard to any good conscience by chance be what is called Bergsonian "mobilism"? There is no holiness in the realm of actuality, and human effort is something always to be renewed: on this point Simmel's relativism, Einstein's nonconformism and Bergson's temporalism would be in agreement.

Men, says Jeremiah, have abandoned the spring of living water to hollow out broken tanks for themselves. And in the same way they abandon the living waters of the living God for ridiculous idols, statues of gold and silver, images carved in stone. The unprecedented, inexplicable, unrelenting dedication with which the prophets and patriarchs track down the ever reemerging temptation of idolatry is proportionate to the irrepressible and protean nature of that idolomania itself. Men, as soon as they are left alone, set about stupidly adoring their cast-iron calves and their golden asses, their crude fetishes, their dolls, and their totems. The temptation of idolatry is the stupid man's permanent tendency on the one hand to fall back into the cult of superficial appearances, on the other to allow himself to be tempted by the fragmentation of plurality and finally to accept the relapse into the inertia of death. The lazy man, for want of élan, no longer follows the movement of life, no longer seeks the unity of essence, no longer penetrates the invisible depths; he thus becomes triply frivolous. If, on the other hand, the specific character of stupidity without any ὁρμή ("momentum") is to stop halfway and wallow blissfully on the landing already reached, we can say that the temptation of smiling appearances, the temptation of plurality, and the temptation of immobility are the three principal forms not only of human futility but above all of human foolishness; the overgrown child smiling at a dappled surface. This is our "stupidity," and it is our psychasthenia, therefore our weakness, which explains the immobilization and fragmentation of the divine and the fascinated attraction to the most peripheral layer. At every moment the living waters tend to get lost in the swamp of stale and stagnant waters. Or if you prefer another image: the living water of faith tends to congeal into idolatry. Idolatry is the name of the eternal human frivolity, the one that makes us take a smile for a virtue, the smell of a rose for a truth, and a wooden beam for a God, the one that makes the superstitious bow down before beasts barely more stupid than them.

In the *Banquet* and the sixth book of the *Republic*, Platonic dialogue also electrified the naïf always ready to interrupt his climb, to fall asleep on the landing, to stop at appearances, to let himself be dazzled by shiny icons and tempted by what the *Meno* calls the "swarm," namely by plurality. Socrates is the vigilant principle that keeps the lazy awake so they go higher, further, always beyond the visible, and without yielding to the temptation of the multiple or appearance. The "Multiple" that Plato warns us against however is not a polytheistic plurality, and as a result indulgence of this plurality, however treacherous its seduction may be, is not strictly speaking a sin. What is condemned in the Bible is the sacrilegious and pagan worship of images: the one who kneels down in front of statuettes or in front of a joist lacerates the divine; he is not only outside of truth but outside of religion.

According to *Creative Evolution* as well, life is tempted at every step to whirl around on the spot: Bergson shows it to be fascinated by the organisms, the masterpieces it succeeds in creating—it asks only to be able to stop at these masterpieces and go no further, only humankind has been able to get over this barrier and sustain the creative élan within itself. Let us say for our part that the temptation to eddy about on the spot is, in its own way, a kind of idolatry and pagan indulgence that hinders the perpetual mobilization of vitality. Man, says Jeremiah (2:27), loves stone and wood as if they had given him life; man, succumbing to middle-class complacency, abandons the spirit for the letter and the elusive model for its static image. Even King Solomon, having become too rich and too powerful, falls into polygamy and polytheism; King Solomon becomes middle class and as stupid as an idolator: the wisdom of Solomon, having lost touch with the movement of life, renounces the infinite restlessness of spirit, turns on the spot, and becomes self-satisfied.

The prophets remained ruthlessly faithful to this exhausting imperative of spirit. Isaiah, before the apostle Paul (Isaiah 29:13; see also Deuteronomy 10:17), contrasts the mouth and the heart and subordinates the ritualism of observances to pneumatic pity. The call to a simplicity, a nakedness of spirit, a stripping away, which will find such a moving echo in *Two Sources*, is the constant demand of Proverbs and the Book of Job. Before the Stoic or Cynical sages, the prophets lambast the pleonexia that exponentially develops the hypertrophy of possessions and adds weight to the excess baggage of luxury. The proprietor, stripped of his possessions, relieved of any inessential or parasitic affiliations, is summoned to deeper things; the frivolous forgets his jewels, his gold plate and luxury silverware to listen to the deeper and more austere voice of his inner core; this voice of a simple heart (Book of Wisdom 1:1), detached and essentialized, speaks to us of the invisible unity and divine mystery hidden beneath the multicolored appearances. It warns us against the disappointment of which Solomon, victim of precious stones and power, is in some ways the symbol.

NOTES

1 On the opposition between the Spinoza's "monism" and Bergson's "dualism," see Gottlieb, "D'une erreur fondamentale dans *Les deux sources* de M. Bergson."

2 See Baudry, *Le problème de l'origine et de l'éternité du monde dans la philosophie grecque de Platon à l'ère chrétienne.*

3 Pascal, *Pensées*, s690/L450: "The God of Christians does not consist in a God who is merely the author of geometrical truths and of the order of the elements; that is the part given by the heathens and Epicureans."

4 Fleg, *Le livre du commencement.* [Translator's note: Where there is a significant difference between the biblical passages cited in French and the most common English versions of these passages, I have translated directly from the French.]

5 See Epictetus, *Discourses*, book I, ch. 15, § 7; *Philebus*, 18 a–b.

6 Compare Genesis 3:19 and Ecclesiastes 3:20. See also Psalms 146:4.

7 The Septuagint translates it: ἵνα τί ("to what end"), the very word of abandonment on Calvary (Matthew 27:46; Mark 15:34: εἰς τι ["why"]).

8 See Exodus 22:18.

9 Isaiah 42:9: "ἀναγγέλλων πρότερον τὰ ἔσχατα πρὶν αὐτὰ γενέσθαι (Behold, the former things have come to pass and new things spring forth)." See also Isaiah 48:3–5.

10 See Revelation 1:8, 1:17; 21:6, and 22:13: "ἐγὼ τό Ἄλφα καὶ τὸ Ὦ, ὁ πρῶτος καὶ ὁ ἔσχατος, ἡ ἀρχὴ καὶ τὸ τέλος [I am the Alpha and the Omega, the First and the Last, the Beginning and the End]."

11 Silesius, *The Cherubinic Wanderer*, part I, 25 and 111.

12 Rauh, "La conscience du devenir."

13 See Simmel, *Zur Philosophie der Kunst*, 146.

14 [Translator's note: See Plotinus, *The First Ennead*, book 6, "On Beauty," § 8.]

15 See Cohen, *Ethik des reinen Willens.*

16 Translator's note: A "garniture de cheminée" (the French phrase is also used in English) is a mantelpiece decoration consisting in a symmetrically arranged set of, most often, a clock with a candlestick on either side.

17 See Revelation 21:4: "ὁ θάνατος οὐκ ἔσται ἔτι [There will be no more death]." See also Revelation 20:14: "ὁ θάνατοςό δεύτερος ἐστιν [It is the second death]." Fleg, *Écoute Israël*, 583.

18 [Translator's note: See Epicurus, *Principal Doctrines*, n. 2.]

19 Huizinga, *Le déclin du Moyen Age*, 164–80

20 See Cohen, *Le Talmud*, 45.

21 See Matthew 22:33; Mark 12:27; Luke 20:38: "θεὸς δὲ οὐκ ἔστιν νεκρῶν ἀλλὰ ζώντων, πάντες γὰρ αὐτῷ ζῶσιν [He is not the God of the dead, but of the living, for to him all are alive]." But, see also Romans 14:8–9.

22 Lewkowitz, *Das Judentum und die geistigen Strömungen des 19.*

23 Gottlieb, "D'une erreur fondamentale dans *Les deux sources* de M. Bergson," 13–14.

24 It is not saying: "τείσομαι δὲ αὐτὸν ἅ με ἠδίκησεν [I'll pay them back for what they did]" (see Romans 12:21; Matthew 5:39; and Pascal, *Pensées*, 14/911).

25 It is the προσωπολημψία ("partiality" or "favouritism") referred to by Paul (Romans 2:11; Eph. 6:9). See also, II Chronicles 19:7.

26 Cohen, *Le Talmud*, 269.

27 Exodus 22:21, 23:9; Leviticus 19:33–34; Deuteronomy 10:18–19.

28 Exodus 33:4–5.

29 Fleg, *Nous de l'espérance*, 64.

30 Boulgakov, *L'orthodoxie*, 247–51.

31 [Translator's note: "Preterition" and "futurition" are terms specific to Jankélévitch. "Preterition" should be understood as related to the "preterite" (past historical) tense, not as the rhetorical device of preterition. See Jankélévitch's *Forgiveness*: "Becoming, in the first place, is essentially futurition and, secondarily, preterition. That is, depending on whether one looks toward the future or toward the past, becoming ceaselessly posits a future and with the same stroke and at the same time it deposits a past behind it" (14).]

32 [Translator's note: Jankélévitch plays here, as elsewhere in his work, on an invented opposition between "survenir," which means to arise or come to pass but which looks like it breaks down into "over" (*sur*) + "come" (*venir*), and "subvenir," which looks like it shares a structure with "souvenir" (memory): "under" (*sub/sou*) + "come" (*venir*).]

33 Compare Wisdom 2:5 and Job 8:9.

34 See Isaiah 43:18 (the Septuagint translate: "μὴ μνημονεύετε τὰ πρῶτα καὶ τὰ ἀρχαῖα μὴ συλλογίζεσθε [Remember ye not the former things, and consider not the ancient things]").

35 Psalm 148; Tolstoy, *Jean Damascène*. [Translator's note: Tolstoy (1817–75) was a Russian poet whose narrative poem "John of Damascus" (1856) was put to verse by Pyotr Ilyich Tchaikovsky (1840–1893). The song "I Bless You, Forests," is the fifth of Tchaikovsky's Seven Romances for voice and piano (Op. 47, n. 5).]

36 See Matthew 22:39; Mark 12:31; Romans 13:9; Galatians 5:14; James 2:8.

TWELVE

Bergson and Nietzsche on Religion

CRITIQUE, IMMANENCE, AND AFFIRMATION

Keith Ansell-Pearson and Jim Urpeth

In order to appreciate the contemporary significance of Bergson's discussion of religion in *The
Two Sources of Morality and Religion* it is instructive to bring
it into a critical dialogue with arguably the only other comparable attempt to articulate a naturalistic account of religion that similarly breaks the confines of a reductive sociobiology, namely, Nietzsche's renaturalization of religion.
We shall begin with an exposition of Bergson's conception
of static and dynamic religion before turning to a consideration of those aspects of Nietzsche's critical evaluation of
religion that seem to complement and challenge Bergson's
claims. In the final section we shall explore points of convergence in Bergson's and Nietzsche's accounts of religion
and consider the radical possibility to which their thought
often seems to tend—the fusion of the theory of life and
religion.

BERGSON ON STATIC RELIGION

We begin with an aspect of Bergson's thinking on religion
that finds a rigorous treatment in his analysis. The phenomenon in question is the "mythmaking function" or
"fabulation" (the fictionalizing of existence or the world
through the telling of stories). Where Nietzsche seems to

treat this as peculiar to a primitive (religious) mentality, Bergson argues that it continues to inform and guide the post-religious mind: it is an element more basic to the operations of the human mind than simply defining it as religious.

Bergson begins his treatment of religion in *Two Sources* by acknowledging that a cursory examination of religions in the past and present provides little more than a farrago of error and folly that is humiliating for human intelligence (TS 102/1061). Religion clings to absurdity and error; it enjoins immorality and prescribes crime. Crass superstition has long been a universal fact of human nature. We find societies existing without science and philosophy but never a society existing without religion. *Homo sapiens*, the only creature on earth endowed with reason and intelligence, is also the only creature able to pin its existence on things unreasonable. Hence, Bergson's initial question: how is it that reasonable beings accept unreasonable beliefs and practices?

He questions the validity of the approach of Lévy-Bruhl who sought to show a primitive mentality at work in early evolution, one that is found in so-called backward peoples. This is not sufficient for Bergson for a number of reasons. The main issue we need to confront is the *psychological origin of superstition*, and this can only be done by examining the general structure of human thought. In fact it is from an observation of civilized man of the present-day that we will find an answer to the question.[1]

What then of Emile Durkheim who lays stress on a "collective mentality" that can explain the workings of religion? Bergson accepts the idea of a "social intelligence" that involves collective representations deposited in language, institutions, and customs. But he argues there are deficiencies in the approaches of both sociology and psychology. Sociology takes the social body as the only reality, regarding the individual as an abstraction. Psychology, on the other hand, underestimates the extent to which the individual is primarily made for society. For Bergson, "our psychical structure originates in the necessity of preserving and developing social and individual life" (TS 108/1066). It is a question of focusing on use or, rather, both function and structure. The mind is not what it is for the fun of it. Bergson is looking for the source of things: mankind has not always had dramas and novels, but it has for most of its history created fictions and myths, and the origins of religion lie in fabulation. How does this mythmaking function come about? His answer is on account of a social need.

Fiction, Bergson notes, resembles an incipient hallucination, one that can thwart our judgment and reason. Nature creates intelligent beings but also needs to guard against certain dangers of intellectual activity without compromising the future of intelligence. In a world of facts where nothing can resist the power of intelligence, there arises a dimension where ghosts of facts appear and a counterfeit of experience is conjured up. Intelligence and superstition, on Bergson's account, go hand in hand and are part of the same (human) being. We need, then, to grasp the utility of the irrational elements of this tendency toward the strange and the absurd in the workings of a certain function of the mind.

The tendency toward the irrational can be likened to a "virtual instinct" (TS 110/1068). What does this mean? It plays a role akin to what instinct plays in animals that are devoid of conceptual intelligence: here all is regulated automatically. In the case of the human, however, psychic inventions are required to ensure mental equilibrium and adaptation to life. This is peculiar to the human animal, and here Bergson is close to the concerns that guide Nietzsche in his analysis in the *Genealogy of Morality* of the human as "the sick animal": man does not simply adapt to his environment and not in the manner of other animals. We are talking of *vital needs* being satisfied and demanding satisfaction, such as having "confidence in life." In part this can explain why religion survives through the ages and survives even in face of the tremendous advances in facts and knowledge of science (Bergson does not offer this as an apology for religion).

Intelligence threatens to break up social cohesion; if society is to continue, there must be a counterpoise to it. If this counterpoise cannot be created by instinct in human beings (intelligence occupies the place it would assume), then the same effect is produced by a virtuality of instinct (or, if one prefers, by the residue of instinct that survives on the fringe of intelligence). It does not exercise direct action but instead calls up imaginary representations. These need to hold their own against the representation of reality and aim to counteract the work of intelligence *through* intelligence. This mythmaking faculty both plays a (vital) social role and serves the individual's need for creative fancy.

Why is there a problem of intelligence? In the case of the anthill and the beehive the individual lives for the community alone. Here instinct is coextensive with life and social instinct is nothing more than the spirit of subordination and coordination animating the cells and tissues and organs of all living bodies. So there is no problem here. However, where the expansion of intelligence reveals itself as in the case of man, the problem becomes acute. Reflection enables the individual to invent and society to develop. But how is society to maintain itself in a situation where, through the license given to individual initiative, social discipline is endangered? What if the individual focuses largely or even solely on himself? The individual cannot work automatically or somnambulistically for the species but will want to seek individual satisfaction and fulfillment. Of course, training in and exposure to formal reasoning will lead him to recognize that he furthers his own interests by promoting the happiness of others, but then as Bergson notes it takes centuries to produce a John Stuart Mill (who has not convinced all philosophers, let alone the mass of mankind). The fact is that intelligence counsels egoism first. This is its logic, if you like. But the virtual instinct of society makes its own demands and places a check on the hyper-individuality of intelligence. This is where religion comes into the picture as a "defensive reaction of nature against the dissolvent power of intelligence" (TS 122/1078).

The first function of religion, therefore, concerns social preservation. It is a kind of instinct (a defensive reaction), but it is also a spiritual intelligence capable of cultivating individuals. Take, for example, death: animals do not know they are mortal and destined to die. Such knowledge is the prerogative of the human animal only. This is not just the sheer brute fact of death, though it is also this. It is the knowledge that all that comes into being is fated to pass away, to turn to dust, to come to nothing. Such is the source of the lament, "all is in vain," and many others too. How can we find the resources for affirming life and for creating new life in the face of such hard knowledge? Bergson argues that religion comes up with the image of life after death or of the eternal or immortal soul that lives on after the earthly body has perished: *"religion is a defensive reaction of nature against the representation, by intelligence, of the inevitability of death"* (TS 131/1086).

Religion then does not have its beginnings or roots in fear as Nietzsche supposes in his positivist period (see *Human, All Too Human,* chapter 3), but more precisely in a reaction against fear, and in its origins it is not a belief in deities (TS 153/1105). At first religion concerns more impersonal forces, and only over time do mythologies grow. Religion exists in order to give man confidence and to support belief: "In default of power, we must have confidence" (TS 164/1114). Bergson's key insight, then, is that (static) religion works against the dissolvent and depressive power of intelligence.

Why does Bergson pass from static religion to dynamic religion? Why not just stop at the static? On the one hand, Bergson has given us a highly interesting account of the sources of religion that seems sufficient, namely: a defensive reaction of nature against what might be depressing for the individual, and dissolvent for society, in the exercise of intelligence (TS 205/1150). So, why does Bergson privilege religion with the positing of *dynamic* religion? This question takes us to the heart of Bergson's thinking, and the answer lies in the problem of intelligence and the insufficiency, as he sees it, of an intellectualist solution to the riddle of humanity's existence. We think Nietzsche locates the same problem or impasse in the third essay of *Genealogy of Morality* where he expresses it as a problem of the will to truth and that science lacks a *faith*, but his response is different.[2] In contrast to Bergson, Nietzsche privileges philosophy but a philosophy of the future that requires new kinds of philosophers. For Nietzsche the future is also a problem of culture and breeding: it is no longer to be left to chance and the higher types of human existence must now be consciously bred.[3] Although Bergson holds that a decision concerning its future is an imperative for humanity (TS 317/1245), he envisages this in quite different terms to Nietzsche. Human beings, he suggests, face the task of determining whether they wish to go on living or not: "Theirs the responsibility, then, for deciding if they want merely to live, or intend to make just the extra effort required for fulfilling, even, on their refractory planet, the essential function of the universe, which is a machine for the making of gods" (TS 317/1245). Although this is open to interpretation, Bergson seems to be suggesting in the final pages of *Two Sources* that humanity needs to curtail its will to power and restrain its aphrodisiacal nature. One might conceive the "gods" here on the model of Epicurus: the task is to learn how to live a simple, modest, and blessed existence.

For Bergson, the human is not only distinguished from the rest of the animal kingdom as the rational animal but also as the sick animal. We are prone to illness and depression, and there are specific reasons why. We know our own morality. Only humans experience problems such as the "futility of existence." The rest of nature exists in "absolute tranquillity"; plants and animals have an unshakeable confidence, such is the nature of their instinctive attachment to life (TS 204/1149). But this attachment to life is what is so complex in the case of the human animal. The nature of our being wedded to life is of a different kind and order.

Bergson holds that religion in its dynamic aspect is superior to philosophy. This is because Bergson thinks philosophy, which is a species of intelligence, is bound up with contemplation and not action. It is also the case that for Bergson religion, again in its dynamic aspect, is vital, or to be more precise, it carries on the *élan vital* that is the creative force or energy of evolution. In its dynamic form religion expresses a superior vitality and a superior attachment to life. Detaching itself from the closed in all its forms, dynamic religion is able to attach itself in this superior way and show the open tendency of each particular thing. Bergson argues that while static religion is foreshadowed in nature, dynamic religion amounts to a leap beyond nature (TS 223/1164). With regards to the former he is largely concerned with identifying its social sources and function; with the latter he believes there is something real at stake in genuine mystic states: they herald new ways of feeling, thinking, being, and are of significance to humanity. To get to the essence of religion and understand the history of humankind, therefore, we need to pass from static to dynamic religion.

Let us explore further Bergson's idea of attachment to life. The human being's "attachment to life" slackens with the rise of intelligence (TS 210/1153). This is because it no longer lives in the present alone. An intelligent being, such as a "human," is one for whom there is no reflection without foreknowledge and no foreknowledge without what Bergson calls "inquietude," and this entails "a momentary slackening of the attachment to life" (TS 210/1153). Intelligence is bound up with culture and social and technical development; it is what Nietzsche calls learning to calculate and compute (see also Nietzsche on mnemotechnics in the *Genealogy of Morality*). However, intelligence does not give us full predictive powers. Bergson writes: "Religion is that element which, in beings endowed with reason, is called upon to make good any deficiency of attachment to life" (TS 210/1153). In static or natural religion, myth counterfeits reality as actually perceived and enables the human animal to recover the confidence it has lost; life is desirable once again.[4]

How does Bergson explain the passage to dynamic religion? The success of religion in giving the human a sense of attachment to life (joy in joy), in the face of the uncertainties and anxieties of intelligence, is the source of this move. In the mystic soul this attachment is felt so deeply that it pervades their whole being as a kind of spirit of life. Bergson's name for this mystical attachment is "love" (TS 38/1007). On this account, pure mysticism is rare (this is not by chance but by reason of its very essence) and is not reached in a series of gradual steps from static religion since a leap is involved. Let us enumerate the key differences and the move that is at work for Bergson. The job or task of religion in its static version is to attach humans to life and the individual to society by telling them tales on a par with those with which children are lulled to sleep. These myths, however, are not like other stories; they are not simply the product of imagination: rather, the mythmaking function responds to a real vital need. Thanks to the fabulating function, we gain a confidence we would otherwise lack. Bergson says that while the creations of the imagination are simply "ideas," the creations of fabulation are "ideo-motory" (they literally get into the nervous system) (TS 211/1154).

In dynamic religion—attained in true mysticism—the confidence in life that static religion gives us is transfigured. Now the attachment to life is not simply of the order of a vital need but of joy or "joy in joy, love of that which is all love" (TS 212/1155). Bergson devotes several pages to tracing the possible development of genuine mysticism or pure mystic states. This does not reside where we might think, for example, in the Eleusian mysteries and Dionysian frenzy. Why not? For Bergson it is because they are part of Greek philosophy's elevation of contemplation over action. In some mystical developments of Greek philosophy, such as Pythagoras, Plotinus, and Neoplatonism, action is held to be a weakening of contemplation, a degradation and degeneration of the perfection attained in the contemplative state. There is an intellectualism endemic to Greek thought, and this means that genuine mysticism is never reached or practiced by it.

For Bergson genuine mysticism is: "the establishment of a contact, consequently of a partial coincidence, with the creative effort which life itself manifests" (TS 220/1162). This is "God" in which, "The great mystic is to be conceived as an individual being, capable of transcending the limitations imposed on the species by its material nature, thus continuing and extending the divine action" (TS 220–21/1162). Bergson's spiritualism is unique since it conceives God as life: the divine force is the creative energy at work in the evolution of life. Life for him is a current of creative energy precipitated into matter that endeavors to wrest from it what it can. This current comes to a halt at specific "points," namely, species and organisms. On one line of evolution the élan vital swerves inward and gets locked into a circle of the eternal return of the same: the society of insects where organization is highly perfected, and although individuals exist they do so on the level of complete automatism. However, on the line of evolution that culminates in the human, or something like it, we can conceive of a superhuman or super-life possibility. As Deleuze puts it, Bergson introduces a capacity for "scrambling the planes, of going beyond his own plane as his own condition, in order to finally express naturing Nature."[5] We should not take this to mean that automatism is not a problem for the human animal. Quite the contrary: for the greater part of our evolutionary history, human beings do in fact exist in closed societies and in accordance with the static religion. Moreover, even once we have attained freedom it is automatism that we still need to work against. Freedom for Bergson, in the very movements by which it is affirmed, creates the very habits that will stifle it if it fails to renew itself by a constant effort.

Now we come to what is perhaps the most contentious aspect of Bergson's thinking. How does the dynamic come into the world? Or rather which religion in particular incarnates the élan vital? The answer for Bergson is Christianity: for him this is a universal religion and not a national religion, although it arises or emerges from one (i.e., Judaism, see TS 240/1179).

For Bergson the great Christian mystics achieve complete mysticism: they radiate extraordinary energy and superabundant activity (St. Paul, St. Teresa, Joan of Arc). Instead of turning inward and closing, the soul opens its gates to a universal love. This gives rise to inventions and organizations that are essentially Western. Why has Christianity taken hold in the West? Why has it had effectively no effect in say India that, says Bergson, has gone over to Islamism? Bergson argues that the development or spread of Christianity is linked to the rise and spread of machine civilization and industrialism: this gives us a growing optimism, at least initially, that human beings are not at the mercy of an indifferent and cruel nature but can control and manipulate it and in the service of human betterment and openness.[6]

Are mystics not crackpots? Should they not be compared to the mentally diseased? We do not know whether Bergson is being deliberately provocative or not, but when he describes these mystics he does so in terms that are decidedly Nietzschean: in them we can locate, "a vast expenditure of energy . . . the superabundance of vitality which it demands flows from a spring which is the very source of life" (TS 232/1172). In short what we find in the great mystics is intellectual vigor: "There is an exceptional, deep-rooted mental healthiness, which is readily recognizable. It is expressed in the bent for action, the faculty of adapting and re-adapting oneself to circumstances, in firmness combined with suppleness, in the prophetic discernment of what is possible and what is not, in the spirit of simplicity which triumphs over combinations" (TS 228/1169). Bergson acknowledges that there are abnormal states at work in mysticism—visions, ecstasies, raptures—that also characterize the mental states of sick people. But he points out that these morbid states can imitate healthy states and prefigure new growth and expansion. There is mystic insanity—for example, the person who thinks they are Jesus or Napoleon and imitates them—but does it follow, he asks, that mysticism is insanity? How do we distinguish between the abnormal and the morbid and sick? Even the great mystics for Bergson warn against visions (pure hallucinations). Visions are explicable solely in terms of the *shock* taking place as the soul passes from the static to the dynamic, from the closed to the open, from everyday life to mystic life: "we cannot upset the regular relation of the conscious to the unconscious without running a risk" (TS 229/1170). Bergson concedes that the image may be pure hallucination and the emotion meaningless agitation (see TS 230–32/1171–72 on the progress of the mystic soul).

Finally, why is the love of God for all humans proclaimed by the great mystic not the same as the fraternity proclaimed by philosophers in the name of reason from Stoics to Kant (TS 233/1173)? Bergson thinks this love is more alive: the rational idea of fraternity is one we can admire and respect but not one we can attach ourselves to with passion. This is the importance of dynamic religion: it touches and teaches us on a level that reason cannot. Does this mean the mystic appeals simply to an intensification of an innate sympathy of man for man (TS 234/1173–74)? No, such an instinct is little more than an imaginary fantasy of philosophers who posit it for reasons of symmetry. We cannot simply pass in a series of discrete steps from the family to the community and nation to the brotherhood of all men and even higher than this. Our social instinct ties us to the local and the national, it does not foster the unity of humankind: "The mystic love of humanity is a very different thing. It is not the extension of an instinct, it does not originate in an idea" (TS 234/1174). Love is neither of the senses nor of the mind but implicitly of both and more than either taken singly; it lies at the root of feeling and reason. More metaphysical than moral in its essence, it contains "the secret of creation" (TS 234/1174).

NIETZSCHE ON RELIGION

Nietzsche, at least for a period of time (the free spirit trilogy), is deeply suspicious of the figure of the saint and the claim to superior insight derived from alleged mystical experiences.[7] He makes this criticism in a number of texts. In *Dawn*, for example, he argues that the very claim that someone has had visions—a so-called genius or superior soul who has seen things the rest of us do not see—should make us cautious.[8] He is suspicious of a teaching of pure spirituality, locating a "chronic over-excitability" in virtuous pure spirits who can only gain pleasure from ecstasy, a precursor of madness, which affords them a standard by which to condemn all earthly things.[9] Furthermore, he holds that behind these states of exaltation and ecstasy there lies human, all too human, motivations and instincts such as vengefulness and self-dissatisfaction: "Mankind owes much that is bad to these wild inebriates: for they are insatiable sowers of the weeds of dissatisfaction with oneself and one's neighbour, of contempt for the age and the world, especially of world-weariness. Perhaps a whole Hell of *criminals* could not produce an affect so oppressive, poisonous to air and land ... as does this noble little community of unruly, fantastic, half-crazy people of genius who cannot control themselves and can experience pleasure only when they have lost themselves."[10] No doubt there is genuine psychological insight here, but Bergson himself insists that ecstasy is not the end point of mysticism. If we take a philosopher-saint such as Plotinus, we find that he goes as far as ecstasy, the state in which the soul feels itself in the presence of the divine or creative source, but he does not go beyond it as the genuine mystic must—that is, to the state where contemplation is engulfed in action (TS 230/1171).

But here we must point to a key difference between Nietzsche and Bergson. Nietzsche has a completely different valuation of the different religions, privileging the free-minded Greeks over Christianity, but also

Buddhism and Islam over Christianity as well. In essence Nietzsche regards Christianity as a pathological religion: it is ruled by an excess of feeling that corrupts head and heart. Christianity, he says, wants to stupefy, intoxicate, and shatter, and as such is devoid of "measure."[11] For Nietzsche, the deepest religious faith is a Dionysian one: "Saying yes to life, even in its strangest and hardest problems. . . . In it the most profound instinct of life, the instinct for the future of life."[12]

Is there anything that resembles dynamic religion in Nietzsche? Perhaps, but for Nietzsche possession or experience of the superior states of the soul is the privilege of the philosopher, not the religious mystic. His definition of the philosopher in *Beyond Good and Evil* resembles Bergson's depiction of the mystic: "A philosopher: that is the person who is constantly experiencing, seeing, hearing, suspecting, hoping, dreaming extraordinary things; who is struck by his own thoughts as if they came from outside, from above or below . . . who may even be himself a thunderstorm, going about pregnant with new lightning."[13] For Nietzsche's philosophy, should we wish to define it, is an affair or activity of spiritual perception or vision entailing the discernment of greatness, significance, importance, what is rare and extraordinary, and so on. In the chapter on religion in *Beyond Good and Evil* Nietzsche maintains that the religious disposition (piety)—that is, a life with God—is a product of a fear of truth; it is "the will to untruth" at any price.[14] Piety has enabled religion to beautify humanity, turning us "so completely into art, surface, and kindness that we no longer suffer when we look at them."[15] In this respect religious human beings belong to the class of artists: burnt children or born artists who find their joy in seeking to falsify life's image. The attempt to transcendentalize or idealize the image is a sign of sickness, and Nietzsche does not wish to be uncharitable about it.

However, he attacks nonreligious Germans—for example, the free thinkers—for being unable to appreciate the possible use of religion and who are simply astonished by the fact that religions exist in the world.[16] He attacks the "presumptuous little dwarf and vulgarian" that he associates with the modern scholar and his faith in his own superiority, in his good conscience for being tolerant in the face of the curiosities of religion.[17] He also holds in contempt the middle-class Protestant who does not know if their interest in going to church should be seen as a new business deal or a new recreational activity. Clearly for Nietzsche religion must be taken seriously. But in what way?

Nietzsche presents the alternative perspective in *Beyond Good and Evil* (61–62) where he speaks of how the free spirit approaches religion. Essentially he views religion as a means of spiritual and social discipline. The essential danger lies when religions seek to establish themselves as sovereign in life, no longer serving as a means of education and cultivation in the hands of the philosopher. His chief concern is with the fate of the higher types of human being and how religion endangers their flourishing. His concern centers on two facts: (1) as in the rest of the animal kingdom, humanity exhibits an excess of failures: the sick, degenerate, and infirm; and (2) successful humans are always the exception: their complicated conditions of life can only be calculated with great subtlety and difficulty. "The economy of mankind," for Nietzsche, is ruled over by the accidental and a law of absurdity. Nietzsche then asks, what is the attitude of religious beings toward the excess of cases that do not turn out right? His answer is that such religious beings seek to, above all, preserve life, "to preserve alive whatever can possibly be preserved."[18] While they can receive credit—"the very highest credit"—for their preserving care, the danger is that such religions, when they exist as sovereign, are among the principal causes that keep the type "man" on a lower rung of the ladder of life. Or, as Nietzsche perhaps dangerously puts it, "they have preserved too much of *what ought to perish.*" Nietzsche immediately goes on to express gratitude toward religions, noting what the spiritual human beings of Christianity have achieved in Europe. But he reiterates his main point: this has been at the cost of worsening *"the European race"* and standing all valuations on their head, for example, breaking the strong, casting suspicion on joy in beauty, turning the instincts of the strong, domineering, and turned-out-well types into uncertainty, agony of conscience, and self-destruction: "invert all love of the earthly and of dominion over the earth into hatred of the earth and the earthly." Has not an attempt been made to apply "a single will" over Europe for eighteen centuries with the aim of turning man into a "sublime miscarriage (*sublime Missgeburt*)?" Such a "monster" is interesting and of a higher, refined kind (hence the word "sublime") but is nevertheless a miscarriage of what could have been bred and educated. With respect to these tasks Nietzsche holds Christianity to be the most presumptuous religion to date, as well as the most calamitous. What has been bred, and whose hegemony now needs contesting, is man as "the herd animal."[19]

As with Nietzsche, Bergson too sees religion as discipline, but only on the level of what he calls "static religion"; he also argues there is a dynamic religion where great spiritual leaders—Jesus, St. Paul, St. Theresa, and so on—bring a new emotion into existence that has the potential to transform humanity. Nietzsche treats this notion of dynamic religion—one that takes mystical states seriously—suspiciously. He does not trust mystical experiences, mystical souls, and their so-called telephone to the beyond. This raises two issues: (1) how are we to interpret the apparently sublime mystical experiences of Zarathustra; and (2) what of Bergson's insight that religious mystics are not about the beyond but the transformation of human life? Mystics for Bergson are not simply humans of vision, raptures, and ecstasies; they are primarily figures of action. Is there not, he asks, a mystic dormant within each one of us, responding to a call (TS 97/1057)?

NATURAL RELIGION: IMMANENCE AND AFFIRMATION

Another approach is possible in which Bergson and Nietzsche can be profitably conjoined as thinkers of immanence and joyous affirmation. Bergson's assertion in *Two Sources* of the preeminence of Christianity (in particular, its mystical aspect)—conceived as the embodiment of the élan vital itself—might seem to preclude any fundamental affinity with Nietzsche's seemingly hostile evaluation of, perhaps, religion per se, but most unequivocally Christianity specifically. However, another, more convergent, configuration of their respective critical discussions of religion can be articulated. We will conclude by sketching such an alternative: our focus is on Bergson's and Nietzsche's positive accounts of religion, that is to say, the extent to which both thinkers suggest that religion can be aligned with, as grounded in, their respective (and arguably very similar) ontologies of natural life in its most affirmative primary process.

As we have seen, both Bergson and Nietzsche accord religion a key role in what they regard as secondary or derivative ontological processes of individual and collective self-preservation; but they also suggest that if religion is inappropriately regarded as primordial, it becomes a life-denying impediment to the flourishing of life. We shall not explore the extent to which Bergson and Nietzsche agree in their respective accounts of the derivative, if nonetheless necessary, role played by such aspects of religion among the (mere) survival strategies of the species. What must be considered now is the possibility that both Bergson and Nietzsche accord religion a role not merely (to use Nietzsche's terms) in the processes of life preservation but also in those of *life enhancement*: that is, both offer not only a naturalistic critique of religion but also a *naturalistic revalidation of it in relation to life affirmation*. Indeed, the possibility must be entertained that both thinkers conclude that natural life has its own indigenous religion of self-affirmation and its own necessity to reassert itself against self-preservation in celebratory gestures of creative becoming. In short do not Bergson and Nietzsche conceive the privilege of the human species to reside in its selection by life for the affirmative return of its dysteleological essence? Is there not a way in which both thinkers' philosophical biologies tend toward the identification of the primary process of life with (or as) non-anthropomorphic religion? From such a perspective religion (in its healthy or dynamic form) is identified as the natural and cultural phenomenon in which the instrumental concerns of the species (i.e., knowledge, measurement, quantification, and so on) are surpassed and a nonobjectifiable creative becoming embraced.

The possibility of such convergence presupposes the plausibility of a "religious" interpretation of Nietzsche. It requires that a credible correlate to Bergson's notion of dynamic religion can be discerned within Nietzsche's texts, something akin to what he might term a healthy religion. While we are confident that such an equivalent exists as a crucial seam in Nietzsche's thought, most obviously in his life-long commitment to identifying the essence of life with the Dionysian, the task of sketching and justifying this claim in any detail cannot be undertaken here.[20] The necessary conditions of so conceiving Nietzsche's thought are that (despite his own occasional lapses in this regard) a distinction between religion and Christianity is maintained and that, whatever might be meant by a positive endorsement of religion in Nietzsche's thought—that is, of its identification with the primordial active forces of life itself—it entails a religion of immanence without a personal God and without reference to morality. For Nietzsche, religion in this affirmative sense marks the achievement of a complete de-anthropomorphization in which thought divests itself of the personification of life (i.e., "God") and acknowledges that life lies beyond good and evil and is irreducible to antithetical thinking (i.e., "morality").

Of course, major textual obstacles seem to exist for such a reading of Nietzsche. In addition to the sober and apparently science friendly mindset of the texts of his so-called positivist period there are also the late texts in which we find an insistent and rigorous pursuit of a "completely de-deified nature."[21] However, it can be plausibly claimed that such a de-deification is not incompatible with, and indeed is a condition of possibility of, the emergence of an impersonal immanent religion of non-anthropomorphic life and that, furthermore, Nietzsche could not be clearer in his late texts that whatever this de-deification might entail, it does not have a scientific or secular trajectory.

Perhaps a productive way of conceiving the confluence of philosophical biology and religion in Bergson and Nietzsche is to consider both to revive and radically reconfigure natural religion. That is to say, both Bergson and Nietzsche urge us to attend to those aspects of nature in which the creative becoming of life is apparent. Such a natural religion is plausibly conceived as religious in that it exceeds the categories of instrumental thought, occurs in and as an affective state (i.e., joy) phenomenologically identifiable as religious and, furthermore, marks life's own self-affirmation regardless of its relationship to human thought. It goes without saying that this is religion without reference to the design argument. As a religion of immanence, the point is not to elaborate analogies with purposive production in order to justify the positing of a transcendent creator. In addition the relevant aspects of natural life are those that exceed the explanatory schemas of any evolutionary theory in which adaptation and self-preservation are particularly emphasized or prioritized. Indeed, part of the significance for contemporary thought and culture of conjoining philosophical biology and religion is the extent to which Bergson and Nietzsche provide resources to displace the moribund debate between intelligent design and evolutionary theory. From this perspective, both parties to this contemporary debate have more in common than they seem to appreciate, as becomes apparent in their shared hostility to the aspects of the natural order prioritized by Bergson and Nietzsche. Hence, Bergson and Nietzsche are viewed as advocates of an atheistic natural religion committed to the self-sufficiency of natural immanence, an order that they credit with a capacity for religious self-affirmation. The religious potential of immanence is thereby acknowledged rather than denied, and the identification of religion per se with the transcendent is disputed.

Nietzsche and Bergson develop two sophisticated philosophical biologies and promote the claim that natural life is religious in essence. They share a monistic conception of life: Nietzsche in terms of the will to power, and Bergson in terms of the élan vital. And both insist on the ontological primacy of time (as eternal recurrence and duration respectively) and of affectivity (which conceives of the real as first and foremost a differential flow of felt difference, not to be confused with the methods by which it is subsequently rendered measurable). On the basis of these shared principles, both Nietzsche and Bergson reject the presumed primacy of a functional and utilitarian conception of life's inherent tendencies. They challenge the assumed primordiality of self-preservation and endeavor to conceive life as creative process irreducible to the anthropomorphic categories of either mechanism or teleology. Both Nietzsche and Bergson are pioneers in the formulation of naturalistic, intra-biological critiques of the philosophical and normative underpinnings of Darwinism, the displacement of which is necessary if the non-transcendent religious nature of life itself is to be accessed and affirmed.

Let us return to Bergson's *Two Sources* to detect the presence of natural religion. On a number of occasions (see TS 205/1150, 207/1152, 222/1163, 250/1188, 262/1198), Bergson notes a kinship between the intellectual ethos and the project of natural religion (if not with its historical alignment with the notion of a transcendent deity that, of course, he like Nietzsche, explicitly refuses). For Bergson, life has an impersonal and immanent source—duration—which ought to be the reference point of all that it makes possible and sustains. On balance, however, Bergson rejects an explicit appropriation (at least in relation to static religion) of the notion of natural religion due to its received meaning and historical provenance. Nonetheless, this should not preclude us from recognizing the profounder sense in which Bergson advances the project of natural religion on the basis of an ontology of life distinct from his deist predecessors.

In this vein it is worth noting the extent to which Bergson insists on an essential feature of natural religion, namely, the claim that there is a universal source of religion intrinsic to natural life that is accessible, in principle, independently of revealed religion. Bergson's allegiance to this key claim of natural religion is apparent in his reference, in relation to the philosophical interpretation and evaluation of mysticism, to an "original content, drawn straight from the very well-spring of religion, independent of all that religion owes to tradition, to theology, to the Churches" (TS 250/1188). In retrieving mysticism as a natural phenomenon and reclaiming it from its ecclesiastical appropriation, the advocate of natural religion must insist that "philosophy . . . confine itself to experience and inference" and forge a partnership with the mystic toward the shared aim of connectedness with the divine process of immanent life (TS 250/1188). As Bergson states, "It would suffice to take mysticism unalloyed, apart from the visions, the allegories, the theological language which express it, to make it a powerful helpmate to philosophical research. . . . We must then find out in what measure mystic experience is a continuation of the experience which led us to the doctrine of the *élan vital*. All the information with which it would furnish philosophy, philosophy would repay in the shape of confirmation" (TS 250–51/1188; translation modified).

For Nietzsche, the religious affirmation of life is identified with bliss and joy. In this regard proximity to Bergson is clearly discernible. Both thinkers accord affectivity an ontological status such that, in relation to certain emotions, the realm of subjective feeling is escaped and a connection is made with the primary tendencies of life. Bergson offers an extended theory of ontological emotion in which a further affinity with Nietzsche can be detected (TS 38–54/1007–20). Both thinkers tend toward the identification of the divine with an asubjective qualitative state in and through which the will to power and élan vital respectively manifest and reaffirm themselves. As Bergson states, "divine love is not a thing of God: it is God Himself" (TS 252/1189).

Bergson seeks to conceive mysticism in "relation to the *élan vital* . . . it is this impulse itself, communicated to exceptional individuals who in turn would fain impart it to all humanity" (TS 213/1156; translation modified). This further underlines Bergson's view of the intrinsically religious nature of reality. As he states, "the ultimate end of mysticism is the establishment of a contact . . . a partial coincidence, with the creative effort which life itself manifests. This effort is of God, if it is not God himself" (TS 220/1162). Indeed, it appears that mysticism is the culmination of the critical trajectory of Bergson's thought as it migrates from a phenomenology of time consciousness to an ontology of life itself: "For this intuition was turned inward; and if, in a first intensification, beyond which most of us did not go, it made us realise the continuity of our inner life, a deeper intensification might carry it to the roots of our being, and thus to the principle of life in general. Now is not this the privilege of the mystic soul" (TS 250/1187)? As indicated, both Nietzsche and Bergson emphasize the ontological significance of joy. Bergson speaks of "a boundless joy, an all-absorbing ecstasy . . . an enthralling rapture" (TS 230/1171). The watchwords in this renaturalization of religious affectivity are, for both thinkers, energy and vitality (as apparent in the passage from *Two Sources* cited above). Religious affectivity in its nonpathological form is here identified with the creative becoming of life itself.

We have suggested that Nietzsche and Bergson develop a biologically grounded account of religion that, unlike so many contemporary attempts, does not beg the question of its origins and status. On the basis of this approach, neither thinker pursues (at least not in relation to healthy or dynamic religion) a reductionist explanation that translates into ultimately nonreligious terms. Neither Nietzsche nor Bergson assumes the primacy within nature of the notions of function and survival, nor do they exclude empirical science from incorporation within the philosophical biologies they propose. They explore the possibility of a naturalistic religion and discriminate between derivative and primary, morbid and non-morbid aspects of various religions (with admittedly significant differences emerging as regards to their evaluation of different religions and aspects thereof). Both thinkers, we suggest, endeavor to identify a becoming religious of the natural life itself, a self-affirmation that occurs as an ontological affectivity that possesses privileged and exceptional members of one of its creative experiments.

NOTES

1 Here Bergson means something broader than what Nietzsche undertakes, for example, in the second essay of *On the Genealogy of Morality* and in the context of tracing developments of bad conscience. In prehistory, argues Nietzsche, the basic creditor-debtor relationship that informs human social and economic activity also finds expression in religious rites and worship in, for example, the way a tribal community expresses thanks to earlier generations. Over time the ancestor is turned into a god and associated with the feeling of fear, and this is the birth of superstition. For a different treatment of superstition, see also Nietzsche, *The Gay Science*, 23.

2 Nietzsche, *Beyond Good and Evil*, 287.

3 Ibid., 203.

4 In *On the Genealogy of Morality* Nietzsche also addresses this function of religion: he sees religion as a response to the problems thrown up by intelligence. For Nietzsche, intelligence takes the form of "culture." Depression and illness have several causes, being produced by the costs of domestication and the internalization of the aggressive drives and instincts; the need for power among the socially and politically oppressed and the fact that this takes the form of metaphysical fictions and fantasy (the "merited" free will of the slaves revolt, for example, the psychical inventions of the priest, and so forth).

5 Deleuze, *Bergsonism*, 107. See also TS 257/1193.

6 On this point we could compare what Nietzsche says about hubris in the third essay of *On the Genealogy of Morality*. Nietzsche holds that it is hubris (what the Greeks understood by overweening pride) that characterizes our whole modern godless existence: it is an awareness of strength or confidence as opposed to weakness or impotence. We moderns consider ourselves to be superior to God and to nature, it is a tremendous elevation of human confidence—and clearly it is this confidence that is now being threatened, whether real or imaginary, today with phenomena such as global warming. Nietzsche, *On the Genealogy of Morality*, III: 9.

7 The "free-spirit trilogy" of 1878–82 refers to Nietzsche's books *Human, All Too Human, Dawn,* and *The Gay Science.*

8 Nietzsche, *Dawn,* 66.

9 Ibid., 39.

10 Ibid., 50.

11 Nietzsche, *Human, All Too Human,* 114, 117. See also *Dawn,* 78.

12 Nietzsche, *Twilight of the Idols,* "What I Owe the Ancients," 5.

13 Nietzsche, *Beyond Good and Evil,* 292.

14 See also the preface in *The Gay Science* on the youthful madness of the will to truth at any price.

15 Nietzsche, *Beyond Good and Evil,* 59.

16 Ibid., 58.

17 Ibid., 58.

18 Ibid., 62.

19 Ibid., 62, 199, 201–2.

20 For an attempt to offer such a reading, see Urpeth, " 'Health' and 'Sickness' in Religious Affectivity." For a more extended discussion of the relationship between Bergson's and Nietzsche's conceptions of religion that takes account of all of Bergson's major works (particularly *Creative Evolution*), see also Urpeth, "Reviving 'Natural Religion.' "

21 See Nietzsche, *The Gay Science,* 109.

THIRTEEN

Assurance and Confidence in
The Two Sources of Morality and Religion

A SOCIOLOGICAL INTERPRETATION OF
THE DISTINCTION BETWEEN STATIC RELIGION
AND DYNAMIC RELIGION

Frédéric Keck
Translated by Alexandre Lefebvre and Perri Ravon

In this chapter, I will offer a commentary on the definition Bergson gives of belief in the chapter titled "Static Religion": "Belief . . . means essentially confidence; the original source is not fear, but a form of assurance against fear" (TS 152/1104; translation modified).

I would like to show what this definition of religion owes to the idea of the social realm as an "insurance scheme,"[1] but I also want to present the split it introduces within this system by claiming that there is a preeminent or "essential" form of confidence. To say that the primary origin of belief is not fear but a form of insurance against fear amounts to saying that religion is a social phenomenon and not the product of the individual imagination: it connects individuals to each other prior to any contract, inasmuch as it collectively reassures them in the face of the threats that weigh on their existence. And yet to say that belief is *essentially* confidence is also to say that there are lesser forms of belief, which, in turn, raise doubts about insurance as a socially organized belief system for finite beings confronted with uncertainty. Bergson puts it succinctly in the first pages of *Two Sources*: "Whether religion be interpreted in one way or another, whether it be social in essence or by accident, one thing is certain, that it has always played a social role" (TS 13/984).

We need to assess the originality of Bergson's thesis, which states both that religion has a social role *and* that this is merely a role, one played by accident more than by essence. This thesis provides a criterion for the sociological study of religions, allowing us to evaluate religions by the yardstick of the essence they should manifest. Bergson's move in *Two Sources* is not to oppose a biological conception of religion, based on the doctrine of the *élan vital*, to a sociological conception of religion, but to distinguish within religion, conceived as a social phenomenon, two forms whose difference in degree becomes a difference in kind—what Bergson calls static religion and dynamic religion. If we want to understand in what sense static religion is a religion "by accident," it is not enough to say that it offers us a form of assurance or insurance against accidents within a systematic risk-sharing scheme that may come to be called static religion. It must also be shown that the essence that manifests itself in the case of accidents can also appear in itself in exceptional situations— which would thus be a definition of dynamic religion.

I will begin by comparing Bergson's analysis to Durkheim's solidarist framework, then go on to show how the encounter between Bergson and Lévy-Bruhl works around the notion of the accident, which will enable us to understand where Bergson departs from Lévy-Bruhl in his analysis of confidence. It is thus a matter of reading *Two Sources* and the major chapters that structure the work by taking the notion of assurance as our point of departure, in order to rediscover a genuine alternative within this framework that perhaps represents one of the most surprising points of convergence between our own philosophical time and the one in which Bergson was writing.

A GENEALOGY OF THE CONCEPT OF INSURANCE IN THE DEBATE ON RESPONSIBILITY

To describe the notion of insurance as it appears in the nineteenth century, we can make use of the genealogy of the welfare state (in French, *l'état-providence*) put forward by François Ewald. According to Ewald, the concept of insurance transforms the concept of responsibility at a time when French legal thought had to legislate on workplace accidents.[2] Workplace accidents provoke a crisis in early nineteenth-century liberal thought, according to which every individual is responsible for his own actions—responsible, that is, for everything falling within the clearly demarcated sphere of his own property. The problem is that a worker cannot be held responsible for the accident he is a victim of: if workers feared liability for work accidents, they would no longer work. Within an increasingly complex social life, the accident introduces the possibility that everything might come to a halt: it represents the possibility of radical discontinuity. The continuity of social life thus obliges recourse to the fiction according to which the employer or state—the guarantors of collective property—are responsible for the accident rather than the worker.

The legal reasoning on workplace accidents transfers responsibility from the worker to the employer or the state by inventing the concept of "no-fault" or "vicarious" liability. Such a concept, however, causes a profound crisis within the concept of causality, because it implies that one can be responsible for an accident (that is to say, required to pay the damages resulting from the accident) without having caused it: while the worker is the direct cause of the accident, society is the cause of the risks incurred by workers who work in more and more dangerous factories. The concept of causality is thus split in two: the worker is the mechanical cause of the accident, while society is the moral cause. In the event of an accident, it is not toward mechanical causality that we must turn but toward the moral causality that should have anticipated the accident. The probabilistic logic of risk thus replaces the mechanical logic of consequences. Society thus appears as a form of "providence" that insures individuals against the risks they incur by anticipating accidents and spreading their cost; in other words, by guaranteeing the material means for social life to resume following the discontinuity of the accident. Insurance is thus an intellectual device that supplements the mechanical causality of individuals with the moral causality of society. This formulation of the social problem in turn requires the involvement of philosophy, because it is a case of understanding how society becomes this very particular subject of responsibility at the moment the discontinuity of the accident interrupts the continuity of life. How can this subject of responsibility be established in such a way that social life is able to continue in its diverse forms? In France much of the dialogue between philosophy and the social sciences turned on this issue of moral causality, as it was framed by responsibility for workplace accidents.

Emile Durkheim responded to the challenge of moral causality with the concept of solidarity. According to the definition given by Léon Bourgeois and the solidarist movement that formed around him, solidarity is the quasi-contract which connects individuals to each other in relation to a primary evil: solidarity is that unbroken chain of generations which forms in response to the possibility of illness. Durkheim, starting with the analysis of criminal law, adapted this framework of solidarity to crime, considered as the socially visible form of illness. In this context, Durkheim defines obligation by its manifestation in the form of sanctions: what makes solidarity visible is the punishment of the act that has transgressed social rules.[3] Society is thus expressed through the figure of the court, which defines what its "proper" scope is and destroys whatever, being "improper," is forbidden.

Society is certainly a moral cause, in that it excises from the social organism whatever it finds unsuitable; but in doing so it acts under the form of the law by assigning a certain number of duties to the individual. To the discontinuity of crime, whereby the individual threatens social life, corresponds the discontinuity of the prohibition, whereby society responds to the individual as a collective tribunal. Granted, Durkheim clearly distinguishes repressive punishment in societies exhibiting mechanical solidarity and restitutive punishment in societies of organic solidarity—the former expressed as a radical discontinuity, the latter as a restoration of continuity. Also, the notion of obligation is broader than that of duty, in that it involves that layer of psychic life where individuals become attached to the rules that constrain them and desire the life of relationships that society represents. But Bergson certainly has a simplified form of Durkheimism in mind when he criticizes the notion of obligation in the first chapter of *Two Sources*: society conceived as an entity closed on itself cannot exercise sufficient moral causality to attract individuals to it; it needs to go further, into the very sources of social life, into the habits by which we follow social rules without even realizing it. In looking for a clear and distinct expression of obligation, we must not take the prohibition as our point of departure but the accident, insofar as its effect is to upset our habits.

From this standpoint, the first sentence of the book—"The remembrance of forbidden fruit is the earliest thing in the memory of each of us, as it is in that of mankind" (*TS* 9/980)—is deceptive. While prohibitions and taboos are what surprise and amaze the philosopher in his scrutiny of society inasmuch as these reveal the fact of obedience and constraint, a closer analysis shows that these must be placed against the broader backdrop of habits, which Bergson calls "the whole of obligation" and which is the truly effective force of social life. To take prohibition as the point of departure is an intellectualist approach to morality, based on its composite and rigid forms: the true focus of moral agents in practice is the accident and the discontinuity it introduces in the continuous fabric of social life. If solidarity constitutes itself in response to the prohibition, insurance emerges to mitigate the effects of the accident.

It was precisely by way of a reflection on accidents that Lévy-Bruhl formulated the problem of responsibility. We can speculate that if Bergson comments at length on Lévy-Bruhl's analyses of "primitive mentality" in the second chapter of *Two Sources*, it is not only because Lévy-Bruhl was, like him, a philosopher interested in ethnographic facts—as opposed to Durkheim, the founder of a school of sociology—it is also because Lévy-Bruhl's thought started out from a reflection on moral causality that was very close to his own concerns. Lévy-Bruhl effectively defended his doctoral thesis in 1884 on "the idea of moral responsibility," taking the following observation as his starting point: the idea of responsibility has become confused because each crime can be referred either to natural causes, as criminology does by bringing innate criminal tendencies to light, or to moral causes, as courts do by appealing to the individual's sense of duty and justice.[4] Lévy-Bruhl's project can be described as a genealogy of the sense of responsibility, showing its development prior to the separation between natural and moral causality. The question of responsibility arises precisely when a phenomenon cannot be classified within the well-defined domains of nature and morality, because it appears at the point where the two domains meet.[5]

In this sense we can understand Lévy-Bruhl's radical thesis, which Bergson has no trouble criticizing as intellectualist, that the primitive mentality is unaware of the principle of contradiction and, as such, is "prelogical." Where we see a separation between two terms, for example, a man and a bird, the primitive mentality sees a relation of identity, the bird acting as the ancestor of a man. Lévy-Bruhl describes a world where the connections between phenomena come before the perception of the phenomena themselves, because these appear as colored by moral significance.

To describe this perception of the world, Lévy-Bruhl uses the term "participation." In the primitive mentality each thing participates in a complex of forces, powers, wills, and properties that all act on the individual in a way that Lévy-Bruhl describes as "mystical," in the sense that they are not perceived through the senses and yet are quite real because they are active.[6] This action at a distance is possible because education has familiarized the primitive subject with these supernatural forces that coexist with natural things and accompany them as ghosts or shadows. What interests Lévy-Bruhl in the primitive mentality is thus the conception of causality at work there and the way it challenges our own: here it is no longer one term that acts on another in a world whose separation is guaranteed by the principle of contradiction, but rather a whole that acts on a term that is one of its parts—thus justifying the use of the term "participation."[7]

Lévy-Bruhl himself acknowledges on two occasions that this conception of causality can be illuminated by Bergson's analyses. In his account of *Time and Free Will* he emphasizes the originality of the Bergsonian concept of causality that, against both Kantianism and associationism, consists in an interpenetration of mental states (even if Lévy-Bruhl admits his difficulty conceiving of an isolated subject of duration, and already looks for a collective genesis of participation).[8] And in *Primitive Mentality* he notes that the representation of time found in primitive cultures escapes the framework of ordered representation and "rather resembles a subjective feeling of duration, not wholly unlike the *durée* described by Bergson."[9] Against the associationist conception of causality held by the British anthropology of Frazer according to which one idea is the cause of another when the latter follows it in the individual mind, Lévy-Bruhl, following Durkheim, describes a new form of causality in which a whole acts on each of its parts by manifesting itself in the form of representations: the individual acts to the extent that he participates in the social. We can therefore see why Bergson took an interest in Lévy-Bruhl at the point when his own reflections on moral causality, hitherto limited to the mental and biological domains, were extending into the social realm. What attracts Bergson's attention, however, is not so much participation itself, which had already been described by Durkheim, but rather the modalities through which it comes into play on the occasion of accidents, which is Lévy-Bruhl's true contribution to the sociological debate on responsibility.

LÉVY-BRUHL'S CRITIQUE: A PSYCHOLOGY
OF ACTION CAUSED BY AN ACCIDENT

Lévy-Bruhl claims in effect that in the primitive mentality there are no accidents, in the sense that every unusual phenomenon is immediately perceived as the intervention of a mystical force. The accident immediately takes us from the order of natural causality, which it disturbs, to the order of supernatural causality, which it reveals. A crocodile that comes too close to the village is not the norm: it must therefore be a sorcerer who has taken the shape of a crocodile. A bird encountered during a ritual hunt is not a bird like other birds; it is the apparition of an ancestor's spirit. Death itself is never accidental, not because men are necessarily unaware of its mechanical causes in the deterioration of the body but because the social effect of the loss of a life is such that this mechanical cause must be supplemented by a will that explains its irruption here and now. The primitive mentality does not explain the "how," it goes directly to the "why": for every accident that disturbs social life, it seeks a cause in the mystic forces that constitute social life.

Bergson understood perfectly well that this description of the primitive mentality had a moral significance. Shortly after his first definition of static religion, he thus writes: "The solidarity between the members of the group is such at first that all are bound to feel that they participate to some degree in the lapse of any single one, at least in such cases as they consider serious: moral evil, if we can use the term at this stage, is regarded much the same as a physical evil spreading from one person to another, until it contaminates the whole society" (TS 124/1080; translation modified). Participation refers here to the bond that unites individuals when one of them is at fault: the fault is not a transgression of a prohibition but a transition to an order of moral causality that unites all individuals in the same current of contamination. As Paul Fauconnet, a student of Durkheim and Lévy-Bruhl, has shown, the notion that the individual is responsible for his act is a modern one because it separates the individual and his act as two contradictory terms. The analysis of the forms of law in primitive societies, by contrast, starts from the act itself insofar as it has interrupted the natural course of things and follows the network of participations by which individuals are morally united until, at last, it comes to a particular individual designated as responsible— what Fauconnet calls "responsibility-generating situations."[10] In the primitive mentality each individual is responsible for everything, because each accident brings into play invisible entities that are shared by the whole group.

Let's isolate the point on which this analysis differs from Durkheim's: there is no contradiction here between accident and rule in the sense that the crime would contradict a preexisting rule; rather, there is participation between the sources of the accident and the set of invisible forces that are expressed through it. Durkheim's intellectualist error is to hold that the individual criminal contradicts the prohibition of the collective conscience because they are constituted on two different planes, whereas we need rather to describe how these two planes interpenetrate in ordinary experience. "In the first place, the prohibitions protecting the social order are put forward," writes Bergson: they are the fallout of a movement that starts with the accident (TS 126; translation modified). The accident is a hub of action around which social life becomes visible, while the prohibition is the formula in which social life is crystallized.

What Bergson finds in Lévy-Bruhl, therefore, is a concept of accident that enables him to analyze moral causality, of which the religious phenomena in primitive societies offer particularly striking examples. Bergson's criticism, however, is that Lévy-Bruhl lacks a sufficiently sophisticated psychology to understand, from the inside, what is truly reassuring about this kind of accident prevention. For Lévy-Bruhl, in effect the primitive mentality is a threatening order of causality, because the wills that are expressed through accidents reflect a vague order with blurry outlines, such as may be found in certain beliefs in witchcraft. On several occasions he cites this statement by an Eskimo shaman: "We don't believe: we're afraid!"[11] From Lévy-Bruhl's standpoint, only the scientific conception of the world is profoundly reassuring insofar as it is based on a natural and entirely predictable causality.

> The uninterrupted feeling of intellectual security is so thoroughly established in our minds that we do not see how it can be disturbed, for even supposing we were suddenly brought face to face with an altogether mysterious phenomenon, the cause of which might entirely escape us at first, we should be convinced that our ignorance was merely temporary; we should know that such causes did exist, and that sooner or later they would declare themselves. Thus the world in which we live is, as it were, intellectualized beforehand. It, like the mind which devises and sets it in motion, is order and reason. Our daily activities, even in their minutest

details, imply calm and complete confidence in the immutability of natural laws. The attitude of the primitive's mind is very different. The natural world he lives in presents itself in quite another aspect to him. All its objects and all its entities are involved in a system of mystic participations and exclusions; it is these which constitute its cohesion and its order.[12]

If Lévy-Bruhl places security entirely on the side of modern science, it is because he makes too clear-cut a distinction between representation and emotion. In primitive mentality he discovers emotions that organize themselves into an order when they are collectively produced. When an accident strikes, Lévy-Bruhl argues, it is no longer representations of nature that come into play; instead, the affective category of the supernatural springs into action. Bergson observes, however, that primitive societies also make use of intellectual representations, and that between modern science and primitive mentality lies a difference of degree and not of kind.

The discussion centers on the notion of chance. According to Lévy-Bruhl, primitives are unaware of chance, in the sense Cournot gives to this term, namely, a random encounter between two independent causal chains. Where "we" invoke chance (for instance, when we trip on a rock, we explain it by the encounter between our movement and the physical presence of the rock), the "primitive" invokes the spell of a sorcerer to explain his lack of attention (the problem being to explain why the individual tripped at that moment rather than another, when he usually walks without tripping). In the same way, when we play roulette, we don't invoke a divinity that acts on the ball and makes it fall on the number we choose; rather, we explain it by chance, that is, the random encounter between our choice and the roulette wheel. In both cases, however, the task is to explain an accident, which is to say not the physical effect of the entities brought together but their significance for the person who finds himself at the point of their encounter. In this sense, chance is analogous to an intention, but an "intention emptied of its content": it is "mechanism behaving as though possessing an intention" (TS 149, 148/1101).

What the primitive man explains here by a "supernatural" cause is not the physical effect, it is its *human significance*, it is its importance to man, and more especially to a particular man, the one who was crushed by the stone. There is nothing illogical, consequently nothing "prelogical" or even anything which evinces an "imperviousness to experience," in the belief that a cause should be proportionate to its effect, that, once having admitted the crack in the rock, the direction and force of the wind— purely physical things which take no account of humanity—there remains to be explained this fact, so momentous to us, the death of a man. The effect is contained pre-eminently in the cause, as the old philosophers used to put it; and if the effect has a considerable human significance, the cause must have at least an equal significance; it is in any case of the same order; it is an *intention*. (TS 145/1098)

Bergson stresses the terms "significance" and "intention" in this passage. These refer to his analysis of language, implicated in the notion of fabulation: it is because intelligence draws a network of linguistic relations around things that it can attribute intentions and a "signification" (in the "scholastic" sense of the "old-time philosophers") to them. Bergson's analysis here is almost phenomenological, in the sense that it analyzes the intentionality of the primitive subject when it must act in an uncertain situation. Let's take the example of a primitive man who shoots an arrow at his prey without knowing if it will hit, and let's see how Bergson describes what we could well call the arrow of primitive intentionality. At issue is a paradox of the human condition: while intelligence must represent the space in which the action of a living being unfolds, the human being undertakes actions whose outcomes are beyond his control. What makes this specifically human intentionality possible is the supplementation of the representation of matter common to all living beings with a specifically mental representation, derived from the fabulation function, namely the distinctively human capacity to make fictional entities appear through language. Added to the sense we share with animals that informs us about things is the "nose," specific to human beings, that informs us about persons. The gap between action and its goal is filled in by the representation of threatening or reassuring personalities: the primitive man invokes the spirit of his prey to compensate for the gap created by his representation of the possibility of failure. It is therefore within a single continuous intentionality that intelligence adds a moral causality of supernatural forces to the mechanical causality of matter. We can thus say that Bergson replaces the Lévy-Bruhlian notion of supernatural cause, still confused in his eyes and too marked by the opposition between magic and science, or between emotion and representation, with that of intentional cause, inscribed within an analysis of the vital functions of language. Man began by explaining things with reference to intentional causes, in light of his attempted action on them, before explaining them by mechanical causes, once he had greater mastery over their effect on him. He therefore explored the entire collection of fictional entities that language makes available to him for himself in a virtual fashion before confronting it with reality by means of science.

AN ANTHROPOLOGY OF UNSURE ACTION

We can understand why Lévi-Strauss was interested in this analysis of primitive intentionality when, in trying to describe totemism from the outside, after Bergson had so well described it from "the inside,"[13] he analyzes the way in which a "classificatory intentionality" cobbles together (*bricole*) pieces of language when faced with events and finally describes it as "tensed by its efforts to transcend itself."[14] The comparison with Lévi-Strauss must, however, be taken further, because it leads us to base the sociology of assurance on a psychology and an anthropology, where the partial forms of assurance taken against fear are related to the manifestation of a whole.

Bergson manages to retain the advances of nineteenth-century social thought—according to which religion is a social phenomenon and not a poor explanation of nature—while avoiding the specifically nineteenth-century illusion according to which the social realm can become entirely predictable in the form of scientific laws. This double overcoming of natural religion and social religion, of naturalism and sociologism, is made possible by a new form of psychology based on the way assurance against fear works intellectually. Bergson bases the sociology of assurance on a psychology of assurance: the need to assure men in their relationships with one another comes from man's need to feel assured in relation to the world. For Bergson, man is a living being like any other; the only difference is that, being more intelligent, he dares to take on a greater number and variety of actions in the world. Animals are more guided by instinct, that is, by automatic habits that lead them to repeat the same actions; man, by contrast, is more intelligent because he always introduces new acts into the world. But because he is more intelligent, he is also less assured, which is to say he cannot rely on the reassurance of habit but must constantly take new risks. Man, therefore, must replace the instinctive assurance of habit with an intellectual and social form of assurance—or "insurance"—provided by religion: "Man is the only animal whose actions are uncertain ["lack assurance"], who hesitates, gropes about and lays plans in the hope of success and the fear of failure. He is alone in realizing that he is subject to illness, alone in knowing that he must die. The rest of nature goes on its expanding course in absolute tranquility" (TS 204/1149).

The type of insurance put in place by human intelligence is always threatened by failure, and that is what radically distinguishes it from the kind that is spontaneously produced by nature. Instinct effectively ensures a perfect adaptation of action to result, as per the model of the bee that spontaneously produces the honeycomb without needing an intellectual model. By contrast, human intelligence produces an image prior to the action to be performed: it thus separates intention from action by giving itself a space of representation of the possibilities of action. That is why intelligence frightens itself: among these possibilities it is led to represent the possibility of the action failing and perhaps even death, a possible outcome of any action.

We must therefore seek the foundations of Bergson's psychology of assurance in the theory of perception that he sets up in the first chapter of *Matter and Memory*. By placing a certain distance between itself and things via the intermediary of the body, the human mind manages to ensure itself against the risks that things pose to the body. Human intelligence reassures itself not by eliminating the possibility of death but by making this possibility merely one among others within a space of possibilities. Intellectual insurance is thus indeed a form of calculation, within a space that establishes distances between beings, but it also establishes healthy distances in our perception of beings in the surrounding world: "In fact, I note that the size, shape, even the color, of external objects is modified as my body approaches or recedes from them; that the strength of an odor, the intensity of a sound, increases or diminishes with distance; finally, that this very distance represents, above all, the measure in which surrounding bodies are insured, in some way, against the immediate action of my body" (MM 21/172).

We now have a better understanding of why Bergson defines fabulation as a "virtual instinct." Within the work of intelligence, which necessarily produces a representation of the possibility of death, religion adds a new form of probability: that an action will succeed because it is supported by a protective divinity. Because the work of intelligence unfolds in the virtual realm, that is, in a space of possibilities, it must rediscover the forces of instinct within itself in order to produce a new action. Instinct is a natural form of providence, of "welfare": it adapts the animal's action to the result; religion is a supernatural form of providence, because it supplements human action with divine intervention. From this perspective, the construction of ever more complex pantheons of gods is a senseless proliferation of the virtual domain, once the goal of the action is lost from view.

THE EXPANSION AND TRANSFIGURATION OF CONFIDENCE

But what then is the significance of the difference in kind that Bergson establishes between static and dynamic religion? The primitive belief in protective divinities appears, from a psychological point of view, analogous to the mystical belief in divine inspiration: both offer assurances to man against the fear of the dangers represented by intelligence. As Bergson states, "[mysticism] may, it is true, lift the soul to another plane: it nonetheless ensures for the soul [*il ne lui en assure pas moins*], to a preeminent degree, the security and the serenity which it is the function of static religion to provide" (*TS* 213/1156). What changes in the transition from one plane to another is that the personality intelligence enters into contact with is no longer partial but total: it is no longer an individual intentionality that fills in the gap opened up by accident, it is instead the intentionality of the élan vital itself, which doesn't need any materiality to manifest itself. The confidence produced by religion is a total confidence: it does not aim to make this or that action possible but rather action in general. Insurance places beings in relation to each other within a space of possibility that is always the product of a calculating intelligence; confidence gathers them together in one simple act. Insurance is thus intelligence's spatial projection of a confidence derived from mystical action: it is the symbolic representation of an act of confidence, which is its transfiguration.

We can thus say that the very essence of religion is expressed in dynamic religion and consider retrospectively that static religion mingled this essence with the accidents of the sensible world. This is, moreover, very much how Lévy-Bruhl defined the notion of participation: the fact of seeing essences at work when accidents occur, insurance thus consists in seeing accidents *sub specie societatis*. But seeing essences here is not just the product of an emotion; it comes at the end of an intentional series that encompasses all the virtual aspects of things in order to gather them together in one simple action. Insurance is conceived in relation to a plurality of possible accidents; confidence is conceived according to the one essential act. Any of the mystics, considered in his own particular journey, subject to suspicions of illness, could himself be considered as an accident, in the sense that mysticism "befalls" him. But we must then conclude that insurance is the form taken by confidence in a finite world filled with accidents. Dynamic religion is only a system of insurance by accident; in its essence it is a system of confidence.

On this point, Bergson once again anticipates one of the central theses of Lévi-Strauss's sociological thought. According to Lévi-Strauss, the semantic structures elaborated at the level of unconscious thought are indeed ways of reassuring the intelligence by referring accidents to categories that predate them. These semantic structures, however, must be placed within a broader dynamic movement that ensures the structures loop back onto themselves and that Lévi-Strauss calls confidence. Thus, when he analyzes the elementary structures of kinship as forms of exchange, where A gives to B so that B gives to A, Lévi-Strauss highlights what Bergson would call a senseless proliferation of the virtual, when the number of clans connected by exchange increases indefinitely and leads to a "generalized exchange." It then becomes necessary to introduce goods that circulate in the opposite direction to women, so as to express the confidence clans have in each other, through the institution of marriage by purchase. Confidence is the primary act that enables relationships to be set up among clans, measured by calculation and money; it is the original impulse that leads societies to exchange women, goods, and words rather than go to war: "Generalized exchange always contains an element of trust. . . . There must be the confidence that the cycle will close again, and that after a period of time a woman will eventually be received in compensation for the woman initially surrendered. *The belief is the basis of trust, and confidence opens up credit.*"[15] If generalized exchange is an act of faith in the possibility of connecting all societies together through exchange, it must nevertheless give way to more limited forms of exchange, such as marriage by purchase, which appear more reassuring because they supplement the exchange of goods with the exchange of women and are projected onto a spatial form that men can master in thought.

Generalized exchange can provide a formula of organization of an exceptional clarity and richness, a formula which can be widened indefinitely and can express the needs of as complex a social group as may be imagined; its theoretical law can function uninterruptedly and without fail. The dangers which threaten it come from outside, from concrete characteristics, and from the formal structure of the group. Marriage by purchase, by substituting itself, then provides a new formula which, while safeguarding the principle of the formal structure, furnishes the means of integrating those irrational factors which arise from chance and from history, factors which the evolution of human society shows to follow—rather than precede—the logical structures which are elaborated by unconscious thought, access to which is often more easily gained through very primitive forms of organization.[16]

We should therefore reconsider Lévi-Strauss's structural anthropology in light of Bergson's philosophy, reintroducing a whole sociology of action into apparently closed symbolic systems, which opens it up to mental possibilities. The relationship between generalized exchange and restricted exchange in Lévi-Strauss is comparable to the relation that governs the dynamic and static in Bergson: exchange is generalized in its essence and restricted by accident. The analysis of totemic classifications will then lead Lévi-Strauss to find the intermediate level in the perception of natural species—a level where intelligence elaborates "composites," in Bergson's words—enabling a transition from the most closed forms to the most open ones, a social organization only opening itself up according to its capacity to integrate the contingency of accidents. The structural anthropology of forms of social organization and systems of religious representation has a moral significance, in that the structures it describes tend toward the moral pole of an indefinite expansion of humanity, but it also has a descriptive value to the extent that it modifies this moral ideal according to the accidents that restrict it in different contexts.[17]

What does the relationship between assurance and confidence imply when considered sociologically? It leads us to reexamine these terms borrowed from religious thought from the perspective of the social intelligence they make visible, in two senses. First in the sense that it is indeed intelligence that works within the social realm in order to connect the beings that make it up, when it instigates systems of assurance or insurance. And second in the sense that the social realm achieves intelligent insight into its own principle when it returns to the sources of action in uncertain situations by producing confidence. Intelligence is at the root of the forms of intentionality that are added onto things, so that men can act on these things even though they are uncertain of the outcome. If accidents always serve as the point of departure of our thinking, if humanity lives in a contingent and precarious world, there are situations in which the very essence of assurance reveals itself by making visible new virtual relationships between things. In this sense, the distinction between static religion and dynamic religion continues to provide a criterion for our assurance-based societies.

NOTES

1 [Translator's note: In French, the same term, "*assurance*," is used for both "assurance" in the general sense of being or feeling assured and the clearly related but narrower concept of "insurance" in the sense of "insurance cover." The author draws on both meanings and the relationship between them.]

2 Ewald, *L'État-providence.*

3 Durkheim, *Division of Labor in Society,* 31.

4 Lévy-Bruhl, *L'Idée de responsabilité.*

5 Lévy-Bruhl's reflection often deals with litigious cases: a man accuses his canoe for being a crocodile that knocked him over; another is accused of eating a child when he was sleeping. See his *Carnets.*

6 Lévy-Bruhl, *How Natives Think,* 78.

7 See my *Contradiction et participation.*

8 Lévy-Bruhl, "Compte rendu de H. Bergson," 527.

9 Lévy-Bruhl, *Primitive Mentality,* 93.

10 See Fauconnet, *La Responsabilité*; Karsenti, "Nul n'est censé ignorer la loi."

11 Lévy-Bruhl, *Primitives and the Supernatural,* 22 (translation modified).

12 Lévy-Bruhl, *Primitive Mentality,* 35.

13 Lévi-Strauss, *Totemism,* 92–93.

14 Lévi-Strauss, *Savage Mind,* 246.

15 Lévi-Strauss, *Elementary Structures of Kinship,* 265 (emphasis added).

16 Ibid., 268.

17 See my *Claude Lévi-Strauss, une introduction.*

FOURTEEN

Tuning into Other Worlds

HENRI BERGSON AND THE
RADIO RECEPTION THEORY
OF CONSCIOUSNESS

G. William Barnard

The metaphysical perspective of Henri Bergson, especially as it appears in *Matter and Memory*, articulates an intriguing and radically unique way of understanding the complex interplay of body and mind, matter and consciousness. Bergson's metaphysics not only dramatically challenges the philosophical materialism that is for the most part tacitly assumed by most academics in Western culture, but it also opens the door to a revisioning of the etiology of a wide range of non-ordinary experiences (e.g., telepathy, clairvoyance, mediumship, possession states, mystical experiences, and so on).[1] As Pete A. Y. Gunter points out: "It may seem a long way from the theories of *Matter and Memory* to the problems of parapsychology, but the two are in fact closely related. Bergson's concept of mind-body relations, with its 'filter' theory of perception and its supposition that nature everywhere 'interpenetrates,' give rise quite naturally to a theory both of how 'psi phenomena' are possible and why we are ordinarily unaware of them."[2]

This chapter is an attempt to continue this (often unacknowledged) aspect of Bergson's philosophical project. It develops his "filter" model of consciousness—along with his fascinating "radio reception" theory that countless different worlds might coexist with our own—as a way to begin to understand the genesis of various religious and paranormal phenomena.

Bergson's willingness to apply his filter theory of consciousness to a variety of non-ordinary phenomena might seem surprising to those scholars who are primarily familiar with Bergson in and through the thought of Gilles Deleuze.[3] However, as I will attempt to show, not only is there a clear-cut historical connection between Bergson's work in *Matter and Memory* and his subsequent interest in paranormal phenomena, but there are also numerous ways in which Bergson's speculations on the metaphysical underpinnings of psi phenomena can be utilized to make sense of phenomena that are exceedingly difficult to explain if they are viewed, as typically happens, through a (frequently tacit and unexamined) materialistic or naturalistic set of metaphysical assumptions.

FILTERING OUT A UNIVERSE OF IMAGES: BERGSON'S THEORY OF PERCEPTION

Before plunging into an examination of Bergson's understanding of the genesis of non-ordinary phenomena, it is necessary to become acquainted with his theory of ordinary perception.

Our commonsense understanding of how we come to know the objective world around us is that physical stimuli from the external world affect our sense organs and these organs then send signals to our brain via the nervous system. Our brain, receiving these signals, promptly translates them into our conscious perceptions. This understanding of the process of perception leads us to assume that we are, in a sense, taking photographs of the universe, using our sense organs as the camera, and developing a picture of the external world by an elaborate chemical process in the brain.

The problem with this commonsense understanding, however, is that our consciousness is nothing like a photograph; it is not a physical piece of paper coated with chemicals. Consciousness is, on the face of it, inherently non-spatial, inner, subjective, and private, whereas the material brain is inherently spatial, outer, objective, and publicly accessible. We are therefore presented with some urgent philosophical questions: How are these two very different "stuffs" related? How is it possible that the inert, squishy, neurochemical activity of the brain somehow manages, almost magically, to change into our conscious perceptual experience?[4]

Bergson offers an ingenious, albeit difficult to grasp, solution to this philosophical dilemma in *Matter and Memory*. He begins by positing a universe that is, below the level of appearances, a pulsating, interconnected field of "images." These images possess qualities that are similar to how both matter and consciousness are often understood. Like matter (at least matter as it is understood by quantum mechanics), images are dynamic patterns of energy, vortices of vibrations that radiate outward, contacting and affecting other complexly patterned vortices of energy. This transmission of energy information is, moment to moment, passed on to other images, automatically, fully, without hesitation. According to Bergson, this measurable, predictable, lawful interaction of images is the basis for the stable, objective world of matter, a world rooted in the dependable, repeatable patterns of cause and effect studied by the natural sciences.

Understood in this way, Bergson's theory of images depicts the way matter is typically thought to behave. However, the universe of images posited by Bergson departs from our commonsense understanding of matter in two ways. First, this universe of images is not inherently divided into a collection of separate objects possessing clear-cut boundaries. According to Bergson, the world of separate objects that we normally perceive is not the true nature of matter. Instead, he argues that the physical world, like our consciousness, is an interconnected, dynamic continuum of becoming, in which "numberless vibrations, all linked together in uninterrupted continuity" travel "in every direction like shivers through an immense body" (MM 208/343).

The second way in which the universe of images posited by Bergson is different from our usual understanding of matter is that we normally think of matter (e.g., a stone) as inert or non-aware. But according to Bergson, consciousness, in a latent form, is already present in the universe of images. The job of the sense organs, the nervous system, and the brain—which are all images—is to receive the pulses of virtually conscious vibrations from the other images of the universe. From this infinitely complex, interpenetrating field of latent consciousness, they select and actualize only those vibrations that serve the needs of our particular organism, letting the rest of the information from the universe pass through unimpeded.

According to Bergson, the raw data of perception (what Bergson refers to as our "pure perceptions," that is, perceptions minus most of the influence of memory) is a filtrate from the totality of the universal flux of potential consciousness in which we find ourselves. Our pure perceptions are, therefore, the result of a radical truncation, a culling process by which we ignore most of what we might potentially know. As a result, we perceive only the "external crust" or the "superficial skin" of what actually surrounds us (MM 36/186).

Nonetheless, Bergson stresses that it is vital that we filter out the vast majority of the streaming universal flux of images in which we are immersed. If we were to perceive and attempt to act upon the physical world at its most fundamental vibratory level we would become incapacitated; if, for example, we no longer saw an oak table as a solid structure of wood but instead consciously perceived and responded to the flux of the almost infinite energetic patterns that underlie the table, we would become lost in the "moving immensity" of what previously had been a motionless, rectangular, solid object (CM 69). We are therefore continually, on subconscious levels, carving out manageable islands of stability in the onrush of universal becoming by choosing to focus only on that level of experience that best serves our needs.

From a Bergsonian perspective, therefore, while we all inhabit the *same* universe (even if that universe, ironically, never ceases to change), it is safe to say that each of us experiences a very *different* universe—a universe that is, to a degree that is difficult to ascertain, partially shaped by the utterly unique and constantly changing lens of how we *interpret* our world.

It is important to stress that how we interpret our world is, itself, partially shaped by the internalization of our psychological background, our physical characteristics, our cultural matrix, our economic status, and so on—that is, by the vast and constantly changing fund of *memories* that we each draw upon to shape our experience. However, it is equally crucial to recognize that Bergson understands memories in a very different way than how they are typically understood. For Bergson, memories are not frozen snapshots of the past tucked away in some cerebral storage chamber. Instead, our memories are interpenetrating fields of consciousness that are inherently creative; they are fields that, while distinct, are not separate from one another; they are fields that can and do combine in unique and unpredictable ways (with varying amounts of freedom) to help create our moment-to-moment experience.

The key point to retain from this discussion is that the interaction between perception and memory that creates our moment-to-moment experience of the world is fundamentally pragmatic: we perceive and interpret only a select subset of the universal flux that surrounds and interpenetrates us, that is, only those aspects of the universe that are necessary in order for us to act in any given situation. Consequently, if our predominant mode of attunement with the world and each other is pragmatic, then it becomes *possible that other worlds of experience exist.*[5] Bergson addresses this possibility in these remarkable lines: "Nothing would prevent other worlds corresponding to another choice, from existing with it in the same place and the same time: in this way twenty different broadcasting stations throw out simultaneously twenty different concerts which coexist without any one of them mingling its sounds with the music of another, each one being heard, complete and alone, in the apparatus which has chosen for its reception the wave-length of that particular station" (CM 69–70).

In these lines, we have what I call Bergson's radio reception theory of consciousness. From this perspective, our everyday, mundane level of consciousness is simply one "channel" out of theoretically unlimited alternate possibilities, a "channel" of consciousness whose function is simply to play the "music" that is appropriate to our day-to-day practical functioning in the physical world.

It is crucial, however, to recognize that according to Bergson these "channels" of consciousness are not made of some sort of Cartesian mental substance that is ontologically distinct from matter. While *Matter and Memory* emphasizes the functional and practical differences between mind and matter, in the final analysis, Bergson asks us to conceive both mind and matter as simply differing manifestations of a unified (albeit continually changing and intrinsically pluralistic) reality: *durée*—the dynamic flow of consciousness writ large or, expressed in different terms, the ongoing flux of time. In this temporal non-dualism, both matter and mind, in the final analysis, are two ends of a single interactive spectrum of temporal becoming. The "stuff" of existence is the creative unfolding, on all levels, of the oneness and manyness of durée.

However, similar to Bergson's radio analogy, this dynamic "stuff" of becoming (i.e., durée or time) is not monolithic; reality does not take place on a single plane. According to Bergson there are multiple dimensions of experience, multiple levels of reality (e.g., quantum, molecular, mineral, vegetal, animal, and human), each possessing a unique, albeit ever-changing, temporal rhythm; there are countless levels of experience (and time) other than our own; there are countless "planes" or, if you will, "channels" of durée.[6] It is to these other channels that we will turn in order to see paranormal phenomena as *extra-ordinary*, that is, phenomena that ordinarily pass above or below our pragmatic experience but that are neither unreal, nor, with the right "tuning," inaccessible to experience.

BERGSON'S INTEREST IN NON-ORDINARY STATES OF CONSCIOUSNESS

As Bergson himself recognizes, given the fact that under the surface of our more prosaic level of awareness there are countless alternative modes of consciousness that are potentially available to us, it should be expected that we would occasionally hear of individuals who claim to have experienced, even if only briefly, non-ordinary modes of perception (e.g., telepathy, clairvoyance, and mystical modes of perception).[7]

In the latter decades of his life, Bergson became increasingly interested in understanding the genesis of these non-ordinary modes of consciousness. This theoretical interest was neither peripheral nor passing. Bergson worked closely for many years with several well-known scholars and scientists who studied psi phenomena in the late nineteenth century and the early twentieth century: his colleague Pierre Janet at the Collège de France; Théodule Ribot and Charles Richet at the Sorbonne; and William James in America. He also worked more obliquely with thinkers such as Fredric Myers, Hans Driesch, Sigmund Freud, and Carl Jung. According to R. C. Grogin, these "psychical researchers" (in addition to Bergson's academic colleagues in philosophy) were the people, "who understood him best. . . . They worked along parallel lines with Bergson, rubbed shoulders with him at conferences, discussion groups and laboratories, and were preoccupied with the same problems that he grappled with. They always recognized that Bergson was one of theirs—that he was one of the truly original theoreticians of psychical research."[8] Bergson's first article on non-ordinary phenomena was, as Leonard Eslick points out, "a skeptical critique of telepathy experiments carried out with hypnotic subjects," published in 1886.[9] Bergson's initial skepticism, however, gradually shifted, and by 1900 Bergson decided to join the Institut psychologique internationale (or, as it was eventually renamed, the Institut général psychologique) a newly formed society dedicated to a careful study of non-ordinary phenomena.[10]

By 1903, in a four-page, rather informal paper published in the *Bulletin de l'Institut général psychologique*, Bergson was clearly curious about how others had examined and tested the fact that some people during séances perceive columns of light and that these columns of light appear to correlate with measurements of high-frequency radiation. In this short piece (M 606–9), as Méheust points out, Bergson is wary of the possibility of deception, yet he also insists that it is crucial to take such phenomena seriously.[11] This attitude of cautious interest in paranormal phenomena is also evident in another short piece published in 1904 in which Bergson asks questions about the study of changes in the respiration of hypnotic subjects during various stages of hypnosis. This interest continues in Bergson's two-page review of Boirac's *La psychologie inconnue*, written in 1908, in which he approvingly notes the author's attempts to classify various non-ordinary phenomena (including hypnosis) (M 639–42, 760–62).

Perhaps most intriguing, however, is the fact that Bergson participated (in 1905 and 1906) in at least four séances (Grogin claims that it was six) designed to test the alleged telekinesis of Eusapia Palladino, a controversial yet allegedly quite powerful medium of that time. Grogin points out that during these séances, Bergson "witnessed the full gamut of the 'phenomena' that made the medium famous: levitations, table-rapping, furniture-moving, flying objects and flashing lights."[12]

Grogin's assessment draws largely on two pages of extremely terse and cryptic notes published in 1906 that all-too-briefly describe what took place during these séances. While the notes are exceedingly elliptical, it is clear that Bergson was an active participant and that he did indeed witness several mysterious and striking phenomena. For example, during one séance Palladino reported that she felt herself becoming physically lighter and asked that her claim be checked using the scale that, fortunately, was present at the séance. (Her claim was subsequently verified.) During another séance various witnesses (including Bergson and Madame Curie) asserted that they clearly saw a dark arm appear beside a curtain and forcibly touch a man several times on the shoulder. Finally, during yet another séance, in which all of the participants sat around a table with their hands clearly visible on the top of the séance table, Palladino asked Bergson, as an outside observer, to closely watch her knees under the séance table—a request that she seemingly made so that it would be clear that she did nothing physically to cause the subsequent phenomena. Bergson, in the interest of science, agreed. Immediately after this request, the séance table rose suddenly into the air, even though another witness asserted that he never let go of Palladino's hand during the entire time that the table was levitating. (Holding the hands of mediums and watching their knees under the table were common, and commonsense, procedures of the time designed to prevent trickery [M 673–74].)

From these notes, it is clear that, while Bergson attended relatively few séances with Palladino, he was able to observe, nonetheless, a relatively wide and dramatic range of telekinetic phenomena. Even so, as Méheust emphasizes, Bergson remained deeply divided about these séances. On the one hand, he was convinced in certain respects that Palladino was trying to trick the researchers. On the other hand, he was equally convinced that some of the phenomena that he witnessed were so extraordinary that they resisted any rational explanation.[13] Méheust also points out that, in an interview with Georges Meunier in 1910 (and Bergson rarely granted interviews), Bergson reiterated his perplexity of the phenomena that he had witnessed during the séances with Palladino, while nonetheless asserting that after examining the various documents published for over twenty-five years on the topic of telepathy, he was convinced that there was stronger evidence in favor of telepathy than against it. In fact, as Bergson put it, if he had to bet for or against the reality of telepathy, he would bet in its favor without any hesitation.[14]

BERGSON'S PRESIDENTIAL ADDRESS: "'PHANTASMS OF THE LIVING' AND PSYCHICAL RESEARCH"

Bergson's stature among the wide-ranging group of philosophers, psychologists, and scientists who were interested in researching non-ordinary phenomena in Europe in the early twentieth century is perhaps most clearly indicated by the fact that he was elected the president of the British Society for Psychical Research in 1913. Bergson's attitudes toward non-ordinary phenomena (especially telepathy and clairvoyance), as well as his belief that his own philosophical understanding of the mind-body relationship offered at least one potentially helpful way to make sense of their genesis, is clearly enunciated in the presidential address that Bergson gave to the Society in London on May 28, 1913: "'Phantasms of the Living' and Psychical Research."

Bergson begins by saying that he is puzzled by the honor that the society bestowed on him because he "has done nothing to deserve it," in that, as he claims, "it is only by reading" that he knows "anything of the phenomena with which the Society deals" (*ME* 75). This claim, which is itself rather interesting given his experiences with Palladino, becomes even more puzzling when he goes on to assert in this public forum: "I have seen nothing myself, I have examined nothing myself" (*ME* 75). Whether reluctant to reveal his rather scant background in this area or simply demurring modestly to the "ingenuity, the penetration, the patience, the tenacity" that has been shown by those present in the hall while studying psi phenomena, it is clear that Bergson admires those who have persevered in their research, especially in the face of "the prejudices of a great part of the scientific world" (*ME* 75, 76). Bergson clearly opposes these prejudices, pointing out how behind the mockery of those who even refuse to examine critically the evidence for psychical phenomena "there is, present and invisible, a certain metaphysic unconscious of itself—unconscious and therefore inconsistent, unconscious and therefore incapable of continually remodeling itself on observation and experience as every philosophy worthy of the name must do" (*ME* 77).

Later in the talk, Bergson offers his own philosophy as a more conscious and therefore suppler and ideally valuable alternative to the taken-for-granted mechanistic materialism that was so prevalent during his day. But before proceeding in this direction, Bergson examines several important methodological issues.

He first asserts (without bothering to give any reasons to support his assertion) that psychical phenomena are facts, facts similar to those studied by natural science. For him, these facts are subject to laws and can therefore be repeated again and again, unlike the specificity and particularity of historical facts (e.g., the battle of Austerlitz) that happen only once and can never repeat themselves. He postulates that, similar to electricity and magnetism, telepathy "is operating at every moment and everywhere, but with too little intensity to be noticed or else in such a way that a cerebral mechanism stops the effect, for our benefit, at the very moment at which it is about to clear the threshold of consciousness" (*ME* 79–80).

Bergson goes on to claim that if and when we finally understand the underlying dynamics of the operation of telepathy, then in much the same way as it is now no longer necessary to wait for a thunderstorm in order to see the effect of electricity, it will no longer be necessary to wait for spontaneous telepathic events, such as the appearance of a "phantasm of the living"—that is, apparitions of individuals, often sick or dying, who appear unexpectedly to friends or loved ones, often miles away, apparitions that are studied in the monumental two-volume work *Phantasms of the Living*, published in 1886, and spearheaded by Edmund Gurney, a founding figure of the Society for Psychical Research.[15]

What Bergson notes, however, is that even though telepathy, to his mind at least, is a lawful and entirely natural phenomenon, nonetheless, it appears that the only way to study it is with "an entirely different method, one which stands midway between that of the historian and that of the magistrate"—that is, a method in which researchers study documents, examine witnesses, assess their reliability, and so forth (*ME* 80). Bergson comments that, after becoming aware of the sheer number of reliable cases and after seeing the care and thoroughness in which these cases were examined, he is "led to believe in telepathy, just as [he] believe[s] in the defeat of the Invincible Armada" (*ME* 81). He admits that this belief has neither "the mathematical certainty" given by a demonstration of the Pythagorean theorem nor the empirical certainty seen in the verification of one of Galileo's laws; however, "it has at least all the certainty which we can obtain in historical or judicial matters" (*ME* 81). Nonetheless, as Bergson notes, this level of evidence is simply not compelling to most scientists. Therefore, because "psychical research" is unable to be produced under strict laboratory conditions, it is considered not only unscientific, but even unreal.

Bergson goes on to give an example of a strategy frequently used by those who are skeptical of the conclusions of psychical research. He describes a dinner party that he attended during which the conversation focused on psychical phenomena. An eminent physician at the party offered a story given to him by a woman whom he considered to be intelligent and trustworthy. This woman's husband, an officer, was killed in battle. According to the doctor, "at the very moment when the husband fell, the wife had the vision of the scene, a clear vision, in all points conformable to the reality" (*ME* 82). The doctor went on to say that this story may *seem* to be evidence for the existence of telepathy or clairvoyance, but as he went on to note, it is important to remember that this was quite likely not the only time that the woman had dreamed that her husband had died—and clearly those other dreams turned out to be false. The physician went on to say, "We notice cases in which the vision turns out to be true, but take no count of the others" (ME 83). The physician concluded that, if we actually took full account of *all* the evidence, then psychical phenomena would be simply understood as the work of coincidence or chance.

Not surprisingly, Bergson disagrees. He comments that after this conversation a young girl said to him, "It seems to me that the doctor argued wrongly just now" (ME 83). Agreeing with the young girl, Bergson notes that there was indeed a fallacy in the doctor's argument (ME 83). According to Bergson, the doctor's fallacy was that he overlooked the specificity of the vision. As Bergson points out, if a painter had, in his imagination, attempted to paint a picture with a level of specificity equal to that of the wife's vision, a picture that showed in minute detail exactly how the real soldiers moved and how they looked, there is absolutely no chance that the painter could succeed because the scene is "decomposable into an infinity of details all independent of one another" so that "an infinite number of coincidences is needed in order that chance should make a fancied scene the reproduction of a real scene" (ME 84).

Bergson further argues that it is mathematically impossible for a painter to produce an utterly accurate picture of the scene even if, as Bergson points out, "we leave out the coincidence *in time,* that is, the fact that two scenes whose content is identical have chosen for their apparition the same moment" (ME 85). Given this double infinity (so to speak) and given the fact that "the lady who had the vision of a part of a battle was in the situation of that painter" in that "her imagination executed a picture," Bergson is willing to conclude that, "if the picture was the reproduction of a real scene, it must, by every necessity, be because she perceived that scene or was in communication with a consciousness that perceived it" (ME 85).

Bergson goes on to claim that, while he has no way to ascertain whether the story that the doctor told was true or false, nonetheless, "if this were proved to me, if I could be sure that even the countenance of one soldier unknown by her, present at the scene, had appeared to her such as it was in reality—then, even if it should be proved to me that there had been thousands of false visions, and even though there had never been a veridical hallucination except this one," then that would be sufficient to prove the possibility of perceiving objects and events at a distance in a way that our senses cannot normally accomplish (ME 85).[16]

Bergson, drawing upon his filter theory of consciousness, suggests that it is possible that "we perceive virtually many more things than we perceive actually, and that here, once more, the part that our body plays is that of shutting out from consciousness all that is of no practical interest to us, all that does not lend itself to our action" (ME 95–96). Given this he asks if it is not also possible that "around our normal perception" there is an unconscious "fringe of perceptions" associated with psi phenomena that occasionally enters into our consciousness "in exceptional cases or in predisposed subjects" (ME 96).

Bergson theorizes that these moments of non-ordinary consciousness may also have another cause. He suggests that the task of the brain is not just to filter out the flood of images that pours in and through us from the physical world. In addition, the brain also attempts to screen out a concurrent, perhaps even more extensive, torrent of coexisting, interpenetrating memories, thoughts, and feelings. To a certain extent these subconscious memories, thoughts, and feelings correlate with our personal biography. However, Bergson emphasizes that our minds, in a way that is far more pronounced than matter, overlap and interpenetrate each other —and in fact transcend spatial boundaries altogether.[17]

Bergson emphasizes that the experimental method is based on the ability to measure physical phenomena, but as he goes on to note, "it is of the essence of mental things that they do not lend themselves to measurement" (ME 87). For Bergson, consciousness by its very nature is not spatial; hence it cannot be measured. Reiterating much of what he explored earlier in *Matter and Memory*, Bergson argues that "consciousness is not a function of the brain"; therefore, it can and does transcend physical boundaries (ME 93). This freedom from spatial limitations means that it is quite possible that our minds are continually blending and overlapping with other minds in a reciprocal flow of mental information below the surface of our awareness. As Bergson notes: "between different minds there may be continually taking place changes analogous to the phenomena of endosmosis. If such intercommunication exists, nature will have taken precautions to render it harmless, and most likely certain mechanisms are specially charged with the duty of throwing back, into the unconscious, images so introduced" (ME 97). However, if this mental "intercommunication" is indeed continually taking place under the surface of our everyday awareness, then he suggests that it is quite possible, even likely, that certain images might occasionally slip past this mechanism, leading to moments of telepathic and clairvoyant knowledge.

It appears, therefore, that Bergson postulates two seemingly distinct ways in which non-ordinary states of consciousness may arise: either (1) they surface when the brain is less "successful" than normal at filtering out the countless images of the *physical world* that are ceaselessly flowing through us, or (2) they occur when the brain fails to keep our personal consciousness screened off from the underlying flux of overlapping *minds* that is present under the surface of our awareness at every moment. However, it is crucial to recall (as was emphasized above) that this seemingly Cartesian division of labor is simply a manifestation of the complexity of Bergson's metaphysical perspective. While Bergson (at least after *Matter and Memory*) acknowledges a *functional* distinction between mind and matter, he also stresses that both mind and matter are simply differing manifestations of a unified (albeit continually changing and intrinsically pluralistic) reality: durée.

Bergson's interest in non-ordinary phenomena did not disappear after 1913.[18] Several decades later, with the publication of *Two Sources*, Bergson comments that he believes that "telepathic phenomena" have been verified by the "mutual corroboration of thousands of statements which have been collected on the subject" (TS 316/1244). He emphasizes that while it is important to be discriminating about what evidence to accept, nonetheless, if only a portion of this evidence was to be accepted as valid, it would have a transforming effect on humanity's willingness to begin to accept the reality of that which it cannot touch or see directly. Bergson admits that the information that we gain from psychical research may well only deal with "the inferior portion" of our consciousness; it may well only focus on "the lowest degree of spirituality" (TS 316/1245). Nevertheless, he argues that the acceptance of psi phenomena would help humanity to open up to the possibility of the existence of other levels of spiritual reality as well.

CONCLUDING BERGSONIAN RUMINATIONS ON THE GENESIS OF NON-ORDINARY PHENOMENA

As a scholar of religious studies, I am struck by how Bergson's philosophical perspective offers a nuanced and sophisticated account of the genesis of the numerous non-ordinary experiences that fill the pages of religious texts and ethnographies (e.g., not only telepathy and clairvoyance but also mediumship, visionary encounters, and so on). Seen from a Bergsonian point of view, these types of powerful (and often transformative) spiritual experiences no longer have to be understood, as numerous theorists have claimed in the past, as evidence of psychological instability (at least in many, if not most cases). They also do not automatically have to be regarded as the meaningless result of the mechanical neurological activity within the brain, nor do they have to be seen as nothing more than the sum total of the psychological, economic, and cultural factors at work within an individual.

Rather, what this Bergsonian point of view allows us to do is to note that, while we need to give careful attention to physiological, psychological, economic, and cultural factors in understanding the genesis of these types of experiences, we can *also* posit that there could be transpersonal, transcultural, transhistorical factors at work as well.[19] Thus, we can suggest that these non-ordinary types of experiences are moments when, for a variety of reasons, individuals "change channels" and tune into dimensions of reality with which they are already connected subconsciously. We can argue that our own subconscious may well overlap with countless "higher" and more inclusive "superconscious strata" of awareness and volition, strata of consciousness that we typically filter out of our daily conscious awareness but that nonetheless might well occasionally manifest themselves powerfully within the psyches of mystics, shamans, and visionaries, levels of consciousness that while interpenetrating our own, might well also possess their own ontological distinctiveness and agency.[20]

In the past, when paranormal and religious phenomena were examined from the context of an Enlightenment mindset, it was often the case that these types of non-ordinary events were frequently ignored, or were dismissed as superstitious relics of backward, irrational cultures, or were reduced to nothing more than a conflux of various psychological, sociological, cultural, economic, or physiological forces. Given the fact that many (if not most) of the Enlightenment (and post-Enlightenment) theorists of religion internalized a highly positivistic and materialistic set of presuppositions, these reductive explanations of paranormal and religious phenomena made quite a bit of sense. However, given a different set of foundational assumptions about the nature of external reality and the nature of the psyche, we can easily begin to understand these types of "atypical" phenomena in much more nonreductive (albeit equally complex and sophisticated) ways.

This Bergsonian understanding of non-ordinary experiences allows us

to claim that it is quite likely that many (if not most) paranormal phenomena are not delusions or superstitious nonsense; in fact we can argue
that they might well be manifestations of a *more* profound, *more* inclusive
quality of perception (or at the very least a level of perception that is an
equally valid and valuable alternative to our more prosaic modes of experience). Seen from a Bergsonian perspective, we are (subconsciously)
connected with the entire universe and the apparent clear-cut separation
between objects is not ontologically real but instead is created by the
filtering mechanisms of the brain as well as by unconscious, deeply en-
grained patterns of memory and belief. Given this alternate set of metaphysical assumptions, then, it makes sense to posit that different spiritual
disciplines (e.g., chanting, fasting, meditation, dancing, ritualized inges-
tion of sacred plants, and so on) simply serve to open up the inner
floodgates in a ritually controlled and culturally sanctioned fashion, allowing practitioners to more easily and effectively absorb and integrate
the powerful information that is pouring into them from different currents of the ocean of the ever-changing images that make up the universe
as we know it. From a Bergsonian perspective, therefore, it can be argued
that many religious, mystical, and visionary experiences are indications
that it is possible to see (and to know) *more*, and even suggest that we can
see and know *better*, than is typically possible from within the context of
our everyday level of consciousness.

It is also important to emphasize that it is not only the more "spectacular" forms of paranormal and/or religious experience that can be reevalu-
ated from a Bergsonian metaphysical framework. If we can begin to let go
of the idea that we are bounded, atomistic, billiard balls of dead matter
that bump against each other in mechanistically predictable ways; if we
can begin, instead, to view ourselves as something closer to a relatively
stable whirlpool in a surging sea of consciousness, then it also becomes
increasingly possible to make sense of a wide range of more prosaic levels
of intuitive awareness as well, modes of experience that frequently occur
within many of us but that we often choose to ignore or deny.

For example, this Bergsonian point of view allows us to argue that our
intuitive insights, while not inevitably accurate, are also not simply psychological in nature but rather have a deeper ontological dimension as
well. Coming from this perspective, we can legitimately claim that our
sense that someone is sexually attracted to us (or conversely, the sense of
danger or wrongness that we pick up from someone) is not irrational, nor

is it simply based on subtle bodily cues, but instead may well be rooted in an accurate perception of what is actually occurring under the surface of our normal sensory perceptions. This Bergsonian perspective also gives us a framework from which to suggest that something more than simply quirks of our psychology underlie those trancelike moments when we are composing a song, or are painting a picture, or are playing the piano, or are writing a story and it seems as if something or someone else is working in and through us: perhaps we are in truth inspired by some deeper strata of the universe (and/or deeper levels of our selfhood). Similarly, we can posit that our empathetic feelings about our pets or even wild animals are not subjective anthropomorphic projections onto other species but actually reflect a genuine, albeit muted, awareness of a deeper underlying ontological connection with these beings. We can argue, in a rational, sophisticated fashion, that it is quite possible that all of these phenomena, in actuality, are simply varieties of ways in which we are tuning into and acknowledging the flow of subliminal information that we constantly receive from the mysterious universe that surrounds and interpenetrates us, but that we (for a variety of evolutionary, cultural, and psychological reasons) typically ignore or choose not to see.

NOTES

1 In this chapter, while I will primarily refer to these phenomena as "non-ordinary," I will at times (following Bergson's terminology) also refer to them as "paranormal" or "psychical" (as well as the more contemporary term "psi").

2 Gunter, "Henri Bergson," 141.

3 Deleuze strongly de-emphasizes the "spiritual" aspects of Bergson's work, as do many commentators who follow in his footsteps. These include Mullarkey, *Bergson and Philosophy*; Ansell-Pearson, *Philosophy and the Adventure of the Virtual*; Lawlor, *The Challenge of Bergsonism*; and Grosz, *The Nick of Time*.

4 These questions are simply one way to confront what David Chalmers calls the "hard problem"; that is, exactly how do "physical processes in the brain give rise to subjective experience"? See "The Puzzle of Conscious Experience," 63.

5 It is perhaps worth reemphasizing that only rarely do we *consciously* choose which images to focus on (and hence which "world of experience" we will inhabit). These choices (if we can stretch the word somewhat), take place with little or no conscious effort of will on our part and occur quasi-instantaneously prompted by subconscious planes of memory, which in turn are dramatically influenced by our biological needs.

6 Bergson speculates that it is possible, and indeed likely, that the human level of *durée* is not the highest that exists in the universe. He muses that these higher and

wider levels of durée would likely be able to condense the entire history of human-ity into a very short period of its own duration in much the same way that we condense the "history" of the vibrations of matter into our conscious experience in any given moment (MM 207/342).

7 There is one form of psi phenomena that Bergson's theoretical perspective would have difficulty explaining, or even acknowledging: precognition. Bergson's repeated emphasis on the open-ended, genuinely creative nature of durée makes it extremely difficult, if not impossible, to conceive of a ready-made future that exists just waiting to be accessed during moments of precognition. The inherent conflict between this theoretical closure to precognition and the (often quite striking) evidence of its existence that has been gathered by parapsychologists over the past few centuries is explored, quite thoughtfully (albeit from a Whiteheadian perspec-tive) in Griffin, *Parapsychology, Philosophy, and Spirituality*, 90–95.

8 Grogin, *Bergsonian Controversy*, 58. Other scholars who are familiar with Bergson's work and life have commented on the overlap between Bergson's philosophy and psychical research and on the degree to which Bergson himself was interested in the paranormal. Bertrand Méheust, for instance, in his magisterial two-volume study of mesmerism in France points out that Bergson's interest in paranormal phenomena was an open secret in the society of his time. See Méheust, *Somnambulisme et médiumnité: Tome 1* and *Tome 2*.

9 Eslick, "Bergson, Whitehead, and Psychical Research," 354. For Bergson's essay "De la simulation inconsciente dans l'état d'hypnotisme," see M 333–41.

10 M. Brady Brower gives a careful and detailed account of the tumultuous formation and development of this society. Originally named the Institut Psychique Interna-tional, its name was almost immediately changed to Institut Psychologique Interna-tional due, in large part, to concerns by several participants that the organization would be perceived as too closely linked to the Society for Psychical Research that was active at the time in England and America. See his *Unruly Spirits*, 51–52.

11 Méheust, *Somnambulisme et médiumnité: Tome 2*, 242.

12 Grogin, *Bergsonian Controversy*, 52. Grogin cites Courtier's "Rapport sur les séances." Grogin also points out that Bergson's stress on empirical research meant that he was not personally involved in occult activities: "According to his brother-in-law, MacGregor Mathers, [who in the 1890s was the leader of the Order of the Golden Dawn, a crucially important esoteric organization], Bergson was not the least bit interested in magic: 'I have shown him everything that magic can do and it has had no effect on him'" (*Bergsonian Controversy*, 43). Grogin goes on to note, however, that "interestingly, Bergson's sister claimed that some of their 'tiresome relatives' were into magic, and years later Bergson's daughter turned to the occult herself" (61n40).

13 Méheust, *Somnambulisme et médiumnité: Tome 2*, 242. Stephen Braude, in a wonder-fully thoughtful examination of the controversies surrounding Palladino, echoes Bergson's assessment. Braude notes that while Palladino was several times caught cheating, nonetheless, her attempts to cheat were very crude and easily detected, and in several rigorously controlled séances that took place in Naples in 1908 three

highly skeptical and experienced investigators were eventually convinced that the phenomena produced by Palladino were genuine. Braude, *Gold Leaf Lady and Other Parapsychological Investigations*, 46–52.

14 Meunier, *Ce qu'ils pensent du "merveilleux,"* 85; and Méheust, *Somnambulisme et médiumnité: Tome 2*, 243.

15 Gurney, Myers, Podmore, *Phantasms of the Living*.

16 William James had a similar attitude toward veridical non-ordinary experiences. For the definitive text on James's exploration of psychic phenomena, see his *Essays in Psychical Research*.

17 Robert Jahn and Brenda Dunne, two prominent parapsychologists, agree with Bergson that one of the primary difficulties that stands in the way of any scientific acceptance of psi phenomena is that "the commonly prevailing conceptualization of consciousness is basically particulate in nature. That is, an individual consciousness is normally presumed to be rather well localized in physical space and time, interacting only with a few specific aspects of its environment and with a few other similarly localized consciousnesses at any given time." They stress that it is only when we can let go of thinking that our consciousness is confined within the boundaries of our physical bodies, and reenvision our consciousness as wavelike in nature (similar to the wavelike nature of quantum realities), that telepathy, clairvoyance, and psychokinesis begin to have the possibility of being understood and accepted as real possibilities. See their "Consciousness, Quantum Mechanics, and Random Physical Processes," 299.

18 Bergson's interest in psi phenomena was also evident in 1919. A secondhand account of Bergson's talk at a Strasbourg conference on the soul, published in 1919, noted Bergson's discussion of psychical research within the larger context of the mind-body problem, as well as his emphasis on the importance of a spiritual point of view (which Bergson associates with France, England, and America) in order to overcome materialism and mechanism (which he, not surprisingly, associates with Germany). See M 1316–19.

19 For a similar methodological perspective, see Kripal, *The Serpent's Gift*; and Ferrer and Sherman, *The Participatory Turn*.

20 From a Bergsonian perspective it is difficult, if not impossible, to make a clear-cut distinction between influxes from previously hidden subconscious (or superconscious) planes of consciousness and the activity of seemingly independent spiritual beings, a difficulty that is also seen in the work of William James, Frederic Myers, and Carl Jung.

FIFTEEN

James, Bergson, and an Open Universe

Paola Marrati
Translated by Alexandre Lefebvre and Perri Ravon

The relationship between Bergson and William James may first appear to be of a historical and personal order: their deep mutual friendship is well known, along with the features of the age they shared. The critique of positivism and intellectualism, as well as an interest in experimental psychology, to give only a few examples, are central to the works of both men but not exclusive to them: many other intellectuals, philosophers, and writers of that generation share them.[1] Yet it is important to understand that there is a deeper philosophical link between these two otherwise very different thinkers, one that cannot be reduced to the features of an age. I would like to go even further and suggest that historical distance enables us today to read Bergson and James in an *untimely* manner, beyond their time if not against it, to paraphrase Nietzsche, and that this distance may make us mindful of aspects of their thought so far unnoticed.

An example of what an untimely reading can offer, to my mind both important and significant, concerns the question of the new. One of the most obvious features James and Bergson share is their repeated and unequivocal affirmation of the ontological, and not merely empirical, reality of change. James's pluralist universe is an "open" universe, just as Bergson's universe is one that "endures," where "not everything is given" and there is a constant creation of the new. For both James and Bergson, this affirmation of the reality of change has consequences that are at once philosophical, political, and ethical. It is not of course a matter of realizing, quite belatedly, that the things of this world change; rather, it is the more difficult—and in many ways still incomplete —task of analyzing the implicit and explicit assumptions behind the age-old privilege afforded to the stable and the eternal and of evaluating their consequences in field of action as much as thought.

It is certainly not by chance that, in his introduction to the French translation of James's *Pragmatism*, Bergson emphasizes, insightfully, that James's famous pragmatist conception of truth makes sense only in the context of a reality conceived as change and becoming, and that any discussion of the former must begin by taking the latter into account:

> The definition that James gives to truth therefore, is an integral part of his conception of reality. If reality is not that economic and systematic universe our logic likes to imagine, if it is not sustained by a framework of intellectuality, intellectual truth is a human invention whose effect is to utilize reality rather than to enable us to penetrate it. *And if reality does not form a single whole, if it is multiple and mobile*, made up of crosscurrents, truth which arises from contact with one of these currents—truth felt before being conceived—is more capable of seizing and storing up reality than truth merely thought. Therefore it is, in fact, with this theory of reality that a critique of pragmatism should first grapple. (CM 218/1449)

Such an affirmation of change and becoming no doubt played a crucial role in the rapid success of pragmatism, as well as in Bergson's extraordinary popularity in prewar America. Celebrated as much in universities as by the educated public, pragmatism (in Dewey's version, as well as in James's) and Bergsonism are cultural phenomena in the broad sense of the term: the debates and interest they provoke go far beyond the philosophical arena and spread to those of literature, art, education, and politics. It is also clear that in this first reception the affirmation of change gives off a certain air of optimism: a confidence in action, in the possibility of social reform, in technical and scientific progress, which all seem to mesh perfectly with the idea of reality as constantly becoming. Such an alliance between faith in progress and a belief in the intrinsic mobility of reality is understandable and not surprising in the context of the times. There is nevertheless nothing necessary about it and, more importantly, it was never affirmed as such by James or Bergson.

A century later, in our own context, the question of change and becoming is more pressing than ever, but the connection—more emotional than logical—between the affirmation of an open universe and faith in scientific and social progress, and an era characterized by optimism, is certainly no longer the order of the day. We fear climate change and rightly so: a little more seasonal stability would be much more reassuring! Other changes wear a more ambiguous face; we are not sure what to make of them. They seem to carry promises as much as threats, such as the striking developments in the biological sciences and biotechnologies. What is certain in any case is that, for us, becoming and change are no longer synonymous with progress: their reality has become, so to speak, normatively neutral, to be evaluated positively or negatively on a case-by-case basis.

It is particularly worthwhile from this standpoint, however, to read, or reread, James and Bergson, for whom the affirmation of the reality of becoming and the necessity of weighing up its philosophical, ethical, and political consequences, goes hand-in-hand with the most rigorous critique of the notion of progress. What was not clearly perceptible for James and Bergson's contemporaries—at least at the beginning of the century, at the time of their greatest success—has now become one of the most stimulating aspects of their thought.

For both philosophers, albeit with different emphases and arguments, taking seriously the idea of an open universe—a "becoming" universe—certainly implies letting go of any ontology or metaphysics that privileges the stability of being or of values and makes the changing world a simple reflection of the eternal world of ideas (whether from a Platonic or Kantian perspective, it matters little here). But, perhaps most importantly, it implies taking leave of any conception or philosophy of history that turns becoming into the unfolding of a teleology. To presuppose an end or an origin that guides history is simply another way of denying the reality of change. It's one that is subtler perhaps, because instead of denying change altogether it "merely" subordinates it to a telos that precedes and directs it, but it is just as misguided.

The fact is that for James as well as Bergson, an ontology of change is inseparable from a radically anti-teleological conception of history: becoming, whether of the universe or of human beings, is not preceded or sustained by anything but itself; nothing guarantees a happy—or un-happy—ending, because becoming is necessarily open. From this point of view, the notion of progress is an illusion, not because there aren't events we can rightly welcome as political, moral, or scientific advances but because such events do not constitute ordered stages, let alone necessary ones, in a supposedly one-way course of history. Likewise, "optimism" and "pessimism" are psychological attitudes that may sometimes be shared by an entire society at a given moment but cannot in any way be tied to a philosophy of the reality of change that, per se, is not and cannot be "optimistic" or "pessimistic" since it does not believe in any script directing "the order of things," nor in any necessity abstracted from becoming.

Of course, this conception of a radically open universe and time affects the way James and Bergson consider almost all the problems and objects they deal with. In what follows, however, I will limit my analysis to just a few of its consequences in the field of moral and political thought.[2]

THE PLURALISTIC UNIVERSE AND THE PLACE OF HOPE

I will begin with James and, more specifically, with his lecture "Pragma-tism and Religion." This piece concludes the series of lectures published as *Pragmatism* (1907), and it succinctly expresses a recurrent theme in *The Pluralistic Universe* and James's other writings.

In this last lecture, James ponders the relationship between pragma-tism and religion. Pragmatism, for James, like any other philosophy, is defined much more by an intellectual and moral attitude—by a way of seeing things, so to speak—than by a set of doctrines, so the question is knowing what differentiates the pragmatist attitude from other philo-sophical temperaments in the field of religion. More precisely, the ques-tion is what differentiates pragmatism from the two fundamental atti-tudes that, according to James, characterize the emotional tone of so many different philosophical doctrines: "tough-mindedness" and "tender-mindedness." All kinds of traditional philosophical divisions can be mapped onto this original difference in affective tone. The "tender-minded" need logical consistency and certainty, seek out a first and ultimate principle that can make sense of the diversity of reality, and are thus inclined toward rationalism and/or monism. The "tough-minded" on the other hand, in James's typology, refuse any form of metaphysical consolation: they want to "face up to things" directly, without submitting them first to a reassuring order, and thus tend to be empiricists and pluralists.[3]

In "Pragmatism and Religion" James explores the consequences of these different temperaments when it comes to thinking about becoming, and his description of the rationalist is what interests me most in this context.[4] This is what he writes:

> Please observe that the whole dilemma revolves pragmatically about the notion of the world's possibilities. Intellectually, rationalism invokes its absolute principle of unity as a ground of possibility for the many facts. Emotionally, it sees it as a container and limiter of possibilities, a guarantee that the upshot shall be good. Taken in this way, the absolute makes all good things certain, and all bad things impossible (in the eternal, namely), and may be said to transmute the entire category of possibility into categories more secure. One sees at this point that the great religious difference lies between the men who insist that the world *must and shall be,* and those who are contented with believing that the world *may be,* saved.[5]

The decision that separates individuals when it comes to religion is the same as the one that separates them when it comes to philosophical temperament: there are those who consider the perfection of the world to be a necessary principle (whether guaranteed by reason or by God makes little difference in this regard) and those who view this perfection as one possible *terminus ad quem,* as a desirable goal worthy of all our efforts, and as a hope that can inspire us but certainly not as an eternally established necessity (*une nécessité établie de tout temps*).[6]

Under James's keen psychological eye, rationalism shows an unexpected face: while intellectually it is characterized, unsurprisingly, by the demand for a principle of unity and coherence, on an affective level, this demand betrays a need to believe in the necessity of a "happy ending." If what is and what *should* be do not as yet coincide, this is simply an empirical fact or a question of time; eventually, they will necessarily coincide because the end, the telos, is guaranteed by the principle, the *arche.* James's genius is to show that an attitude that is intellectually or philosophically "strong," an uncompromising rationalism, is necessarily accompanied by —or is simply the result of—a "tender-minded" psychological attitude, the emotional need for certainty. The less we are able to accept the uncertainty of becoming, the more we project an unshakeable logic.

James's pluralistic conception of the universe does not offer such guarantees, as he explicitly states in his discussion of the problem of "the One and the Many":

> Pluralism, accepting a universe unfinished, with doors and windows open to possibilities uncontrollable in advance, gives us less religious certainty than monism, with its absolutely closed-in world. . . . In point of fact, however, monism is usually willing to exert this optimistic faith: its world is certain to be saved, yes, is saved already, unconditionally and from eternity, in spite of all the phenomenal appearances of risk. A world working out an uncertain destiny, as the phenomenal world appears to be doing, is an intolerable idea to the rationalistic mind. *Pluralism, on the other hand, is neither optimistic nor pessimistic, but melioristic, rather. The world, it thinks, may be saved, on condition that its parts shall do their best. But shipwreck in detail, or even on the whole, is among the open possibilities.*[7]

Whereas on a rationalist and monistic approach the world is always already saved, eternally saved as it were, the pluralistic universe is a universe in the making, an open universe with an uncertain fate, offering no certainty. While optimism is crucial for the "tender-minded," it is incompatible with pluralism: the open-ended nature of the becoming it affirms cannot exclude outright an "unhappy ending." But this does not mean that pluralism encourages despair. Optimism and pessimism, according to James, resemble each other more than we think: they are the twin symmetrical reactions to the one and the same belief that privileges stability over movement, eternity over becoming, and necessity over the uncertainty of the possible. If pluralism is not and cannot be "optimistic," then neither is it destined to play the role of the doomsayer who confidently (at times, one might even say happily) awaits the coming apocalypse.

Pluralism, as James conceives it, is not a philosophy of progress. Rather, and this is quite different, it is a "melioristic" philosophy that sees in the reality of change the possibility, with no guarantees, for individual and collective human action to be effective, to guide becoming and introduce the new.[8] While rationalism protects us from the anxiety of an uncertain fate, its "optimism," according to James, risks leading us to not recognize what responsibility we do have as humans in relation to a world that's a work in progress. No doubt our actions only represent a tiny portion of the pluralistic universe, yet they do or can have their effect, just as hope requires no certainty to be what it is: hope.

In the pluralistic universe, as in the Bergsonian universe, "not every-thing is given": the new can spring forth; we can even produce it. It must be stressed once again, however, that the emphasis placed on confidence in human action, on the possibility of cooperating with others, on the hope of being able to contribute, as much as possible, to the "redemp-tion" of the world—in short, all of the melioristic themes of James's pragmatism—does not rely on any ontological, moral, or religious opti-mism that would be intrinsic to a philosophy of change and becoming. Precisely the opposite, in fact: because the course becoming takes is not given in advance, hope takes on all of its moral, political, and religious significance. It is because things can always take a turn for the worse that we must act, and there is a place for both responsibility and hope.

It must also be noted that this aspect of James's pragmatism has pro-foundly marked contemporary American philosophy, well beyond those authors who explicitly claim his legacy, and even sometimes those who otherwise express their reservations about pragmatism in general. Richard Rorty is a telling example of the first category. Having always proclaimed himself a pragmatist, Rorty nevertheless entertains a privileged relationship with Dewey's thought: he finds James in a way too religious and mystical and, perhaps more decisively, does not find the same social and political forcefulness in James's thought as he does in Dewey's work. And yet, in *Hope in Place of Knowledge*, as in many other of his texts, Rorty emphatically advances the ethical and political spirit of James's pluralism when he re-minds us, in such a convincing manner, that no epistemological certainty can guarantee a more just and inclusive society, and that hope, in and of itself, is the only foundation—itself unfounded—required for us to be en-gaged in civic life.[9] For his part, Stanley Cavell—who to be sure does not consider himself a pragmatist, and who is more interested in Henry than William James—also underscores, through his reinterpretation of modern skepticism, the limitations of a conception of knowledge grounded in a strict notion of epistemological certainty. Such a model cannot grasp—and, worse, tends to disqualify—forms of reason and reasoning specific to moral and political life, where the absence of agreement and certainty is not due to limited knowledge but to the very nature of the moral and political conversation.[10]

DURATION AND RESPONSIBILITY

We find in Bergson the same affirmation of the reality of change and the new, as well as a critique of the notion of progress and of all metaphysical "optimism" or "pessimism." If James's starting point is an analysis of the philosophical temperament underlying rationalism and its need for reassuring certainties, Bergson's critique of the notion of progress is initially in response to a philosophical problem, whose consequences for moral and political thought only become explicit with the publication of *The Two Sources of Morality and Religion* in 1932. The consistency of his position on this subject is nevertheless remarkable.

In a lecture given at Oxford in 1920, and published in 1934 as "The Possible and the Real" in *Creative Mind,* Bergson gives us the most detailed version of his critique of the category of the possible and establishes a link between the retrospective illusion of the possible and the notion of progress as one of its forms. Bergson returns in this text to the importance of the formulation of problems in philosophy and once again he claims that because solutions are always presupposed by the very statement of the problem, the correct formulation of a problem is not just a matter of good methodology but absolutely decisive. Poorly posed problems produce all sorts of metaphysical confusions, whereas when they are correctly stated they resolve themselves of their own accord (CM 95/1335). The category of the possible represents, in his opinion, the very paradigm of a poorly posed problem and the confusions that stem from it. In the history of philosophy, just as in everyday language, we assume that the category of the possible contains something less than that of the real or, in other words, we assume that a possibility is necessarily lesser than its real counterpart. For Bergson, however, the exact opposite is true: it is the possible that contains more than the real, and the question is to understand where this error comes from and what other false ideas stem from this poorly posed problem. Bergson gives an example, not without a certain humor, of what he means:

> During the Great War certain newspapers and periodicals sometimes turned aside from the terrible worries of the day to think of what would happen later once peace was restored. They were particularly preoccupied with the future of literature. Someone came one day to ask me my ideas on the subject. A little embarrassed, I declared I had none. "Do you not at least perceive," I was asked, "certain possible directions? Let us

grant that one cannot foresee things in detail; you as a philosopher have at least an idea of the whole. How do you conceive, for example, the great dramatic work of tomorrow?" I shall always remember my interlocutor's surprise when I answered, "If I knew what was to be the great dramatic work of the future, I should be writing it." I saw distinctly that he conceived the future work as being already stored up in some cupboard reserved for possibles; because of my long-standing relations with philosophy, I should have been able to obtain from it the key to the storehouse. "But," I said, "the work of which you speak of is not yet possible."—"But it must be, since it is to take place."—"No, it is not. I grant you, at most, that it will have been possible." "What do you mean by that?"—"It's quite simple. Let a man of talent or genius come forth, let him create a work: it will then be real, and by that very fact it becomes retrospectively or retroactively possible. It would not be possible, it would not have been so, if this man had not come upon the scene. That is why I tell you that it will have been possible today, but that it is not yet so. (CM 100–101/1339–40)

We believe that the possibility of things precedes their existence, in the manner of the set of possible worlds contemplated by Leibniz's God before the best one is chosen to bring into existence; or like the a priori structures that shape in advance the form of all possible experience. Our attitude toward the future is guided by this belief, even when we are unaware of it: it has the force of a habit. It is thus not hard to understand why we imagine the concept of the possible contains less than that of the real: one being the image of the other, existence would seem to give body to possibility's ghost and bring the one thing it lacks: a little reality. As Deleuze stresses in *Difference and Repetition*, the consequence of this habit of thought is that existence becomes incomprehensible: because it adds nothing to the possible concept that supposedly precedes it, existence remains outside the concept, without justification and, paradoxically, without importance.[11] According to Bergson, the possible is only the real with, in addition, an act of thought that projects it backwards: "the possible is nothing but the mirage of the present in the past," and, as such, it contains more than the real—it contains the real *and* the intellectual act that constitutes it retrospectively, in a retroactive fashion (CM 101/1341; translation modified).

What is at stake for Bergson is much more than a simple question of method or conceptual analysis: behind the illusion of the possible lies an error that threatens the very task of philosophy, as he conceives it, or, more specifically, the task of conversion that philosophy must undertake. Philosophy must learn to turn its gaze away from the eternal—whether in another world or in this one, because there is also a modern way of disregarding time—and turn instead toward movement, toward newness in the making, and attempt, finally, to think them. It is in this context that the Bergsonian critique of the possible takes on its full importance. Philosophy's inability to give conceptual determination to existence is a direct consequence of its desire to grasp what is eternal in time, to understand movement only as the realization of a preexisting possibility outside of time. In his interpretation of the history of ancient and modern philosophy, Bergson highlights the fact that, despite some important and obvious differences, the Platonic idea that knowledge is knowledge of the eternal continues to hold sway and impose its ideal explicitly or implicitly even in our own time. What comes to exist, what is born in time, must have its law, reason, or cause of existence elsewhere: it is simply the incarnation of a preexisting possibility. The conversion that Bergson so earnestly hopes and prays for (*appeler de tous ses vœux*) is thus a conversion of philosophy to time. As the term "conversion" suggests, it is less about changing the "objects" that philosophy concerns itself with (time, after all, is a very ancient object of thought), than changing its attitude, its way of conceiving them, or, if you will, its *desire*. Philosophy must become capable of turning away from its desire for eternity in order to think the power [*puissance*] of time, which, as Bergson writes, is "invention or it is nothing at all" (CE 341/784). The fact that such a conversion is not an easy task, or that such an assertion is not easy to comprehend, is evident when we see that so many remarkable philosophers and readers—from Heidegger to Adorno, from Merleau-Ponty to Foucault, to name just a few—are unsuccessful in their readings of Bergson. They criticize the Bergsonian conception of time for its supposed subjectivism, for its dichotomy between time and space, and they sidestep the whole question of the new and, with it, Bergson's entire philosophical project.

To believe that the possibility of things precedes their existence thus amounts to denying the reality of newness and change, to speaking about time without thinking it, to erasing the one feature that truly defines it: its creative force. But how can we think this power that time has? As is well known, in *Creative Evolution* Bergson seeks to demonstrate that his project is not an abstract metaphysical hypothesis. The Darwinian discovery of the evolution of life and the production of new and unpredictable life-forms, along with the new ideas and concepts required to think them, oblige philosophy and science, in Bergson's view, to rethink their conception of time. Time can no longer be thought of as the external framework in which events unfold but must instead be conceived as a truly active force: time is active in and of itself. When Bergson claims, "if [time] does nothing, it is nothing," he appeals to what could be described as a properly ontological pragmatism (CE 39/784). The being of time is nothing apart from its specifically active power. The criticism of the category of the possible is thus a necessary consequence of a theory of duration. In his first book, *Time and Free Will* (1889), Bergson explores the psychological and subjective dimension of duration. In *Matter and Memory* (1896), he develops a metaphysics and ontology of time as duration. But it is only with *Creative Evolution* that Bergson establishes the missing link between a subjective experience of temporality and a philosophical hypothesis: the "fact" of the evolution of life provides the means for this transition. The concept of duration and the criticism of the concept of the possible it implies were developed in an area between psychology and biology, which does not mean they have no consequences for Bergson's moral, religious, and political thought. On the contrary, they constitute one of its chief components.

Without being able to embark here on a detailed analysis of *Two Sources*, I would nevertheless like to show that the very way Bergson poses the problem of the development—the "becoming"—of human societies depends upon his non-finalistic conception of time.[12] The question Bergson poses in *Two Sources* is the origin of human society and some of its essential features, namely, morality and religion. But, writing at one of the darkest moments in history, Bergson is also concerned with the *future* of these societies. What about change and newness in human history? What can we expect, or learn, from this history? Bergson's task is made even harder by the fact that he cannot rely on either a purely rationalist conception or any form of historicism. He cannot adopt either a Kantian standpoint or a Hegelian one: on his account, human history, that is, the development of societies and moral and religious forms, is caught up in the evolutionary movement of life and shares its complete lack of teleology. Already in *Creative Evolution*, Bergson stresses the decided absence of any preestablished direction that could guide the evolution of living things. According to Bergson, the finalistic and deterministic interpretations of evolution only appear to conflict with each other, because in reality they share the same misplaced notion that "everything is given." For determinism, "everything is given" in the past, in the form of a causal chain that would reduce the evolution of life to the unfolding of a set program. Finalism, on the other hand, subordinates evolution to an end to be reached and is thus oriented toward the future, but it is a future whose shape is known in advance and is already determined by and contained in the finality it aspires to. Whether driven by the past or attracted by the future, in both cases the evolution of species and life-forms is conceived as a superficial phenomenon. Time is once again stripped of its creative force and is reduced to a neutral framework in which events unfold—events whose law is removed from time (CE 39–45/528–32).

According to Bergson, every attempt to think the development of human societies in terms of a philosophy of history shares the same teleological illusion of finalism. Human becoming is not an exception to evolution; no law of history outlines its steps in advance. Viewed in this light, the notion of progress is only one manifestation of the retrospective illusion of the possible. However, a Kantian-style approach, which would ground the autonomy of morality on pure reason, is equally unacceptable for Bergson, not only because the ideas of reason reintroduce a form of teleology but most of all because reason itself is a product of evolution. Bergson's attempt to think two different, and in many ways opposed, sources of morality and religion aims to account not only for what links human history to the evolution of the species but also for what goes beyond it.[13] One of the two sources, "closed" morality and religion, has a near-biological function: to preserve the unity of society, the clan mental-ity that brings together members of a group and induces them, when necessary, to sacrifice themselves for the "common good." The love for family, for city, and for nation sustained by closed morality and religion reflects the necessity of this link. In times of peace it can take the univer-salist form of "rights toward humanity," but this form is deceptive, accord-ing to Bergson: every society is *closed* by nature; that is to say, every society defines itself through the *inclusion* of a certain number of individ-uals and the *exclusion* of all others. To convince ourselves, we need only consider what happens as soon as a war breaks out: human solidarity without limits or borders disappears; in its place we witness unrestrained violence against the enemy—murder, rape, torture, and cruelty. Accord-ing to Bergson, the reply that these are rare and exceptional events is an illusion: there is nothing exceptional about war, despite our desire not to see it coming and to exclude it from the normal course of things as if it were merely an unfortunate accident.

No closed society, democratic or not, escapes the instinct to be cohesive, the clan mentality that, for Bergson, is fundamentally a warring instinct. The exclusion that forms the foundation of closed societies is thus not neutral, and even less benevolent, but essentially hostile. This explains why Bergson does not believe we can move from the love of family and nation to the love of all humanity in a series of quantitative expansions, by the continual progress of a sentiment that would expand in scope without changing in nature. While "open" morality and religion, perhaps even an open form of society, are possible, it is only on the condition of being derived from another source, a second source, distinct in principle from the first with its quasi-biological function of ensuring the survival of the group. The analysis of this second source goes beyond the scope of this chapter, but one of its aspects must be highlighted here. The openness that interests Bergson, namely the possibility of a morality and religion not grounded in a communitarian principle of inclusion and exclusion, cannot be achieved by degrees. Men and women dream of it from time to time, and sometimes this dream of an open society manages to break through the enclosure and realize a part of itself before society once again closes itself up and falls back into that network of habits that constitutes the whole of social obligation. What takes place during such moments is a *qualitative* rather than a *quantitative* change, a *leap* rather than a step forward in a given direction. Bergson insists on this point: we can call these moments "progress" if we hold to such ideas, but the fact is that there is no sense in which they link up with each other, one following from the other, in an well-ordered course of history. They are, rather, moments of rupture that are active for a time before they are reabsorbed within the moral and religious forms of closed society.

The problem with this type of retrospective illusion of the possible that is constituted by the idea of progress is the same as that described by James: as with rationalistic optimism, the belief in progress may be reassuring, but this reassurance is bought at too high a price. In Bergson's view, if progress really existed, it would mean that moral and political changes would be able to be foretold in advance and as a result there would be no need to create them, namely to invent and produce anything new in terms of human modes of existence.

To think becoming requires that we renounce both the dream of knowledge as certainty and our despair when faced with the absence of absolute knowledge. It asks us, in the old language of the Enlightenment, that we accept to become adults, face our responsibilities as well as our dreams, and understand that the choice is not between absolute knowledge and impotence. That other paths are open to us, perhaps less reassuring, but more concrete. James, Bergson, and their legacy are without question still ahead of us.

NOTES

1 For a biography of Bergson, see Soulez and Worms, *Bergson*.

2 While there is no "political philosophy," in the strict sense of the term in either James or Bergson, it is hard to deny that *Two Sources* is an attempt by Bergson to reflect on the political domain as much as on morality and religion. As for James's notion of pluralism, which itself has political echoes, it continues to be at the center of debate in political philosophy in the United States. See, for example, Connolly, *Pluralism*.

3 James does not claim to describe specific doctrines but rather certain traits, a certain affective configuration common to different authors. With his notion of *Befindlichkeit* in *Being and Time*, Heidegger also stresses the importance of affects in the way *Dasein* is in the world, but unlike James he does not establish any link between affects and philosophical positions, as though the life of the mind was unconcerned by anything but itself.

4 For James, pragmatism in a way takes on the role of mediator here inasmuch as it recognizes that the principle upheld by the "tender-minded" of an eternal, perfect, and absolute universe that coexists with—some would say duplicates—our own, has no doubt proved useful in the course of human history.

5 James, *Pragmatism and the Meaning of Truth*, 135.

6 Bergson, as we shall see, criticizes the category of the possible but in a way that contradicts the letter rather than the spirit of James's passage.

7 James, *Some Problems of Philosophy*, 141–42 (emphasis added).

8 According to James, whose argument is very close to Bergson's on this point, monism implies that the temporal content of the universe is already given, and therefore that the possibility of the new emerging is ruled out.

9 See Rorty, *Hope in Place of Knowledge*.

10 See Cavell, *The Claim of Reason*.

11 Deleuze, *Difference and Repetition*, 211.

12 For a detailed analysis of the relationship between duration and politics in *Two Sources*, allow me to refer to my "Mysticism and the Foundation of the Open Society."

13 On this note Bergson refers to the Spinozist distinction between *natura naturans* and *natura naturata*: while the closed society depends on nature as it is, the open society displays a natura naturans, a creative force that does not exhaust itself with what it creates (see *TS* 58/1024).

Adorno, Theodor. *Metaphysics: Concept and Problems*. Trans. Edmund Jephcott. Stanford: Stanford University Press, 2002.

Agamben, Giorgio. *Homo Sacer: Sovereign Power and Bare Life*. Trans. Daniel Heller-Roazen. Stanford: Stanford University Press, 1998.

Ansell-Pearson, Keith. *Philosophy and the Adventure of the Virtual: Bergson and the Time of Life*. London: Routledge, 2002.

——. "The Transfiguration of Existence and Sovereign Life: Sloterdijk and Nietzsche on Posthuman and Superhuman Futures." *Environment and Planning D: Society and Space* 27, no. 1 (2009): 139–56.

Antliff, Mark. *Bergson: Cultural Politics and the Parisian Avant-Garde*. Princeton: Princeton University Press, 1993.

Arendt, Hannah. *The Human Condition*. Chicago: University of Chicago Press, 1958.

——. *On Revolution*. New York: Penguin, 1990.

——. *The Origins of Totalitarianism*. New York: Harcourt, Brace and Company, 1951.

Azouvi, Francis. *La gloire de Bergson: Essai sur le magistère philosophique*. Paris: Gallimard, 2007.

Badiou, Alain. *Being and Event*. Trans. Oliver Feltham. London: Continuum, 2005.

——. *Ethics: An Essay on the Understanding of Evil*. Trans. Peter Hallward. London: Verso, 2001.

——. *Saint Paul: The Foundation of Universalism*. Trans. Ray Brassier. Stanford: Stanford University Press, 2003.

Balibar, Etienne. "Citizen Subject." In *Who Comes after the Subject?* Ed. Eduardo Cadava, Peter Connor, and Jean-Luc Nancy, 33–57. London: Routledge, 1991.

——. " 'Rights of Man' and 'Rights of the Citizen': The Modern Dialectic of Equality and Freedom." In *Masses, Classes, Ideas: Studies on Politics and Philosophy Before and After Marx*. Ed. James Swenson, 39–59. London: Routledge, 1994.

Barden, Garrett. "Method in Philosophy." In *The New Bergson*. Ed. John Mullarkey, 32–65. Manchester: Manchester University Press, 1999.

Baudry, Jules. *Le problème de l'origine et de l'éternité du monde dans la philosophie grec-que de Platon à l'ère chrétienne.* Paris: Société d'édition 'Les belles lettres,' 1931.

Belloy, Camille de. "Une mise au point de Bergson sur *Les Deux Sources.*" In *Annales bergsoniennes I, Bergson dans le siècle.* Ed. Frédéric Worms, 133–42. Paris: PUF, 2002.

Bergson, Henri. *Correspondances.* Paris: PUF, 2002.

——. *Creative Evolution.* Trans. Arthur Mitchell. New York: Dover, 1998.

——. *The Creative Mind.* New York: Citadel Press, 2002.

——. *Les deux sources de la morale et de la religion.* Paris: PUF, 2008.

——. "Henri Bergson on Moral Values and Other Subjects." *Personalist* 42 (1961): 178–80.

——. *Laughter: An Essay on the Meaning of the Comic.* Trans. Cloudesely Brereton and Fred Rothwell. Rockville, MD: Arc Manor, 2008.

——. *Matter and Memory.* Trans. Nancy Margaret Paul and W. Scott Palmer. New York: Zone Books, 1991.

——. *Mélanges.* Paris: PUF, 1972.

——. *Mind-Energy: Lectures and Essays.* Trans. H. Wildon Carr. Santa Barbara: Greenwood Press, 1975.

——. *Œuvres.* Ed. André Robinet, with an introduction by Henri Gouhier. Paris: PUF, 1959.

——. *Time and Free Will: An Essay on the Immediate Data of Consciousness.* Trans. F. L. Pogson. New York: Dover, 2001.

——. *The Two Sources of Morality and Religion.* Trans. R. Ashley Audra and Cloudesely Brereton. Notre Dame: University of Notre Dame Press, 1977.

Bernstein, Hermann. *With Master Minds: Interviews.* New York: Universal Series Publishing Company, 1913.

Blackman, Lisa. "Reinventing Psychological Matters: The Importance of the Suggestive Realm in Tarde's Ontology." *Economy and Society* 36, no. 4 (2007): 574–96.

Bloch, Ernst. *Heritage of Our Times.* Trans. Neville Plaice and Stephen Plaice. Berkeley: University of California Press, 1991.

Bloom, Howard K. *The Global Brain: The Evolution of Mass Mind from the Big Bang to the 21st Century.* New York: Wiley, 2000.

Boulgakov, Sergei. *L'orthodoxie.* Paris: Balzon, d'Allonnes et Cie, 1958.

Boyd, Brian. *On the Origin of Stories: Evolution, Cognition, and Fiction.* Cambridge: Harvard University Press, 2009.

Braude, Stephen E. *The Gold Leaf Lady and Other Parapsychological Investigations.* Chicago: University of Chicago Press, 2007.

Brower, M. Brady. *Unruly Spirits: The Science of Psychic Phenomena in Modern France.* Champaign: University of Illinois Press, 2010.

Butler, Judith. *Gender Trouble: Feminism and the Subversion of Identity.* London: Routledge, 1990.

Cariou, Marie. *Bergson et le fait mystique.* Paris: Aubier, 1976.

Carr, David. *Interpreting Husserl: Critical and Comparative Studies.* Dordrecht: M. Nijhoff, 1987.

Carr, Nicholas. *The Shallows: What the Internet Is Doing to Our Brains.* New York: Norton, 2010.

Carroll, Joseph. "Human Nature and Literary Meaning: A Theoretical Model Illustrated with a Critique of *Pride and Prejudice*." In *The Literary Animal: Evolution and the Nature of Narrative*. Ed. Jonathan Gottschall and David Sloan Wilson, 76–106. Chicago: Northwestern University Press, 2005.

——. "Three Scenarios for Literary Darwinism." *New Literary History* 41, no. 1 (2010): 53–67.

Cavell, Stanley. *The Claim of Reason: Wittgenstein, Skepticism, Morality, and Tragedy*. Oxford: Oxford University Press, 1999.

Chalmers, David. "The Puzzle of Conscious Experience." *Scientific American* (1995): 62–68.

Chevalier, Jacques. *Entretiens avec Bergson*. Paris: Plon, 1959.

Cohen, Abraham. *Le Talmud*. Trans. Jacques Marty. Paris: Payot, 1950.

Cohen, Hermann. *Ethik des reinen Willens*. Berlin: Cassirer, 1904.

Cohen, Tom. *Hitchcock's Cryptonymies*. Minneapolis: University of Minnesota Press, 2005.

Connolly, William. *The Ethos of Pluralization*. Minneapolis: University of Minnesota Press, 1995.

——. *Neuropolitics: Thinking, Culture, Speed*. Minneapolis: University of Minnesota Press, 2002.

——. *Pluralism*. Durham: Duke University Press, 2005.

Copleston, Frederick C. "Bergson on Morality." *Proceedings of the British Academy* 41 (1955): 247–66.

Courtier, Jules. "Rapport sur les séances d'Eusapia Palladino à l'Institut général psychologique, 1905–1908." *Bulletin de l'Institut général psychologique* 8, nos. 5–6 (1908): 415–546.

Critchley, Simon. *The Ethics of Deconstruction: Derrida and Levinas*. Oxford: Blackwell, 1992.

Curle, Clinton. *Humanité: John Humphrey's Alternative Account of Human Rights*. Toronto: University of Toronto Press, 2007.

Damasio, Antonio. *Descartes' Error: Emotion, Reason, and the Human Brain*. New York Penguin, 2005.

——. *The Feeling of What Happens: Body and Emotion in the Making of Consciousness*. New York: Harcourt Brace, 1999.

Dehaene, Stanislas. *The Number Sense: How the Mind Creates Mathematics*. Oxford: Oxford University Press, 1997.

Deleuze, Gilles. *Bergsonism*. Trans. Hugh Tomlinson and Barbara Habberjam. New York: Zone Books, 1988.

——. *Cinema 2: The Time-Image*. Trans. Hugh Tomlinson and Barbara Habberjam. Minneapolis: University of Minnesota, 1989.

——. *Difference and Repetition*. Trans. Paul Patton. New York: Columbia University Press, 1994.

——. *Spinoza: Practical Philosophy*. Trans. Robert Hurley. San Francisco: City Lights Books, 1988.

Deleuze, Gilles, and Félix Guattari. *A Thousand Plateaus*. Minneapolis: University of Minnesota Press, 1987.

——. *What Is Philosophy?* Trans. Hugh Tomlinson and Graham Burchell. New York: Columbia University Press, 1994.

DeLillo, Don. *Point Omega: A Novel*. New York: Scribner, 2010.

Derrida, Jacques. "Faith and Knowledge: The Two Sources of 'Religion' at the Limits of Reason Alone." In *Religion*. Ed. Jacques Derrida and Gianni Vattimo, 1–78. Stanford: Stanford University Press, 1998.

———. *The Politics of Friendship*. Trans. George Collins. London: Verso, 1997.

———. *Rogues: Two Essays on Reason*. Trans. Pascale-Anne Brault and Michael Nass. Stanford: Stanford University Press, 1998.

Dews, Peter. "Uncategorical Imperatives: Adorno, Badiou and the Ethical Turn." *Radical Philosophy* 111 (2002): 33–37.

Durkheim, Emile. *L'Allemagne au-dessus de tout. La mentalité allemande et la guerre*. Paris: Librairie Armand Collin, 1916.

———. *The Division of Labor in Society*. Trans. Lewis Coser. New York: Free Press, 1984.

———. *The Elementary Forms of Religious Life*. Trans. Karen Fields. New York: Free Press, 1995.

———. *Moral Education: A Study in the Theory and Application of the Sociology of Education*. Trans. Everett Wilson and Herman Schnurer. New York: Free Press, 1961.

———. *Professional Ethics and Civic Morals*. Trans. Cornelia Brookfield. London: Routledge, 1992.

Ellmann, Maud. *The Poetics of Impersonality: T.S. Eliot and Ezra Pound*. Cambridge: Harvard University Press, 1987.

Epictetus. *Discourses*. Trans. Robert F. Dobbin. Oxford: Clarendon Press, 1998.

Epicurus. *Letters, Principal Doctrines, and Vatican Sayings*. Indianapolis: Bobbs-Merrill, 1964.

Eslik, Leonard. "Bergson, Whitehead, and Psychical Research." In *Bergson and Modern Thought*, edited by Andrew C. Papanicolaou and P. A. Y. Gunter, 353–68. New York: Harwood Academic Publishers, 1987.

Ewald, François. *L'État-providence*. Paris: Grasset, 1986.

Fauconnet, Paul. *La Responsabilité*. Paris: Alcan, 1920.

Ferrer, Jorge N., and Jacob H. Sherman, ed. *The Participatory Turn*. Albany: SUNY, 2008.

Fink, Eugen. *Sixth Cartesian Meditation: The Idea of a Transcendental Theory of Method*. Bloomington: Indiana University Press, 1995.

Fleg, Edmond. *Écoute Israël*. Paris: Flammarion, 1954.

———. *Le livre du commencement: Genèse*. Paris: Éditions de Minuit, 1959.

———. *Nous de l'espérance*. Angers: Au Masque d'Or, 1949.

Foucault, Michel. *The History of Madness*. Trans. Jonathan Murphy and Jean Khlafa. London: Routledge, 2006.

———. *The History of Sexuality, Volume Two: The Use of Pleasure*. New York: Pantheon Books, 1985.

Freud, Sigmund. *Moses and Monotheism*. Trans. James Strachey. New York: Penguin, 1990.

Goddard, Jean-Christophe. *Mysticisme et folie. Essai sur la simplicité*. Paris: Desclée de Brouwer, 2002.

Goodin, Robert E. "Enfranchising All Affected Interests, and Its Alternatives." *Philosophy and Public Affairs* 35, no. 1 (2007): 40–68.

Gottlieb, Noé. "D'une erreur fondamentale dans *Les deux sources* de M. Bergson." *Revue des Études Juives* 95, no. 189 (1933): 1–22.

Gouhier, Henri. *Bergson et le Christ des évangiles*. Paris: Vrin, 1961.

——. *Les méditations métaphysiques de Jean-Jacques Rousseau*. Paris: Vrin, 1969.

Goux, Jean-Joseph. *Symbolic Economies: After Marx and Freud*. Trans. Jennifer Curtiss Gage. Ithaca: Cornell University Press, 1990.

Greenfield, Susan. *I.D.: The Quest for Meaning in the 21st Century*. London: Sceptre, 2008.

Greer, John Michael. *The Ecotechnic Future: Envisioning a Post-Peak World*. Gabriola Island: New Society Publishers, 2009.

Griffin, David Ray. *Parapsychology, Philosophy, and Spirituality*. New York: SUNY, 1997.

Grogin, R. C. *The Bergsonian Controversy in France, 1900–1914*. Calgary: University of Calgary Press, 1988.

Grosz, E. A. *The Nick of Time: Politics, Evolution, and the Untimely*. Durham: Duke University Press, 2004.

Guerlac, Suzanne. *Thinking in Time: An Introduction to Henri Bergson*. Ithaca: Cornell University Press, 2006.

Guerlac, Suzanne, and Pheng Cheah, ed. *Derrida and the Time of the Political*. Durham: Duke University Press, 2007.

Guizot, François. *Histoire de la civilisation en Europe*. Paris: Didier et Cie, 1875.

Gunter, Pete A. Y. "Henri Bergson." In *Founders of Constructive Postmodern Philosophy: Peirce, James, Bergson, Whitehead, and Hartshorne*. Ed. David Ray Griffin, John B. Cobb Jr., Marcus P. Ford, Pete A. Y. Gunter, and Peter Ochs, 133–64. Albany: SUNY, 1993.

Gurney, Edmund, Frederic W. H. Myers, and Frank Podmore. *Phantasms of the Living*. 2 vols. London: Rooms of the Society for Psychical Research, 1886.

Habermas, Jürgen. *Between Facts and Norms: Contributions to a Discourse Theory of Law and Democracy*. Trans. William Rehg. Cambridge: MIT Press, 1996.

——. "Constitutional Democracy: A Paradoxical Union of Contradictory Principles." *Political Theory* 29, no. 6 (2001): 766–81.

——. *Moral Consciousness and Communicative Action*. Trans. Christian Lenhardt and Shierry Weber Nicholsen. Cambridge: MIT Press, 1999.

——. *The Philosophical Discourse of Modernity*. Trans. Frederick Lawrence. Cambridge: MIT Press, 1987.

Hansen, Mark. "Becoming as Creative Involution? Contextualizing Deleuze and Guattari's Biophilosophy." *Postmodern Culture* 11, no. 1 (2000).

Hardt, Michael, and Antonio Negri. *Empire*. Cambridge: Harvard University Press, 2000.

Höffding, Harald. *La philosophie de Bergson: Exposé et critique*. Paris: Alcan, 1916.

Honig, Bonnie. "Between Decision and Deliberation: Political Paradox in Democratic Theory." *American Political Science Review* 101, no. 1 (2007): 1–17.

Horkheimer, Max. "On Bergson's Metaphysics of Time." *Radical Philosophy* 131 (2005): 9–19.

Huizinga, Johan. *Le déclin du Moyen Age*. Paris: Payot, 1932.

Husserl, Edmund. *Cartesian Meditations*. Trans. Doris Cairns. Hague: M. Nijhoff, 1965.

——. *The Phenomenology of Internal Time-Consciousness*. Trans. James S. Churchill. Bloomington: Indiana University Press, 1964.

Ignatieff, Michael. *Human Rights as Politics and Idolatry*. Princeton: Princeton University Press, 2003.

Ishay, Micheline. *The History of Human Rights: From Ancient Times to the Globalization Era*. Berkeley: University of California Press, 2004.

Jahn, Robert G., and Brenda J Dunne. "Consciousness, Quantum Mechanics, and Random Physical Processes." In *Bergson and Modern Thought: Towards a Unified Science*. Ed. Andrew Papanicalaou and Pete A. Y. Gunter, 271–304. New York: Harwood Academic Publishers, 1987.

James, William. *Essays in Psychical Research*. Cambridge: Harvard University Press, 1986.

———. *Pragmatism and the Meaning of Truth*. Cambridge: Harvard University Press, 2000.

———. *Some Problems of Philosophy: A Beginning of an Introduction to Philosophy*. Lincoln: University of Nebraska Press, 1996.

Jankélévitch, Vladimir. *Forgiveness*. Trans. Andrew Kelley. Chicago: University of Chicago Press, 2005.

———. *Henri Bergson*. Paris: PUF, 1959.

———. *Premières et dernières pages*. Paris: Editions du Seuil, 1994.

Kant, Immanuel. *Critique of Practical Reason*. Trans. Mary J. Gregor. Cambridge: Cambridge University Press, 1997.

———. "Idea for a Universal History with a Cosmopolitan Aim." Trans. Robert B. Louden and Günter Zöller. *Anthropology, History, and Education*. Cambridge: Cambridge University Press, 2007.

———. *Perpetual Peace*. Trans. Mary J. Gregor. Cambridge: Cambridge University Press, 1999.

Karsenti, Bruno. "Nul n'est censé ignorer la loi: Le droit pénal, de Durkheim à Fauconnet." *Archives de philosophie* 67 (2004): 557–81.

Keck, Frédéric. "Bergson et l'anthropologie: Le problème de l'humanité dans *Les deux sources de la morale et de la religion*." In *Annales bergsoniennes I: Bergson dans le siècle*. Ed. Frédéric Worms, 195–214. Paris: PUF, 2002.

———. *Claude Lévi-Strauss, une introduction*. Paris: La Découverte, 2004.

———. *Contradiction et participation: Lucien Lévy-Bruhl, entre philosophie et anthropologie*. Paris: Editions du CNRS, 2008.

Kelly, Michael R., ed. *Bergson and Phenomenology*. London: Palgrave Macmillan, 2010.

Korsgaard, Christine. *The Sources of Normativity*. Cambridge: Cambridge University Press, 1996.

Kripal, Jeffrey J. *The Serpent's Gift*. Chicago: Chicago University Press, 2007.

Lafrance, Guy. *La philosophie sociale de Bergson: Sources et interprétation*. Ottawa: Editions de l'Université d'Ottawa, 1974.

Lalande, André. "Philosophy in France, 1932." *Philosophical Review* 43, no. 1 (1934): 1–26.

Latour, Bruno. "Gabriel Tarde and the End of the Social." In *The Social in Question, New Bearings in History and the Social Sciences*. Ed. Patrick Joyce, 117–32. London: Routledge, 2002.

——. "A Plea for the Earthly Sciences." In *New Social Connections, Sociology's Subjects and Objects*. Ed. Judith Burnett, Syd Jeffers, and Graham Thomas, 72–84. London: Palgrave Macmillan, 2010.

——. *The Politics of Nature: How to Bring the Sciences into Democracy*. Trans. Catherine Porter. Cambridge: Harvard University Press, 2004.

——. *Reassembling the Social: An Introduction to Actor Network Theory*. Oxford: Oxford University Press, 2005.

Latour, Bruno, and Pasquale Gagliardi, eds. *Les atmospheres de la politique: Dialogue pour un monde commun*. Paris: Seuil, 2006.

Lawlor, Leonard. "Asceticism and Sexuality: The 'Trumpery of Nature' in Bergson's *The Two Sources of Morality and Religion*." Special SPEP issue, *Philosophy Today* (2002): 92–101.

——. "Auto-affection and Becoming (Part I): Who Are We?" *Environmental Philosophy* 6, no. 1 (2009): 1–20.

——. "Becoming and Auto-affection (Part II): Who Are We?" *Graduate Faculty Philosophy Journal* 30, no. 2 (2010): 219–37.

——. *The Challenge of Bergsonism: Phenomenology, Ontology, Ethics*. London: Continuum, 2003.

——. *Early Twentieth-Century Continental Philosophy*. Bloomington: Indiana University Press, 2011.

Lawlor, Leonard, and Valentine Moulard. "Henri Bergson." *Stanford Encyclopedia of Philosophy*, 2004. http://plato.stanford.edu/entries/bergson/.

Lecky, W. E. H. *History of European Morals from Augustus to Charlemagne*, part 1. Kila, MT: Kessinger Publising, 2003.

Lefebvre, Alexandre. "Human Rights in the Later Philosophy of Deleuze and Bergson." *Theory and Event* 14 (2011).

——. *The Image of Law: Deleuze, Bergson, Spinoza*. Stanford: Stanford University Press, 2008.

Lefebvre, Alexandre, and Melanie White. "Bergson on Durkheim: Society *Sui Generis*." *Journal of Classical Sociology* 10, no. 4 (2010): 457–77.

——. "Religion within the Bounds of Mere Emotion: Bergson and Kant." In *Emotions Matter*. Ed. Alan Hunt, Dale Spencer, and Kevin Walby, 102–23. Toronto: University of Toronto Press, 2012.

Levinas, Emmanuel. *Entre Nous: Thinking-of-the-Other*. Trans. Michael B. Smith and Barbara Harshav. New York: Columbia University Press, 2000.

Lévi-Strauss, Claude. *The Elementary Structures of Kinship*. Trans. James Harle Bell, John Richard von Sturmer, and Rodney Needham. Boston: Beacon Press, 1971.

——. *The Savage Mind*. Trans. George Weidenfeld. Oxford: Oxford University Press, 1996.

——. *Totemism*. Trans. Rodney Needham. London: Merlin Press, 1964.

Lévy-Bruhl, Lucien. *Carnets*. Paris: PUF, 1998.

——. "Compte rendu de H. Bergson, *Essai sur les données immédiates de la conscience*." *Revue philosophique* 29, no. 5 (1890).

——. *How Natives Think*. Trans. Lilian A. Clare. London: Allen and Unwin, 1926.

——. *L'Idée de responsabilité*. Paris: Hachette, 1884.

——. *Primitive Mentality*. Trans. Lilian A. Clare. New York: AMS Press, 1978.

——. *Primitives and the Supernatural*. Trans. Lilian A. Clare. New Work: Haskell House Publishers, 1973.

Lewkowitz, Albert. *Das Judentum und die geistigen Strömungen des 19 Jahrhvnderts*. Breslau: M. and H. Marcus, 1935.

Llewelyn, John. *The Middle Voice of Ecological Conscience*. London: Macmillan, 1991.

Lovelock, James. *The Vanishing Face of Gaia: A Final Warning*. New York: Basic Books, 2009.

Mannheim, Karl. *Conservatism: A Contribution to the Sociology of Knowledge*. New York: Routledge, 1986.

Marion, Jean-Luc. *The Erotic Phenomenon*. Trans. Stephen E. Lewis. Chicago: University of Chicago Press, 2008.

Maritain, Jacques. *Bergsonian Philosophy and Thomism*. Trans. Mabelle L. Andison and J. Gordon Andison. New York: Greenwood Press, 1968.

——. *De Bergson à Thomas d'Aquin*. Paris: Flammarion, 1947.

Marrati, Paola. "Mysticism and the Foundation of the Open Society: Bergsonian Politics." In *Political Theologies*. Ed. Hent de Vries, 591–601. New York: Fordham University Press, 2006.

Maurras, Charles. *De la politique naturelle au Nationalisme intégral*. Paris: Vrin, 1972.

May, Todd. *The Moral Theory of Poststructuralism*. University Park: Pennsylvania State University Press, 1995.

Méheust, Bertrand. *Somnambulisme et médiumnité: Tome 1, Le défi du magnétisme*. Paris: Institut Synthélabo pour le progrès de la connaissance, 1999.

——. *Somnambulisme et médiumnité: Tome 2, Le choc des sciences psychiques*. Paris: Institut Synthélabo pour le progrès de la connaissance, 1999.

Menary, Richard, ed. *The Extended Mind*. Cambridge: MIT Press, 2010.

Meunier, Georges. *Ce qu'ils pensent du "merveilleux."* Paris: Albin Michel, 1910.

Michelman, Frank I. "Constitutional Authorship." In *Constitutionalism: Philosophical Foundations*. Ed. L. Alexander, 64–98. Cambridge: Cambridge University Press, 1998.

Montesquieu, Charles de Secondat. *The Spirit of the Laws*. Trans. Anne M. Cohler, Basia C. Miller, and Harold Stone. Cambridge: Cambridge University Press, 1989.

Mossé-Bastine, Rose-Marie. *Bergson, éducateur*. Paris: PUF, 1995.

Mouffe, Chantal. *The Democratic Paradox*. London: Verso, 2000.

Mullarkey, John. *Bergson and Philosophy*. Edinburgh: Edinburgh University Press, 1999.

——, ed. *The New Bergson*. Manchester: Manchester University Press, 2000.

Nietzsche, Friedrich. *Beyond Good and Evil*. Trans. Marion Faber. Oxford: Oxford University Press, 1998.

——. *Dawn*. Trans. Brittain Smith. Stanford: Stanford University Press, 2011.

——. *The Gay Science*. Trans. Josefine Nauckhoff. Cambridge: Cambridge University Press, 2001.

——. *Human, All Too Human*. Trans. R. J. Hollingdale. Cambridge: Cambridge University Press, 1984.

——. *On the Genealogy of Morality.* Trans. Carol Diethe. Cambridge: Cambridge University Press, 2006.

——. *Twilight of the Idols.* Trans. Duncan Large. Oxford: Oxford University Press, 1998.

Nussbaum, Martha. *Women and Human Development: The Capabilities Approach.* Cambridge: Cambridge University Press, 2000.

Ochoa Espejo, Paulina. *The Time of Popular Sovereignty: Process and the Democratic State.* University Park: Pennsylvania State University Press, 2011.

Olson, Kevin. "Paradoxes of Constitutional Democracy." *American Journal of Political Science* 51, no. 2 (2007): 330–43.

O'Neill, Onora. *Acting on Principle: An Essay on Kantian Ethics.* New York: Columbia University Press, 1975.

Pascal, Blaise. *Pensées.* Trans. Roger Ariew. Indianapolis: Hackett, 2005.

Patton, Paul. *Deleuzian Concepts: Philosophy, Colonization, Politics.* Stanford: Stanford University Press, 2010.

Paulhan, Jean. *The Flowers of Tarbes, or, Terror in Literature.* Trans. Michael Syrotinski. Champaign: University of Illinois Press, 2006.

Pippen, Robert. *The Persistence of Subjectivity: On the Kantian Aftermath.* Cambridge: Cambridge University Press, 2005.

Plato. *Philebus.* In *Plato: Complete Works.* Ed. John M. Cooper. Indianapolis: Hackett Publishing, 1997.

Popper, Karl. *The Open Society and Its Enemies.* London: Routledge, 2011.

Rabinow, Paul, and Nikolas Rose. "Biopower Today." *BioSocieties* 1, no. 2 (2006): 195–217.

Rauh, Frédéric. "La conscience du devenir." *Revue de métaphysique et de morale* 5 (1897): 659–81.

Rawls, John. *The Law of Peoples.* Cambridge: Cambridge University Press, 2001.

——. *A Theory of Justice.* Cambridge: Harvard University Press, 1999.

Ricoeur, Paul. *The Symbolism of Evil.* Trans. Emerson Buchanan. New York: Harper and Row, 1967.

Riquier, Camille. *Archéologie de Bergson: Temps et métaphysique.* Paris: PUF, 2009.

Rorty, Richard. *Hope in Place of Knowledge: The Pragmatics of Tradition in Philosophy.* Taipei: Academica Sinica, 1999.

Russell, Bertrand. "The Philosophy of Bergson." *The Monist* 22 (1912): 321–47.

Salmon, Wesley C., ed. *Zeno's Paradoxes.* Indianapolis: Hackett, 2001.

Schmitt, Carl. *The Crisis of Parliamentary Democracy.* Trans. Ellen Kennedy. Cambridge: MIT Press, 1985.

Servier, Jean. *Histoire de l'utopie.* Paris: Gallimard, 1967.

Shklar, Judith N. "Bergson and the Politics of Intuition." In *Political Thought and Political Thinkers.* Ed. Stanley Hoffmann, 317–38. Chicago: University of Chicago Press, 1998.

Silesius, Angelus. *The Cherubinic Wanderer.* Mahwah, NJ: Paulist Press, 1986.

Simmel, Georg. *Zur Philosophie der Kunst.* Potsdam: Kiepenheuer, 1922.

Singer, Peter. "All Animals Are Equal." In *Animal Rights and Human Obligations.* Ed. Tom Regan and Peter Singer, 148–62. Upper Saddle River: Prentice-Hall, 1989.

——. *Animal Liberation.* 4th ed. London: Pimlico, 1995.

——. *Practical Ethics.* 2nd ed. Cambridge: Cambridge University Press, 1993.

Sitbon-Peillon, Brigitte. "Bergson et le primitif: Entre métaphysique et sociologie." In *Annales bergsoniennes I: Bergson dans le siècle.* Ed. Frédéric Worms, 171–94. Paris: PUF, 2002.

Sorel, Georges. *Reflections on Violence.* Trans. Jeremy Jennings. Cambridge: Cambridge University Press, 1999.

Soulez, Philippe. *Bergson politique.* Paris: PUF, 1989.

Soulez, Philippe, and Frédéric Worms. *Bergson.* Paris: PUF, 2002.

Surya, Michel. *De l'argent: La ruine de la politique.* Paris: Editions Payot and Rivages, 2009.

Tarde, Gabriel. *Les lois de l'imitation: Etude sociologique.* Paris: Félix Alcan, 1911.

Taylor, Charles. *Sources of the Self: The Making of Modern Identity.* Cambridge: Cambridge University Press, 2000.

Tristan, Flora. *The Workers' Union.* Trans. Beverly Livingstone. Chicago: University of Illinois Press, 2007.

Urpeth, Jim. " 'Health' and 'Sickness' in Religious Affectivity: Nietzsche, Otto and Bataille." In *Nietzsche and the Divine.* Ed. J. Lippitt and J. Urpeth, 226–51. Manchester: Clinamen Press, 2000.

——. "Reviving 'Natural Religion': Nietzsche and Bergson on Religious Life." In *Nietzsche and Phenomenology.* Ed. A. Rehberg, 185–206. Newcastle upon Tyne: Cambridge Scholars Press, 2011.

Varela, Francisco J., Evan T. Thompson, and Eleanor Rosch. *The Embodied Mind: Cognitive Science and Human Experience.* Cambridge: MIT Press, 1991.

Vieillard-Baron, Jean-Louie. *Bergson.* Paris: PUF, 1991.

Vries, Hent de. "Of Miracles and Special Effects." *International Journal for Philosophy of Religion* 50, no. 1/3 (2001): 41–56.

Waal, Frans de. *The Age of Empathy: Nature's Lessons for a Kinder Society.* New York: Three Rivers Press, 2009.

——. "Morally Evolved: Primate Social Instincts, Human Morality, and the Rise and Fall of 'Veneer Theory.' " In *Primates and Philosophers.* Ed. Josiah Ober and Stephen Macedo, 1–58. Princeton: Princeton University Press, 2006.

Waal, Frans de, and Frans Lanting. *Bonobo: The Forgotten Ape.* New York: Columbia University Press, 1998.

Warren, Nicolas de. "Miracles of Creation: Bergson and Levinas." In *Bergson and Phenomenology.* Ed. Michael R. Kelly, 174–200. London: Palgrave Macmillan, 2010.

Waterlot, Ghislain, ed. *Bergson et la religion: Nouvelles perspectives sur* Les Deux Sources de la morale et de la religion. Paris: PUF, 2009.

——. "Penser avec et dans le prolongement des *Deux Sources de la morale et de la religion.*" In *Bergson et la religion. Nouvelles perspectives sur* Les Deux Sources de la morale et de la religion. Ed. Ghislain Waterlot, 1–42. Paris: PUF, 2009.

Weisman, Alan. *The World Without Us.* New York: St. Martin's Press, 2007.

Whelan, Frederick G. "Prologue: Democratic Theory and the Boundary Problem." In

Liberal Democracy. Ed. J. R. Pennock and J. W. Chapman, 13–47. New York: NYU Press, 1983.

Wiggins, David. *Needs, Values, Truth: Essays in the Philosophy of Value.* Oxford: Clarendon Press, 1998.

Wittgenstein, Ludwig. *Philosophical Investigations.* Trans. G. E. M. Anscombe, P. M. S. Hacker, and Joachim Schulte. Oxford: Blackwell, 2009.

Worms, Frédéric, ed. *Annales bergsoniennes I: Bergson dans le siècle.* Paris: PUF, 2002.

——. *Bergson et les deux sens de la vie.* Paris: PUF, 2004.

——. "L'intelligence gagnée par l'intuition? La relation entre Bergson et Kant." *Les études philosophiques* 4, no. 59 (2001): 453–64.

——. " 'Terrible réalité' ou 'faux problème'? Le mal selon Bergson." In *Bergson et la religion: Nouvelles perspectives sur* Les deux sources de la morale et de la religion. Ed. Ghislain Waterlot, 379–88. Paris: PUF, 2008.

Žižek, Slavoj. *First as Tragedy, Then as Farce.* London: Verso, 2009.

CONTRIBUTORS

KEITH ANSELL-PEARSON holds a personal chair in philosophy at the University of Warwick. He is the author and editor of books on Bergson, Deleuze, and Nietzsche. He is the co-editor (with John Mullarkey) of *Bergson: Key Writings* (Continuum, 2002) and editor of the Henri Bergson Centennial Series (Palgrave Macmillan, 2007).

G. WILLIAM BARNARD is associate professor of religious studies at Southern Methodist University. He is the author of *Exploring Unseen Worlds: William James and the Philosophy of Mysticism* (SUNY Press 1997), and *Living Consciousness: Reclaiming the Metaphysical Vision of Henri Bergson* (SUNY Press, 2011).

CLAIRE COLEBROOK is professorial research fellow, Centre for Modernism Studies in Australia, at the University of New South Wales. She has written books and articles on literary theory, literary history, contemporary philosophy, feminist theory, and poetry. Her most recent books are *Deleuze and the Meaning of Life* (Continuum, 2010) and *Milton, Evil and Literary History* (Continuum, 2008).

HISASHI FUJITA is lecturer in the faculty of international studies of culture at Kyushu Sangyo University.

SUZANNE GUERLAC is professor of French at UC Berkeley. She is author of *Thinking in Time: An Introduction to Henri Bergson* (Cornell University Press, 2006) and co-editor (with Pheng Cheah) of *Derrida and the Time of the Political* (Duke University Press, 2009).

VLADIMIR JANKÉLÉVITCH (1903–85) held the chair in moral philosophy at the Sorbonne from 1951 to 1978. He is the author of more than twenty books on philosophy and music, including *Henri Bergson* (PUF, 1959).

FRÉDÉRIC KECK is researcher at the CNRS, attached to the Laboratoire d'anthropologie sociale in Paris. He is the author of *Lucien Lévy-Bruhl, entre philosophie et anthropologie* (CNRS, 2008) and co-editor of the works of Lévi-Strauss in the Bibliothèque de la Pléiade (Gallimard, 2007).

LEONARD LAWLOR is Edwin Erle Sparks Professor of Philosophy at Penn State University. He is the author of numerous books on modern and contemporary continental philosophy, including *The Challenge of Bergsonism* (Continuum, 2003).

ALEXANDRE LEFEBVRE is lecturer in the Department of Government and International Relations and the Department of Philosophy at the University of Sydney. He is author of *The Image of Law: Deleuze, Bergson, Spinoza* (Stanford University Press, 2008).

PAOLA MARRATI is professor of humanities and philosophy and director of the Program for the Study of Women, Gender, and Sexuality at the Johns Hopkins University. She is author of *Genesis and Trace: Derrida Reading Husserl and Heidegger* (Stanford University Press, 2005) and *Gilles Deleuze: Cinema and Philosophy* (Johns Hopkins University Press, 2008).

JOHN MULLARKEY is professor of film and television studies at Kingston University, London. He is author of *Bergson and Philosophy* (University of Edinburgh Press, 1999), *Post-Continental Philosophy* (Continuum, 2006), and *Philosophy of the Moving Image: Refractions of Reality* (Palgrave Macmillan, 2010). He is editor of *The New Bergson* (Manchester University Press, 1999) and co-editor (with Keith Ansell-Pearson) of *Bergson: Key Writings* (Continuum, 2002).

PAULINA OCHOA ESPEJO is assistant professor in the department of political science at Yale University. She is the author of *The Time of Popular Sovereignty: Process and the Democratic State* (Penn State University Press, 2011).

CARL POWER received a PhD from the University of Sydney for his work on the social theory of Henri Bergson. He is currently researching and writing about the history and science of regenerative medicine.

PHILIPPE SOULEZ (1943–94) was professor of philosophy at the Université de Paris VIII. He is author of several books, including *Bergson politique* (PUF, 1989) and (with Frédéric Worms) *Bergson: Biographie* (Flammarion, 1997).

JIM URPETH is senior lecturer in philosophy in the School of Humanities and Social Sciences, University of Greenwich. He is co-editor (with John Lippitt) of *Nietzsche and the Divine* (Clinamen, 2000).

MELANIE WHITE is senior lecturer in social theory in the school of social sciences at the University of New South Wales.

FRÉDÉRIC WORMS is professor of philosophy at the Université de Lille III and director of the Centre international d'étude de la philosophie française contemporaine at the Ecole Normale Supérieure. He is author of several books on Bergson, including (with Philippe Soulez) *Bergson: Biographie* (Flammarion, 1997) and *Bergson ou les deux sens de la vie* (PUF, 2004), and he is editor of the *Annales bergsoniennes* (PUF).

moral causality, 266–72; of supernatural forces, 274

"Moral creators," 72. *See also* mystics and mysticism

Moral Education (Durkheim), 41, 45

morality, 20n7; biological foundation of, 29, 177–79, 185; closed and open distinction, 179, 191; energetics of, 101–2; first-person demands on, 177–78; forces behind, 101; intellectualism and, 177, 185; intelligence and, 102–3; intentionality and, 183; intuition and, 177; justification of, 174–75; motivations in, 181; mysticism and, 179; "normative question" in, 175, 178; of the organism, 87; primitive mentality, 271; as pseudo-instinct, 182; shift to ethics from, 186; two sources of, 163–64; universal extension of, 198–99. *See also* freedom

moral obligation, 101–2, 151, 163, 213n9, 268; versus aspiration, 178–79; biological interpretation of, 103–5; infra and supra intellectual forces in, 178–79, 183; Kantian reason and, 180; loan repayment example of Kant, 184; motivation in, 181; resistance to, 175–76; supra-social forces in, 44

"Moral Obligation" (chapter 1, *Two Sources*), 149–50, 196–97

moral philosophy: critique of Kantian, 179–83; empiricists, 181; rational intuitionists, 182

moral reciprocity, 209

motivation for morality, 181–82; poststructuralists and, 186–87

movement, 52, 54, 61, 63, 67–68, 70, 72–73, 111, 124n31; Zeno's paradox and, 162–63

music, 55, 75, 77, 79, 91

Myers, Fredric, 286

mystical love, 49, 55–57, 125n37, 129–30, 158n10, 252; versus fraternity, 254–55

mystics and mysticism, 35–38, 233–34, 269; action and, 147; Bergson qualification of, 106; Christian, 156; contemplation versus action in, 252; defined, 72, 147; as disequilibrium, 152, 156; elimination of the political by, 12; Greek philosophy and, 252; human as species and, 105, 107; impetus to love and, 151; versus mental illness, 254; morality and, 106, 179; mystical versus morbid states, 152; Nietzsche on, 255–56; Nietzsche versus Bergson on, 258; pagan seers, 224–25; in political philosophy, 11–12, 45, 106; in politics and political institutions, 18; progress and, 111–12; religion and, 204. *See also* dynamic religion; Jewish prophecy and prophets

myth, 128; Sorelian definition of, 135–36

mythmaking function. *See* fabulation function

narcissism of humans, 91

naturalistic religion. *See* biological foundations: of religion

natural religion, 275

natural selection, 90

nature, 83, 148; "cheating nature," 145, 153–55, 157; de-deification of, in Nietzsche, 259–60; dynamic religion as leap beyond, 251; representations of, 273; as source of static religion, 149. *See also* biological foundations

Nietzsche, Frederich, 40, 155; on mysticism, 255–56. *See also* religion, Bergson versus Nietzsche

non-ordinary phenomenon. *See* paranormal

"normative question," 175, 178

nothingness as false problem, 226–28

ontology: of change, 299, 301; of creativity, 13; joy and, 262

open morality, 9–10, 186–87, 241; conscience and, 209–10; creation and, 150; as disposition of the soul, 69

ALEXANDRE LEFEBVRE is lecturer in the Department of Government and International Relations and the Department of Philosophy at the University of Sydney.

MELANIE WHITE is senior lecturer in social theory in the School of Social Sciences at the University of New South Wales.

Library of Congress Cataloging-in-Publication Data

Bergson, politics, and religion /
Alexandre Lefebvre and Melanie White, editors.
p. cm.
Includes bibliographical references and index.
ISBN 978-0-8223-5256-3 (cloth : alk. paper)
ISBN 978-0-8223-5275-4 (pbk. : alk. paper)
1. Bergson, Henri, 1859–1941—Political and social views.
2. Bergson, Henri, 1859–1941—Religion.
I. Lefebvre, Alexandre.
II. White, Melanie Allison
B2430.B43B426 2012
194—dc23   2011053301